AN INTRODUCTION TO POLITICAL IDEAS

Peter M.R. Stirk
and
David Weigall

PINTER

Distributed in the United States by St. Martin's Press

First published in 1995 by
Pinter Publishers Limited, *A Cassell Imprint*
Wellington House, 125 Strand, London, WC2R OBB, United Kingdom

Distributed exclusively in the USA by St. Martin's Press, Inc.,
Room 400,175 Fifth Avenue, New York, NY10010, USA

British Library Cataloguing in Publication Data

A CIP catalogue record for this book is available from The British Library

ISBN 1855671581 (hbk)
ISBN 185567162 X (pbk)

Library of Congress Cataloging-in-Publication Data

Printed in Great Britain by
SRP Ltd, Exeter

CONTENTS

PREFACE

This book is an introduction to political ideas and their various interpretations. At the same time it aims to provide the reader with an introduction to, and practice in reading, political texts. These are arranged thematically and range from classical antiquity to the present day. The readings in each chapter are arranged chronologically. Together, they embody a wide variety of usages and interpretations, from very different contexts.

As an introduction, it is intended in particular for students of politics, history and international Relations who are studying political thought for the first time, and should be regarded as an encouragement to read further rather than as a substitute for more detailed study of the texts in their original context. Above all, we hope that this book will provide the student with practice in coming to terms with political texts and growing confidence in evaluating them.

ACKNOWLEDGEMENTS AND LIST OF SOURCES

The editors have benefited from the helpful advice of several colleagues and would like to thank Clarissa Campbell Orr, Dr. Julia Stapleton, John Sutton, Henry Tudor and Dr Michael Woodhouse. We are grateful to Diana Gonzalez and Wendy Redhead for their help in preparing the typescript. The Research Committee of the Department of Politics, University of Durham, contributed to the costs of preparing the typescript.

The editors are grateful to the following publishers for permission to reproduce copyright material: Blackwell Publishers (documents 1.3, 3.9, 4.10, 5.3, 6.9, 6.10, 6.11, 8.2, 8.3, 8.12, 9.2, 9.6, 12.2); Cambridge University Press (documents 1.4, 2.7, 5.7, 5.11, 6.2, 8.5, 8.11, 10.9); Everyman's Library, David Campbell Publishers Limited (documents 3.3, 4.7, 6.6); HarperCollins Publishers (documents 2.6, 3.12, 11.8, 10.10), Lawrence & Wishart Ltd. (documents 2.10, 9.16); Longman Group Limited (document 1.13); Macmillan Press Limited (documents 3.15, 8.8, 11.11, 12.13, 12.14, 12.16); Macmillan Publishing Company (document 2.12); The MIT Press (document 8.10); New Left Review (document 9.18); W.W. Norton & Company, Inc. (documents 1.2, 7.3); Oxford University Press (documents 1.1, 3.1, 3.2, 4.3, 5.5, 7.1, 7.9, 8.1, 8.7, 10.1, 12.4, 12.5); Penguin UK (documents 2.1, 4.1, 5.10, 6.1, 6.7, 9.13, 10.2, 12.1, 12.3); Penguin Books USA Inc. (document 5.12); Routledge, Chapman & Hall Limited (documents 3.10, 4.8, 6.8, 10.10, 10.13, 11.13); Scandinavian University Press (documents 7.14, 11.14); Simon & Schuster (document 6.4); Sweet & Maxwell Limited (document 1.12); University of Toronto Press (documents 3.8, 7.15, 10.6); Weidenfeld and Nicolson (documents 9.8, 9.10); Yale University Press (document 8.4). The editors are also grateful to Professor Charles Lindblom and Mr. S. Maclure and Professor Bikhu Parekh for permission to reproduce material from their works.

Every effort has been made to contact possible copyright holders. Should any extracts from works still in copyright have been included inadvertently without acknowledgement the publishers should be notified so that any omissions may be rectified in future editions.

Chapter 1: The Origin and nature of political order

1.1   Aristotle, *The Politics*, trans. B. Jowett (Oxford, Clarendon Press, 1905), pp. 1-5.

1.2   Reprinted from *St. Thomas Aquinas on Politics and Ethics*, translated and edited by Paul E. Sigmund with the permission of W.W. Norton and Company, Inc.

Copyright (c) 1988 by W.W. Norton and Company, Inc., pp. 14-17

1.3 Thomas Hobbes, *Leviathan*, edited by Michael Oakeshott (Oxford, Basil Blackwell, 1946), pp. 80-4.

1.4 J.P. Sommerville (ed.), *Filmer, Patriarcha and other Writings*, (Cambridge, Cambridge University Press, 1991), pp. 235-6.

1.5 *Locke's Two Treatises of Government*, edited with an introduction by Peter Laslett (Cambridge, Cambridge University Press, 1960), pp. 368-71.

1.6 *Hume-Theory of Politics*, edited by F. Watkins (London, Nelson, 1954), pp. 202-3

1.7 Jean-Jacques Rousseau, *The Social Contract*, translated by Wilmore Kendall (Chicago, Henry Regenery and Co., 1954), p. 19

1.8 *The Complete Writings of Thomas Paine*, edited by Philip S. Foner (New York, The Citadel Press, 1945), pp. 4-7.

1.9 Edmund Burke, *Reflections on the Revolution in France*, edited by Conor Cruise O'Brien (London, Pelican, 1988), pp. 150-1.

1.10 M. Oakeshott (ed.), *The Social and political Doctrines of Contemporary Europe* (Cambridge, Cambridge University Press, 1939), pp. 18-19

1.11 Friedrich Engels, *The Origins of the Family, Private Property and the State* (Moscow, Foreign Languages Publishing House, 1954), pp. 277-8.

1.12 Lord Denning, *The Road to Justice* (London, Stevens and Sons, 1954), pp. 7-9.

1.13 Bernard Crick, *Political Education and Political Literacy* (London, Longman, 1987), pp. 54-5.

Chapter 2: Authority and obligation

2.1 Plato, *The Last Days of Socrates* (Penguin, 1969), pp.89-93

2.2 St Paul, Romans 13.

2.3 Robert C. Schultz (ed), *Luther's Works*, vol. 46 The Christian in Society III (Philadelphia, Fortress, 1967), pp. 24-7

2.4 The Political Works of James I, Reprinted from the edition of 1616, with an Introduction by Charles Howard McIlwain (New York, Russel and Russel Inc., 1965) Copyright 1918, Harvard University Press.

2.5 *The Works of John Locke*, Vol. 5 (London, 1801), pp. 409-11.

2.6 David Hume, *A Treatise of Human Nature*, Books Two and Three, edited by Pall S. Ardall (London, Fontana Press, 1972), pp. 271-3. Reprinted by permission of HarperCollins Publishers.

2.7 *Kant's Political Writings*, edited by Hans Reiss (Cambridge University Press, 1970), p. 54

2.8 *The French Right from De Maistre to Maurras*, edited by J.S. McClelland (London, Cape, 1970), pp. 45-7 Reproduced from *The Works of Joseph de Maistre*, translated by Jack Lively (Allen and Unwin Ltd. 1965 and the Macmillan Company, Free Press of Glencoe, 1965).

2.9 *Auguste Comte and Positivism. The Essential Writings* (New York, Harper, 1975), pp. 275-7

2.10 Karl Marx, Friedrich Engels, *Collected Works*, Vol. 23 (London, Lawrence and Wishart, 1988), pp. 422-5

2.11 H. H. Gerth and C. Wright Mills (eds), *From max Weber:Essays in Sociology* (London, Routledge and Kegan Paul, 1948), pp. 78-9.

2.12 Reprinted with the permission of Scribner's, an imprint of Simon & Schuster from

H.B. Davis and R.C. Good (eds), *Reinhold Niebuhr on Politics* (New York, Charles Scribner, 1960), pp. 268-70, 272.

2.13 Arend Lijphart (ed), *Politics in Europe: Comparisons and Interpretations* (Englewood Cliffs, NJ, Prentice Hall, 1969), ch.11. (c) 1969 Eva Tamm Lijphart.

2.14 Carl J. Friedrich, 'Authority, Reason and Decision', in Carl J. Friedrich (ed.), *Nomos I. Authority* (Harvard University Press, 1952), pp.35-7

Chapter 3: Forms of government

3.1 Aristotle, *The Politics*, translated by Benjamin Jowett (Oxford, Clarendon Press, 1905), pp. 79-80.

3.2 Aristotle, *The Politics,* translated by Benjamin Jowett (Oxford, Clarendon Press, 1905), pp. 123-31

3.3 John Milton, *Prose Writings* (London, Dent, 1954), pp. 191-5.

3.4 *Locke's Two Treatises of Government*, edited with an introduction by Peter Laslett (Cambridge, Cambridge University Press, 1960), pp. 373-5

3.5 Montesquieu, *The Spirit of the Laws*, translated by T. Nugent (London, G. Bell, 1914), pp. 151-2, 154. 156, 159-60.

3.6 Gareth Jones (ed.), *The Sovereignty of the Law* (Basingstoke, Macmillan, 1973), pp. 65-6.

3.7 Jean-Jacques Rousseau, *The Social Contract*, translated by G.D.H. Cole (London, Dent, 1913), pp. 32-3

3.8 Vittorio Alfieri, *Of Tyranny*, translated by J.A. Molinaro and B. Corrigan (Toronto, Toronto University Press, 1961), pp. 111-14.

3.9 *The Federalist*, edited by M. Beloff (Oxford, Basil Blackwell, 1987), pp. 245-48.

3.10 *Bentham's Political Thought*, edited by B. Parekh (London, Croom Helm, 1973), pp. 294-8.

3.11 James Mill, *Essay on Government* (Cambridge, Cambridge University Press, 1937), pp. 8-13.

3.12 F.C. Mather (ed.), *Chartism and Society* (London, Bell and Hyman, 1980), pp. 67-8.

3.13 Alexis de Tocqueville, *Democracy in America*, translated by Henry Reeve (London, Saunders and Otley, 1863)

3.14 Sir Henry Maine, *Popular Government* (London, John Murray, 1909), pp. 211-13.

3.15 *Selected Writings of Pierre-Joseph Proudhon*, edited by Stewart Edwards and translated by Elizabeth Fraser (London, Macmillan, 1979), pp. 107-10.

3.16 James Bryce, *The American Commonwealth*, Vol. II ((London, Macmillan, 1898), pp. 225-6.

Chapter 4: Rights

4.1 Plato, *The Republic* (Harmondsworth, Penguin), pp. 66-7

4.2 Henry de Bracton, *De legibus et consuetudinibus Angliae,* edited by George E. Woodbine (New Haven, Yale University Press, 1915), Vol. 2, pp. 19, 21-2

4.3 Samuel Pufendorf, *Elementorium Jurisprudentiae Universalis Libro Duo*, translated by William Abbott Oldfather (Oxford, Clarendon Press, 1931), pp. 58-60

4.4 Richard Overton, *An Arrow Against All Tyrants* (London, 1646), pp. 3-4.

4.5 *The Works of John Locke*, Vol. 5 (London, 1801), pp. 341-2, pp. 311-12

4.6   Declaration of the Rights of Man and of the Citizen, 1791, in Philip S. Foner (ed.), *The Complete Writings of Thomas Paine,* (New York, Citadel Press, 1945), Vol. 1, pp. 313-15

4.7   Thomas Paine. *The Rights of Man* (London, Dent, 1906), pp. 10-17, 44-5

4.8   Bikhu Parekh (ed.), *Bentham's Political Thought* (London, Croom Helm, 1973), pp. 262-70

4.9   William Cobbett, *Rural Rides* (Harmondsworth, Penguin, 1967), pp. 433-4

4.10   David McLellan (ed.), *Karl Marx. Early Texts* (Oxford, Blackwell, 1973), pp. 102-4

4.11   John Rae, 'State Socialism and Social Reform', *Contemporary Review*, Vol. 58 (1890), pp. 438-9

4.12   Thomas Hill Green, *Lectures on the Principle of Political Obligation* (London, Longmans, Green and Co., 1921), p.44

4.13   Eleanor Rathbone, 'The Remuneration of Women', in Victor Gollancz (ed.), *The Making of Women* (London, Allen and Unwin, 1917), pp. 114-17

4.14   Wesley Newcomb Hohfeld, *Fundamental Legal Conceptions As Applied in Judicial Reasoning and Other Cases* (New Haven, Yale University Press, 1920), pp. 96-7.

4.15   *The Treaty of Versailles* (Washington, US Government Printing Office, 1944)

4.16   International Convention on Economic, Social and Cultural Rights (1966)

Chapter 5: Ideas of Liberty

5.1   Niccoló Machiavelli, *The Discourses*, edited by Bernard Crick (London, Penguin, 1970), pp. 277-9.

5.2   L.H. Berens, *The Digger Movement in the Days of the Commonwealth* (London, Simpkin, Marshall and Co., 1906), pp. 1880-2.

5.3   Thomas Hobbes, *Leviathan*, edited by Michael Oakeshott (Oxford, Basil Blackwell, 1946), pp. 136-45.

5.4   Montesquieu, *The Spirit of the Laws*, translated by T. Nugent (London, Encyclopedia Britannica Inc., 1952), pp. 68-9

5.5   *Free Government in the Making* (New York, Oxford University Press, 1985), edited by A.T. Mason and G.E. Baker, pp. 126-9. Copyright (c) 1985. Reprinted by permission of Oxford University Press, Inc.

5.6   *Hume-Theory of Politics*, edited by F. Watkins (London, Nelson, 1954), pp. 129-34.

5.7   John Stuart Mill, *On Liberty*, edited by S. Collini (Cambridge, Cambridge University Press. 1989), pp. 5-16

5.8   Claudia Carlen Ihm (ed.), *The Papal Encyclicals 1878-1903* (New York, Pierian Press, 1990), pp. 173-4, 176

5.9   Alfredo Rocco, 'The Political Doctrine of Fascism', *International Conciliation* (1926).

5.10   Lord Hailsham, *The Case for Conservatism* (London, Penguin, 1947), pp. 62-4

5.11   T.E. Utley and J.S. Maclure (eds), *Documents of Modern Political Thought* (Cambridge, Cambridge University Press, 1957), pp. 62-5.

5.12   From *Between Past and Future* by Hannah Arendt (New York, Viking Press Inc. 1968), pp. 148-52. Copyright 1954, 1956, 1957, 1958, 1960, 1961 by Hannah Arendt. Used by permission of Viking Penguin, a division of Penguin Books USA Inc.

5.13   Ivo D. Duchacek, *Rights and Liberties in the World Today* (Santa Barbara, ABC Clio, 1973), p. 77.

Chapter 6: Justice and Equality

6.1 Plato, *The Republic* (Penguin, 1955), pp. 89-90
6.2 J.A.G. Pocock (ed.), *The Political Works of James Harrington* (Cambridge University Press, 1977), p. 172
6.3 Thomas Hobbes, *Leviathan* (Harmondsworth. Pelican, 1968), pp. 201-3, 208, 211-12
6.4 Reprinted with the permission of Simon & Schuster from *Moral and Political Philosophy* by David Hume, edited by Henry D. Aiken, pp. 63-7. Copyright 1948 by Macmillan Publishing Company.
6.5 Phillippe Buonarotti, *Babeuf's Conspiracy for Equality* (London, Hetherington, 1836), pp. 318-23
6.6 J.S. Mill, *Utilitarianism, On Liberty, and Considerations on Representative Government* (Dent, 1972), pp. 40-2, 45, 47-8.
6.7 Karl Marx, *The First International and After* (Harmondsworth, Penguin, 1974), pp. 341, 344-7
6.8 R.H. Tawney, *Equality* (London, Allen and Unwin: 4th edition), pp. 35-41, 47
6.9 John Rawls, 'Distributive Justice', in Peter Laslett and W.G. Runciman (eds), *Philosophy, Politics and Society*, Third Series (Oxford, Basil Blackwell, 1967), pp. 58-9, 61, 67.
6.10 Robert Nozick, *Anarchy, State and Utopia* (Oxford, Basil Blackwell, 1974), pp. 171-2 and 238
6.11 Michael Walzer, *Spheres of Justice. A Defence of Pluralism and Equality* (Oxford, Blackwell, 1983), pp. 16-20.

Chapter 7: Property

7.1 Aristotle, *The Politics*, trans. B. Jowett (Oxford, Clarendon Press, 1905), pp. 5-9.
7.2 *The New Testament*
7.3 Reprinted from *St. Thomas Aquinas on Politics and Ethics*, translated and edited by Paul E. Sigmund with the permission of W.W. Norton and Company, Inc. Copyright (c) 1988 by W.W. Norton and Company, Inc., pp. 72-3.
7.4 James Harrington, *Oceana* (London, Routledge and Kegan Paul, 1887), Part 1, pp. 18-19 and Part 3, pp. 14-15.
7.5 *Locke's Two Treatises of Government*, edited with an introduction by Peter Laslett (Cambridge, Cambridge University Press, 1960), pp. 304-6, 308-9, 317-19.
7.6 Jean-Jacques Rousseau, *The Social Contract*, translated by Wilmore Kendall (Chicago, Henry Regenery and Co., 1954), pp. 20-3.
7.7 Edmund Burke, *Reflections on the Revolution in France*, edited by Conor Cruise O'Brien (London, Pelican, 1988), pp. 140-1.
7.8 P. Garside (ed.), *The Visionary* (Cardiff, Cardiff University Press, 1984), pp. 11-15
7.9 *Free Government in the Making* (New York, Oxford University Press, 1985), edited by A.T. Mason and G.E. Baker, pp. 366-7. Copyright (c) 1985. Reprinted by permission of Oxford University Press, Inc.
7.10 Karl Marx and Friedrich Engels, *The Communist Manifesto* (London, Penguin, 1967), pp. 96-8.
7.11 A.T. Mason and G.E. Baker (eds), *Free Government in the Making* (New York, Oxford University Press, 1985), pp. 534-5.

7.12   Ramsay Macdonald, *Socialism: Critical and Constructive* (London, Cassall, 1924), pp. 131-2

7.13   Morris Cohen, 'Property and Sovereignty', *Cornell Law Quarterly* (December 1927), pp. 11-13.

7.14   Charles E. Lindblom, *Democracy and Market System* (Oslo, Norwegian University Press, 1988), pp. 117-19

7.15   C.B. Macpherson, *Property* (Toronto, University of Toronto Press, 1978), pp. 4-7.

Chapter 8: The State and Sovereignty

8.1   Niccoló Machiavelli, *The Prince*, translated by L. Ricci and E. R. Vincent (Oxford, Oxford University Press, 1934), pp. 65-7.

8.2   Jean Bodin, *The Six Books of the Republic*, edited by J.M. Tooley (Oxford, Basil Blackwell, 1955), pp. 25-9.

8.3   Thomas Hobbes, *Leviathan*, edited by Michael Oakeshott (Oxford, Basil Blackwell, 1946), pp. 109-20, 129-36.

8.4   *Samuel Johnson: Political Writings*, edited by D.J. Greene (Yale University Press, 1977), pp. 422-5.

8.5   *Richard Price: Political Writings*, edited by D.O. Thomas (Cambridge, Cambridge University Press, 1991), pp. 30-5.

8.6   *The Works of Edmund Burke*, Vol. 8 (London, Bell, 1868), pp. 3-5, 7-8.

8.7   G.W.F. Hegel, *The Philosophy of Right*, translated by T.M. Knox (Oxford, Oxford University Press, 1952), pp. 182-3

8.8   Dicey, T*he Law of the Constitution*, edited by E.C.S. Wade (London, Macmillan, 1985), p. 39

8.9   Michael Oakeshott (ed.), *The Social and Political Doctrines of Contemporary Europe* (Cambridge, Cambridge University Press, 1939), pp. 166-8.

8.10   Carl Schmitt, *Political Theology*, translated by George Schwab (Massachusetts, Massachusetts Institute of Technology, 1985), pp. 5-9.

8.11   F.H. Hinsley, *Sovereignty* (Cambridge, Cambridge University Press, 1986), p. 222.

8.12   Robert Nozick, *Anarchy, State and Utopia* (Oxford, Basil Blackwell, 1974), pp. ix and 113-14.

Chapter 9: The idea of revolution

9.1   *The Statesman's Book of John of Salisbury* (New York, Alfred A. Knopf, 1928), pp. 258, 367-9, 372-3

9.2   A.P. D'Entreves, *Aquinas. Selected Political Writings* (Oxford, Basil Blackwell, 1948), pp. 29-33

9.3   N. Machiavelli, *The Discourses*, edited by Bernard Crick (Harmondsworth, Penguin, 1970), pp. 106-9.

9.4   Francis Bacon, *The Essays* (London, Cassell, 1907), pp. 55-9

9.5   *Killing No Murder* (Edinburgh, 1741)

9.6   John Locke, *The Second Treatise of Civil Government*, edited by J.W. Gough (Oxford, Blackwell, 1946), pp. 103-5, 107-8.

9.7   Alexander Hamilton, *A Full Vindication* (1774), in A.T. Mason and G.E. Baker (eds), *The Government in the Making. Readings in American Political Thought* (Oxford University Press, 1985: 4th edition), pp. 104-5.

9.8   Marquis de Condorcet, 'On the Meaning of the Word "Revolutionary"', in

Krishan Kumar (ed.), *Revolution. The Theory and Practice of a European Idea* (London, Weidenfeld and Nicolson, 1971), pp. 93-5

9.9 *The Writings of Henry David Thoreau*, Vol. 10 (Cambridge, Mass., Riverside Press, 1894)

9.10 Alexis de Tocqueville, *On the State of Society in France Before the Revolution of 1789* (London, Henry Reeve, 1865), reprinted in Krishan Kumar (ed.), *Revolution. The Theory and Practice of a European Idea* (London, Weidenfeld and Nicolson, 1971), pp. 113-14

9.11 Stewart Edwards (ed.), *Selected Writings of Pierre-Joseph Proudhon* (London, Macmillan, 1970), pp. 159-60.

9.12 Sam Dolgoff (ed.), *Bakunin on Anarchy* (London, Allen and Unwin, 1973), pp. 99-101

9.13 Karl Marx, *Capital*, Vol. 1 (Harmondsworth, Penguin, 1976), pp. 928-9

9.14 *Marx Engels Selected Correspondence* (Moscow, Progress Publishers, 1975), pp.

9.15 V.I. Lenin, *What is to be done?* (Peking, Foreign Languages Press, 1973), pp. 37, 48-51

9.16 V.I. Lenin, *Collected Works*, Vol. 24, April-June 1917 (London, Lawrence and Wishart, 1964), pp. 43-6

9.17 Hermann Rauschning, *Germany's Revolution of Destruction* (London, Heinemann, 1939), pp. 20-1

9.18 Herbert Marcuse, 'Re-examination of the Concept of Revolution', *New Left Review*, No. 56 (July-August 1969), pp. 30-3

Chapter 10: Democracy

10.1 Aristotle, *The Politics*, trans. B. Jowett (Oxford, Clarendon Press, 1905), pp. 329-41.

10.2 David Wooton (ed.), *Divine Right and Democracy* (London, Penguin, 1986), pp. 285-8.

10.3 *The Letters of Noah Webster*, edited by Harry L. Werfel (New York, Library Publishers, 1953), pp. 207-8.

10.4 John Plamenatz (ed.), *Readings from Liberal Writers* (London, Allen and Unwin, 1965), pp. 211-15.

10.5 *Northern Star* (2 January 1841)

10.6 *The Collected Works of John Stuart* Mill, Vol. XIX, edited by J.M. Robson (University of Toronto Press, 1977), pp. 403-6.

10.7 Mrs Hugo Reid, *A Plea for Women* (Edinburgh, W.Tait, 1843), pp. 49, 53, 64, reprinted in Patricia Hollis (ed.), Women in Public 1850-1900 (London, George Allen & Unwin, 1979), p. 293.

10.8 Barbara Leigh Smith Bodichon, *Reason for and Against the Enfranchisement of Women* (1866), reprinted in Patricia Hollis (ed.), Women in Public 1850-1900 (London, George Allen & Unwin, 1979), pp. 295-6

10.9 Sir James FitzJames Stephen, *Liberty, Equality Fraternity*, edited by R.J. White (Cambridge, Cambridge University Press, 1967), pp. 210-11.

10.10 Joseph Schumpeter, *Capitalism, Socialism and Democracy* (New York, Harper and Row, 1942), pp. 250-2. Copyright 1942, 1947 by Joseph A. Schumpeter. reprinted by permission of HarperCollins Publishers, Inc.

10.11 G.D.H. Cole, *The Social Theory* (London, Methuen, 1920), pp. 103-6.

10.12 Harold Laski, *Democracy in Crisis* (London, Allen and Unwin, 1933), pp. 49-52.

10.13 F.A. von Hayek, *The Constitution of Liberty* (London, Routledge and Kegan Paul, 1960), pp. 107-9.
10.14 Lord Hailsham in *The Listener* (21 October 1976), pp. 496-7

Chapter 11: State and economy

11.1   Adam Smith, *The Wealth of Nations* (Harmondsworth, Penguin, 1970), pp. 442-3
11.2   *Karl Marx. Early Writings* (Harmondsworth, Penguin, 1974), pp. 411-13
11.3   Friedrich List, *The National System of Political Economy* (London, Longmans, 1885), pp. 140, 142-5
11.4   Bismarck. Sydney Pollard and Colin Homes (eds), *Documents of European Economic History, Vol. 2, Industrial Power and National Rivalry* (London, Arnold, 1972), pp. 128-9.
11.5   Herbert Spencer, *Social Statics and The Man Versus the State* (London, Williams and Norgate, 1892), pp. 306-10
11.6   Henry Steele Commager (ed.), *Documents of American History* (New York, Appleton-Century-Crofts, 1949: 5th edition), pp. 143-5
11.7   Leon Duguit, *Law in the Modern State* (New York, Howard and Fertig, 1974), pp. 44-8
11.8   G.D.H. Cole, *Self Government in Industry* (London, Bell and Sons, 1917), pp. 84-5
11.9   N. Bukharin and E. Preobrazhensky, *The ABC of Communism* (Harmondsworth, Penguin, 1969, pp. 114-5
11.10 Henry Steele Commager (ed.), *Documents of American History* (New York, Appleton-Century-Crofts, 1949: 5th edition), pp. 403-4
11.11 John Maynard Keynes, *The General Theory of Employment*, Interest and Money (London, Macmillan, 1936), pp. 377-81
11.12 William Beveridge, *Full Employment in a Free Society* (London, Allen and Unwin, 1944), p. 38
11.13 F.A. Hayek, *The Road to Serfdom* (London, George Routledge, 1944), pp. 27-31
11.14 Charles E. Lindblom, *Democracy and Market System* (Oslo, Norwegian University Press, 1988), pp. 125-6

Chapter 12: The international order

12.1   Thucydidees, *History of the Peloponnesian War* (London, Penguin, 1954), pp. 360-1
12.2   A.P. D'Entreves, *Aquinas. Selected Political Writings* (Oxford, Basil Blackwell, 1948), pp. 159, 161
12.3   N. Machiavelli, *The Prince* (Penguin, 1961), pp. 119-21
12.4   Alberico Gentili, *De Iuri Belli*, Vol. 2, Translation of the edition of 1612 (Oxford, Clarendon Press, 1933), pp. 31-2
12.5   Hugo Grotius, *De Jure Ac Paci Libri Tres* (Oxford, Clarendon Press, 1925), pp. 17-19
12.6   E de Vattel, *The Law of Nations or the Principles of Natural Law*, Vol. 3, Translation of the edition of 1758 (Washington, Carnegie Institution, 1916), pp. 251-2

12.7   Lord Palmerston, House of Commons 1 March 1848

12.8   *The Political Writings of Richard Cobden*, Vol. 1 (London, William Ridgeway, 1867), pp. 258-260, 262-360, 278-83

12.9   Joseph Mazzini, *Life and Writings*, Vol. 4 Critical and Literary (London, Smith, Elder and Co., 1867), pp. 275-6 and 277

12.10 Lord Acton, *The History of Nationality and Other Essays* (London, Macmillan, 1909), p. 284-5, 288, 289, 298.

12.11 Heinrich von Treitschke, *Politics*, Vol. 1 (London, Constable, 1916), pp. 595-8, 609-11

12.12 *The Treaty of Versailles* (Washington, US Government Printing Office, 1944)

12.13 Alfred Zimmern, *The League of Nations and the Rule of Law* (London, Macmillan, 1939), pp. 2-7

12.14 E.H. Carr, *The Twenty Years Crisis* (London, Macmillan, 1939), pp. 108-11

12.15 E.F. Penrose, *Economic Planning for Peace* (Princeton, Princeton University Press, 1953), pp. 126-7

12.16 Hedley Bull, *The Anarchical Society. A Study of Order in World Politics* (London, Macmillan, 1977), pp. 8-10, 13, 16-19

INTRODUCTION: READING POLITICAL TEXTS

Political ideas are the means by which we assert our membership of communities or nations, define our position within them, set out their purposes and ends, and make claims upon each other and institutions within society. They are also a way in which we express our disagreement with each other about these things and sometimes the means by which we seek to justify our use of violence against each other. Without political ideas and the language in which they are expressed political or civic culture would have neither rationale nor articulated purpose.

The language and the ideas themselves are both familiar and unfamiliar. Normally we use them – liberty, democracy, justice, for instance – without much reflection. We are only partially aware of their implications and underlying assumptions, to say nothing of their provenance.

This is not a peculiar feature of modern civilization. In ancient Greece, Socrates's standard approach to argument, and education, was to begin with an apparently simple question, eliciting an apparently simple and customary response. He would then proceed to lay bare the assumptions and implications of that answer until his hapless interlocutor confessed that the original answer was misguided.

Although Socrates' approach is, by no means, a universally valid model of political argument, all political texts seek to persuade us of something, to obey or to rebel, to hold on to our 'property' or to relinquish it for someone else's benefit, to recognize someone's right or to deny that there is any such right at all. In doing so they must be close enough to our own unreflective use of ideas and language to be intelligible yet they must also seek to stretch or redefine our ideas and language. One of the purposes of this book is to help to bridge that gap between our unreflective use of ideas and language and the political texts which form an important part of our collective intellectual inheritance.

When we refer to ideas and language, ideas and terminology, it is important for us to realize that the two do not necessarily coincide. Our word 'revolution', for example, is, in its current political meaning, relatively novel. Yet that does not mean that people born before 'revolution' acquired its contemporary meaning had no understanding of what we now designate as 'revolution'. They could well have the idea without using our contemporary term for it. By the same token we have to take care that on seeing the familiar term we do not automatically assume that the meaning is the same or that the evaluation placed on the term is the same. For example, while we would now probably assume that calling someone a democrat signified approval, this has not always been the implication. Until recent times it was common for people to condemn democracy as leading to ungovernability, licence and anarchy. In the past a 'democrat' was usually perceived as a threat to established order and hierarchy. To call someone a 'democrat' was to villify them.

There are a number of good reasons for bringing together extracts from works with a wide variety of different meanings, assumptions and implications. In the first place, many of the authors form part of the intellectual inheritance which has contributed to, influenced and informed contemporary as well as past argument on these themes. Secondly, the authors concerned have usually put their case with great clarity or rhetorical force and have, in these respects, not been bettered.

To become aware of the discrepancy between contemporary and past usage provides perspective. It means that our customary interpretation is not the only one. It offers us the opportunity to establish some critical distance from our own perceptions and prejudices. It can, for example, remind us of what we have lost in the process of refining and redefining our political ideas. We are reminded of this by the late Hannah Arendt when she claims we have lost sight of the original meaning of the ideas of authority and freedom (see document 5.12). It can also make us more aware of the ambiguities in our contemporary understanding of ideas, for these are rarely, if ever, single and clear cut.

The major changes of meaning of terms and the broad transformation of ideas is indicated in the introductions to the chapters. The extracts are organized chronologically in each of the chapters to give an idea of range, development and tradition. Yet it has been argued by some that the difference in meaning of terms and ideas and the great variety of contexts in which they have been expressed are so great that to bring together political theorists divided by vast stretches of time and diversity of circumstances is to invite misunderstanding at best, and probably outright distortion. The basic problem, it is claimed, is that the diverse thinkers are likely to be addressing quite different questions when, for example, they talk about 'justice'. According to Quentin Skinner, 'The mistake, in short, lies in supposing that there is any one question to which these various thinkers are all addressing themselves'.[1]

At one level this is true. The question, what is justice?, was, for Plato, equivalent to asking what is the best form of the state and his answer pointed towards, in the words of one commentator, 'a moral reordering of the whole of society'.[2] Even Aristotle found this too expansive and suggested a narrower conception and classification of justice. Much later Hobbes criticized Aristotle's classification, further narrowing the idea of justice in his attempt to answer the question: is justice derivable from the laws of nature? The difference is compounded by the fact that the Greek Plato did not use the word 'justice' and the fact that there is some dispute about whether the word he did use can be properly translated as 'justice'.[3]

Are we then limited to discussing, at most, the Greek concept of justice, the seventeenth-century concept of justice, and so on? To do more than this we need enough similarity to claim that these authors touch upon a common problem – even if they do so by asking different questions and coming up with radically different answers. This they clearly do. When Plato writes about returning what we have borrowed and Hobbes about 'giving to every man his own' they are talking about something recognizably similar. They are both talking about the distribution of goods. The fact that Plato will subordinate the distribution of goods to wider considerations of justice is quite compatible with his coming up with an account of justice which does, in his eyes, provide for a just distribution of goods, among other things. Hobbes, for his part, was so concerned to elevate the keeping of contracts to the mechanism for deciding what belonged to whom that he rejected the idea of distributing goods according to merit (the traditional idea of distributive justice) and redefined distributive justice to conform with his emphasis on keeping contracts. But Hobbes comes up with an account which does, in his eyes, provide for a just distribution of goods.

The following pages are intended as an encouragement to read further. A full understanding of Plato's concept of 'justice' will lead one to read at least *The Republic* and other writings, and place that in the context of the political thought of the fifth century BC. The purpose here, though, is introduction. It is, in the first place, to bridge the gap between the familiar assumptions and language of political ideas and the assumptions and language of political texts. The second aim is precisely to indicate, and often all that can be done is to indicate, that there are radically different approaches to the perennial problems of political theory. Radical questioning of one idea, say of justice, will not infrequently lead us to question other ideas about the nature of rights or the idea of the state and the relation between the state and the economy.

Two other intentions should be mentioned. Political ideas are not confined to the great texts of political philosophy. They are embodied in the works of minor figures, in the manifestos of political parties, in international treaties, in legal advocacy, speeches at trials and so on. We have sought to include a range of such texts to illustrate this fact. Political ideas do not inhabit some kind of ghetto. They pervade the realm of politics and much more besides.

Political ideas are usually advanced in order to persuade and part of that persuasion lies in the way that they are advanced. It lies in their rhetorical force as well as the intrinsic content of the ideas. Some political thinkers, like Edmund Burke, have seen so close a connection between these two elements that rhetoric takes on a key role in their understanding of what politics itself is.[4] Others, who have claimed to be more dispassionate, have nevertheless written to persuade and have argued in a style which they believed to be appropriate to their age and their specific audience. Political ideas can also be set out in the form of a record of an agreement, as in constitutions and treaties. Again our intention has been to provide a wide enough range of styles, from the legal language of international treaties to the biting sarcasm of Marx or Bentham, to bring out this aspect of political texts.

There are, of course, costs involved in such diversity. Space precludes our demonstrating the importance of traditions of political thought *in a strict sense*. There is a broader sense in which one might call the set of discussions on justice a 'tradition'.[5] But a stricter sense of tradition exists where different political theorists share basic values or assumptions, conceptions of what constitutes a valid argument or a political community.

To illustrate this kind of tradition would require a far narrower focus than is possible here. Nor is it only a question of the focus of discussion. Most societies contain competing traditions, or at the least competing interpretations of a tradition which stretch their boundaries to the point of breaking. Which traditions are operative, what their essential traits are and who belongs in which tradition, are all questions which are far from easy to answer.[6] Nevertheless, traditions in this narrower sense may well provide a bridge between the broad political ideas introduced here and the particular thinkers in their specific society and time.[7]

In reflecting on contemporary problems and disputes we will, intentionally or not, use political ideas drawn from some, at least, of these traditions – whether traditions in the broad or narrow sense. In considering the merits of alternative electoral systems we will use ideas of representation and democracy, in discussing the welfare state we will invoke rights, justice, property and assumptions about the proper extent of government. In our reaction to the collapse of political order in neighbouring, or distant, countries we will talk of liberty, sovereignty and the international order.

To that extent political ideas cannot be isolated from other aspects of politics, nor simply divided, on the one hand, into histories of political thought, and on the other, of contemporary political philosophy.[8] We cannot act politically, as citizens, without the motivation of political ideas and assumptions, and we derive our ideas, willingly or not, from our intellectual inheritance. Learning to clarify ideas, to evaluate and to debate, are skills that the study of political thought can strongly reinforce.

NOTES

1 Quentin Skinner, 'A Reply to My Critics', in James Tully (ed.), *Meaning and Context. Quentin Skinner and His Critics* (Cambridge, Polity, 1988), p. 283. The volume contains a good survey of what has often been an acrimonious dispute.

2 Julia Annas, *An Introduction to Plato's Republic* (Oxford University Press, 1981), p. 13.

3 On this see Annas, *An Introduction to Plato's Republic*

4 See Iain Hampsher-Monk, 'Rhetoric and Opinion in the Politics of Edmund Burke', *History of Political Thought,* Vol. 9 (1988), pp. 455–84.

5 This seems to be the position taken by Andrew Lockyer who describes this type of tradition as a 'tradition of discourse'. '"Traditions" as Context in the History of Political Theory', *Political Studies,* Vol. 27 (1979), pp. 201–17

6 See Iain Hampsher-Monk, 'Review Article: Political Languages in Time – The Work of J.G.A. Pocock', *British Journal of Political Science,* Vol. 14 (1984), pp. 89-116.

7 Ibid.

8 For a good survey of the state of political theory see David Miller, 'The Resurgence of Political Theory', *Political Studies,* Vol. 38 (1990), pp. 421–37.

1

THE ORIGINS AND NATURE OF POLITICAL ORDER

INTRODUCTION

The student of politics can readily find numerous works on the 'state' or 'obligation' or 'revolution' but few explicitly devoted to the concept of political order. Moreover, it has been periods of disorder, civil strife and revolution, which have done most to stimulate thought upon the political process. Despite this, the idea of order is crucial to political thought. Without some kind of order political life is inconceivable. Even advocates of the most violent revolution have held out the prospect of a new order, once the old has been swept away. The fact that order is necessary does not, of course, tell us what kind of order is desirable.

The term order is most likely to appear in contemporary political discourse in the call for 'law and order', which usually implies a demand for more vigorous policing and harsher punishment of offences. Behind the alarmism which accompanies the cry for law and order stands the reliance of the political community upon observance of the law. Even political systems of which we disapprove have laws for regulating the behaviour of their members. As Lord Denning pointed out, however, it makes a great deal of difference whether the government, too, is subject to the rule of law and whether the government is allowed to act as judge in its own case.

Ancient Greek use of the idea of order recognized the importance of law but set this in a much wider context. Then, human behaviour was seen as part of a natural and divine universe. In Plato's words, 'And philosophers tell us, Callicles, that communion and friendship, and orderliness and temperance and justice bind together heaven and earth and gods and men, and that this universe is therefore called Cosmos or order, not disorder or misrule'.[1] This broader concept of order, linking the human, the natural and the divine worlds, was still widespread enough in the sixteenth century for Shakespeare to invoke:

> Take but degree away, untune that string,
> And hark what discord follows. Each thing meets
> In mere oppugnancy The bounded waters
> Should lift their bosoms higher than the shores
> And make a sop of all this solid globe.
> Strength should be lord to imbecility,
> And the rude son should strike his father dead.
> This chaos, when degree is suffocate,
> Follows the choking.

For the Greeks the order underlying the universe was accessible to human reason. The world was, in principle, intelligible. Within this universe men could pursue the 'good life' as members of a political community, and only as members of a political community. Hence Aristotle accepted that political communities arose from the natural weakness of men, from their dependence upon each other and because of the advantages to be gained by cooperation. But the purpose of political life was distinct from these natural origins. For Aristotle, the truly human life was essentially a political one; only gods and animals could develop their potential without a political community.

With the advent of Christianity these concepts of order and politics were challenged. Saint Augustine, although he initially shared the Platonic vision, came to doubt the human capacity to grasp the broader order of the universe. Man was now said to be corrupted by original sin. The cosmological order was defined as a gift of God which men might hope to participate in only after their death. This pessimistic view of human nature was to become the dominant model for much of western political thought. Because of the Fall of Man ecclesiastical and secular institutions were said to be necessary counterweights to untamed human nature. The political community was not an arrangement for the pursuit of the good life. The good life was equated with the after life. Political institutions were necessary to mitigate sin. That was all they could do.

This conservative view of the essential imperfections of human beings stressed that it is precisely too much hope and too much trust in human capacities which constitutes the most dangerous manifestations of this imperfection. The French anti-revolutionary theorist, Joseph de Maistre, summed this up when he referred to original sin as 'explaining everything and without which nothing can be explained'. The consequence of human imperfection is that people acting on their own uncontrolled impulses will, on the whole, act badly. Hence Edmund Burke's insistence that government was necessary to restrain human nature.

This pessimistic theory of human nature had not gone unchallenged even within the medieval church. St Thomas Aquinas helped revive an Aristotelian perspective. As a Christian he naturally emphasized the supernatural end of man, the salvation of his soul, but he also held that the state could make men good. Government was once more seen as a means of promoting good, not simply of checking evil and harm. While Aquinas's relatively benign view of human nature was held in check, later political theorists exhibited less restraint. As the idea of progress came to grip the mind, human nature came to be seen not only as basically benign but, more importantly, as capable of improvement. As the anarchist William Godwin put it in *An Enquiry Concerning Political Justice* (1793), 'Man is perfectible or in other words susceptible of perpetual improvement'. So great indeed was this potential improvement that government was, to Godwin's mind, a hindrance. Whereas Aristotle had held that the political community was the indispensable means for the good life and Augustine accepted it as a necessary consequence of human wickedness, Godwin saw government as an unmitigated evil.

As confidence in human nature and progress grew, so too did suspicion of government. Suspicion of government did not necessarily lead to the anarchist conclusion that government was a dispensable evil. For many, it was a necessary evil which had to be kept in check lest it exceed its allotted functions. Central to this suspicion of government was the contrast between society and government. The two, warned Thomas Paine, should not be confused (see document 1.8). In making this warning Paine reflected a growing assumption that societal and political order were distinct. Men, it was argued, had reason enough to cooperate in order to improve their material conditions and had the emotional inclinations to facilitate that cooperation. But Paine parted company from the anarchist principle in denying that men were virtuous enough to manage without political institutions. The societal impulse towards cooperation and order had to be supplemented by a political order, which, in turn, had to be closely watched lest it develop into a tyranny worse than no government at all.

The possibility of social order without a political community had played an important part in political debate since at least the seventeenth century. The debate involved both explanations of the origins of political societies and arguments for the nature (see document 1.6) and limits of political obligation. As David Hume pointed out, there are dangers in conflating the two. The fact that political order arose amidst 'the fury of revolutions, conquests and public convulsion' did not mean that its citizens would not eventually accept it.

Hume was also attacking the argument that the origins of political order lay in a contract or agreement made by its citizens. The argument that political order was the product of deliberate artifice had played an important role in undermining the idea that political order was a natural condition into which men were born. The supposition that order was the natural experience drew heavily upon aspects of life closer to daily experience. For Filmer, the origins of political order lay in the family. The first kings, he argued, were the fathers of families.

This patriarchal conception of order was bolstered by analogy with the human body: kings were the heads which directed the lower organs. These images, of patriarchal authority and the analogy of the political and individual body, exercised a powerful influence upon political debate for several centuries. At the time of Filmer's defence of patriarchal authority, however, their influence was waning.

The doctrine which emphasized the artificial character of order pointed, however, in different directions. Much depended upon the picture which political theorists painted of the state of nature, the condition of men prior to the establishment of political order. For Hobbes, writing against the background of the English Civil War, the state of nature was one of savage insecurity. In it, life would be 'solitary, poor, nasty, brutish and short'. The only escape was to form a political community in which men elevated one of their number to a position of absolute authority. Quite how thorough Hobbes was in ascribing order to this sovereign or Leviathan is evident from the fact that the sovereign was to set down the meaning of the key terms of political discourse, the meaning of right and wrong, mine and yours, good and bad. Without this sovereign imposition there would be a mere tower of Babel in which men disputed the meaning of the basic concepts regulating their cohabitation. The strength of Hobbes' insistence that order was derived from the sovereign may seem extreme. It is, however, worth noting that modern historians of the nation-state have placed considerable emphasis upon the role of the state in enforcing common standards and types of law, a 'national' language and respect for common symbols.

John Locke painted a substantially different picture of the state of nature. It was still insecure enough to prompt men to want to establish a political community. But a political community was necessary in order to guarantee what men already had. It was necessary, above all, for the 'preservation of their property'. Which view one took about the origins of political order made a great difference to the nature of political order and, consequently, to the prospects of its collapse. For Hobbes, the collapse of political order meant an immediate return to the state of nature. Short of the certainties established by the sovereign, there was only the anarchy of civil war. Locke, however, could contemplate the dissolution of the established political order with more equanimity. If government transgressed the limits imposed upon it, it could be dissolved and another political order instituted in its place.

For most of the history of political thought the question of how did political order arise has been answered either by reference to myths, legends and religions, or by citing the advantages of human cooperation and the certainties created by political order. Seventeenth-century reflection upon the state of nature was largely an extension of the latter, refined by more systematic argument about man's social and political nature. In the eighteenth century, this kind of explanation began to give way to accounts which emphasizsed the evolution of human societies through several stages, culminating in the formation of complex societies and political institutions.

In these accounts economic development played a key role. Thus, the eighteenth-century Scotsman, Adam Ferguson, distinguished between a 'savage' stage, lacking any conception of property or political authority, a 'barbarous' stage, in which distinctions of property were drawn but in which political disorder was rife, and a 'polished' stage, in which political order complimented economic specialization. Although much in these accounts was speculative, their authors were moving towards an empirical explanation of the origins of political order recognizably similar to contemporary political sociology.

They were also pointing with increasing regularity to the relationship between political order and economically defined classes. The idea of conflict between rich and poor was hardly new. It had been all too evident to the inhabitants of the Greek city-states. In the eighteenth century, however, concepts of class were being utilized within histories of 'civil society' as key explanatory elements. This theme was to be most fully developed by Karl Marx and Friedrich Engels. In their more simplistic formulations the political order, the state, was portrayed as the instrument of the ruling class. The political order was merely a system for preserving the property of the most powerful class of society. There were, however, other interpretations which appeared in their work. The state was presented sometimes as a relatively autonomous body which served to hold the conflicts of social classes in check. Finally, the state was presented as fulfilling certain communal tasks which were beyond the capacities of individuals or, indeed, of the various classes of society.

Although Marx and Engels were inclined to ask in whose interest does the state act?, even where they did not construe its origin in terms of the interests of the ruling class, their ambiguity points to an enduring problem. Political order is both distinct from and related to other kinds of order. We do not now expect political disorder to be accompanied by the 'raging of the sea', and the 'shaking of the earth', but we do expect it to be accompanied by the disruption of the economy. If severe and prolonged enough, we might worry about its impact upon the education of our children or even its psychological impact. In brief, political order seems bound up with order in other spheres of human activity. Yet, contrary to Hobbes, societies are capable of tolerating high levels of political disorder without experiencing total collapse. How we assess the relationship between political order and other forms of order will depend upon our conception of the origins of political order and what purpose we expect political order to serve.

DOCUMENTS

Document 1.1

Aristotle on the State as a Natural Institution

Although he spent most of his life in Athens and founded the Lyceum there, Aristotle (384–321 BC), as a Macedonian by origin, was only a resident alien and did not enjoy Athenian citizenship. For Aristotle, direct participation in the *polis*, or city-state, was the essence of citizenship. He presented the *polis* as a natural institution brought about by a natural social process rooted in human potentiality. He explicitly rejected the idea that political authority rested upon a social contract. The *polis* was the natural further evolution from the smaller communities of the household.

Every state is a community of some kind, and every community is established with a view to some good; for mankind always act in order to obtain that which they think good. But, if all communities aim at some good, the state or political community, which is the highest of all, and which embraces all the rest, aims, and in a greater degree than any other, at the highest good.

Now there is an erroneous opinion that a statesman, king, householder, and master are the same, and that they differ, not in kind, but only in the number of their subjects …

But all this is a mistake; for governments differ in kind, as will be evident to any one who considers the matter according to the method which has hitherto guided us. As in other departments of science, so in politics, the compound should always be resolved into the simple elements or least parts of the whole. We must therefore look at the elements of which the state is composed, in order that we may see in what they differ from one another, and whether any scientific distinction can be drawn between the different kinds of rule.

He who thus considers things in their first growth and origin, whether a state or anything else, will obtain the clearest view of them. In the first place (1) there must be a union of those who cannot exist without each other; for example, of male and female, that the race may continue; and this is a union which is formed, not of deliberate purpose, but because, in common with other animals and with plants, mankind have a natural desire to leave behind them an image of themselves. And (2) there must be a union of natural ruler and subject that both may be preserved. For he who can foresee with his mind is by nature intended to be lord and master, and he who can work with his body is a subject, and by nature a slave; hence master and slave have the same interest. Nature, however, has distinguished between the female and the slave. For she is not niggardly, like the smith who fashions the Delphian knife for many uses; she makes each thing for a single use, and every instrument is best made when intended for one and not for many uses. But among barbarians no distinction is made between women and slaves, because there is no natural ruler among them: they are a community of slaves, male and female. Wherefore the poets say, –

'It is meet that Hellenes should rule over barbarians'; as if they thought that the barbarian and the slave were by nature one.

Out of these two relationships between man and women, master and slave, the family first arises, and Hesiod is right when he says, -

'First house and wife and an ox for the plough, 'for the ox is the poor man's slave. The family is the association established by nature for the supply of men's every day wants, and the members of it are called by Charondas 'companions of cupboard' and by Epimenides the Cretan, 'companions of the manger'. But when several families are united, and the association aims at something more than the supply of daily needs, then comes into existence the village … When several villages are united in a single community, perfect and large enough to be nearly or quite self-sufficing, the state comes into existence, originating in the bare needs of life, and continuing in existence for the sake of a good life. And therefore, if the earlier forms of society are natural, so is the state, for it is the end of them, and the (completed) nature is the end. For what each thing is when fully developed we call its nature, whether we are speaking of a man, a horse, or a family. Besides, the final cause and end of a thing is the best, and to be self-sufficing is the end and the best.

Hence it is evident that the state is a creation of nature, and that man is by nature a political animal. And he who by nature and not by mere accident is without a state, is either above humanity, or below it; he is the 'Tribeless, lawless, heartless one,' whom Homer denounces – the outcast who is a lover of war; he may be compared to a bird which flies alone.

Now the reason why man is more of a political animal than bees or any other gregarious animals is evident. Nature, as we often say, makes nothing in vain, and man is the only animal whom she has endowed with the gift of speech. And whereas mere sound is but an indication of pleasure or pain, and is therefore found in other animals (for their nature attains to the perception of pleasure and pain and the intimation of them to one another, and no further), the power of speech is intended to set forth the expedient and inexpedient, and likewise the just and the unjust. And it is a characteristic of man that he alone has any sense of good and evil, of just and unjust, and the association of living beings who have this sense makes a family and a state.

Thus the state is by nature clearly prior to the family and to the individual, since the whole is of necessity prior to the part; for example, if the whole body be destroyed, there will be no foot or hand, except in an equivocal sense, as we might speak of a stone hand; for when destroyed the hand will be no better. But things are defined by their working and power; and we ought not to say that they are the same when they are no longer the same, but only that they have the same name. The proof that the state is a creation of nature and prior to the individual is that the individual, when isolated, is not self-sufficing; and therefore he is like a part in relation to the whole. But he who is unable to live in society, or who has no need because he is sufficient for himself, must be either a beast or a god: he is not part of a state. A social instinct is implanted in all men by nature, and yet he who first founded the state was the greatest of benefactors. For man, when perfected, is the best of animals, but, when separated from law and justice, he is the worst of all; since armed injustice is the more dangerous, and he is equipped at birth with the arms of intelligence and with moral qualities which he may use for the worst ends. Wherefore, if he have not virtue, he is most unholy and the most savage of animals, and the most full of lust and gluttony.

Document 1.2

St Thomas Aquinas, *On Kingship*

St Thomas Aquinas (1225–74), one of the greatest leading figures in medieval philosophy and theology, wrote *On Kingship* (sometimes also known as *On the Governance of Rulers*) as the earliest of his political works between 1265 and 1267. It drew heavily on Aristotle. It asserted the naturalness of the political community while arguing for the superiority of monarchy over other forms of government, distinguishing tyranny from proper kingship and specifying the duties incumbent on good rulers.

We must first explain what is meant by the term, king. When a thing is directed towards an end, and it is possible to go one way or another, someone must indicate the best way to proceed toward the end. For example, a ship that moves in different directions with the shifting winds would never reach its destination if it were not guided into port by the skill of its helmsman. Man too has an end towards which all the actions of his life are directed, since all intelligent beings act for an end. Yet the diversity of men's pursuits and activities means that men proceed to their intended objectives in different ways. Therefore man needs someone to direct him towards his end. Now every man is naturally endowed with the light of reason to direct his actions towards his end. If men were intended to live alone as do many animals, there would be no need for anyone to direct him towards his end, since every man would be his own king under God, the highest king, and the light of reason given to him from on high would enable him to act on his own. But man is by nature a political and social animal. Even more than other animals he lives in groups (*multitudine*). This is demonstrated by the requirements of his nature. Nature has given other animals food, furry covering, teeth, and horns and claws – or at least speed of flight – as means to defend themselves. Man however, is given none of these by nature. Instead he has been given the use of his reason to secure all these things by the work of his hands. But a man cannot secure all these by himself, for a man cannot adequately provide for his life by himself. Therefore it is natural for man to live in association with his fellows.

In addition, nature has instilled in other animals the ability to perceive what is useful or harmful to them. For example, a sheep knows by nature that the wolf is its enemy. Some animals even have the natural ability to know the medicinal herbs and other things necessary to their existence. Man, on the other hand, has a natural knowledge of what is necessary to his life only in a general way, using his reason to move from general principles to the knowledge of particular things that are necessary for human life. And it is not possible for one man to arrive at the knowledge of all these things through the use of his reason. Thus it is necessary for him to live in society so that one person can help another and different men can employ their reasons in different ways, one in medicine, and others in this or that endeavor. This is most clearly demonstrated by the fact that man uses words to communicate his thoughts fully to others. It is true that other animals express their feelings in a general way. Dogs express their anger by barking and other animals express their feelings in other ways. But man is more able to communicate with others than other gregarious animals such as cranes, ants, or bees. [King] Solomon refers to this when he says 'It is better for two to live together than alone, for they have the advantage of mutual company.'

Therefore if it is natural for man to live in association with others, there must be some way for them to be governed. For if many men were to live together and each to provide what is convenient for himself, the group (*multitudo*) would break up unless one of them had the responsibility for the good of the group, just as the body of a man or an animal would disintegrate without a single controlling force in the body that aimed at the common good of all the members. As Solomon says, 'Where there is no ruler, the people will be dispersed'. This is reasonable since the private good and the common good are not the same. Private concerns divide the community, while common concerns unite it. Those differences exist for different reasons. Therefore besides what moves each person to his own private good there must be something that moves everyone to the common good of the many. Therefore in everything that is ordered to a single end, one thing is found that rules the rest. In the physical universe, by the intention of divine providence all the other bodies are ruled by the first or heavenly body, as divine providence directs, and all material bodies are ruled by rational creatures. In each man the soul rules the body and within the soul reason rules over passion and desire. Likewise among the parts of the body there is one ruling part, either the heart or the head that moves all the others. So in every group, there must be something that rules.

When things are ordered to some end, one can proceed in the right way and the wrong way. So the government of a group can be carried out in the right way or the wrong way. Something is done in the right way when it is led to its appropriate end, and in the wrong way when it is led to an inappropriate end. The proper end of a group of free men is different from that of a group of slaves, for a free man determines his own actions while a slave, *qua slave*, is one who belongs to another. If then a group of free men is directed by a ruler to the common good of the group, his government will be right and just because it is appropriate for free men, but if the government is directed not at the common good of the group but at the private good of the ruler it will be unjust and a perversion. God warns such rulers in the Book of Ezekiel, 'Woe to shepherds that feed themselves (because they seek their own benefit). Should not the flocks be fed by the shepherd?' Shepherds must seek the good of their flocks, and rulers, the good of those subject to them.

If a government is under one man who seeks his own benefit and not the good of those subject to him, the ruler is called a tyrant. The word is derived from *tyro*, the Greek word for 'strength,' because he uses force to oppress the people instead of justice to rule. Hence among the ancients all powerful men were called tyrants. But if an unjust government is exercised not by one but by more than one, if they are few it is called an oligarchy which means 'rule by the few'. In this case a few rich men oppress the people. Such a government differs only in number from a tyranny. An unjust government exercised by the many is called a democracy, that is, 'rule by the people', which occurs when the common people use the force of numbers to oppress the rich. In this case the whole people acts like a tyrant.

We can also classify the types of just government. If the government is carried out by a large number, as when a group of warriors governs a city or province, it is usually called a polity. But if a few virtuous men carry out the administration, a government of this kind is called an aristocracy, that is the best rule, or rule of the best, who for this reason are called the aristocrats. But if a good government is in the hands of one man alone it is appropriate to call him a king. So the Lord said in [the Book of] Ezekiel, 'My servant David will be king all over, and there will be one shepherd over all of them.' Thus it is very clear that it is the nature of kingship that there should be one to rule and that he should be a shepherd who seeks the common good of all and not his own benefit.

Since men must live together because they cannot acquire what is needed to live if they remain by themselves, a social group is more perfect if it provides better for the necessities of life. A family in a single household provides adequately for some of the needs of life such as the natural acts of nourishment and the procreation of children, etc. In a single locality you will find self-sufficiency in a given manufacture. But a city which is a perfect community contains whatever is needed for life, and even more so a province because of the need for common defense and mutual aid against enemies. Therefore the right name for someone who rules a perfect community, whether a city or a province, is a king. while someone who directs a household is not called a king but the father of a family. Yet there is a certain resemblance to a king in his position so that sometimes kings are called the fathers of their people.

From what we have said it is clear that a king is one who rules over the people of a city or a province for the common good. So Solomon says in [the Book of] Ecclesiastes. 'A king commands all the lands subject to him.'

Thomas Hobbes, Of the Natural Condition of Mankind, as Concerning Their Felicity, and Misery

Thomas Hobbes (1588–1679) was a philosopher and political theorist. His doctrines were understood by some to be supportive of the monarchy in its dispute with Parliament and Hobbes fled to France in 1640. The English royalists however regarded his *Leviathan* (1651) with considerable suspicion and Hobbes fled back to England. The uncertainty about his thought is reflected by the fact that, on the one hand, he received a pension from Charles II and, on the other, his work was condemned by the University of Oxford in 1683. He included this famous analysis of the State of Nature in *Leviathan*, in which he portrays 'what manner of life there would be where there was no common power to fear'. Men by nature are proud and assertive, but also fearful, creatures. The English Civil War mirrors the State of Nature and he uses this analysis of man and his natural passions to justify his conception of sovereignty.

Nature hath made men so equal, in the faculties of the body, and mind; as that though there be found one man sometimes manifestly stronger in body, or of quicker mind than another; yet when all is reckoned together, the difference between man, and man, is not so considerable, as that one man can thereupon claim to himself any benefit, to which another may not pretend, as well as he. For as to the strength of body, the weakest has strength enough to kill the strongest, either by secret machination, or by confederacy with others, that are in the same danger with himself.

And as to the faculties of the mind, ... I find yet a greater equality amongst men, than that of strength ... That which may perhaps make such equality incredible, is but a vain conceit of one's own wisdom, which almost all men think they have in a greater degree, than the vulgar; that is, than all men but themselves, and a few others, whom by fame, or for concurring with themselves, they approve ... But this proveth rather that men are in that point equal than unequal. For there is not ordinarily a greater sign of the equal distribution of any thing, than that every man is contented with his share.

From this equality of ability, ariseth equality of hope in the attaining of our ends. And therefore if any two men desire the same thing, which nevertheless they cannot both enjoy, they become enemies; and in the way to their end, which is principally their own conservation, and sometimes their delectation only, endeavour to destroy, or subdue one another. And from hence it comes to pass, that where an invader hath no more to fear, than another man's single power; if one plant, sow, build, or possess a convenient seat, others may probably be expected to come prepared with forces united, to dispossess, and deprive him, not only of the fruit of his labour, but also of his life, or liberty. And the invader again is in the like danger of another.

And from this diffidence of one another, there is no way for any man to secure himself, so reasonable as anticipation; that is, by force, or wiles, to master the persons of all men he can, so long, till he see no other power great enough to endanger him: and this is no more than his own conservation requireth, and is generally allowed. Also because there be some, that taking pleasure in contemplating their own power in the acts of conquest, which they pursue farther than their security requires; if others, that otherwise would be glad to be at ease within modest bounds, should not by invasion increase their power, they would not be able, long time, by standing only on their defence, to subsist. And by consequence, such augmentation of dominion over men being necessary to a man's conservation, it ought to be allowed him.

Again, men have no pleasure, but on the contrary a great deal of grief, in keeping company, where there is no power able to over-awe them all. For every man looketh that his companion should value him, at the same rate he sets upon himself: and upon all signs of contempt, or undervaluing, naturally endeavours, as far as he dares, (which amongst them that have no common power to keep them in quiet, is far enough to make them destroy each other), to extort a greater value from his contemners, by damage; and from others, by the example.

So that in the nature of man, we find three principal causes of quarrel. First, competition; secondly, diffidence; thirdly, glory.

The first, maketh men invade for gain; the second, for safety; and the third, for reputation. The first use violence, to make themselves masters of other men's persons, wives, children, and cattle; the second, to defend them; the third, for trifles, as a word, a smile, a different opinion, and any other sign of undervalue ...

Hereby it is manifest, that during the time men live without a common power to keep them all in awe, they are in that condition which is called war; and such a war, as is of every man, against every man. For WAR, consisteth not in battle only, or the act of fighting; but in a tract of time, wherein the will to contend by battle is sufficiently known ...

Whatsoever therefore is consequent to a time of war, where every man is enemy to every man; the same is consequent to the time, wherein men live without other security, than what their own strength, and their own invention shall furnish them withal. In such condition, there is no place for industry; because the fruit thereof is uncertain: and consequently no culture of the earth; no navigation, nor use of the commodities that may be imported by sea; no commodious building; no instruments of moving, and removing, such things as require much force; no knowledge of the face of the earth; no account of time; no arts; no letters; no society; and which is worst of all, continual fear, and danger of violent death; and the life of man, solitary, poor, nasty, brutish, and short.

It may seem strange to some man, that has not well weighted these things; that nature should thus dissociate, and render men apt to invade, and destroy one another: and he may therefore, not trusting to this inference, made from the passions, desire perhaps to have the same confirmed by experience. Let him therfore consider with himself, when taking a journey, he arms himself, and seeks to go well accompanied; when going to sleep, he locks his doors; when even in his house he locks his chests; and this when he knows there be laws, and public officers, armed, to revenge all injuries shall be done him; what opinion he has of his fellow subjects, when he rides armed; of his fellow citizens, when he locks his doors; and of his children, and servants, when he locks his chests. Does he not there as much accuse mankind by his actions, as I do by my words? ...

It may peradventure be thought, there was never such a time, nor condition of war as this; and I believe it was never generally so, over all the world: but there are many places, where they live so now. For the savage people in many places of America, except the government of small families, the concord whereof dependeth on natural lust, have no government at all; and live at this day in that brutish manner, as I said before. Howsoever, it may be perceived what manner of life there would be, where there were no common power to fear, by the manner of life, which men that have formerly lived under a peaceful government, use to degenerate into, in a civil war ...

To this war of every man, against every man, this also is consequent; that nothing can be unjust. The notions of right and wrong, justice and injustice have there no place. Where there is no common power, there is no law: where no law, no injustice. Force, and fraud, are in war the two cardinal virtues ... It is consequent also to the same condition, that there be no property, no domination, no mine and thine distinct; but only that to be every man's, that he can get: and for so long, as he can keep it. And thus much for the ill condition, which man by mere nature is actually placed in; though with a possibility to come out of it, consisting partly in the passions, partly in his reason.

The passions that incline men to peace, are fear of death; desire of such things as are necessary to commodious living; and a hope by their industry to obtain them. And reason suggesteth convenient articles of peace, upon which men may be drawn to agreement. These articles, are they, which otherwise are called the Laws of Nature ...

Document 1.4

Robert Filmer on the Patriarchal View (*Observations upon Aristotle's Politics Touching Forms of Government*)

Sir Robert Filmer (1588–1653) was a Royalist political theorist whose best-known work, *Patriarcha*, although published in 1680, was originally written in the early 1630s. Filmer argued that the political authority of the monarch was absolute and had its origin in the divine establishment of patriarchal power. He rejected any idea of original natural liberty, or social contract. The state was a family and the monarch had fatherly authority over it. *The Observations*, from which this extract is taken, was published in 1652. Filmer attempted to show that Aristotle had favoured the doctrine of royal absolutism even if he had sometimes been unclear in expressing the theory.

(From the Preface)

It is not probable that any sure direction of the beginning of government can be found either in Plato, Aristotle, Cicero, Polybius, or in any other of the heathen authors, who were ignorant of the manner of the creation of the world: we must not neglect the scriptures and search in philosophers for the grounds of dominion and property, which are the main principles of government and justice. The first government in the world was monarchical, in the father of all flesh. Adam being commanded to multiply, and people the earth, and to subdue it, and having dominion given him over all creatures, was thereby the monarch of the whole world; none of his posterity had any right to possess anything, but by his grant or permission, or by succession from him. The earth (says the Psalmist) has he given to the children of men: which shows the title comes from the fatherhood. There never was any such thing as an independent multitude who at first had a natural right to a community. This is but a fiction or fancy of too many in these days, who please themselves in running after the opinions of philosophers and poets, to find out such an original of government as might promise them some title to liberty, to the great scandal of Christianity and bringing in of atheism, since a natural freedom of mankind cannot be supposed without the denial of the creation of Adam. And yet this conceit of original freedom is the only ground upon which not only the heathen philosophers, but also the authors of the principles of the civil law, and Grotius, Selden, Hobbes, Ascham and others, raise and build their doctrines of government, and of the several sorts of kinds, as they call them, of commonwealths.

Adam was the father, king and lord over his family: a son, a subject, and a servant or a slave were one and the same thing at first. The father had power to dispose or sell his children or servants; whence we find that, at the first reckoning up of goods in scripture, the manservant and the maidservant are numbered among the possessions and substance of the owner, as other goods were. As for the names of subject, slave and tyrant, they are not found in scripture, but what we now call a subject of a slave is there named no other than a servant. I cannot learn that either the Hebrew, Greek or Latin have any proper and original word for a tyrant or a slave: it seems these are names of later invention and taken up in disgrace of monarchial government.

I cannot find any one place or text in the Bible where any power or commission is given to a people either to govern themselves, or to choose themselves governors, or to alter the manner of government at their pleasure. The power of government is settled and fixed by the commandment of 'honour thy father'; if there were a higher power than the fatherly, then this commandment could not stand and be observed. Whereas we read in scripture of some actions of the people in setting up of kings, further than to a naked declaration by a part of the people of their obedience such actions could not amount, since we find no commission they have, to bestow any right. A true representation of the people to be made is as impossible as for the whole people to govern. The names of an aristocracy, a democracy, a commonwealth, a state, or any other of like signification are not to be met either in the law or gospel.

That there is a ground in nature for monarchy, Aristotle himself affirms, saying the first kings were fathers of families. As for any ground of any other form of government, there has been none yet alleged but a supposed natural freedom of mankind; the proof whereof I find none do undertake, but only beg it to be granted. We find the government of God's own people varied under the several titles of Patriarchs, Captains, Judges and Kings, but in all these the supreme power rested still in one person only. We nowhere find any supreme power given to the people, or to a multitude, in scripture, or ever exercised by them. The people were never the Lord's anointed, nor called gods, nor crowned, nor had the title of nursing fathers (Genesis xxxv, ii). The supreme power, being an indivisible beam of majesty, cannot be divided among, or settled upon, a multitude. God would have fixed in one person, not sometimes in one part of the people, and sometimes in another, and sometimes, and that for the most part, nowhere, as when the assembly is dissolved it must rest in the air, or in the walls of the chamber where they were assembled.

If there were anything like a popular government among God's people, it was about the time of the Judges, when there was no king in Israel. For they had then some small show of government, such as it was, but it was so poor and beggarly that the scripture brands it with this note, that every man did what was right in his own eyes, because there was no king in Israel. It is not said, because there was no government but because there was no king. It seems no government, but the government of a king, in the judgement of the scriptures, could restrain men from doing what they liked. Where every man does what he pleases, it may be truly said, there is no government; for the end of government is that every man should not do what he pleases, or be his own judge in his own case. For the scripture to say there was no king, is to say, there was no form of government in Israel.

(From the Observations)

Those that are willing to be persuaded that the power of government is originally in the people, finding how impossible it is for any people to exercise such power, do surmise that though the people cannot govern, yet they may choose representers or trustees that may manage this power for the people, and such representers must be surmised to be the people. And since such representers cannot truly be chosen by the people, they are fain to divide the people into several parts, as of provinces, cities and borough-towns, and to allow to every one of those parts to choose one representer or more of their own. And such representers, though not any of them be chosen by the whole, or major part, of the people, yet still must be surmised to be the people; nay, though not one of them be chosen either by the people or the major part of the people of any province, city or borough for which they serve, but only a smaller part, still it must be said to be the people.

Now when such representers of the people do assemble or meet, it is never seen that all of them can at one time meet together; and so there never appears a true or full representation of the whole people of the nation, the representers of one part or other being absent, but still they must be imagined to be the people. And when such imperfect assemblies be met, though not half be present, they proceed; and though their number be never so small, yet it is so big that in the debate of any business moment, they know not how to handle it, without referring it to a fewer number than themselves though themselves are not so many as they should be. Thus those that are chosen to represent the people are necessitated to choose others to represent the representers themselves. A trustee of the north does delegate his power to a trustee of the south; and one of the east may substitute one of the west for his proxy. Hereby it comes to pass that public debates which are imagined to be referred to have a general assembly of a kingdom, are contracted into a particular or private assembly, than which nothing can be more destructive or contrary to the nature of public assemblies. Each company of such trustees has a prolocutor, or speaker; who, by the help of three or four of his fellows that are most active, may easily comply in gratifying one the other, so that each of them in their turn may sway the trustees, whilst one man, for himself or his friend, may rule in one business, and another man for himself or his friend prevail in another cause, till such a number of trustees be reduced to so many petty monarchs as there be men of it. So in all popularities, where a general council or great assembly of the people meet, they find it impossible to dispatch any great action either with expedition or secrecy if a public free debate be admitted; and therefore are constrained to epitomize, and sub-epitomize themselves so long, till at last they crumble away into the atoms of monarchy, which is the next degree to anarchy; for anarchy is nothing else but a broken monarchy, where every man is his own monarch or governor.

It is believed by many that, at the very first assembling of the people, it was unanimously agreed in the first place that the consent of the major part should bind the whole; and that though this first agreement cannot possibly be proved, either how or by whom it could be made, yet it must necessarily be believed or supposed, because otherwise there could be no lawful government at all. That there could be no lawful government, except a general consent of the whole people be first surmised, is no sound proposition; yet true it is that there could be no popular government without it. But if there were at first a government without being beholden to the people for their consent, as all men confess there was, I find no reason but that there may be so still, without asking leave of the multitude.

If it be true that men are by nature free-born, and not to be governed without their own consents, and that self-preservation is to be regarded in the first place, it is not lawful for any government but self-government to be in the world: it were sin in the people to desire, or attempt to consent to, any other government. If the fathers will promise to themselves to be slaves, yet for their children they cannot, who have always the same right to set themselves at liberty which their fathers had to enslave themselves.

To pretend that a major part, or the silent consent of any part, may be interpreted to bind the whole people is both unreasonable and unnatural; it is against all reason for men to bind others where it is against nature for men to bind themselves. Men that boast so much of natural freedom are not willing to consider how contradictory and destructive the power of a major part is to the natural liberty of the whole people; the two grand favourites of the subjects, liberty and property (for which most men pretend to strive), are as contrary as fire to water, and cannot stand together. Though by human laws in voluntary actions a major part may be tolerated to bind the whole multitude, yet in necessary actions, such as those of nature are, it cannot be so. Besides, if it were possible for the whole people to choose their representers, then either every (and) each one of these representers ought to be particularly chosen by the whole people, and not one representer by one part, and another representer by another part of the people, or else it is necessary that continually the entire number of the representers be present, because otherwise the whole people is never represented.

Again, it is impossible for the people, though they might and would choose a government, or governors, ever to be able to do it: for the people, to speak truly and properly, is a thing or body in continual alteration and change. It never continues one minute the same, being composed of a multitude of parts whereof divers continually decay and perish, and others renew and succeed in their places. They which are the people this minute are not the people the next minute. If it be answered that it is impossible to stand so strictly, as to have the consent of the whole people, and therefore that which cannot be, must be supposed to be the act of the whole people, this is a strange answer: first to affirm a necessity of having the people's consent, then to confess an impossibility of having it. If but once that liberty, which is esteemed so sacred, be broken, or be taken away but from one of the meanest or basest of all the people, a wide gap is thereby opened to many multitude whatsoever that is able to call themselves, or whomsoever they please, the people …

Document 1.5

John Locke, Of the Ends of Political Society and Government

Locke (1632–1704) gained access to the world of high politics as a protégé of the Earl of Shaftesbury whose life Locke saved by an operation whose success has been described as a medical miracle of the age. He was involved in several dangerous conspiracies to restrain royal power and eventually fled into exile. He did not return until the Glorious Revolution of 1689. Locke published his *Two Treatises of Government* after the Glorious Revolution, although they were composed at the time of the Exclusion Crisis (1679–80). He follows the example of Hobbes in contrasting political society with the state of nature, and though he has a more benign view of the latter, which he describes as being 'properly' a condition where men live together 'according to reason without a common superior on earth', he is aware of its inadequacies. In contradiction of Filmer's patriarchal view, Locke states that 'all peaceful beginnings of Government have been laid in the consent of the people'.

If man in the state of nature be so free, as has been said; if he be absolute lord of his own person and possessions, equal to the greatest, and subject to nobody, why will he part with his freedom? Why will he give up this empire, and subject himself to the dominion and control of any other power? To which 'tis obvious to answer, that though in the state of nature he hath such a right, yet the enjoyment of it is very uncertain, and constantly exposed to the invasion of others. For all being kings as much as he, every man his equal, and the greater part no strict observers of equity and justice, the enjoyment of the property he has in this state is very unsafe, very unsecure. This makes him willing to quit a condition, which, however free, is full of fears and continual dangers; and 'tis not without reason that he seeks out and is willing to join in society with others, who are already united, or have a mind to unite, for the mutual preservation of their lives, liberties, and estates, which I call by the general name, property.

The great and chief end, therefore, of men's uniting into commonwealths, and putting themselves under government, is the preservation of their property; to which in the state of nature there are many things wanting.

First, There wants an established, settled, known law, received and allowed by common consent to be the standard of right and wrong, and the common measure to decide all controversies between them. For though the law of nature be plain and intelligible to all rational creatures; yet men, being biased by their interest, as well as ignorant for want of study of it, are not apt to allow of it as a law binding to them in the application of it to their particular cases.

Secondly, In the state of nature there wants a known and indifferent judge, with authority to determine all differences according to the established law. For every one in that state, being both judge and executioner of the law of nature, men being partial to themselves, passion and revenge is very apt to carry them too far, and with too much heat in their own cases, as well as negligence and unconcernedness, to make them too remiss in other men's.

Thirdly, In the state of nature there often wants power to back and support the sentence when right, and to give it due execution. They who by any injustice offended will seldom fail, where they are able, by force to make good their injustice; such resistance many times makes the punishment dangerous, and frequently destructive to those who attempt it.

Thus mankind, notwithstanding all the privileges of the state of nature, being but in an ill condition while they remain in it, are quickly driven into society … And in this we have the original right and rise of both the legislative and executive power, as well as of the governments and societies themselves.

For in the state of nature, to omit the liberty he has of innocent delights, a man has two powers.

The first is to do whatsoever he thinks fit for the preservation of himself and others within the permission of the laws of nature, by which law, common to them all, he and all the rest of mankind are of one community, make up one society, distinct from all other creatures. And were it not for the corruption and viciousness of degenerate men there would be no need of any other, no necessity that men should separate from this great and natural community, and by positive agreements combine into smaller and divided associations.

Document 1.6

David Hume on The Foundation of Government

David Hume (1711–76), Scottish philosopher and historian, was sceptical of 'natural rights' or an original 'social contract'. He argued that to postulate a state of nature antecedent to society in which isolated individuals come together to forge a social contract was a fiction that was of no use in explaining how or why men behave as they do in society. Social and political institutions should be understood as devices developed in response to the exigencies of the human condition. He showed less interest in who was morally entitled to rule than in who was likely to rule well and command the allegiance of the people.

My intention here is not to exclude the consent of the people from being one just foundation of government where it has place. It is surely the best and most sacred of any. I only pretend that it has very seldom had place in any degree and never almost in its full extent. And that therefore some other foundation of government must also be admitted.

Were all men possessed of so inflexible a regard to justice that, of themselves, they would totally abstain from the properties of others, they had forever remained in a state of absolute liberty, without subjection to any magistrate or political society; but this is a state of perfection of which human nature is justly deemed incapable. Again, were all men possessed of so perfect an understanding as always to know their own interests, no form of government had ever been submitted to, but what was established on consent, and was fully canvassed by every member of the society; but this state of perfection is likewise much superior to human nature. Reason, history, and experience show us that all political societies have had an origin much less accurate and regular; and were one to choose a period of time when the people's consent was the least regarded in public transactions, it would be precisely on the establishment of a new government. In a settled constitution, their inclinations are often consulted; but during the fury of revolutions, conquests, and public convulsions, military force or political craft usually decides the controversy.

When a new government is established, by whatever means, the people are commonly dissatisfied with it, and pay obedience more from fear and necessity, than from any idea of allegiance or of moral obligation. The prince is watchful and jealous, and must carefully guard against every beginning or appearance of insurrection. Time, by degrees, removes all these difficulties, and accustoms the nation to regard as their lawful or native princes that family which, at first, they considered as usurpers or foreign conquerors. In order to found this opinion, they have no recourse to any notion of voluntary consent or promise, which, they know, never was in this case either expected or demanded. The original establishment was formed by violence, and submitted to from necessity. The subsequent administration is also supported by power, and acquiesced in by the people, not as a matter of choice, but of obligation. They imagine not that their consent gives their prince a title; but they willingly consent, because they think that, from long possession, he has acquired a title, independent of their choice or inclination.

Should it be said that by living under the dominion of a prince, which one might leave, every individual has given a tacit consent to his authority, and promised him obedience, it may be answered that such an implied consent can only have place where a man imagines that the matter depends on his choice. But where he thinks (as all mankind do who are born under established governments) that by his birth he owes allegiance to a certain prince or certain form of government, it would be absurd to infer a consent or choice which he, expressly in this case, renounces and disclaims.

Can we seriously say that a poor peasant or artisan has a free choice to leave his country, when he knows no foreign language or manners, and lives from day to day, by the small wages which he acquires? We may as well assert that a man, by remaining in a vessel, freely consents to the dominion of the master, though he was carried on board while asleep, and must leap into the ocean, and perish, the moment he leaves her.

Document 1.7

Jean-Jacques Rousseau on the Civil State

The following extract is from *The Social Contract* (1762). Rousseau (1712–78) discusses the benefits of participation in a civil association and appears to follow Aristotle in believing human beings reach their moral fulfilment through citizenship. The emphasis on community and the bonds of sentiment, as contrasted with individualism and rationalism, are key elements in his thought.

The transition from the state of nature to the civil state produces a quite remarkable transformation within man – i.e., it substitutes justice for instinct as the controlling factor in his behaviour, and confers upon his actions a moral significance that they have hitherto lacked.

Only when this transformation has come about does the voice of duty take the place of physical motivation, and law that of appetite. Only then, therefore, does man, who hitherto has considered himself alone, find himself obliged to act on other principles, and to consult his reason before he heeds his desires.

In the civil state man foregoes, to be sure, numerous benefits that he has been enjoying as grants from nature. So great, however, are the benefits that he acquires in their stead – such is the extent to which his faculties are mobilized and developed, such the degree to which his concepts are broadened and his sentiments ennobled, such the level to which his soul is lifted up – that we are justified in saying this: if only the abuses associated with his new condition did not often reduce him to a condition even lower than the state of nature, he would have to bless incessantly the happy moment that has snatched him, once and for all, from that state, and made out of a stupid and dull-witted animal an intelligent being and a man.

Let us reduce the items on each side of the ledger to terms easy to compare: Man loses, through the social contract, his natural liberty, along with an unlimited right to anything that he is tempted by and can get. He gains civil liberty, along with ownership of all he possesses. Lest we fail to grasp the extent of his gains, however, we must distinguish sharply between natural liberty, which is limited only by the individual's own powers, and civil liberty, which is limited by the general will – as also between possession, which rests either upon might or upon the right of the first occupant, and ownership, which can have no basis other than positive title.

Nor is that all. One might add to the gains from the civil state that of moral freedom, in the absence of which nothing can make man truly his own master. For just as motivation by sheer appetite is slavery, so obedience to self-imposed law is liberty. But I have already dwelt all too long upon this topic – besides which the philosophical meaning of the word liberty is, at this point, no part of my problem.

Document 1.8

Thomas Paine on Society and Government

Thomas Paine (1737–1809), the English radical, political propagandist and revolutionary, spent most of his active political career in America and France. His *Rights of Man* (1791–92) made him the foremost radical thinker in Britain in the late eighteenth century. That was inspired by Edmund Burke's attack on the French Revolution. The extract below comes from his earlier publication *Common Sense* (1776), which pleaded the case for American Independence and first appeared in Philadelphia. It went through twenty-five impressions in its first year of publication alone. Although he did not necessarily persuade with his republicanism, he convinced many who had played little part in politics previously that they had the right to discuss political principles and agitate for political reform. The following extract contains the gist of Paine's view of government as a necessary evil to be reduced to a minimum and rendered safe by means of representative government involving frequent elections.

Some writers have so confounded society with government, as to leave little or no distinction between them; whereas they are not only different, but have different origins. Society is produced by our wants, and government by our wickedness; the former promotes our happiness *positively* by uniting our affections, the latter *negatively* by restraining our vices. The one encourages intercourse, the other creates distinctions. The first is a patron, the last a punisher. Society in every state is a blessing, but government, even in its best state, is but a necessary evil; in its worst state an intolerable one: for when we suffer, or are exposed to the same miseries *by a government*, which we might expect in a country *without government*, our calamity is heightened by reflecting that we furnish the means by which we suffer. Government, like dress, is the badge of lost innocence; the palaces of kings are built upon the ruins of the bowers of paradise. For were the impulses of conscience clear, uniform and irresistibly obeyed, man would need no other lawgiver; but that not being the case, he finds it necessary to surrender up a part of his property to furnish means for the protection of the rest; and this he is induced to do by the same prudence which in every other case advises him, out of two evils to choose the least. Wherefore, security being the true design and end of government, it unanswerably follows that whatever form thereof appears most likely to ensure it to us, with the least expense and greatest benefit, is preferable to all others.

In order to gain a clear and just idea of the design and end of government, let us suppose a small number of persons settled in some sequestered part of the earth, unconnected with the rest; they will then represent the first peopling of any country, or of the world. In this state of natural liberty, society will be their first thought. A thousand motives will excite them thereto; the strength of one man is so unequal to his wants, and his mind so unfitted for perpetual solitude, that he is soon obliged to seek assistance and relief of another, who in his turn requires the same. Four or five united would be able to raise a tolerable dwelling in the midst of a wilderness, but one man might labour out the common period of life without accomplishing any thing; when he had felled his timber he could not remove it, nor erect it after it was removed; hunger in the mean time would urge him to quit his work, and every different want would call him a different way. Disease, nay even misfortune, would be death; for, though neither might be mortal, yet either would disable him from living, and reduce him to a state in which he might rather be said to perish than to die.

Thus necessity, like a gravitating power, would soon form our newly arrived emigrants into society, the reciprocal blessings of which would supersede, and render the obligations of law and government unnecessary while they remained perfectly just to each other; but as nothing but Heaven is impregnable to vice, it will unavoidably happen that in proportion as they surmount the first difficulties of emigration, which bound them together in a common cause, they will begin to relax in their duty and attachment to each other: and this remissness will point out the necessity of establishing some form of government to supply the defect of moral virtue.

Some convenient tree will afford them a State House, under the branches of which the whole colony may assemble to deliberate on public matters. It is more than probable that their first laws will have the title only of Regulations and be enforced by no other penalty than public disesteem. In this first parliament every man by natural right will have a seat.

But as the colony increases, the public concerns will increase likewise, and the distance at which the members may be separated, will render it too inconvenient for all of them to meet on every occasion as at first, when their number was small, their habitations near, and the public concerns few and trifling. This will point out the convenience of their consenting to leave the legislative part to be managed by a select number chosen from the whole body, who are supposed to have the same concerns at stake which those have who appointed them, and who will act in the same manner as the whole body would act were they present. If the colony continue increasing, it will become necessary to augment the number of representatives, and that the interest of every part of the colony may be attended to, it will be found best to divide the whole into convenient parts, each part sending its proper number: and that the *elected* might never form to themselves an interest separate from the *electors*, prudence will point out the propriety of having elections often: because as the *elected* might by that means return and mix again with the general body of the electors in a few months, their fidelity to the public will be secured by the prudent reflection of not making a rod for themselves. And as this frequent interchange will establish a common interest with every part of the community, they will mutually and naturally support each other, and on this, (not on the unmeaning name of king,) depends the *strength of government, and the happiness of the governed*.

Here then is the origin and rise of government; namely, a mode rendered necessary by the inability of moral virtue to govern the world; here too is the design and end of government, viz. Freedom and security. And however our eyes may be dazzled with show, or our ears deceived by sound; however prejudice may warp our wills, or interest darken our understanding, the simple voice of nature and reason will say, 'tis right.

I draw my idea of the form of government from a principle in nature which no art can overturn, viz. that the more simple any thing is, the less liable it is to be disordered, and the easier repaired when disordered; and with this maxim in view I offer a few remarks on the so much boasted constitution of England. That it was noble for the dark and slavish times in which it was erected, is granted. When the world was overrun with tyranny the least remove therefrom was a glorious rescue. But that it is imperfect, subject to convulsions, and incapable of producing what it seems to promise, is easily demonstrated …

Document 1.9

Edmund Burke on Government and Human Nature

Edmund Burke (1729–97) had been a Whig politician for many years before he published *Reflections on the Revolution in France* (1790). This, from which the following extract is taken, made him one of the founding fathers of Conservative political thought. He attacked the assumptions underlying the French Revolution, rationalism, abstract thought and utopianism and asserted the value of tradition, custom and evolutionary development. Government should be related to human nature as it was. It existed to restrain the effects of human imperfection.

... One of the first motives to civil society, and which becomes one of its fundamental rules, is, that no man should be judge of his own cause. By this each person has at once divested himself of the first fundamental right of an uncovenanted man, that is, to judge for himself, and to assert his own cause. He abdicates all right to be his own governor. He inclusively, in a great measure, abandons the right of self-defence, the first law of nature. Men cannot enjoy the rights of an uncivil and of a civil state together. That he may obtain justice he gives up his right of determining what it is in points the most essential to him. That he may secure some liberty, he makes a surrender in trust of the whole of it.

Government is not made in virtue of natural rights, which may and do exist in total independence of it; and exist in much greater clearness, and in a much greater degree of abstract perfection: but their abstract perfection is their practical defect. By having a right to everything they want everything. Government is a contrivance of human wisdom to provide for human wants. Men have a right that these wants should be provided for by this wisdom. Among these wants is to be reckoned the want, out of civil society, of a sufficient restraint upon their passions. Society requires not only that the passions of individuals should be subjected, but that even in the mass and body as well as in the individuals, the inclinations of men should frequently be thwarted, their will controlled, and their passions brought into subjection. This can only be done by a power out of themselves; and not, in the exercise of its function, subject to that will and to those passions which it is its office to bridle and subdue. In this sense the restraints on men, as well as their liberties, are to be reckoned among their rights. But as the liberties, and the restrictions vary with times and circumstances, and admit of infinite modifications, they cannot be settled upon any abstract rule: and nothing is so foolish as to distress them upon that principle.

Document 1.10

Abraham Lincoln on the Nature of Government

Abraham Lincoln (1809–65), President of the United States of America, wrote the following in 1834. In this year he entered on his political career, joining the state legislature.

Government is a combination of the people of a country to effect certain objects by joint efforts. The best framed and best administered governments are necessarily expensive; while by efforts in frame and maladministration most of them are more onerous than they need be, and some of them very oppressive. Why, then, should we have government? Why not each individual take to himself the whole fruit of his labour without having any of it taxed away, in services, corn or money? Why not take just so much land as he can cultivate with his own hands, without buying it of anyone?

The legitimate object of government is 'to do for the people what needs to be done, but which they cannot, by individual effort, do at all, or do so well, for themselves'. There are many such things – some of them exist independently of the injustice of the world. Making and maintaining roads, bridges and the like; providing for the helpless young and afflicted; common schools; and disposing of deceased men's property, are instances.

But a far larger class of objects springs from the injustice of men. If one people will make war upon another, it is a necessity with that other to unite and cooperate for defence. Hence the military department. If some men will kill, or beat, or constrain others, or despoil them of property, by force, fraud or non-compliance with contracts, it is a common object with peaceful and just men to prevent it. Hence the criminal and civil departments.

Document 1.11

Friedrich Engels on Barbarism and Civilization

Friedrich Engels (1820–95) published the following in 1884 in *The Origin of the Family, Private Property and the State*. His assertion that the state is 'as a rule, the state of the most powerful economically dominant class' is consistent with the position he and Marx took up during their long collaboration. In 1852, for instance, in *The Eighteenth Brumaire of Louis Bonaparte*, Marx had argued how Louis-Napoleon had been the representative of the very large class of small peasants. In *The German Ideology* (1845–6) Marx had written: 'the state is nothing more than the form of organization which the bourgeois by necessity adopts for both internal and external purposes as a mutual guarantee of their property and interests. The independence of the state is found today only in countries where estates have not fully developed into classes...'.

... The state is, therefore, by no means a power forced on society from without; just as little is it 'the reality of the ethical idea', 'the image and reality of reason', as Hegel maintains. Rather, it is a product of society at a certain stage of development; it is the admission that this society has become entangled in an insoluble contradiction with itself, that it is cleft into irreconcilable antagonisms which it is powerless to dispel. But in order that these antagonisms, classes with conflicting economic interests, might not consume themselves and society in sterile struggle, a power seemingly standing above society became necessary for the purpose of moderating the conflict, of keeping it within the bounds of 'order'; and this power, arisen out of society, but placing itself above it, and increasingly alienating itself from it, is the state ...

... As the state arose from the need to hold class antagonisms in check, but as it arose, at the same time, in the midst of the conflict of these classes, it is, as a rule, the state of the most powerful, economically dominant class, which, through the medium of the state, becomes also the politically dominant class, and thus acquires new means of holding down and exploiting the oppressed class. Thus, the state of antiquity was above all the state of the slave owners for the purpose of holding down the slaves, as the feudal state was the organ of the nobility for holding down the peasant serfs and bondsmen, and the modern representative state is an instrument of exploitation of wage labour by capital. By way of exception, however, periods occur in which the warring classes balance each other so nearly that the state power, as ostensible mediator, acquires, for the moment, a certain degree of independence of both. Such was the absolute monarchy of the seventeenth and eighteenth centuries, which held the balance between the nobility and the class of burghers; such was the Bonapartism of the First, and still more of the Second French Empire, which played off the proletariat against the bourgeoisie and the bourgeoisie against the proletariat. The latest performance of this kind, in which ruler and ruled appear equally ridiculous, is the new German Empire of the Bismarck nation: here capitalists and workers are balanced against each other and equally cheated for the benefit of the impoverished Prussian cabbage junkers.

... Only under the second Bonaparte does the state seem to have made itself completely independent. As against civil society, the state machine has consolidated its position so thoroughly that the chief of the Society of December 10 suffices for its head, an adventurer blown in from abroad, raised on the shield by a drunken soldiery, which he has bought with liquor and sausages, and which he must continually ply with sausage anew. Hence the downcast despair, the feeling of most dreadful humiliation and degradation that oppresses the breast of France and makes her catch her breath. She feels dishonoured.

And yet the state power is not suspended in mid air. Bonaparte represents a class, and the most numerous class of French society at that, the small-holding peasants.

Document 1.12

Lord Denning on the Rule of Law

Lord Denning (born 1899) has been High Court Judge and Master of the Rolls. This extract is taken from *The Road to Justice* (1954).

Every country which is under the rule of law must have courts to try persons who offend against the law. It cannot allow private individuals to take the law into their own hands. This applies to all modern countries: East as well as West, North as well as South. Each of them is under the rule of law in this sense, that each has an organized government which keeps order among the people by means of laws which must be observed. Soviet Russia has laws against murder, rape and theft just as England has. No private individual is allowed to take the law into his own hands and exact his own private vengeance for the wrong done to him. If order is to be kept in any country it is fundamental that any person who is accused of an offence must be brought before the courts of the land and tried and punished by those courts, and not by the relatives or friends of the person whom he has murdered, raped or robbed. The so called 'lynch law', whereby a gang of people summarily put an offender to death without trial, is no law at all. It is the negation of law, and is not permitted in any modern country, because of the disorders which would ensue. If people were allowed to exact their own private vengeance for real wrongs, they would soon exact it for supposed wrongs and the country would be in a state of anarchy.

There is, however, another sense in which we say that a country is under the rule of law: and that is when not only private individuals, but also the policy and even the Government departments themselves, are not allowed to take the law into their own hands, but must bring to trial every person whom they accuse. Most modern countries recognise this rule so far as ordinary crimes are concerned. Even if the police catch a man red-handed, they are not allowed to punish him without trial. Even if he has been seen to commit a murder, the police must not shoot him dead. They must only arrest him and bring him for trial. The only exception is when there is no other way to arrest him but to shoot him dead. The reason for this rule is the fundamental principles of natural justice that no man can be a judge in his own cause. The policy in such cases are the accusers and cannot therefore also be judges. They must bring the accused person for trial before the courts of the land and not punish him summarily themselves.

POLITICAL OFFENCES

It is when we come to political offences, such as treason or sedition, that we find the great difference. These are offences against the Government itself, and according to the principles of natural justice they ought to be tried by independent judges and not by the

Government, which is an interested party. The Government cannot be a judge in its own cause any more than anyone else. But here is the point where divergent political philosophies come into play. The totalitarian philosophy puts the safety of the Government above all else and says that the police and judges are only instruments to secure its safety and to carry out the Government policy. The individualist philosophy regards human personality as the supreme value and says that every individual in the country is entitled to be protected by the judges against arbitrary action on the part of the Government. Everyone is entitled therefore to a fair trial even when he is accused of a political offence: and he can only be assured of this if the judges are independent of the Government. The totalitarian countries pay, however, a delicate tribute to the individualist philosophy in that they often go to the trouble of putting political offenders on trial. They go through the form of a trial even though the result is a foregone conclusion in which the judges have been told by the Government what they are to do. The totalitarian countries thus implicitly recognise that no man should be condemned without a trial, even when he is accused by the Government. But when they hold a trial, we who stand by may well ask, What is the use of any trial unless it is a fair trial? An unfair trial condemns those who hold it; and not those who are condemned by it. Individualist countries have been known, however, to return the compliment by adopting sometimes totalitarian methods. They have allowed their agents to adopt inquisitorial methods and to condemn men for their political past without going through the formalities of a trial – without indeed any specific charge being made against them. I venture to assert that nothing is more important in our civilisation today than that we should insist on this fundamental principle that no one should be condemned without a trial, by which I mean of course a fair trial.

Document 1.13

Bernard Crick on the Concept of Order

Bernard Crick (born 1929), Emeritus Professor of Politics at London University, is author of *In Defence of Politics* and many other works, and has shown a particular interest in political education.

Order is the most general perception that rational expectations about political, social and economic relationships, almost whatever they are, will be fulfilled. Disorder is when one doesn't know what is going to happen next, or more strictly when uncertainties are so numerous as to make rational premeditation or calculation appear impossible. Faced with disorder, the radical philosopher Bentham said, 'mankind will choose any kind of "order", however unjust'. 'Order' is, in this sense, a prerequisite of any kind of government at all, good or bad. Justice, rights, welfare, all need 'order', and even freedom … becomes trivial or simply ineffective if there is no reasonably settled context. But the concept is morally completely neutral. It is simply knowing where one stands, however bad and oppressive the system ('at least one knows where one stands' – which is no excuse, for the same could be true in a better system). Only a lunatic would attack order as such, or could possibly adjust to a complete breakdown of expectations; but those who justify order as such, rather than simply point to its minimal necessity, are usually smuggling into the concept their own particular ideas of the best form that 'order' should take. And prophecies that 'all order will break down if something isn't done about it' – whatever it is, are notoriously rhetorical and alarmist. Concepts of disorder can best be elaborated as specific negations of 'order'. I mean that different types of disorder are best understood in terms of what they are challenging rather than as things in themselves; and nor should we necessarily assume that they are instruments to some other purpose. Their main purpose may be to protest against the existing form of 'order'. I would suggest that these negations of 'order' could be seen as some kind of continuum from public opinion, pressure, strike, boycott, parade, demo, rebellion, *coup d'état*, war of independence, civil war, through to revolution. And that each of these concepts has specific and limiting characteristics; in other words, violence is rarely uncontrolled and explosive, it is usually intended and specific. 'Ungovernable fury' is usually fairly deliberate. Ideas of how much types of violence threaten 'order' are highly conventional and historically specific. Some people today fear 'a breakdown of law and order' from a degree of violence on the streets which was easily tolerable (if disliked) in the eighteenth century. And in some of the Arab kingdoms of the early Muslim era, civil war and fratricide were the recognized institutions for settling the succession to the throne.

Questions for discussion

1. Can political systems improve men or merely restrain them from harming each other?
2. What do you understand by the term political order?
3. How important are conceptions of human nature in different accounts of the origins of political order.
4. How important is the rule of law to political order?
5. How important is political order to other kinds of order in society?

Notes

1. Quoted in Sheldon S. Wolin, *Politics and Vision* (London, Allen and Unwin, 1961), p. 34

Further Reading

The importance of the idea of order to the political vision is emphasized in Sheldon S. Wolin, *Politics and Vision* (London, Allen and Unwin, 1961). For an attempt by a contemporary political scientist to deal with the concept see U. Rosenthal, *Political Order* (Alphen aan den Rijn, Sijthoff & Noordhoff, 1978). On the rule of law and related conceptions see J.Y. Morin, 'The Rule of Law and the Rechtstaat Concept', in E. McWhinnney et al. (eds), *Federalism in the Making* (Dordrecht, Kluwer, 1992). For medieval conceptions of order see J.H. Burns (ed.), *The Cambridge History of Medieval Political Thought c.1350–1450* (Cambridge, Cambridge University Press, 1988). For more recent reflections upon human imperfection see Michael Oakeshott, *Rationalism and Politics* (London, Methuen, 1962) and A.M. Quinton, *The Politics of Imperfection* (London, Faber, 1978). There is a rich literature on sixteenth–and seventeenth-century conceptions: see E.M.W. Tillyard, *The Elizabethan World Picture* (London, Penguin, 1963); W.H. Greenleaf, *Order, Empiricism and Politics 1500–1700* (Hull, University of Hull Press, 1964); P. King, *The Ideology of Order–A Comparative Analysis of Jean Bodin and Thomas Hobbes* (London, Allen and Unwin, 1974); and Robert Eccleshall, *Order and Reason in Politics* (Oxford, Oxford University Press, 1978). The use of order in a later political theorist can be found in M. Viroli, 'The Concept of *ordre* and the Language of Classical Republicanism in Jean–Jaques Rousseau', in A. Pagden (ed.), *The Languages of Political Theory in Early-Modern Europe* (Cambridge, Cambridge University Press, 1987). For studies of the eighteenth-century innovation see David Kettler, *The Social and Political Thought of Adam Ferguson* (Ohio, Ohio State University Press, 1965) and Ronald L. Meek, *Smith, Marx and After*

(London, Chapman and Hall, 1977). H. Draper, *Karl Marx's Theory of Revolution* (New York, Monthly Review Press, 1978) is a comprehensive survey of the ideas of Marx and Engels.

For a modern attempt to reassert the distinctiveness of political life see H. Arendt, *On Revolution* (Harmondsworth, Penguin, 1973). There are some helpful comments in chapter 2 of F.A. Hayek, *Law, Legislation and Liberty*, Vol. 1 *Rules and Order* (London, Routledge and Kegan Paul, 1973). For the underlying preconceptions see also: Michael Oakeshott, *Rationalism in Politics*, (London, Methuen, 1962) and A.M. Quinton, *The Politics of Imperfection*, (London, Faber, 1978).

2

AUTHORITY AND OBLIGATION

INTRODUCTION

The idea of authority is central to any political order, but in contemporary usage
the distinctive features of authority are, it is argued, blurred by the confusion of
authority with power.[1] This confusion arises partly because power and authority
are related – both are essential to political order. Hence, we readily speak of a
government losing its authority when it cannot enforce its policies. Yet we also
refer to the 'legitimate' government of a country in circumstances where that
government has been driven into exile as a result of foreign invasion or a *coup
d'état*.

The mere fact that the citizens of this hapless state obey the new rulers, foreign
or indigenous, will not necessarily persuade us that they have the authority to
issue commands or that the citizens are under an obligation to obey them. In
drawing these distinctions we are pointing to the association of authority with a
right. Authority in this sense is a right to issue a command and, because the
command is rightfully issued, citizens are under an obligation to obey. Shorn of
this association with right, we lose the ability to distinguish between legitimate
and illegitimate power, between authority and sheer might.

Although we still distinguish between authority and power the distinction was
once drawn in much sharper terms than is customary now. It was possible for the
Roman political theorist Cicero to argue that 'unless there is in the State an even
balance of rights, duties, and functions, so that the magistrates have enough
power, the counsels of the eminent citizens enough authority, and the people
enough liberty, this kind of government cannot be safe from revolution'.[2]
Authority here signified the tradition and values of Rome and was closely bound
up with the foundation of the city. Something of this distinction is still evident in
the political experience of the United States. There the Founding Fathers and the
Constitution they produced enjoy an authority bound up with the act of founding
the state. There are, of course, crucial differences as well as similarities. Although
in both cases authority was located in a specific institution, the Roman Senate
and the American Supreme Court, their functions are radically different.

Whereas, as Hannah Arendt describes, the Roman Senate gave political advice, the Supreme Court's function is one of judicial interpretation.[3]

For much of our history it has not been a political event that has been identified as the source of authority, but rather a divine instance. Obedience was commanded by the god or gods of the community. In the Christian form, this doctrine opened up a gap between the obligation to obey God himself and the obligation to obey political rulers. One solution to this problem was to argue that Christians should carry out their obligations to both, the underlying hope being that the two would prove compatible. An alternative was to try to close the gap by presenting political rulers as the agents of God (see documents 2.2, 2.3 and 2.4). This option added greatly to the authority of political rulers for revolt became a sin as well as a risky political act.

Defining authority in terms of its source, especially when that source was a transcendent god, put authority beyond question. Authority was explicitly contrasted with reason as a motive for believing something or doing something. Although this has always been an element of authority, the rigorous contrast has been questioned. There have been numerous attempts to reconcile reason and authority. Among Christian political theorists St Thomas Aquinas stands out as an early attempt to do precisely this. More recently, Carl J. Friedrich has explicitly sought to divorce authority from its source, from the person issuing the command or instruction (see document 2.14). What endows the utterances with authority is, according to this version, the potential to supply persuasive reasons for the utterance. The reasons will not typically be supplied, but the presumption that they can be is what matters. Thus, we acknowledge the authority of the doctor on the assumption that he could justify his prescriptions.

Authority here is associated with knowledge. We speak of someone being an authority on something and defer to his judgement on those grounds. There is, however, a distinction between being an authority on something and being *in* authority. Being in authority gives one the right to issue commands, or at least advice, or something between the two, as in the case of the doctor. Being an authority does not, at least not necessarily.

It has, however, been argued that authority should be derived from knowledge, that being an authority should mean that one is in authority. This epistemocratic (rule based on knowledge) or technocratic approach to authority can be traced back to Plato's advocacy of 'philosopher-kings', but it was really only in the early nineteenth century, in the ideas of the Frenchmen Saint-Simon and Auguste Comte, that it came into its own.[4] Saint-Simon acknowledged that in the medieval era the clergy had exercised 'spiritual power' by virtue of being the most knowledgeable and enlightened class. Now, however, authority had passed to 'scientists' for 'they alone today have the power to command universal credence'.[5]

Underlying this assertion is the belief that political problems are much the same as other problems, that political problems have solutions or answers which can be discerned by scientific method. Yet, despite pitting science against metaphysics, the ethos of the industrial age against the rule of priests, Saint-Simon's interpreter, Comte, faced a similar problem to the early Christian churchmen. The latter were not willing to trust each individual to discern the commandments of God. The majority of the population would have to accept the truths of religion on the authority of the clergy. He was not convinced that the mass of the populace were well-enough informed to be aware of the need to defer to his technocrats. Hence he advocated buttressing technocracy with the trappings of religion.

Another problem facing defenders of authority was how to preserve the gap between those in authority and those subject to it without giving the appearance that they were advocating tyranny. The difficulty is reflected in James I's defence of his divine right to rule. He was not asserting that his right was completely unlimited. He too was bound by law and, he noted, a king who violated that law was no more than a tyrant. But at the same time he denied that his subjects had any right to decide when lawful royal government prevailed and when tyranny prevailed. This balancing act was becoming increasingly difficult to maintain in seventeenth-century England. Defenders of authority had, however, two other arguments which they could turn to. One was the analogy between political government within the civil order and patriarchal authority within the family. Indeed, at its height the patriarchal doctrine asserted not simply the analogy between the authority of the king and that of the father, but also that the moral authority of the ruler was identical to that of the *pater familias*. Although now rarely used in reasoned argument, the analogy has been employed in the symbolism and rhetoric of charismatic rulers of the twentieth century; by, for example, the French leaders Marshal Pétain and General de Gaulle. Earlier it was used more systematically. The second, more enduring, argument was to point to the weakness of their critics. The critics claimed that men could only be placed under an obligation by their own free will. In brief, men were obliged to obey governments because they had promised to do so. (See also document 4.3.)

In the early formulations this consent or contract theory of obligation was bound up with arguments about the origin of political order (see Chapter 1). But the theory could be freed from having to carry this burden. It could be read as a hypothetical account of what men might reasonably agree to.[6] Depending upon the assumptions made about human nature and the assumptions made about the hypothetical pre-political state, it appeared that men could reasonably agree to very diverse political arrangements. Using the same basic model of a theory of consent, Hobbes and Locke came up with radically different institutional models: the Leviathan with sword in hand and limited government. This is one of the reasons for insisting upon the importance of actual consent.[7]

Actual consent was also important because it gave substance to the idea of individual freedom and because it served to rebut the suggestion that whatever freedom men might have had they had surrendered it long ago. Locke's answer to this was that even had our ancestors consented to some particular political arrangement they in no way bound future generations. By opening up the question of how each individual came to consent to government, a new dimension had been added to the debate. What counts as consent? In some cases there are formal procedures, as for example when someone becomes a citizen of a state other than the one in which he was born. But most of us are born within, and remain within, an existing polity. Are we under an obligation to obey it? Locke's argument was that even where some formal, express, consent could not be identified, there were other ways in which we could be said tacitly to consent, for example by obeying the rules of a society or enjoying property under its protection.

For this to be persuasive there have to be alternatives to consenting to the existing political structure; there has to be, at the least, the possibility of emigration. The Scottish philosopher and historian David Hume, among others, denied that this was a real option for the poor. Nor did he accept that most people even considered that their consent was necessary to justify authority. Not consent but utility was the answer to the authority of government. Men accepted that they were under an obligation to obey government because they recognized that it was in their long-term interest to do so. But utilitarian justifications of obligation bring their own problems. Consider the case of the country which has experienced a *coup d'état* and suppose that the new rulers do in fact fulfil the utilitarian criterion of maximizing the happiness of the greatest number of the population. Do the citizens then have an obligation to obey them?

Hume had not relied entirely upon utility in order to justify or explain obligation. Utility was, he argued the original and underlying motive for obligation. But with the passage of time any explicit reflection upon the benefits of government diminished. Authority was accepted, he argued, out of habit. The habit, however, was soon to be challenged radically and authority called into question more thoroughly than ever before by the French Revolution.

The philosophical temper which accompanied these events is well reflected in Kant's comments upon enlightenment. Where Hume saw the congenial influence of custom, Kant saw immaturity. In his examples, even the authority of the doctor is suspect. The imagery of paternal authority was being employed in order to criticize authority. Accepting guidance from another was to remain at the level of the child; short of intellectual deficiency, the only reasons for doing so were lethargy and cowardice.

The attack upon the idea of authority which is reflected in Kant's paean to enlightenment was in large measure successful. The idea of authority became increasingly difficult to defend. At the level of the state, the idea of authority was displaced by that of sovereignty. The defence of authority became associated with the political reaction against the ideas of the French Revolution. In France itself, Joseph de Maistre sought to stem the rising tide, invoking the old arguments. Into the twentieth century authoritarians would, rightly, pose as enemies of the ideas of the French Revolution.

Henceforth, reasoned argument for authority would usually take a technocratic form. The problem of political obligation would be dealt with in terms of consent or utility or justice. We obey, the arguments run, because we have promised to, because we benefit from the arrangement, or because the political system is just and we have a natural obligation to abide by just arrangements. None of these arguments was new. All of them can be found in the mouth of Plato's Socrates. What was new was that the terms of the debate had shifted. This is reflected in the fact that the reader is as likely to encounter 'authoritarian' or 'authoritarianism' in a title as 'authority'.

From the sixteenth to the nineteenth century, in philosophy, science and politics, reason was pitted against authority, custom and tradition. In the nineteenth century, authority seemed to many to be succumbing to the twin attacks of science and democracy. As Engels had occasion to complain, the starting point of debate was that authority was illegitimate. Authority was held to be incompatible with reason and autonomy or self-determination. Engels defended authority but in a limited sense. Authority was necessary because of the complexity of social and economic activity. Authority was justified by the division of labour. It is no longer political authority strictly speaking, that is being justified here. Engels did resist the anarchistic inclination to see even the revolution as an anti-authoritarian process, but his assumption was that political authority would disappear along with the class division of society. That would, however, still leave the authority of the factory director over the worker, of the ship's captain over the passengers and crew.

Engels, even as he defended authority, reflected the disrepute into which the idea had fallen. In this he was premature. The twentieth century would witness a reassertion of authority by the theories of elitism, theories in which authority was increasingly shorn of any justification and presented as a fact of nature or as something obtained by manipulating the sentiments and interests of the populace.[8] On the political stage, the fascist regimes proclaimed the authority of the charismatic leader with a lack of restraint which was proper, in the eyes of James I to tyrants rather than divinely appointed kings. This violent reassertion of the idea of authority effectively equated authority with power and did much to confirm the disrepute into which the idea had fallen.

DOCUMENTS

Document 2.1

Plato, *Crito*

Plato (427–347 BC) was a member of a powerful Athenian family. He lived through the Peloponnesian War which saw the defeat of Athens. He engaged in several, unsuccessful attempts to educate rulers and founded the Academy as a school for statesmen in 386 BC. He was greatly influenced by Socrates. The *Crito* was one of several works by Plato which were written to vindicate the memory of Socrates. Socrates had been found guilty in 399 BC on charges of impiety and corrupting the minds of the young. While imprisoned, awaiting execution, friends tried to persuade him to escape and go into exile. The extract below forms part of Socrates' reply to one such friend, Crito.

SOCRATES: Then consider the logical consequence. If we leave this place without first persuading the State to let us go, are we or are we not doing an injury, and doing it in a quarter where it is least justifiable? Are we or are we not abiding by our just agreements?

CRITO: I can't answer your question, Socrates; I am not clear in my mind.

SOCRATES: Look at it in this way. Suppose that while we were preparing to run away from here (or however one should describe it) the Laws and Constitution of Athens were to come and confront us and ask this question: 'Now Socrates, what are you proposing to do? Can you deny that by this act which you are contemplating you intend, so far as you have the power, to destroy us, the Laws, and the whole State as well? Do you imagine that a city can continue to exist and not be turned upside down, if the legal judgements which are pronounced in it have no force but are nullified and destroyed by private persons?' – how shall we answer this question, Crito, and others of the same kind? There is much that could be said, especially by a professional advocate, to protest against the invalidation of this law which enacts that judgements once pronounced shall be binding. Shall we say 'Yes, I do intend to destroy the laws, because the State wronged me by passing a faulty judgement at my trial'? Is this to be our answer, or what?

CRITO: What you have just said, by all means, Socrates.

SOCRATES: Then what supposing the Laws say 'Was there provision for this in the agreement between you and us, Socrates? Or did you undertake to abide by whatever judgements the State pronounced?' If we expressed surprise at such language, they would probably say: 'Never mind our language, Socrates, but answer our questions; after all, you are accustomed to the method of question and answer. Come now, what charge do you bring against us and the State, that you are trying to destroy us? Did we not give you life in the first place? Was it not through us that your father married your mother and begot you? Tell us, have you any complaint against those of us Laws that deal with marriage?'

'No, none', I should say. 'Well, have you any against the laws which deal with children's upbringing and education, such as you had yourself? Are you not grateful to those of us Laws which were instituted for this end, for requiring your father to give you a cultural and physical education?' 'Yes', I should say. 'Very good. Then since you have been born and brought up and educated, can you deny, in the first place, that you were our child and servant, both you and your ancestors? And if this is so, do you imagine that what is right for us is equally right for you, and that whatever we try to do to you, you are justified in retaliating? You did not have equality of rights with your father, or your employer (supposing that you had one), to enable you to retaliate; you were not allowed to answer back when you were scolded or to hit back when you were beaten, or to do a great many other things of the same kind. Do you expect to have such licence against your country and its laws that if we try to put you to death in the belief that it is right to do so, you on your part will try your hardest to destroy your country and us its Laws in return? and will you, the true devotee of goodness, claim that you are justified in doing so? Are you so wise as to have forgotten that compared with your mother and father and all the rest of your ancestors your country is something far more precious, more venerable, more sacred, and held in greater honour both among gods and among all reasonable men? Do you not realize that you are even more bound to respect and placate the anger of your country than your father's anger? that if you cannot persuade your country you must do whatever it orders, and patiently submit to any punishment that it imposes, whether it be flogging or imprisonment? And if it leads you out to war, to be wounded or killed, you must comply, and it is right that you should do so; you must not give way or retreat or abandon your position. Both in war and in the law-courts and everywhere else you must do whatever your city and your country commands, or else persuade it in accordance with universal justice; but violence is a sin even against your parents, and it is far greater sin against your country.' – What shall we say to this, Crito? – that what the Laws say is true, or not?

CRITO: Yes, I think so.

SOCRATES: 'Consider, then Socrates,' the Laws would probably continue, 'whether it is also true for us to say that what you are now trying to do to us is not right. Although we have brought you into the world and reared you and educated you, and given you and all your fellow-citizens a share in all the good things at our disposal, nevertheless by the very fact of granting our permission we openly proclaim this principle: that any Athenian, on attaining to manhood and seeing for himself the political organization of the State and us its Laws, is permitted, if he is not satisfied with us, to take his property and go away wherever he likes. If any of you chooses to go to one of our colonies, supposing that he should not be satisfied with us and the State, or to emigrate to any other country, not one of us Laws hinders or prevents him from going away wherever he likes, without any loss of property. On the other hand, if any one of you stands his ground when he can see how we administer justice and the rest of our public organization, we hold that by so doing he has in fact undertaken to do anything that we tell him; and we maintain that anyone who disobeys is guilty of doing wrong on three separate counts: first because we are his parents, and secondly because we are his guardians; and thirdly because, after promising obedience, he is neither obeying us nor persuading us to change our decision if we are at fault in any way; and although all our orders are in the form of proposals, not of savage commands, and we give him the choice of either persuading us or doing what we say, he is actually doing neither. These are the charges, Socrates, to which we say that you will be liable if you do what you are contemplating; and you will not be the least culpable of your fellow-countrymen, but one of the most guilty.' If I said 'Why do you say that?' they would no doubt pounce upon me with perfect justice and point out that there are very few people in Athens who have entered into this agreement with them as explicitly as I have. They would say 'Socrates, we have substantial evidence that you are satisfied with us and with the State. You would not have been so exceptionally reluctant to cross the borders of your country if you had not been exceptionally attached to it. You have never left the city to attend a festival or for any other purpose, except on some military expedition; you have never travelled abroad as other people do, and you have never felt the impulse to acquaint yourself with another country or constitution; you have been content with us and with our city. You have definitely chosen us, and undertaken to observe us in all your activities as a citizen; and as the crowning proof that you are satisfied with our city, you have begotten children in it. Furthermore, even at the time of your trial you could have proposed the penalty of banishment, if you had chosen to do so: that is, you could have done then with the sanction of the State what you are now trying to do without it. But whereas at that time you made a noble show of indifference if you had to die, and in fact preferred death, as you said, to banishment, now you show no respect for your earlier professions, and no regard for us, the Laws, whom you are trying to destroy; you are behaving like the lowest type of menial, trying to run away in spite of the contracts and undertakings by which you agreed to live as a member of our State. Now first answer this question: 'Are we or are we not speaking the truth when we say that you have undertaken, in deed if not in word, to live your life as a citizen in obedience to us?' What are we to say to that, Crito? Are we not bound to admit it?

Document 2.2

St Paul on Christian Obedience

Paul (d. 67 AD) was born a Roman citizen in Tarsus. A Pharisee, he participated in the persecution of Christians before his conversion. He undertook several extensive journeys to spread the Christian religion and wrote extensively to the various Christian communities. He was arrested in 58 AD, subsequently released before being re-arrested and executed on the order of Emperor Nero. The extract below, from his Letter to the Romans, has been described as 'the most influential political judgement in the New Testament'.

1. Let every soul be subject unto the higher powers. For there is no power but of God: the powers that be are ordained of God.
2. Whosoever therefore resisteth the power, resisteth the ordinance of God: and they that resist shall receive to themselves damnation.
3. For rulers are not a terror to good works, but to the evil. Wilt thou then not be afraid of the power? Do that which is good, and thou shalt have praise of the same.
4. For he is the minister of God to thee for good. But if thou do that which is evil, be afraid; for he beareth not the sword in vain: for he is the minister of God, a revenger to execute wrath upon him that doeth evil.
5. Wherefore ye must needs be subject, not only for wrath, but also for conscience sake.
6. For this cause pay ye tribute also: for they are God's ministers, attending continually upon this very thing.
7. Render therefore to all their dues: tribute to whom tribute is due; custom to whom custom, fear to whom fear; honour to whom honour.

Document 2.3

Martin Luther on Authority

Martin Luther (1483–1546) led the Protestant Reformation in Germany. At this time of intense religious debate the Peasants War (1524–26) occurred. Both sides sought religious justification. Luther's *Admonition to Peace* was a reply to *The Twelve Articles of the Swabian Peasants,* written in early 1523, which was the most widely circulated of the rebels' manifestos. In the first part of his *Admonition,* Luther castigated the German princes for their 'raging and obstinate tyranny'. Despite this, in the second part, he denied the peasants any right to resort to force. The extract is a strong assertion of the centrality of authority to political and economic order.

Second, it is easy to prove that you are taking God's name in vain and putting it to shame; nor is there any doubt that you will, in the end, encounter all misfortune, unless God is not true. For here is God's word, spoken through the mouth of Christ, 'All who take the sword will perish by the sword' [Matt. 26:52]. That means nothing else than that no one, by his own violence, shall arrogate authority to himself; but as Paul says, 'Let every person be subject to the governing authorities with fear and reverence' [Rom. 13:1].

How can you get around these passages and laws of God when you boast that you are acting according to divine law, and yet take the sword in your own hands, and revolt against 'the governing authorities that are instituted by God?' Do you think that Paul's judgment in Romans 13 [:2] will not strike you, 'He who resists the authorities will incur judgment'? You take God's name in vain when you pretend to be seeking divine right, and under the pretence of his name work contrary to divine right. Be careful, dear sirs. It will not turn out that way in the end.

Third, you say that the rulers are wicked and intolerable, for they will not allow us to have the gospel; they oppress us too hard with the burdens they lay on our property, and they are ruining us in body and soul. I answer: The fact that the rulers are wicked and unjust does not excuse disorder and rebellion, for the punishing of wickedness is not the responsibility of everyone, but of the worldly rulers who bear the sword. Thus Paul says in Romans 13 [:4] and Peter, in 1 Peter 3 [2:14], that the rulers are instituted by God for the punishment of the wicked. Then, too, there is the natural law of all the world, which says that no one may sit as judge in his own case or take his own revenge. The proverb is true, 'whoever hits back is in the wrong.' Or as it is said, 'It takes two to start a fight.' The divine law agrees with this, and says, in Deuteronomy 32 [:35], 'Vengeance is mine; I will repay, says the Lord.' Now you cannot deny that your rebellion actually involves you in such a way that you make yourselves your own judges and avenge yourselves. You are quite unwilling to suffer any wrong. That is contrary not only to Christian law and the gospel, but also to natural law and all equity …

It is true that the rulers do wrong when they suppress the gospel and oppress you in temporal matters. But you do far greater wrong when you not only suppress God's word, but tread it underfoot, invade his authority and law, and put yourselves above God. Besides, you take from the rulers their authority and right, indeed, everything they have. What do they have left when they have lost their authority?

I make you the judges and leave it to you to decide who is the worse robber, the man who takes a large part of another's goods, but leaves him something, or the man who takes everything that he has, and takes his life besides. The rulers unjustly take your property; that is the one side. On the other hand, you take from them their authority, in which their whole property and life and being consist. Therefore you are far greater robbers than they, and you intend to do worse things than they have done. 'Indeed not', you say, 'We are going to leave them enough to live on.' If anyone wants to believe that, let him! I do not believe it. Anyone who dares go so far as to use force to take away authority, which is the main thing, will not stop at that, but will take the other, smaller thing that depends upon it. The wolf that eats a whole sheep will also eat its ear. And even if you permitted them to keep their life and some property, nevertheless, you would take the best thing they have, namely, their authority, and make yourselves lords over them. That would be too great a robbery and wrong. God will declare you to be the greatest robbers …

And now we want to move on and speak of the law of Christ, and of the gospel, which is not binding on the heathen, as the other law is. For if you claim that you are Christians and like to be called Christians and want to be known as Christians, then you must also allow your law to be held up before you rightly. Listen, then, dear Christians, to your Christian law! Your Supreme Lord Christ, whose name you bear, says, in Matthew 6 [5:39–41], 'Do not resist one who is evil. If anyone forces you to go one mile, go with him two miles. If anyone wants to take your coat, let him have your cloak too. If anyone strikes you on one cheek, offer him the other too.' Do you hear this, O Christian association? How does your program stand in light of this law? You do not want to endure evil or suffering, but rather want to be free and to experience only goodness and justice. However, Christ says that we should not resist evil or injustice but always yield, suffer, and let things be taken from us. If you will not bear this law, then lay aside the name of Christian and claim another name that accords with your actions, or else Christ himself will tear his name away from you, and that will be too hard for you.

Document 2.4

James VI and I on the Authority of Kings

James VI and I (1566–1625) became king of Scotland in 1567 and king of England in 1603. James had set out his ideas of the divine right of kings in *The Trew Law of Free Monarchies* (1598). The assertion of the divine right of kings was a reaction against the emergence of theories of popular resistance. It was also intended to free monarchs from the constraints of feudal law and claims of papal authority. James was a prominent participant in these debates. In the extract, from a speech to Parliament in 1609, James modified the ideas of the *Trew Law* but sought to maintain the substance of his absolutism.

The State of MONARCHIE is the supremest thing vpon earth: For Kings are not only GODS Lieutenants vpon earth, and sit vpon GODS throne, but euen by GOD himselfe they are called Gods. There bee three principall similitudes that illustrates the state of MONARCHIE: one taken out of the word of GOD; and the two other out of the grounds of Policie and Philosophie. In the Scriptures Kings are called Gods, and so their power after a certaine relation compared to the Diuine power. Kings are also compared to Fathers of families: for a King is trewly *Parens patriae*, the politique father of his people. And lastly, Kings are compared to the head of this Microcosme of the body of man...But now in these times we are to distinguish betweene the state of Kings in their first originall, and betweene the state of setled Kings and Monarches, that doe at this time gouerne in their ciuill Kingdomes: For euen as God, during the time of the olde Testament, spake by Oracles, and wrought by Miracles; yet how soone it pleased him to setle a *Church* which was bought, and redeemed by the blood of his onely Sonne *Christ*, then there was a cessation of both; He euer after gouerning his people and Church within the limits of his reueiled will. So in the first originall of Kings, whereof some had their beginning by Conquest, and some by election of the people, their wills at that time serued for Law; Yet how soone Kingdoms began to be setled in ciuilitie and policie, then did Kings set downe their minds by Lawes, which are properly made by the King onely; but at the rogation of the people , the Kings grant being obtained thereunto. And so the King became to be *Lex loquens* [a speaking law], after a sort, binding himselfe by a double oath to the obseruation of the fundamentall Lawes of his kingdome: *Tacitly*, as by being a King, and so bound to protect aswell   the people , as the Lawes of his Kingdome; And *Expresely,* by his oath at his Coronation...In which case the Kings conscience may speak vnto him, as the poore widow said to Philip of Macedon; Either gouerne according to your Law, *Aut ne Rex sis* [or your are no king]. And though no Christian man ought to allow any rebellion of people against their Prince, yet doeth God neuer leaue Kings vnpunished when they transgresse these limits: For in that same Psalme where God saith to Kings, *Vos Dij estis* [you are gods], hee immediately thereafter concludes, *But ye shall die like men.* The higher wee are placed, the greater shall our fall be. *Vt causus sic dolor:* the taller the trees be, the the more in danger of the winds; and the tempest beats sorest vpon the highest mountains. Therefoe all Kings that are not tyrants, or periured, wil be glad to bound themselues within the limits of their Laws; and they that perswade them the contrary, are vipers and pests, both against them and the Commonwealth. For it is a great difference bwteene a Kings gouernment in a setled State, and what Kings in their originall might doe in *Individuo vago* [as unrestrained individuals]. As for my part, I thanke God, I haue euer giuen good proofe, that I neuer had intention to the contrary: And I am sure to go to my graue with that reputation and comfort, that neuer King was in all time more carefull to haue his Lawes duely obserued, and himselfe to gouerne thereafter, then I.

I conclude then this point touching the power of Kings, with this Axiome of Diuinitie, That as to dispute what God may doe, is Blasphemie; but *quid vult Deus* [what God wishes], that Diuines may lawfully, and doe ordinarily dispute and discusse; for to dispute *A Posse ad Esse* [form potential to actual] is both against Logicke and Diuinitie: So it is sedition in Subjects, to dispute what a King may do in the height of his power: But iust Kings wil euer be willing to declare what they wil do, if they wil not incurre the curse of God. I wil not be content that my power be disputed vpon: but I shall euer be willing to make the reason appeare of all my doings, and rule my actions according to my Lawes.

Document 2.5

John Locke on the Theory of Consent

John Locke's (see introduction to document 1.5) interest in consent arose from his need to counter the arguments of Sir Robert Filmer (1588–1653) which were repeatedly published in the 1680s by supporters of the king. Filmer claimed that men acquire political obligation by virtue of being born in a certain country and could not renounce that obligation. The extract illustrates Locke's alternative account of the origins of political obligation

Every man being, as has been shewed, naturally free, and nothing being able to put him into subjection to any earthly power, but only his own consent; it is to be considered, what shall be understood to be a sufficient declaration of a man's consent, to make him subject to the laws of any government. There is a common distinction of an express and a tacit consent, which will concern our present case. Nobody doubts but an express consent, of any man, entering into any society, makes him a perfect member of that society, a subject of that government. The difficulty is, what ought to be looked upon as a tacit consent, and how far it binds, *i.e.* how far any one shall be looked on to have consented, and thereby submitted to any government, where he has made no expressions of it at all. And to this I say, that every man, that hath any possession, or enjoyment, of any part of the dominions of any government, doth thereby give his tacit consent, and is as far forth obliged to obedience to the laws of that government, during such enjoyment, as any one under it; whether this his possession be of land, to him and his heirs for ever, or a lodging only for a week; or whether it be barely travelling freely on the highway; and in effect, it reaches as far as the very being of any one within the territories of that government.

To understand this the better, it is fit to consider that every man, when he at first incorporates himself into any commonwealth, he, by his uniting himself thereunto, annexed also, and submits to the community those possessions, which he has, or shall acquire, that do not already belong to any other government. For it would be a direct contradiction, for any one, to enter into society with others for the securing and regulating of property. And yet to suppose his land, whose property is to be regulated by the laws of the society, should be exempt from the jurisdiction of that government, to which he himself the proprietor of the land, is a subject. By the same act therefore, whereby any one unites his person, which was before free, to any commonwealth; by the same he unites his possessions, which were before free, to it also; and they become, both of them, person and possession, subject to the government and dominion of that commonwealth, as long as it hath a being. Whoever therefore, from thenceforth, by inheritance, purchase, permission, or otherways enjoys any part of the land, so annext to, and under the government of that commonwealth, must take it with the condition it is under; that is, of submitting to the government of the commonwealth, under whose jurisdiction it is, as far forth as any subject of it.

But since the government has a direct jurisdiction only over the land, and reaches the possessor of it, (before he has actually incorporated himself in the society) only as he dwells upon, and enjoys that: the obligation any one is under, by virtue of such enjoyment, to 'submit to the government, begins and ends 'with the enjoyment'; so that whenever the owner, who has given nothing but such a tacit consent to the government, will by donation, sale, or otherwise, quit the said possession, he is at liberty to go and incorporate himself into any other commonwealth; or to agree with others to begin a new one, in vacuis locis, in any part of the world they can find free and unpossessed: whereas he, that has once, by actual agreement, and any express declaration, given his consent to be of any commonwealth, is perpetually and indispensably obliged to be and remain unalterably a subject to it, and can never be again in the liberty of the state of nature; unless by any calamity, the government, he was under, comes to be dissolved; or else by some publick act cuts him off from being any longer a member of it.

But submitting to the laws of any country, living quietly, and enjoying privileges and protection under them, makes not a man a member of that society: this is only a local protection and homage due to, and from all those, who, not being in a state of war, come within the territories belonging to any government, to all parts whereof the force of its law extends. But this no more makes a man a member of that society, a perpetual subject of that commonwealth, than it would make a man a subject to another in whose family he found it convenient to abide for some time; though, whilst he continued in it, he were obliged to comply with the laws, and submit to the government he found there. And thus we see, that foreigners, by living all their lives under another government, and enjoying the privileges and protection of it, though they are bound, even in conscience, to submit to its administration, as far forth as any denison; yet do not thereby come to be subjects or members of that commonwealth. Nothing can make any man so, but his actually entering into it by positive engagement, and express promise and compact. This is that, which I think, concerning the beginning of political societies, and that consent which makes any one a member of any commonwealth.

Document 2.6

David Hume on the Habit of Obedience

David Hume (1711–1776) was born in Edinburgh. He published the *Treatise of Human Nature*, still accounted as a major work of British philosophy, in 1739–40. According to Hume the *Treatise* 'Fell dead-born from the Press' though many consider it to be more superior to his more popular later works. In the extract Hume rejects the theory of consent as the source of political obligation.

Lest those arguments should not appear entirely conclusive (as I think they are) I shall have recourse to authority, and shall prove, from the universal consent of mankind, that the obligation of submission to government is not derived from any promise of the subjects …

A man, who acknowledges himself to be bound to another, for a certain sum, must certainly know whether it be by his own bond, or that of his father; whether it be of his mere goodwill, or for money lent him; and under what conditions, and for what purposes he has bound himself. In like manner, it being certain, that there is a moral obligation to submit to government, because everyone thinks so; it must be as certain that this obligation arises not from a promise; since no one, whose judgement has not been led astray by too strict adherence to a system of philosophy, has ever yet dreamed of ascribing it to that origin. Neither magistrates nor subjects have formed this idea of our civil duties.

We find, that magistrates are so far from deriving their authority, and the obligation to obedience in their subjects, from the foundation of a promise or original contract, that they conceal, as far as possible, from their people, especially from the vulgar, that they have origin from thence. Were this the sanction of government, our rulers would never receive it tacitly, which is the utmost that can be pretended; since what is given tacitly and insensibly can never have such influence on mankind, as what is performed expressly and openly. A tacit promise is, where the will is signified by other more diffuse signs than those of speech; but a will there must certainly be in the case, and that can never escape the person's notice, who exerted it, however silent or tacit. But were you to ask the far greatest part of the nation, whether they had ever consented to the authority of their rulers, or promised to obey them, they would be inclined to think very strangely of you; and would certainly reply, that the affair depended not on their consent, but that they were born to such an obedience. In consequence of this opinion, we frequently see them imagine such persons to be their natural rulers, as are at that time deprived of all power and authority, and whom no man, however foolish, would voluntarily choose; and this merely because they are in that line, which ruled before, and in that degree of it, which used to succeed; though perhaps in so distant a period, that scarce any man alive could ever have given any promise of obedience. Has a government, then, no authority over such as these, because they never consented to it, and would esteem the very attempt of such a free choice a piece of arrogance and impiety? We find by experience, that it punishes them very freely for what it calls treason and rebellion, which, it seems, according to this system, reduces itself to common injustice. If you say, that by dwelling in its dominions, they in effect consented to the established government; I answer, that this can only be, where they think the affair depends on their choice, which few or none, beside those philosophers, have ever yet imagined. It never was pleaded as an excuse for a rebel, that the first act he performed, after he came to years of discretion, was to levy war against the sovereign of the state; and that while he was a child he could not bind himself by his own consent, and having become a man, showed plainly, by the first act he performed, that he had no design to impose on himself any obligation to obedience. We find, on the contrary, that civil laws punish this crime at the same age as any other, which is criminal, of itself, without our consent; that is, when the person is come to the full use of reason; whereas to this crime they ought in justice to allow some intermediate time, in which a tacit consent at least might be supposed. To which we may add, that a man living under an absolute government, would owe it no allegiance; since, by its very nature, it depends not on consent. But as that is as *natural* and *common* a government as any, it must certainly occasion some obligation; and it is plain from experience, that men, who are subjected to it, do always think so.

Document 2.7

Immanuel Kant on Maturity and Autonomy

Immanuel Kant (1724–1804), a German philosopher, is better known for his epistemological and moral theories than his political writings. The latter did, however, play an important part in advancing the idea of the *Rechtstaat* (an approach making law the heart of the state) which challenged the prevailing authoritarian structure of contemporary Prussia. *What is Enlightenment?* was first published in 1784.

Enlightenment is man's emergence from his self-incurred immaturity. Immaturity is the inability to use one's own understanding without the guidance of another. This immaturity is self-incurred if its cause is not lack of understanding, but lack of resolution and courage to use it without the guidance of another. The motto of enlightenment is therefore: *Sapere aude!* have courage to use your *own* understanding!

Laziness and cowardice are the reasons why such a large proportion of men, even when nature has long emancipated them from alien guidance (*naturaliter maiorennes*), nevertheless gladly remain immature for life. For the same reasons, it is all too easy for others to set themselves up as their guardians. It is so convenient to be immature! If I have a book to have understanding in place of me, a spiritual adviser to have a conscience for me, a doctor to judge my diet for me, and so on, I need not make any efforts at all. I need not think, so long as I can pay; others will soon enough take the tiresome job over for me. The guardians who have kindly taken upon themselves the work of supervision will soon see to it that by far the largest part of mankind (including the entire fair sex) should consider the step forward to maturity not only as difficult but also as highly dangerous. Having first infatuated their domestic animals, and carefully prevented the docile creatures from daring to take a single step without the leading-strings to which they are tied, they next show them the danger which threatens them if they try to walk unaided. Now this danger is not in fact so very great, for they would certainly learn to walk eventually after a few falls. But an example of this kind is intimidating, and usually frightens them off from further attempts.

Document 2.8

Joseph de Maistre on the Need for Submission

Joseph de Maistre (1753-1821) was born in the Kingdom of Sardinia. He fled from the invading armies of revolutionary France to Lausanne where he wrote his *Études sur la souveraineté* (1794–96). His works, along with those of Edmund Burke and Louis de Bonald, constituted the intellectual reaction to the

Enlightenment and the French Revolution. The *Études* were not published till 1884.

Human reason left to its own resources is completely incapable *not only of creating but also of conserving any religious or political association,* because it can only give rise to disputes and because, to conduct himself well, man needs beliefs, not problems. His cradle should be surrounded by dogmas; and, when his reason awakes, all his opinions should be given, at least all those relating to his conduct. Nothing is more vital to him than *prejudices.* Let us not take this word in bad part. It does not necessarily signify false ideas, but only, in the strict sense of the word, any opinions adopted without examination. Now, these kinds of opinion are essential to man; they are the real basis of his happiness and the palladium of empires. Without them, there can be neither religion, morality, nor government. There should be a state religion just as there is a state political system; or rather, religion and political dogmas, mingled and merged together, should together form a *general* or *national mind* sufficiently strong to repress the aberrations of the individual reason which is, of its nature, the mortal enemy of any association whatever because it gives birth only to divergent opinions.

All known nations have been happy and powerful to the degree that they have faithfully obeyed this national mind, which is nothing other than the destruction of individual dogmas and the absolute and general rule of national dogmas, that is to say, useful prejudices. Once let everyone rely on his individual reason in religion, and you will see immediately the rise of anarchy of belief or the annihilation of religious sovereignty. Likewise, if each man makes himself the judge of the principles of government you will see immediately the rise of civil anarchy or the annihilation of political sovereignty. Government is a true religion; it has its dogmas, its mysteries, its priests; to submit it to individual discussion is to destroy it; it has life only through the national mind, that is to say, political faith, which is a *creed.* Man's primary need is that his nascent reason should be curbed under a double yoke; it should be frustrated, and it should lose itself in the national mind, so that it changes its individual existence for another communal existence, just as a river which flows into the ocean still exists in the mass of water, but without name and distinct reality.

What is patriotism? It is this national mind of which I am speaking; it is individual *abnegation.* Faith and patriotism are the two great thaumaturges of the world. Both are divine. All their actions are miracles. Do not talk to them of scrutiny, choice, discussion, for they will say that you blaspheme. They know only two words, *submission* and *belief;* with these two levers, they raise the world. Their very errors are sublime. These two infants of Heaven prove their origin to all by creating and conserving; and if they unite, join their forces and together take possession of a nation, they exalt it, make it divine and increase its power a hundredfold …

Document 2.9

Auguste Comte on the Social Bases of Authority

Auguste Comte (1798–1857) was influenced by Saint-Simon (1760–1825) although he later broke with him. Both have been described as the founding fathers of sociology and have had a strong influence upon France's administrative élites. Comte admired medieval catholicism, but instead of advocating a restoration he advocated the development of a new 'spiritual power' which would combine technocratic and mystical elements. The extract is taken from his major work, *Cours de philosophie positive* (1830–42).

If the dispersive tendency arising from the distribution of functions naturally propagates itself, it is clear that any influence capable of neutralizing it must also be constantly expanding. In fact, an elementary subordination must always be growing out of the distribution of human operations, which gives birth to government, in the bosom of society itself, as we could easily discover by analyzing any marked subdivision that has just taken place in any employment whatever. This subordination is not only material, but yet more intellectual and moral; that is, it requires, besides practical submission, a corresponding degree of real confidence in both the capacity and the probity of the special organs to whom a function, hitherto universal, is confided …

   This elementary subordination discloses its own law, which is that the various operations in which individuals are engaged fall naturally under the direction of those that are next above them in generality …

   The eminent regularity of military associations renders the law obvious at once, and when the law is once admitted, it discloses the spontaneous connection of this elementary social subordination with that political subordination, properly so called, that is the basis of government and presents itself as the last degree in the hierarchy formed by the subjection of the more special to the more general classes of phenomena. For, as the various particular functions of the social economy are naturally implicated in relations of greater generality, all must at length be subject to the direction of the most general function of all, which is characterized, as we have seen, by the constant action of the whole upon the parts. On the other hand, the organs of this direction must be much strengthened by the encouragement afforded to intellectual and moral inequality under a system of division of employments. It is clear that while men were obliged to do everything for themselves, they must have been confined to domestic life, devoting all their activity to supply the wants of the family; and there could be little expansion of individual ability and character. Though marked individuality must always have made itself felt, in every state of society, the division of labour and the leisure that it brings have been needful to the conspicuous development of that intellectual superiority on which all political ascendancy must mainly rest. We must observe, moreover, that there can be no such division of intellectual as of material labour, so that the intellectual functions must be less affected than the industrial by the dispersive tendencies of such a division. We are familiar with the effect of civilization in developing moral and, even more, intellectual inequalities; but we must bear in mind that moral and intellectual forces do not admit, like the physical, of being accumulated and compounded; so that, eminently as they can concur, and clearly as they are the creators of social concurrence, they are much less adapted for direct cooperation. A sufficient coalition of the most insignificant individuals can easily carry any point of physical conflict, or of acquisition of wealth, against the highest superiority in an individual or a family; so that, for example, the most enormous private fortune cannot sustain any competition with the financial power of a nation, whose treasury is filled by a multitude of the smallest contributions. But, on the contrary, if the enterprise depends on a high intellectual power, as in the case of a great scientific or poetical conception, there can be no association of ordinary minds, however extensive, that can compete with a Descartes or a Shakespeare. It is the same in the moral case – as, for instance, if society is in need of any great resource of devotedness, the want cannot be supplied by accumulating any amount of moderate zeal furnished by individuals. The only use of a multitude in such a case is that it improves the chance of finding the *unique* organ of the proposed function, and when that singular agent is once found, there is no degree of multitude that can weigh down its preponderance. It is through this privilege that intellectual and moral forces tend to an ever-increasing social authority, from the time when a due division of employments admits of their proper development.

Such then, is the elementary tendency of all human society to a spontaneous government. This tendency accords with a corresponding system, inherent in us as individuals, of special dispositions towards command in some and towards obedience in others. We must not, with regard to the first, confound the desire to rule with the fitness to do so, though the desire is one element of the fitness; and, on the other hand, there is a much stronger inclination to obedience in the generality of men than it is customary in our day to suppose. If men were as rebellious as they are at present represented, it would be difficult to understand how they could ever have been disciplined; and it is certain that we are all more or less disposed to respect any superiority, especially any intellectual or moral elevation, in our neighbours, independently of any view to our own advantage – and this instinct of submission is, in truth, only too often lavished on deceptive appearances. However excessive the desire of command may be in our revolutionary day, there can be no one who, in his secret mind, has not often felt, more or less vividly, how sweet it is to obey when he can have the rare privilege of consigning the burdensome responsibility of his general self-conduct to wise and trustworthy guidance, and probably the sense of this is strongest in those who are best fitted for command. In the midst of political convulsion, when the spirit of revolutionary destruction is abroad, the mass of the people manifest a scrupulous obedience towards the intellectual and moral guides from whom they accept direction, and upon whom they may even press a temporary dictatorship, in their primary and urgent need of a preponderant authority. Thus do individual dispositions show themselves to be in harmony with the course of social relations as a whole, in teaching us that political subordination is as inevitable, generally speaking, as it is indispensable.

Document 2.10

Friedrich Engels on Revolution and Authority

Friedrich Engels (1820–95) was the son of a German textile manufacturer and Karl Marx's closest friend until Marx's death in 1883. Engels represented his father's business in Manchester while collaborating with Marx in analysing the capitalist system and seeking to overthrow it. His article 'On Authority' formed part of a bitter dispute within the International Working Men's Association (the First International) between the followers of Marx and the followers of Bakunin. 'On Authority' was first published in Italy, a stronghold of Bakunin's 'anti-authoritarians'.

A number of socialists have latterly launched a regular crusade against what they call the *principle of authority*. It suffices to tell them that this or that act is *authoritarian* for it to be condemned. This summary mode of procedure is being abused to such an extent that it has become necessary to look into the matter somewhat more closely.

Authority, in the sense in which the word is used here, means the imposition of the will of another upon ours; on the other hand, authority presupposes subordination. Now since these two words sound bad and the relationship which they represent is disagreeable to the subordinated party, the question is to ascertain whether there is any way of dispensing with it, whether – given the conditions of present-day society – we could not create another social system, in which this authority would be given no scope any longer and would consequential have to disappear. On examining the economic, industrial, and agricultural conditions which form the basis of present-day bourgeois society, we find that they tend more and more to replace isolated action by combined action of individuals. Modern industry with its big factories and mills, where hundreds of workers supervise complicated machines driven by steam, has superseded the small workshops of the separate products, the carriages and wagons of the highways have been replaced by railway trains, just as the small schooners and sailing feluccas have been by steamboats. Even agriculture falls increasingly under the dominion of the machine and of steam, which slowly but relentlessly put in the place of the small proprietors big capitalists, who with the aid of hired workers cultivate vast stretches of land. Everywhere combined action, the complication of processes dependent upon each other, displaces independent action by individuals. But whoever mentions combined action speaks of organisation; now is it possible to have organisation without authority?

Supposing a social revolution dethroned the capitalists, who now exercise their authority over the production and circulation of wealth. Supposing, to adopt entirely the point of view of the anti-authoritarians, that the land and the instruments of labour had become the collective property of the workers who use them. Will authority have disappeared or will it only have changed its form? Let us see …

The automatic machinery of a big factory is much more despotic than the small capitalists who employ workers ever have been. At least with regard to the hours of work one may write upon the portals of these factories: *Lasciate ogniautonomia, voi che entrate!* [Leave, ye that enter in, all autonomy behind!] If man, by dint of his knowledge and inventive genius, has subdued the forces of nature, the latter avenge themselves upon him by subjecting him, in so far as he employs them, to a veritable despotism, independent of all social organisation. Wanting to abolish authority in large-scale industry is tantamount to wanting to abolish industry itself, to destroy the power loom in order to return to the spinning wheel …

When I submitted arguments like these to the most rabid anti-authoritarians, the only answer they were able to give me was the following: Yes, that's true, but here it is not a case of authority which we confer on our delegates, *but of a commission entrusted!* These gentlemen think that when they have changed the names of things they have changed the things themselves. This is how these profound thinkers mock at the whole world.

We have thus seen that, on the one hand, a certain authority, no matter how delegated, and, on the other hand, a certain subordination are things which, independent of all social organisation, are imposed upon us together with the material conditions under which we produce and make products circulate.

We have seen, besides, that the material conditions of production and circulation inevitably develop with large-scale industry and large-scale agriculture, and increasingly tend to enlarge the scope of this authority. Hence it is absurd to speak of the principle of authority as being absolutely evil and of the principle of autonomy as being absolutely good. Authority and autonomy are relative things, whose spheres vary with the various phases of the development of society. If the autonomists confined themselves to saying that the social organisation of the future would restrict authority solely to the limits within which the conditions of production render it inevitable, we could understand each other; but they are blind to all facts that make the thing necessary and they passionately fight the word.

Why do the anti-authoritarians not confine themselves to crying out against political authority, the state? All socialists are agreed that the political state, and with it political authority, will disappear as a result of the coming social revolution, that is, that public functions will lose their political character and be transformed into the simple administrative functions of watching over the true interests of society. But the anti-authoritarians demand that the authoritarian political state be abolished at one stroke, even before the social conditions that gave birth to it have been destroyed. They demand that the first act of the social revolution shall be the abolition of authority. Have these gentlemen ever seen a revolution? A revolution is certainly the most authoritarian thing there is; it is the act whereby one part of the population imposes its will upon the other part by means of rifles, bayonets, and cannon – authoritarian means, if such there be at all; and if the victorious party does not want to have fought in vain, it must maintain this rule by means of the terror which its arms inspire in the reactionaries. Would the Paris Commune have lasted a single day if it had not made use of this authority of the armed people against the bourgeois? Should we not, on the contrary, reproach it for not having used it freely enough?

   Therefore, either one of two things: either the anti-authoritarians don't know what they are talking about, in which case they are creating nothing but confusion, or they do know, and in that case they are betraying the movement of the proletariat. In either case they serve the reaction.

Document 2.11

Max Weber on Three Forms of Domination

Max Weber (1864–1920) was a universal scholar as well as an active participant in the political debates of his day. He held academic posts at Freiburg, Heidelberg and Munich. His views on authority were derived from an extensive knowledge of economic and legal history and political and religious systems. In this extract from *Politics as a Vocation*, a lecture of 1918, he gave a summary of his classification of *Herrschaft* (translated variously as authority, domination, legitimacy).

Like the political institutions historically preceding it, the state is a relation of men dominating men, a relation supported by means of legitimate (i.e. considered to be legitimate) violence. If the state is to exist, the dominated must obey the authority claimed by the powers that be. When and why do men obey? Upon what inner justifications and upon what external means does this domination rest?

   To begin with, in principle, there are three inner justifications, hence basic *legitimations* of domination.

   First, the authority of the 'eternal yesterday', i.e. of the mores sanctified through the unimaginably ancient recognition and habitual orientation to conform. This is 'traditional' domination exercised by the patriarch and the patrimonial prince of yore.

   There is the authority of the extraordinary and personal *gift of grace* (charisma), the absolutely personal devotion and personal confidence in revelation, heroism, or other qualities of individual leadership. This is 'charismatic' domination, as exercised by the prophet or – in the field of politics – by the elected war lord, the plebiscitarian ruler, the great demagogue, or the political party leader.

   Finally, there is domination by virtue of 'legality', by virtue of the belief in the validity of legal statute and functional 'competence' based on rationally created *rules*. In this case, obedience is expected in discharging statutory obligations. This is domination as exercised by the modern 'servant of the state' and by all those bearers of power who in this respect resemble him.

It is understood that, in reality, obedience is determined by highly robust motives of fear and hope, fear of the vengeance of magical powers or of the power-holder, hope for reward in this world or in the beyond - and besides all this, by interests of the most varied sort. Of this we shall speak presently. However, in asking for the 'legitimations' of this obedience, one meets with these three 'pure' types: 'traditional,' 'charismatic,' and 'legal.'

Document 2.13

Reinhold Niebuhr on Legitimacy

Reinhold Niebuhr (1892–1971) was an American Protestant theologian. He gained public prominence with *Moral Man and Immoral Society* (1932) which was highly sceptical about the ability of social groups to pursue a moral course of action. He was also an advocate of what became known as the Realist approach to international relations (see Chapter 12).

The question of the sources of governmental power or authority has been consistently raised in history. A simple cynical answer to this question is given by many. It is that authority stems from force and that the government or nation has authority which has the capacity to compel obedience to its decisions. But this answer rests upon a too simple identification of physical force and authority. It neglects the factor of prestige as a source of authority.

It is true that no government can either exercise internal authority or marshal the community's strength for conflict with other communities without a minimal degree of physical force as one of the ingredients of its power. Indeed force alone may be a tentative source of power, at the beginning of a reign or after a revolution. Coercion enforces obedience until the authority of government has been established, when it may win uncoerced consent by its prestige. But authority dependent purely upon force is rightly regarded as insufferable in the long run because force connotes unwilling obedience against the inclinations of the members of the community. In short, authority must rest upon either implicit or explicit consent rather than merely upon the force to compel conformity to its will.

This is to say that the attempt of a government to exercise internal authority without at least implicit consent destroys community. It generates resentments which require more and more force to suppress. Hence despotisms are short-lived even if they combine fraud with force to generate a spurious consent. In conflict situations *among* communities it is taken for granted that military force is the *ultima ratio*. But it is equally true, though not equally obvious, that force alone is subject to a law of diminishing returns even in the external relations of communities.

We have suggested that the 'consent' ingredient of authority may be either implicit or explicit. The prestige of political authority in traditional communities seems so absurd to the modern mind that a great chasm would seem to exist between democratic governments deriving the authority of the 'ruler' from 'the consent of the governed' and the traditional rulers who derive their prestige from such claims as that of incorporating the cosmic order. But while the chasm is great it is not as great as the modern imagination assumes. Traditional government is more legitimate than pure democrats are inclined to believe because it has enough implicit consent to dispense with fraud and to rely on only a minimum of force. And while democratic government relies upon explicit consent for the authority of a particular government, it must also rely on implicit consent for the authority of the system of government which permits the alternation of particular governments by popular will.

Indeed, the democratic principle which derives the authority of government from the 'consent of the governed' and exalts the 'sovereign people' as the source of all authority does not describe so simple a process as Locke and other rationalist democratic theorists assumed. The explicit consent which is given or withheld from particular parliamentary governments, expressing the will of a people at a given moment, may be more or less rational. But the authority and majesty of a governmental system which allows this alternation of particular governments is not so simply rational. As other theorists such as Hume, Burke and Montesquieu have shown, this authority rests upon habits of loyalty and confidence in its stability; in short, upon an implicit consent derived not so much from rational calculations as from emotions, habits and traditions, growing out of organic and historical experiences, and analogous to the sources of loyalty in traditional communities.

In any case, if we define majesty or prestige as the principal source of the community's consent, and thus of the government's authority, it is necessary to identify the component elements of prestige. These differ somewhat as between traditional and modern democratic polities.

Before the rise of democracy, legitimate governments drew their authority from various ideological systems which were identical in their emphasis upon justifying the authority of government chiefly by its ability to maintain peace and order, providing the order was not bought at too great a price of justice. Justice is always a secondary, but not a primary, source of authority and prestige. The primary source is the capacity to maintain order, because order is tantamount to existence in a community and chaos means non-existence.

The ability to maintain order in traditional governments since the rise of the first empires in Egypt and Babylon rested on the authority derived on the one hand from the prestige of continued rule and on the other hand from the prestige gained through the claim that the political order was an extension and an application of the cosmic order. In the one case the 'legitimacy' of dynastic inheritance guaranteed the transmission of authority from generation to generation. In the other case idolatrous claims were made for the priest-kings and God-kings of Egypt and Babylon in order that both legitimacy in the narrow sense and in the sense of the ultimacy of the order would guarantee the 'majesty' necessary to prevent chaos. In both cases, reverence for an order which a given generation could not create but from which it could benefit was involved. This is the valid religious element in the majesty of government. The priests did not create this reverence for Providence but they could manipulate it. They were, therefore, the chief agents of the 'organization of consent' in the ancient empires.

The substance of the prestige of the national kings rests on the legitimacy of their rule, and that legitimacy is established by dynastic succession. Kings of the Christian nations were never thought to be divine, yet they still claimed to rule by 'divine right'. The right was inherited from their fathers. The principle of dynastic legitimacy is so absurd a principle of selection of men fit to rule that its persistence throughout all history, despite the weight of injustice which absolute monarchy created, must have some fairly obvious cause. That cause is the prevention of anarchy, the avoidance of competing claims to the throne upon the death of the monarch …

But the authority of traditional community produced injustice as well as order. And so the modern democratic society slowly came into being, in which the prestige of justice was added to that of order as a source of authority, and freedom and equality were adopted as standards of justice. A free society must have a proper reverence for the principle of government as a source of order, but also a proper insistence that the power of government be brought under control of the people and that the majesty of government be partly derived from its capacity for justice.

Document 2.13

Charles De Gaulle, the Bayeux Manifesto

Charles de Gaulle (1901–70) was a military officer and strategist who gained fame as the leader of the Free French in the Second World War. He headed a government of national unity in 1944 but resigned in January 1946 as it became clear that the political parties would not agree to a presidential style constitution. The extract is from the Bayeux Manifesto (June 1946) in which de Gaulle set out his ideas on government. They were to be partially implemented after de Gaulle returned to power in 1958.

It goes without saying that the executive power cannot emanate from a parliament composed of two chambers and exercising legislative power without the danger of leading to a confusion of powers in which the government would soon be reduced to nothing but a gathering of delegations. In the present period of transition it was undoubtedly necessary for the constituent National Assembly to elect the president of the provisional government because, with a clean slate, there was no other acceptable method of selection. But this can only be a temporary arrangement. Truly, the unity, the cohesion, and the internal discipline of the French government must be sacred, or else the very leadership of the country will rapidly become powerless and disqualified.

But how could this unity, this cohesion, and this discipline be maintained in the long run, if the executive power emanated from the other power, with which it must be in balance, and if each member of the government, which is collectively responsible to the entire national representation, held his position solely as the delegate of a party?

Hence the executive power ought to emanate from the chief of state, placed above the parties, elected by a body which includes the parliament but which is much larger and is composed in such a manner as to make him the president of the French Union, as well as of the Republic. The chief of state must have the responsibility to reconcile, in the choice of men, the general interest with the direction given by the parliament; he must have the task of appointing the ministers, and first, of course, the premier, who will have to direct the policy and the work of the government; the chief of state must have the function of promulgating laws and issuing decrees, because it is towards the state as a whole that these obligate the citizens; he must have the task of presiding over meetings of the government and of exercising that influence of continuity there which is indispensable to a nation; he must serve as arbiter above political contingencies, either normally through the council or, in moments of grave confusion, by inviting the country to make known its sovereign decision through elections; he must have the duty, if the Fatherland should be in danger, to be the guarantor of the national independence and of the treaties concluded by France.

Document 2.14

Carl J. Friedrich on Authority and Reason

Carl Joachim Friedrich (b. 1901) was born in Leipzig but became an American citizen. A prominent political scientist, he was instrumental in formulating the concept of totalitarianism in the 1950s. The extract is taken from his 'Authority, Reason and Decision' (1952).

It has, I hope, become apparent that I not only reject the use of the word 'authority' for the purpose of designating any kind of power, but that when I speak of authority, I wish to say that the communications of a person possessing it exhibit a very particular kind of relationship to reason and reasoning. Such communication, whether opinions or commands, are not demonstrated through rational discourse, but they possess the *potentiality of reasoned elaboration* – they are 'worthy of acceptance.' Seen in this perspective, authority is a *quality* of communication, rather than of persons, and when we speak of the authority of a person, we are using a short-hand expression to indicate that he possesses the capacity to issue authoritative communications. And furthermore, when we say X possesses authority, we thereby propose to suggest that the communications which X addresses to A, B, and C are based upon reasoning that has meaning not only to X, but also to A, B, and C, in the sense of being related to knowledge which they all possess, or to opinions, beliefs, and values which they all share. But we are not concerned with the problem of persuasion; it is not a matter of X's ability to 'influence' the thinking or acting of the others, though this usually is involved in the situation. What matters is that this capacity to issue communications which may be elaborated by reasoning is a decisive phenomenon in a great many social and more particularly political relationships. We should like to call it authority, but, whatever it is called, this potentiality of reasoned elaboration would appear to play a vital role in situations which involve authority. Perhaps one should be content to call it the 'rational factor' in authority ...

Now it is important that this 'reasoning' is not necessarily, nor even usually, employed in fact, though it may be hinted at or suggested by symbols. But it is important that the 'potentiality of reasoned elaboration' of the communication exists. In other words, not the psychological concomitant of a *belief* in the capacity of the authority for such reasoned elaboration is decisive, but the actual existence of such a capacity. This does not mean that there could not arise situations wherein the capacity was erroneously believed to exist. Such errors are a common occurrence in relations among men. But such situations are properly and meaningfully described as involving 'false' or 'faked' authority. Genuine authority, on the other hand, requires that the capacity actually is present. The respect, esteem, or other psychological concomitants, while undoubtedly present as well, are not a distinctive feature of authority. Power, wealth, and a host of other qualities likewise occasion these psychological reactions.

Questions for discussion.

1. Is authority essentially irrational?
2. Should religious authority be separated from political authority?
3. How do we consent to political authority?
4. Was Socrates right to refuse to escape?
5. Can one be an anti-authoritarian in a modern society?
6. Why do people obey governments?

Notes

1 On this see Carl J. Friedrich, 'Authority, Reason and Decision', in Carl J. Friedrich (ed.), *Nomos I. Authority* (Cambridge MA, Harvard University Press, 1958), pp. 28–48. For a similar point, but without insisting on the terminological distinction between power and authority, see David Beetham, *The Legitimation of Power* (London, Macmillan, 1991).

2 Marcus Tulius Cicero, *De Re Publica De Legibus* (London, Heinemann, 1928), p. 169 (translation modified). I am grateful to Henry Tudor for drawing this to my attention. See also Hannah Arendt, 'What Was Authority?', in Carl J. Friedrich (ed.), *Nomos I. Authority* (Cambridge, MA., Harvard University Press, 1958).

3 Hannah Arendt, *On Revolution* (Harmondsworth, Penguin, 1973), p. 200. For some of the problems involved here see the divergent interpretations of the contributions by Michael J. Perry, Austin Sarat and Martin P. Golding in J.R. Pennock and J.W. Chapman (eds), *Nomos XXIX. Authority Revisited* (New York, New York University Press,1983), pp. 221–301.

4 See Terence Ball, 'Authority and Conceptual Change', in Pennock and Chapman (eds), *Authority Revisited*.

5 Ghita Ionescu (ed.), *The Political Thought of Saint Simon* (Oxford, Oxford University Press, 1976), p. 176.

6 On this see Jules Steinberg, *Locke, Rousseau and the Idea of Consent* (Westport, Greenwood Press, 1978).

7 For others see Harry Beran, *The Consent Theory of Obligation* (London, Croom Helm, 1987), especially chapters 4 and 5.

8 See Vilfredo Pareto, *The Mind and Society,* Vol. 4 (London, Jonathan Cape, 1935).

Further Reading

The best critical assessments of the evolution of the idea of authority are to be found in two essays written in the 1930s: Max Horkheimer, 'Authority and the

Family', in *Critical Theory* (New York, Seabury, 1972) and Herbert Marcuse, 'A Study on Authority', in *Studies in Critical Philosophy* (London, NLB, 1972). A defence of older ideas of authority can be found in Hannah Arendt, *On Revolution* (Harmondsworth, Penguin, 1973) and 'Authority', in Carl J. Friedrich (ed.), *Nomos I. Authority* (Cambridge, MA., Harvard University Press, 1958). The latter volume and J.R. Pennock and J.W. Chapman (eds), *Nomos XXIX. Authority Revisited* (New York, New York University Press 1987) contain several useful analytical essays, as does Paul Harris (ed.), *On Political Obligation* (London, Routledge, 1990). A good recent survey is John Horton, *Political Obligation* (London, Macmillan, 1992). There are useful comments in the contributions by R.S. Peters and Peter Winch in Anthony Quinton (ed.), *Political Philosophy* (Oxford, Oxford University Press, 1967). Contrasting approaches to the golden age of consent theory can be found in Jules Steinberg, *Locke, Rousseau and the Idea of Consent* (Westport, Greenwood Press, 1978) and Harry Beran, *The Consent Theory of Obligation* (London, Croom Helm, 1987). On the origins of the technocratic vision of authority see George C. Iggers, *The Cult of Authority. The Political Philosophy of the Saint-Simonians* (The Hague, Martinus Nijhoff, 1970). Paul Thomas, *Karl Marx and the Anarchists* (London, Routledge and Kegan Paul, 1980) provides a detailed survey of its theme. David Beetham, *The Legitimation of Power* (London, Macmillan, 1991) is critical of the influence of Max Weber.

3

FORMS OF GOVERNMENT AND THE SEPARATION OF POWERS

INTRODUCTION

The diversity of forms of government has been a persistent theme in reflections upon political order. The purpose of this reflection has been to determine which forms of government are more desirable, which are more stable, and which are more appropriate for a particular state or people. The answers to these three questions have not necessarily been the same; for example, the most desirable form of government has not always been seen as the most stable.

For much of human history the predominant form of government has been rule by one person. Rule by one person has, in turn, been divided into several forms. For Aristotle rule by one person could be either good or bad depending upon whether he ruled in the interests of the community or in his own interest: in the former case Aristotle designated the ruler as a monarch; in the latter case as a tyrant who had usurped power by the use of force or deception. Tyrannies, he added, were unstable because of the hostility which they inevitably aroused, although he did note that Asiatic peoples were typically slavish and accepted despotic rule. His prejudices against 'oriental' despotism were to be revived in the eighteenth century by Montesquieu.

A similar dichotomy was followed in examining the other forms of rule: rule by the few and rule by the many. Aristocracy and the polity corresponded to the good versions of these two and oligarchy and democracy to the perverse forms where they rule in their own interest. Since Aristotle construed political conflict primarily in terms of the conflict of classes, he recommended a mixed form of government as appropriate for most cities. The point was to grant some satisfaction to the wealthy élite and to the poorer majority. This did not, however, entail any separation of powers in the modern sense. According to Aristotle 'the same persons ... may act as a deliberative council and a judicial court'.[1]

This idea of a mixed government or constitution waned during the early middle ages. The predominant form of government became monarchical. Initially an elective element was often present in the choice of the monarch but the hereditary principle established itself as the prime mechanism for transferring power. Even at the height of its authority and influence, though, monarchy was never entirely absolutistic. It was limited by custom and constrained by its capacity to encourage obedience. In an age before modern communications it relied upon widespread acceptance and compliance as mediated by the support of the leaders of the community, magistrates and justices.

Moreover, the thirteenth century saw a revival of argument in favour of a mixed constitution, although with a significantly different emphases. According to one version, the mixed government was necessary in order to check the accumulation of power. The various forces within the community would act to balance each other. According to another version, the virtue of mixed government lay in the fact that it combined the strengths of the various elements. The one, the king, supplied unity, the few, wisdom and the many, power.[2]

Even in the fifteenth and much of the sixteenth centuries, however, these proposals for the basic structure of government and the restraint of power were not designated by the term 'constitutions'. Constitutions were, in the prevailing meaning of the term, merely whatever had been decreed and judged. Despite the absence of the term the concerns were recognizably the same. The term, constitution was used extensively in seventeenth-century England to challenge what was seen as the excessive claims of the monarchy. Here the 'ancient constitution' was invoked. The 'ancient constitution' was a compound of laws, some being dated back before the Norman Conquest. English kings had, it was argued, confirmed and accepted this constitution in their coronation oaths and charters. The constitution was, in effect, a contract between king and people.

The seventeenth century also witnessed increasing clarity about the functions of government. The medieval era had worked largely with the conceptions of government and jurisdiction, with the monarch having a greater discretionary power in the former, while, with regard to jurisdiction, he was supposed to act in accordance with the law. The modern distinction between legislation and adjudication was not insisted upon. By the end of the seventeenth century, greater distinction between the functions of government and a new doctrine of the separation of powers had transformed the language of constitutionalism into a form comparable to that used today.

It was, in fact, to be the eighteenth-century Frenchman, Montesquieu, who became seen as the authoritative source for the division of government into the three functions: the executive, the legislative and the judicial. Montesquieu was not entirely consistent in this threefold division. In part he followed John Locke in distinguishing between legislative, executive and, in Locke's words, federative functions. The contrast between legislation the executive function, the implementation of law, is clear enough, though it tends to conflate the judicial function and executive functions in the sense of what we would now call administration. By the federative function, Locke meant a sphere of activity, largely associated with foreign affairs, which by its very nature could not be subject to law in the same way as domestic government (see also Chapter 12). Elsewhere, Locke did insist that judges be independent. The radicals at the time of the English Civil War had, if anything, been even more clear cut in their assertion of the importance of separating out legislative and judicial functions.

There was, then, some disagreement about how power should be separated. Alongside the distinction between executive, legislative and judicial functions there was a distinction between two types of executive function. One type was governed by law set down by the legislature. The other type was largely discretionary and was concerned typically with foreign affairs. There was general agreement between these various authors that the separation of powers, however defined, was essential for the preservation of liberty.

While individual authors, like Montesquieu, ran together arguments concerning the separation of powers and arguments concerning a mixed constitution and the operation of checks and balances these two are logically distinct. The doctrine of the separation of powers relied primarily upon the idea that liberty was to be preserved by keeping each branch of government within its appropriate sphere. The doctrine of mixed government or checks and balances relied upon setting up one branch of government, or section of society, to watch over or to balance another.

Both doctrines were invoked in the great constitutional debate surrounding the foundation of the United States of America, with the separation of powers initially gaining ascendancy, only to be moderated later by arguments invoking checks and balances. The compromise outcome reflected the commitment in principle to a separation of powers but allowed, for example, for judicial scrutiny of legislation.

The doctrine of the separation of powers was not universally welcomed. The eighteenth-century English jurist, William Blackstone, saw positive dangers in the separation of powers. The interference of one branch in another was necessary, he argued, to prevent each from overreaching itself and becoming tyrannical. When Blackstone wrote, monarchies were still the typical form of government and the clash between advocates of monarchy and critics was still intense (see documents 3.6 and 3.7).

The problem posed by monarchical power formed an important backcloth to the emergence of the ideas of constitutional government and the doctrine of the separation of powers which still constitute the material of contemporary political argument. Nor did the fading of monarchical power in the nineteenth century solve the problems which had animated earlier political theorists. As monarchs disappeared or were increasingly confined to largely ceremonial roles, the executive branch of government stepped into its shoes, although in diverse forms. The two main democratic systems of executive power which emerged were the collegial cabinet system and the constitutional presidential system. The former is typically selected by the legislature and is dependent upon it for continued office. The latter is typically selected by the electorate and is not dependent upon legislative confidence.

The choice between presidential and cabinet governments was part of that wider set of choices about how to constrain power and how to manage the conflict of interests within political communities. In most political theories the interests have been seen as those of the one, the few and the many. That is, they have been seen as the interest of the monarch or dictator, the interests of the rich and those of the poor. One solution has been to postulate a common interest which, it was hoped, might override the particular interests. Alternatively, political theorists postulated some overarching moral framework or purpose of government beyond which government, whether monarchical, oligarchic or democratic, could not go without forfeiting its authority. Few however, have been content to rely upon these restraints of principle and the fear that, in the last resort, excess may provoke revolt. Most have sought more specific constraints and guarantees.

These problems, of the definition of common interest or purpose and the institutional form of polities, have been particularly acute where the polity itself is a compound of political communities, that is, in the case of confederations and federations. As forms of government these have proved highly resistant to definition. The reason is not hard to find. The term 'foedus' meant covenant or treaty. A federation, therefore, might mean no more than an alliance between two or more states. A federation or confederation, however, entails more than that. It entails the creation of a common government by means of a treaty. Although the precise difference between federation and confederation has been disputed they can be roughly distinguished according to whether the new political community drives its authority from the member states (confederation) or directly from the individual citizens within the territory of the new political unit (federation).

It was this latter element in the United States of America which so impressed Alexis de Toqueville. Here he saw the strength of the new union. Of course, the direct authority of the union over its citizens did not mean that the member states were without any constitutional powers and status. Otherwise there would simply be a state as opposed to a federation. The trend in the United States of America was towards emphasizing common identities and towards giving priority to the union of the nation. It would, however, take a bloody civil war before that centralizing trend triumphed over those who argued that the United

States was in fact a confederacy.

While the federal principle in the United States ultimately led to the strengthening of central power, the federal principle could be invoked in favour of radical decentralization. It was this emphasis which attracted the French socialist Pierre Joseph Proudhon. Proudhon did not accept the guarantees provided by a separation of powers, nor those of checks and balances, whether of institutions or classes. The state itself was the oppressive Moloch which exploited its citizens. This 'integral federalism', as it has been called, sought not so much to divide or check power as to dissolve it amidst an array of diverse associations, preferably as small as possible.

Proudhon's anarchistic federalism reflected a loss of faith in the attempt to constrain power. It reflected a hatred of the increasing power of the modern state, regardless of the precise form of government, over the individual citizen. For all the eccentricities of Proudhon's federalism, his evocation of a radically decentralizing federalism suggests that government should not automatically be assumed to be good. The question, which is the best form of government?, is preceded by the question, why do we need government at all?

DOCUMENTS

Document 3.1

Aristotle on the Classification of Constitutions

The ancient Greek philosopher Aristotle (384–321 BC) devoted considerable space in his *Politics* to the classification of constitutions, the different forms of state and the ways of ordering or allocating offices. What distinguished the bad from the good, in his view, was the pursuit of sectional as opposed to universal benefit. His review of the six main kinds of constitution and of the different manifestations of each is very detailed and illustrated by many references to actual historical states. This categorization was a fundamental contribution to political thought.

The conclusion is evident: that governments, which have a regard to the common interest, are constituted in accordance with strict principles of justice, and are therefore true forms; but those which regard only the interest of the rulers are all defective and perverted forms, for they are despotic, whereas a state is a community of freemen.

Having determined these points, we have next to consider how many forms of government there are, and what they are; and in the first place what are the true forms, for when they are determined the perversions of them will at once be apparent. The words constitution and government have the same meaning, and the government, which is the supreme authority in states, must be in the hands of one, or of a few, or of many. The true forms of government, therefore, are those in which the one, or the few, or the many, govern with a view to the common interest; but governments which rule with a view to the private interest, whether of the one, or of a few, or of the many, are perversions. For citizens, if they are truly citizens, ought to participate in the advantages of a state. Of forms of government in which one rules, we call that which regards the common interests, kingship or royalty; that in which more than one, but not many, rule, aristocracy (the rule of the best); and it is so called, either because the rulers are the best men, or because they have at heart the best interests of the state and of the citizens. But when the citizens at large administer the state for the common interest the government is called by the generic name, – a constitution. And there is a reason for this use of language. One man or a few may excel in virtue; but of virtue there are many kinds: and as the number increases it becomes more difficult for them to attain perfection in every kind, though they may in military virtue, for this is found in the masses. Hence, in a constitutional government the fighting-men have the supreme power, and those who possess arms are the citizens.

Of the above-mentioned forms, the perversions are as follows: of royalty, tyranny; of aristocracy, oligarchy; of constitutional government, democracy. For tyranny is a kind of monarchy which has in view the interest of the monarch only; oligarchy has in view the interest of the wealthy; democracy, of the needy: none of them the common good of all.

Document 3.2

Aristotle on the Polity

The political thought of Aristotle (384–321 BC) is permeated by the assumption that the *polis*, city-state, is the most developed unit of human association. He took as one of the central facts in the city-states of his own time the struggle between rich and poor. His prescription for harmony among citizens is 'polity' and for stability is a mixed constitution blending democratic and oligarchic features.

Next we have to consider how by the side of oligarchy and democracy the so-called polity or constitutional government springs up, and how it should be organized. The nature of it will be at once understood from a comparison of oligarchy and democracy; we must ascertain their different characteristics, and taking a portion from each, put the two together, like the parts of an indenture. Now there are three modes in which fusions of government may be effected. The nature of the fusion will be made intelligible by an example of the manner in which different governments legislate, say concerning the administration of justice. In oligarchies they impose a fine on the rich if they do not serve as judges, and to the poor they give no pay; but in democracies they give pay to the poor and do not fine the rich. Now (1) the union of these two modes is a common or middle term between them, and is therefore characteristic of a constitutional government, for it is a combination of both. This is one mode of uniting the two elements. Or (2) a mean may be taken between the enactments of the two: thus democracies require no property qualification, or only a small one, from members of the assembly, oligarchies a high one; here neither of these is the common term, but a mean between them. (3) There is a third mode, in which something is borrowed from the oligarchical and something from the democratical principles. For example, the appointment of magistrates by lot is democratical, and the election of them oligarchical, democratical again when there is no property qualification, oligarchical when there is. In the aristocratical or constitutional state, one element will be taken from each – from oligarchy the mode of electing to offices, from democracy the disregard of qualification. Such are the various modes of combination ...

We have now to enquire what is the best constitution for most states, and the best life for most men, neither assuming a standard of virtue which is above ordinary persons, nor an education which is exceptionally favoured by nature and circumstances, nor yet an ideal state which is an aspiration only, but having regard to the life in which the majority are able to share, and to the form of government which states in general can attain. As to those aristocracies, as they are called, of which we were just now speaking, they either lie beyond the possibilities of the greater number of states, or they approximate to the so-called constitutional government, and therefore need no separate discussion. And in fact the conclusion at which we arrive respecting all these forms rests upon the same grounds. For if it has been truly said in the Ethics that the happy life is the life according to unimpeded virtue, and that virtue is a mean, then the life which is in a mean, and in the mean, attainable by every one, must be the best. And the same principles of virtue and vice are characteristic of cities and of constitutions, for them constitution is in a figure the life of the city.

Now in all states there are three elements; one class in very rich, another, very poor, and a third is a mean. It is admitted that moderation and the mean are best, and therefore it will clearly be best to possess the gifts of fortune in moderation, for in that condition of life men are most ready to listen to reason. But he who greatly excels in beauty, strength, birth or wealth, or on the other hand who is very poor, or very weak, or very much disgraced, finds it difficult to follow reason. Of these two the one sort grow into violent and great criminals, the other into rogues and petty rascals. And two sorts of offences correspond to them, the one committed from violence, the other from roguery. The petty rogues are disinclined to hold office, whether military or evil, and their aversion to these two duties is as great an injury to the states as their tendency to crime. Again, those who have too much of the goods of fortune, strength, wealth, friends, and the like, are neither willing nor able to submit to authority. The evil begins at home: for when they are boys, by reason of the luxury in which they are brought up, they never learn, even at school, the habit of obedience. On the other hand, the very poor, who are in the opposite extreme, are too degraded. So that the one class cannot obey, and can only rule despotically; the other knows not how to command and must be ruled like slaves. Thus arises a city, not of freemen, but of masters and slaves, the one despising, the other envying; and nothing can be more fatal to friendship and good fellowship in states than this: for good fellowship tends to friendship; when men are at enmity with one another, they would rather not even share the same path. But a city ought to be composed, as far as possible, of equals and similars; and these are generally the middle classes. Wherefore the city which is composed of middle-class citizens is necessarily best governed; they are, as we say, the natural elements of a state. And this is the class of citizens which is most secure in a state, for they do not, like the poor, covet their neighbours' goods; nor do others covet theirs, as the poor covet the goods of the rich; and as they neither plot against others, nor are themselves plotted against, they pass through life safely. Wisely then did Phocylides pray, – 'Many things are best in the mean; I desire to be of a middle condition in my city'.

Thus it is manifest that the best political community is formed by citizens of the middle class, and that those states are likely to be well-administered. In which the middle class is large, and larger is possible than both the other classes, or at any rate than either singly; for the addition of the middle class turns the scale, and prevents either of the extremes from being dominant. Great then is the good fortune of the state in which the citizens have a moderate and sufficient property; for where some possess much, and the others nothing, there may arise an extreme democracy, or a pure oligarchy; or a tyranny may grow out of either extreme, – either out of the most rampant democracy, or out of an oligarchy; but it is not so out of a middle and nearly equal condition. I will explain the reason of this hereafter, when I speak of the revolutions of states. The mean condition of states is clearly best, for no other is free from faction; and where the middle class is large, there are least likely to be factions and dissensions. For a similar reason large states are less liable to faction than small ones, because in them the middle class is large; whereas in small states it is easy to divide all the citizens into two classes who are either rich or poor, and to leave nothing in the middle. And democracies are safer and more permanent than oligarchies, because they have a middle class which is more numerous and has a greater share in the government; for when there is no middle class, and the poor greatly exceed in number, troubles arise, and the state soon comes to an end. A proof of the superiority of the middle class is that the best legislators have been of a middle condition; for example, Solon, as his own verses testify; and Lycurgus, for he was not a king; and Charondas, and almost all legislators ...

The legislator should always include the middle class in his government, if he makes his laws oligarchical, to the middle class let him look; if he makes them democratical, he should equally by his laws try to attach this class to the state. There only can the government ever be stable where the middle class exceeds one or both the others, and in that case there will be no fear that the rich will unite with the poor against the rulers. For neither of them will ever by willing to serve the other, and if they look for some form of government more suitable to both, they will find none better than this, for the rich and the poor will never consent to rule in turns, because they mistrust one another. The arbiter is always the one trusted, and he who is in the middle is an arbiter. The more perfect admixture of the political elements, the more lasting will be the state.

Document 3.3

John Milton, *The Tenure of Kings and Magistrates*

John Milton (1608–74), poet, political thinker and publicist, wrote *The Tenure of Kings and Magistrates* in January 1649. It was the first major defence of the trial and execution of Charles I. He argued that government is a trust, not a possession, and that tyranny should be avenged. Only good government legitimated the exercise of power. This led to his appointment as Secretary for Foreign Tongues in the Commonwealth, in which capacity he set out to justify the English Revolution to the peoples of the Continent. His justification was inspired by his belief in Christian liberty, believing that people first 'entered into a polity' in order 'to live safe and free, without suffering violence and wrong' and into a church 'to live piously and religiously'.

No man who knows aught, can be so stupid to deny that all men naturally were born free, being the image and resemblance of God himself, and were, by privilege above all the creatures, born to command, and not to obey; and that they lived so, till from the root of Adam's transgression falling among themselves to do wrong and violence, and foreseeing that such courses must needs tend to the destruction of them all, they agreed by common league to bind each other from mutual injury; and jointly to defend themselves against any that gave disturbance or opposition to such agreement. Hence came cities, towns, and commonwealths, and because no faith in all was found sufficiently binding, they saw it needful to ordain some authority that might restrain by force and punishment what was violated against peace and common right.

This authority and power of self-defence and preservation being originally and naturally in every one of them, and unitedly in them all, for ease, for order, and lest each man should be his own partial judge, they communicated and derived either to one whom for the eminence of his wisdom and integrity they chose above the rest, or to more than one whom they thought of equal deserving. The first was called a king, the other, magistrates: not to be their lords and masters (though afterwards those names in some places were given voluntarily to such as had been authors of inestimable good to the people), but to be their deputies and commissioners, to execute, by virtue of their intrusted power, that justice which else every man by the bond of nature and of covenant must have executed for himself, and for one another. And to him that shall consider well why among free persons one man by civil right should bear authority and jurisdiction over another, no other end or reason can be imaginable.

These for a while governed well and with much equity decided all things at their own arbitrament, till the temptation of such a power, left absolute in their hands, perverted them at length to injustice and partiality. Then did they who now by trial had found the danger and inconveniences of committing arbitrary power to any, invent laws, either framed or consented to by all, that should confine and limit the authority of whom they chose to govern them: that so man, of whose failing they had proof, might not more rule over them, but law and reason, abstracted as much as might be from personal errors and frailties: while, as the magistrate was set above the people, so the law was set above the magistrate. When this would not serve, but that the law was either not executed, or misapplied, they were constrained from the time, the only remedy left them, to put conditions and take oaths from all kings and magistrates at their first instalment to do impartial justice by law: who, upon those terms and no other, received allegiance from the people, that is to say, bond or covenant to obey them in execution of those laws which they, the people had themselves made or assented to. And this oft-times with express warning, that if the king or magistrate proved unfaithful to his trust, the people would be disengaged.

They added also counsellors and parliaments, not to be only at his beck, but, with him or without him, at set times, or at all times when any dangers threatened, to have care of the public safety ...

It being thus manifest that the power of kings and magistrates is nothing else but what is only derivative, transferred, and committed to them in trust from the people to the common good of them all, in whom the power yet remains fundamentally and cannot be taken from them without a violation of their natural birthright, and seeing that from hence Aristotle, and the best of political writers, have defined a king, 'him who governs to the good and profit of his people, and not for his own ends' – follows from necessary causes that the titles of sovereign lord, natural lord, and the like, are either arrogances or flatteries, not admitted by emperors and kings of best note, and disliked by the church …

It follows, lastly, that since the king or magistrate holds his authority of the people, both originally and naturally for their good in the first place, and not his own, then may the people, as oft as they shall judge it for the best, either choose him or reject him, retain him or depose him, though no tyrant, merely by the liberty and right of freeborn men to be governed as seems to them best. This, though it cannot but stand with the plain reason, shall be made good also by Scripture (Deut xvii. 14): 'When thou art come into the land which the Lord thy God giveth thee, and shalt say, I will set a king over me, like as all the nations about me'. These words confirm us that the right of choosing, yea of changing their own government, is by the grant of God himself in the people.

Document 3.4

John Locke on the Legislative Power

In Locke's view, if any arm of government exceeds its authority, or invades the basic natural rights and liberties of its citizens, or fails to carry out effectively its responsibilities then the whole structure of government is dissolved and power reverts to the people. Although he sees the executive as the main source of oppression and misrule in political communities, he accepts that a popularly elected legislature may also forfeit its authority if it abuses its powers.

The great end of men's entering into society being the enjoyment of their properties in peace and safety, and the great instrument and means of that being the laws established in that society: the first and fundamental positive law of all commonwealths, is the establishing of the legislative power; as the first and fundamental natural law, which is to govern even the legislative itself, is the preservation of the society, and (as far as will consist with the public good) of every person in it. This legislative is not only the supreme power of the commonwealth, but sacred and unalterable in the hands where the community have once placed it; nor can any edict of anybody else, in what form so ever conceived, or by what power so ever backed have the force and obligation of a law, which has not its sanction from that legislative which the public has chosen and appointed. For without this the law could not have that, which is absolutely necessary to its being a law, the consent of the society over whom nobody can have a power to make laws; but by their own consent, and by authority received from them; and therefore all the obedience, which by the most solemn ties any one can be obliged to pay, ultimately terminates in this supreme power, and is directed by those laws which it enacts; nor can any oaths to any foreign power whatsoever, or any domestic subordinate power discharge any member of the society from his obedience to the legislative, acting pursuant to their trust, nor oblige him to any obedience contrary to the laws so enacted, or farther than they do allow, it being ridiculous to imagine one can be tied ultimately to obey any power in the society which is not the supreme.

Though the legislative, whether placed in one or more, whether it be always in being, or only by intervals, though it be the supreme power in every commonwealth, yet, it is not nor can possibly be absolutely arbitrary over the lives and fortunes of the people. For it being but the joint power of every member of the society given up to that person, or assembly, which is legislator; it can be no more than those persons had in a state of nature before they entered into society, and gave it up to the community. For nobody can transfer to another more power than he has in himself, and nobody has an absolute arbitrary power over himself, or over any other to destroy his own life, or take away the life or property of another. A man, as has been proved, cannot subject himself to the arbitarary power of another; and having in the state of nature no arbitrary power over the life, liberty, or possession of another, but only so much as the law of nature gave him for the preservation of himself, and the rest of mankind; this is all he doth, or can give up to the commonwealth, power in the utmost bounds of it, is limited to the public good of the society. It is a power that hath no other end but preservation, and therefore can never have a right to destroy, enslave, or designedly to impoverish the subjects.

Document 3.5

Montesquieu on the English Constitution

Charles-Louis de Secondat Baron de Montesquieu (1689–1755) the French philosopher, political and social theorist concluded, after a stay in England, that the key to the liberty of Englishmen was the division of political power among three distinct bodies, and that only in a political order in which power is divided could citizens enjoy true liberty. Every government had three sorts of power – legislative, executive and judicial. There could be no liberty at all if all three were united in one person. In England the old monarchical government had been integrated into a broader and more effective system of checks and balances. The English nation as painted by Montesquieu set a standard by which other nations might be judged. Although he thought that England offered the best single case of constitutional liberty, he believed that the English constitution had evolved without plan or conscious construction. By making explicit its principles, he opened the way for the deliberate construction of constitutions, as during the American and French Revolutions.

In every government there are three sorts of power: the legislative; the executive in respect to things dependent on the law of nations; and the executive in regard to matters that depend on the civil law.

By virtue of the first, the prince or magistrate enacts temporary or perpetual laws, and amends or abrogates those that have been already enacted. By the second he makes peace or war, sends or receives embassies, establishes the public security, and provides against invasions. By the third, he punishes criminals, or determines the disputes that arise between individuals. The latter we shall call the judiciary power, and the other simply the executive power of the state.

The political liberty of the subject is a tranquillity of mind arising from the opinion each person has of his safety. In order to have this liberty, it is requisite the government be so constituted as one man need not be afraid of another.

When the legislative and executive powers are united in the same person, or in the same body of magistrates, there can be no liberty; because apprehensions may arise, lest the same monarch or senate should enact tyrannical laws, to execute them in a tyrannical manner.

Again, there is no liberty, if the judiciary power be not separated from the legislative and executive. Were it joined with the legislative, the life and liberty of the subject would be exposed to arbitrary control; for the judge would be then the legislator. Were it joined to the executive power, the judge might behave with violence and oppression.

There would be an end of everything, were the same man or the same body, whether of the nobles or of the people, to exercise those three powers, that of enacting laws, that of executing the public resolutions, and of trying the causes of individuals ...

As in a country of liberty, every man who is supposed a free agent ought to be his own governor; the legislative power should reside in the whole body of the people. But since this is impossible in large states, and in small ones, is subject to many inconveniences, it is fit the people should transact by their representatives what they cannot transact by themselves.

The inhabitants of a particular town are much better acquainted with its wants and interests than with those of other places; and are better judges of the capacity of their neighbours than of that of the rest of their countrymen. The members, therefore, of the legislature should not be chosen from the general body of the nation; but it is proper that in every considerable place a representative should be elected by the inhabitants. The great advantage of representatives is, their capacity of discussing public affairs. For this people collectively are extremely unfit, which is one of the chief inconveniences of a democracy ...

The body of the nobility ought to be hereditary. In the first place it is so in its own nature; and in the next there must be a considerable interest to preserve its privileges – privileges that in themselves are obnoxious to popular envy, and of course in a free state are always in danger.

But as a hereditary power might be tempted to pursue its own particular interest and forget those of the people, it is proper that where a singular advantage may be gained by corrupting the nobility, as in the laws relating to the supplies, they should have no other share in the legislation than the power of rejecting, and not that of resolving ...

The executive power ought to be in the hands of a monarch, because this branch of government, having need of despatch, is better administered by one than by many: on the other hand, whatever depends on the legislative power is often at times better regulated by many than by a single person.

But if there were no monarch, and the executive power should be committed to a certain number of persons selected from the legislative body, there would be an end then of liberty; by reason the two powers would be united, as the same persons would sometimes possess, and would be always able to possess, a share in both.

The executive power, pursuant of what has been already said, ought to have a share in the legislature by the power of rejecting; otherwise it would soon be stripped of its prerogative. But should the legislative power usurp a share of the executive, the latter would be equally undone.

If the prince were to have a part in the legislature by the power of resolving, liberty would be lost. But as it is necessary he should have a share in the legislature for the support of his own prerogative, this share must consist in the power of rejecting ...

Here, then, is the fundamental constitution of the government we are treating of. The legislative body being composed of two parts, they check one another by the mutual privilege of rejecting. They are both restrained by the executive power, as the executive is by the legislative.

Document 3.6

Sir William Blackstone on the Balanced Constitution

Sir William Blackstone (1723–80) was Vinerian Professor of Law at Oxford University, judge and jurist. In his famous *Commentaries on the Laws of England* (1756–59), from which the extract below is taken, he expressed with particular clarity the Old Whig perception of the eighteenth-century constitutional order established in the Glorious Revolution of 1688.

It is highly necessary for preserving the balance of the constitution, that the executive power should be a branch, though not the whole, of the legislative. The total union of them, for the present, would in the end produce the same effects, by causing that union against which it seems to provide. The legislature would soon become tyrannical, by making continual encroachments, and gradually assuming to itself the rights of the executive power. Thus the Long Parliament of Charles the First, while it acted in a constitutional manner, with the royal concurrence, redressed many heavy grievances and established many salutary laws. But when the two houses assumed the power of legislation, in exclusion of the royal authority, they soon after assumed likewise the reins of administration; and, in consequence of these united powers, overturned both church and state, and established a worse oppression than any they pretended to remedy. To hinder therefore any such encroachments, the king is himself a part of the parliament: and, as this is the reason of his being so, very properly therefore the share of legislation, which the constitution has placed in the crown consists in the power of rejecting rather than resolving; this being sufficient to answer the end proposed. For we may apply to the royal negative, in this instance, what Cicero observes of the negative of the Roman tribunes, that the crown has not any power of doing wrong, but merely of preventing wrong from being done. The crown cannot begin of itself any alterations in the present established law; but it may approve or disapprove of the alterations suggested and consented to by the two houses. The legislative therefore cannot abridge the executive power of any rights which it now has by law, without its own consent; since the law must perpetually stand as it now does, unless all the powers will agree to alter it. And herein indeed consists the true excellence of the English government, that all the parts of it form a mutual check upon each other. In the legislature, the people are a check upon the nobility, and the nobility a check upon the people; by the mutual privilege of rejecting what the other has resolved: while the king is a check upon both, which preserves the executive power from encroachments. And this very executive power is again checked and kept within due bounds by the two houses, through the privilege they have of inquiring into, impeaching, and punishing the conduct (not indeed of the king, which would destroy his constitutional independence; but, which is more beneficial to the public) of his evil and pernicious counsellors. Thus every branch of our civil polity supports and is supported, regulates and is regulated, by the rest: for the two houses naturally drawing in two-directions of opposite interest, and the prerogative in another still different from them both, they mutually keep each other from exceeding their proper limits; while the whole is prevented from separation, and artificially connected together by the mixed nature of the crown, which is a part of the legislative, and the sole executive magistrate. Like three distinct powers in mechanics, they jointly impel the machine of government in a direction different from what either acting by itself, would have done; but at the same time in a direction partaking of each, and formed out of all; a direction which constitutes the true line of the liberty and happiness of the community.

Document 3.7

Jean-Jacques Rousseau on the Role of the Legislator

For Rousseau (1712–78) the role of the legislator should be to create a sense of common identity and shared sentiment. The primary concern of any society should be the institution of laws which will bind it together. The legislator is necessary because individuals are unlikely to have a clear comprehension of the common good of society as distinct from their perception of their own individual advantage and self-interest. Rousseau makes a fundamental distinction between the idea of a 'general will' and 'the will of all'.

In order to discover the rules of society best suited to nations, a superior intelligence beholding all the passions of men without experiencing any of them would be needed. The intelligence would have to be wholly unrelated to our nature, while knowing it through and through, its happiness would have to be independent of us, and yet ready to occupy itself with ours; and lastly, it would have, in the march of time, to look forward to a distant glory, and working in one century, to be able to enjoy in the next. It would take gods to give men laws ...

The legislator occupies in every respect an extraordinary position in the State. If he should do so by reason of his genius, he does so no less by reason of his office, which is neither magistracy, nor Sovereignty. This office, which sets up the Republic, nowhere enters into its constitution; it is an individual and superior function, which has nothing in common with human empire; for if he who holds command over men ought not to have command over the laws, he who has command over the laws ought not any more to have it over men; or else his laws would be the ministers of his passions and would often merely serve to perpetuate his injustices: his private aims would inevitably mar the sanctity of his work ...

He, therefore, who draws up the laws has, or should have, no right of legislation, and the people cannot, even if it wishes, deprive itself of this incommunicable right, because according to the fundamental compact, only the general will can bind the individuals, and there can be no assurance that a particular will is in conformity with the general will, until it has been put to the free vote of the people.

Document 3.8

Vittorio Alfieri, What Is Tyranny?

Vittorio Alfieri (1749–1803), was a Piedmontese poet and dramatist, many of whose writings called for an independent and united Italy. His two important political treatises followed his plays in contrasting freedom and tyranny. The extract below analyzes despotism. Until the outbreak of the French Revolution Alfieri, like many other eighteenth-century intellectuals, believed that all evil in society resulted from absolutism. After 1789 he came to hate the Revolution and France and demanded unity and freedom for Italy.

Tyranny is the name that applies without distinction to any government in which he who is charged with the execution of the laws may make, destroy, break, interpret, hinder, and suspend them, or even only evade them with assurance of impunity. And so, in any case the lawbreaker, whether he be hereditary or elective, usurper or legitimate, good or bad, one or many, who has sufficient force to do this is a tyrant; every society which accepts him is a tyranny; every nation which endures him is servile.

And vice versa, that government must be considered a tyranny in which he who is charged with creating laws can execute them himself. And here it must be observed that laws, that is, mutually accepted solemn social contracts, must be only the simple product of the will of the majority, expressed through the duly elected representatives of the people. If, therefore, the elected, on setting down in laws the will of the majority, can themselves execute them at their will, they become tyrants because they alone have the power to interpret, annul, change, and carry them out either badly or not at all. For the difference between tyranny and just government is not (as some state stupidly, others maliciously) that established laws exist or do not exist, but that in good government it has been made impossible not to put the laws into effect.

Not only, then, is every government a tyranny in which he who executes the laws makes them, or he who makes them executes them, but indeed any government is an absolute tyranny in which he who is responsible for carrying out the laws never even gives an account of their execution to those who created them.

But since there are so many kinds of tyranny which under different names attain the same end, I shall not undertake to distinguish between them, much less to distinguish them from so many other moderate and just governments, distinctions which are known to all.

Whether it is easier to endure many tyrants or one alone is a very debatable problem. I shall put it aside for the present, because, since I was born and reared under the tyranny of one man, and since this is the most common type in Europe, it may be that I am better suited to discuss it with more ease and less inexperience, perhaps to the even greater benefit of my many fellow-serfs. I shall note in passing only that the tyranny of many, although more lasting because of its nature (as the example of Venice shows us), seems nevertheless to be much less harsh and terrible to one who endures it than the tyranny of one man alone. I attribute this to the very nature of man, in which his hatred is diminished by being divided among many, just as the fear one feels for the many can never be compared with that felt for one man alone. In short, the many can indeed be continually the unjust oppressors of the whole nation, but never of separate individuals for private whims. In these governments of the many (which the corruption of the times, the confusion of terms, and the perversion of ideas have induced us to call republics), the people, no less enslaved than in the MONO-TYRANNY, enjoy nevertheless a certain appearance of liberty and dare to utter her name without guilt. Unfortunately the people, when corrupt, ignorant, and not free, are satisfied with appearances alone.

But returning to the tyranny of one man alone, I say that it takes several forms. It may be hereditary or even elective. Among modern nations, the pontifical states and many other ecclesiastical states are of the second type. In such governments, the people, having reached the final stage of political stupidity, see their own liberty, which they neither recognize nor value, falling once more into their hands whenever one of their celibate tyrants dies. And then they see it taken away at once by a few electors who create for them another tyrant, who has usually all the vices of hereditary tyrants, but not sufficient power to compel his subjects to endure him. I shall set aside this tyranny too, since it has fallen to the lot of very few men who, through their unlimited baseness, are entirely unworthy of such a name.

I intend, therefore, to discuss now that hereditary tyranny which, rooted more or less for long centuries in various parts of the globe, never or rarely or temporarily suffered injury from reborn liberty, and was not altered or destroyed except by another tyranny. In this class I reckon all the present kingdoms of Europe, with the single exception so far of England. I would except Poland if, assuming that some part of it should be saved from dismemberment and should still persist in desiring to have slaves and to be called a republic, the nobles became slaves and the people free.

MONARCHY is the sweet name that ignorance, adulation, and fear gave and still give to governments of this kind. In order to demonstrate how invalid it is, I believe that the simple interpretation of the name will be enough. Monarchy means either the exclusive and preponderant authority of one man; and then monarchy is synonymous with tyranny; or else it means the authority of one man restrained by laws, which, so as to be able to restrain authority and power, must necessarily possess, too, a power and effective authority equal at least to that of the monarch. At that very moment in which there are in a government two forces and authorities counterbalancing one another, it plainly ceases at once to be a monarchy. This Greek word does not mean anything else but the government and authority of one man, in addition to laws of course, for without some form of law no society exists. But even here the authority of one man above the law is implied: for no one is a monarch where there exists an authority greater than or equal to his own.

Now, I ask, in what way does the government and authority of one man in a tyranny differ from the government and authority of one man in a monarchy? Someone will answer: 'In abuse.' I will reply: 'And who can prevent abuse?' Someone will add: 'The laws''. I will retort: 'Do these laws have power and authority in themselves, entirely independent from that of the prince?' No one will be able to supply a further answer. Then, since the authority of these so-called laws (though they may be divine) is allied to the authority of one powerful armed man, what power will they have, miserable and impotent as they are, against his absolute power and force whenever he conflicts with them? The laws will be subjugated. And indeed they are subjugated every day. But if any effective legitimate force is introduced into the state to create, defend, and maintain the laws, it is very clear that such a government will no longer be a monarchy because the authority of one man will no longer be enough to make laws and annul them. So this name of monarchy, a perfect synonym for tyranny, but so far not as abhorrent, is applied to our governments only to confirm princes in their absolute rule and to deceive subjects by allowing or compelling them to doubt their own absolute servitude.

The proof of all that I assert is continually observed in the opinion of modern kings themselves. They glory in the name of monarch and pretend to detest that of tyrant, but at the same time they consider quite inferior to themselves those other few princes and kings who, finding infrangible limits to their power, share their authority with the laws. These absolute kings know very well, then, that there is no difference between monarchy and tyranny. Would that this were known by peoples who even now are painfully experiencing it! But European princes hold dear the power of tyrants and only the name of monarchs. The people, on the contrary, despoiled and humiliated and oppressed by monarchy, stupidly detest tyranny alone.

But the few men who are neither kings nor slaves (if by chance they do not consider equally base all princes, monarchs as well as tyrants, and limited princes, too, who are always likely to become tyrants), these few true thinking men realize, nevertheless, how much more honourable, important, and glorious a dignity it is to preside with laws over a free nation of men, rather than to mislead capriciously a cowardly flock of sheep.

I shall omit all further proof (for it is unnecessary) to demonstrate that a limited monarchy cannot exist without immediately ceasing to be a monarchy, and that every unlimited monarchy is a tyranny, although the monarch sometimes, in not abusing in any way his power to harm, may not be a tyrant.

Document 3.9

James Madison, *The Federalist* No. 47

James Madison (1751–1836), was an American statesman and political thinker. During the eight months following the adjournment of the Constitutional Convention of 1787 he, together with Alexander Hamilton and John Jay, wrote a series of eighty-five essays in support of the proposed Constitution. They were intended to influence voters electing delegates to the ratifying convention and the delegates themselves. *The Federalist,* numbers 37–87, explain the 'conformity of the proposed Constitution to the true principles of republican government'.

The accumulation of all powers, legislative, executive, and judiciary, in the same hands, whether of one, a few, or many, and whether hereditary, self-appointed, or elective, may justly be pronounced the very definition of tyranny. Were the federal Constitution, therefore, really chargeable with the accumulation of power, or with a mixture of powers, having a dangerous tendency to such an accumulation, no further arguments would be necessary to inspire a universal reprobation of the system. I persuade myself, however, that it will be made apparent to every one, that the charge cannot be supported, and that the maxim on which it relies has been totally misconceived and misapplied. In order to form correct ideas on this important subject, it will be proper to investigate the sense in which the preservation of liberty requires that the three great departments of power should be separate and distinct.

The oracle who is always consulted and cited on this subject is the celebrated Montesquieu. If he be not the author of this invaluable precept in the science of politics, he has the merit at least of displaying and recommending it most effectually to the attention of mankind. Let us endeavour, in the first place, to ascertain his meaning on this point.

The British Constitution was to Montesquieu what Homer has been to the didactic writers on epic poetry. As the latter have considered the work of the immortal bard as the perfect model from which the principles and rules of the epic art were to be drawn, and by which all similar works were to be judged, so this great political critic appears to have viewed the Constitution of England as the standard, or to use his own expression, as the mirror of political liberty; and to have delivered, in the form of elementary truths, the several characteristic principles of that particular system.

That we may be sure, then, not to mistake his meaning in this case, let us recur to the source from which the maxim was drawn.

On the slightest view of the British Constitution, we must perceive that the legislative, executive, and judiciary departments are by no means totally separate and distinct from each other. The executive magistrate forms an integral part of the legislative authority. He alone has the prerogative of making treaties with foreign sovereigns, which, when made, have, under certain limitations, the force of legislative acts. All the members of the judiciary department are appointed by him, can be removed by him on the address of the two Houses of Parliament, and form, when he pleases to consult them, one of his constitutional councils. One branch of the legislative department forms also a great constitutional council to the executive chief, as, on another hand, it is the sole depositary of judicial power in cases of impeachment, and is invested with the supreme appellate jurisdiction in all other cases. The judges, again, are so far connected with the legislative department as often to attend and participate in its deliberations, though not admitted to a legislative vote. From these facts, by which Montesquieu was guided, it may clearly be inferred that, in saying 'There can be no liberty where the legislative and executive powers are united in the same person, or body of magistrates,' or, 'if the power of judging be not separated from the legislative and executive powers,' he did not mean that these departments ought to have no partial agency in, or no control over, the acts of each other. His meaning, as his own words import, and still more conclusively as illustrated by the example in his eye, can amount to no more than this, that where the whole power of one department is exercised by the same hands which possess the whole power of another department, the fundamental principles of a free constitution are subverted. This would have been the case in the constitution examined by him if the king, who is the sole executive magistrate, had possessed also the complete legislative power, or the supreme administration of justice; or if the entire legislative body had possessed the supreme judiciary, or the supreme executive authority. This, however, is not among the vices of that constitution. The magistrate in whom the whole executive power reside cannot of himself make a law, though he can put a negative on every law; nor administer justice in person, though he has the appointment of those who do administer it. The judges can exercise no executive prerogative, though they are shoots from the executive stock; nor any legislative function, though they may be advised by the legislative councils. The entire legislative can perform no judiciary act, though by the joint act of two of its branches the judges may be removed from their offices, and though one of its branches is possessed of the judicial power in the last resort. The entire legislative, again, can exercise no executive prerogative, though one of its branches constitutes the supreme executive magistracy, and another, on the impeachment of a third, can try and condemn all the subordinate officers in the executive department.

The reasons on which Montesquieu grounds his maxim are a further demonstration of his meaning. 'When the legislative and executive powers are united in the same person or body,' says he, 'there can be no liberty, because apprehensions may arise lest the same monarch or senate should enact tyrannical laws to execute them in a tyrannical manner.' Again: 'Were the power of judging with the legislative, the life and liberty of the subject would be exposed to arbitrary control, for the judge would then be the legislator. Were it joined to the executive power, the judge might behave with all the violence of an oppressor.' Some of these reasons are more fully explained in other passages; but briefly stated as they are here, they sufficiently establish the meaning which we have put on this celebrated maxim of this celebrated author.

Document 3.10

Jeremy Bentham, *Summary of Basic Principles*

Jeremy Bentham (1748–1832) was the founder of the doctrine of utilitarianism. His initial interest lay in law and penal reform. He became committed to political reform and democracy after meeting James Mill in 1808. He died in 1832 just before the Great Reform Bill was passed and donated his body to the Webb School of Anatomy for dissection. In his view major institutions should be subjected to the continual test whether they produced 'benefit, advantage, pleasure, good and happiness'. The following is an extract from his *Summary of Basic Principles* written in 1820.

A general political catechism: containing a bird's eye view of the field of law and government as it is contrasted throughout with government as it ought to be.

Q. What is the best form of govenment?
A. That which is most conducive to the proper end of government.

Q. What is the proper end of government?

A. The greatest happiness of the greatest number.

Q. What is the form of government most conducive to that end?

A. Pure democracy.

Q. How many pure and simple forms of government are there?

A. Three: namely pure monarchy, pure aristocracy and pure democracy.

Q. What is the circumstance by which these three forms are distinguished from one another?

A. Number: monarchy being the government of one; aristocracy, that of the few; democracy, that of the many.

Q. How many fixed forms of government may there be?

A. As many that are capable of being made by the mixture of those three simple forms.

Q. How many forms of government are there to which the term monarchy is commonly applied?

A. Two: namely pure monarchy and mixed monarchy.

Q. What is the most common sort of mixed monarchy?

A. That in which the power of the monarch is more or less checked and lessened by portions of power possessed by aristocratical bodies or democratical bodies or both.

Q. What is the form of government in Great Britain and Ireland?

Q. What is the actual end actually pursued by man in general?

A. His own greatest happiness.

Q. What is the actual end of government under a democracy?

A. The greatest happiness of the greatest number.

Q. What is the actual end of government under every other form of government?

A. The greatest happiness of those among whom the powers of government are shared.

Q. Under the English monarchy who are those among whom the powers of government are shared?

A. The king and those under his command, the House of Lords and the House of Commons.

Q. What are the means by which under a democracy the possessors of the powers of government pursue their ends and support themselves?

A. A free consent of the people or the subject many as signified by their representatives, whom they have freely chosen as such.

Q. What are the means by which, in a pure monarchy, those who possess the powers of government pursue their ends and support themselves?

A. Force (military force) and intimidation.

Q. What are the means by which in the English monarchy, the possessors of the powers of government pursue their ends and support themselves?

A. Force (military force), intimidation, corruption and deceit (delusion).

Q. [What is] the form most conducive to the proper end of government?

A. Democracy – pure representative democracy.

Q. What is the form least conducive, and most adverse, to that only proper end?

A. Pure monarchy.

Q. Amongst mixed governments, what are the forms which are most conducive, and least adverse, to that same proper end?

A. Those in which the mixture has most of pure representative democracy, and least of pure monarchy in it.

Q. What are the causes by which pure monarchy is rendered thus adverse to the proper end of government?

A. Its vices.

Q. What are those vices?

A. They are all collected in that one all-comprehensive view which constitutes its essence – viz. despotism. The uncontrollableness of its power, whereby the despot, adding to the inclination the power of making a constant sacrifice of the happiness of all other members of the community to his own individual happiness, does accordingly, on all occasions, make that sacrifice.

Q. What are the vices by which mixed monarchy is rendered, in the next degree, least conducive to that same proper end?

A. They consist of, or are constituted by, the means by which the monarch and those under his command and influence, are enabled, and, in a manner, necessitated to employ, in pursuit of their several particular ends – viz. force, intimidation, corruption, and deceit as above.

Q. Considering that, to pure monarchy, there belong but those two vices, viz. force and intimidation, i.e. the employing of the instruments so denominated as means, how is it that mixed monarchy which, in addition to those two vices, has two others, viz. corruption and deceit, is not, in a still higher degree, more adverse to the proper end of government than monarchy is?

Q. What are the advantages of monarchy as compared with representative democracy?

A. None.

Q. How comes it then to have place?

A. By its being established as such, almost all men are born under it, all men are used to it, few men are used to anything else: till of late years nobody ever dispraised it, everybody praised it, nobody saw anything better, nobody knew of anything better, few had heard of anything better: men are reconciled to mixed monarchy in England by the same causes by which they were reconciled to pure monarchy in Morocco, Turkey and Industan. No state of things so bad, but that acquiescence under it may be produced by ignorance of better, in a word, by habit, by authority, and by the instruments of corruption and delusion by which it became surrounded and with which it became equipped.

Q. By what causes was it originally established?

A. First by necessity, then by force and intimidation.

Q. How by necessity?

A. In the early stages of society all men were at war with one another: warring like brutes for the means of subsistence and sexual intercourse; united by chance in bands associated for that purpose. But no band could on any occasion act in concert without submitting and paying obedience, on that occasion at least, to the orders of a leader. As the occasions of war multiplied the habit of obedience, obsequiousness, strengthened; as wars multiplied, war or expectation of war became permanent and perpetual: and thus chieftainship became monarchy.

Q Monarchy being thus established, how came it to be hereditary?

A. It was hereditary first in males, then at last in females.

Among males first in the children of the last monarchy, then failing them in others of his kindred according as they were mixed akin to his. Among his children first to one in entirety, then in some instances where the country was large enough in shares; when in entirety at first in the eldest son, then incidentally as circumstances give occasion to choice in this or that other of the sons.

Document 3.11

James Mill, *An Essay on Government*

James Mill (1773–1836) published *An Essay in Government* in 1819. It was one of a series of articles which he wrote for the *Encyclopedia Britannica*. It subsequently became recognized as the classic statement of the political theory of British Utilitarianism. In this extract he argues the inadequacy of monarchical and aristocratic government as well as the impossibility of the classical model of democracy. His remedy was representative government with a greatly extended franchise, regular elections and a secret ballot. Under such a representative system, he believed, it would be possible to achieve 'the greatest happiness of the greatest number'.

There are three modes in which it may be supposed that the powers for the protection of the community are capable of being exercised. The community may undertake the protection of itself, and of its members. The powers of protection may be placed in the hands of a few. And, lastly, they may be placed in the hands of an individual. The Many, The Few, The One; These varieties appear to exhaust the subject. It is not possible to conceive any hands, or combination of hands, in which the powers of protection can be lodged, which will not fall under one or other of those descriptions. And these varieties correspond to the three forms of government, the Democratical, the Aristocratical, and the Monarchical.

It will be necessary to look somewhat closely at each of these forms in their order.

1. THE DEMOCRATICAL. It is obviously impossible that the community in a body can be present to afford protection to each of its members. It must employ individuals for that purpose. Employing individuals, it must choose them; it must lay down the rules under which they are to act; and it must punish them, if they act in disconformity to those rules.In these functions are included the three great operations of Government – Administration, Legislation, and Judicature. The community, to perform any of these operations, must be assembled. This circumstance alone seems to form a conclusive objection against the democratical form. To assemble the whole of a community as often as the business of Government requires performance would almost preclude the existence of labour; hence that of property; and hence the existence of the community itself.

There is another objection, not less conclusive. A whole community would form a numerous assembly. But all numerous assemblies are essentially incapable of business. It is unnecessary to be tedious in the proof of this proposition. In an assembly, every thing must be done by speaking and assenting. But where the assembly is numerous, so many persons desire to speak, and feelings by mutual inflammation become so violent, that calm and effectual deliberation is impossible.

It may be taken, therefore, as a position from which there will be no dissent, that a community in mass is ill-adapted for the business of government. There is no principle more in conformity with the sentiments and the practice of the people than this. The management of the joint affairs of any considerable body of the people they never undertake for themselves. What they uniformly do is to choose a certain number of themselves to be the actors in their stead. Even in the case of a common benefit club, the members choose a committee of management and content themselves with a general control.

2. THE ARISTOCRATICAL. This term applies to all those cases in which the powers of government are held by any number of persons intermediate between a single person and the majority. When the number is small, it is common to call the government an oligarchy; when it is considerable, to call it an aristocracy. The cases are essentially the same, because the motives which operate in both are the same. This is a proposition which carries, we think, its own evidence along with it. We, therefore, assume it as a point which will not be disputed. The source of evil is radically different in the case of aristocracy from what it is in that of democracy.

The community cannot have an interest opposite to its interest. To affirm this would be a contradiction in terms. The community within itself, and with respect to itself, can have no sinister interest. One community may intend the evil of another; never its own. This is an indubitable proposition, and one of great importance. The community may act wrong from mistake. To suppose that it could from design, would be to suppose that human beings can wish their own misery.

The circumstances from which the inaptitude of the community, as a body, for the business of government arises – namely, the inconvenience of assembling them, and the inconvenience of their numbers when assembled – do not necessarily exist in the case of aristocracy. If the number of those who hold among them the powers of government is so great as to make it inconvenient to assemble them, or impossible for them to deliberate calmly when assembled, this is only an objection to so extended an aristocracy and has no application to an aristocracy not too numerous, when assembled, for the best exercise of deliberation.

The question is whether such an aristocracy may be trusted to make that use of the powers of government which is most conducive to the end for which government exists?

There may be a strong presumption that any aristocracy monopolizing the powers of government would not possess intellectual powers in any very high perfection. Intellectual powers are the offspring of labour. But a hereditary aristocracy are deprived of the strongest motives to labour. The greater part of them will, therefore be defective in those mental powers. This is one objection, and an important one, though not the greatest.

We have already observed that the reason for which government exists is that one man, if stronger than another, will take from him whatever that other possesses and he desires. But if one man will do this, so will several. And if powers are put into the hands of a comparatively small number, called an aristocracy – powers which make them stronger than the rest of the community – they will take from the rest of the community as much as they please of the objects of desire. They will thus defeat the very end for which government was instituted. The unfitness, therefore, of an aristocracy to be entrusted with the powers of government rests on demonstration.

3. THE MONARCHICAL.   It will be seen, and therefore words to make it manifest are unnecessary, that in most respects the monarchical form of government agrees with the aristocratical and is liable to the same objections. If government is founded upon this, as a law of human nature, that a man if able will take from others anything which they have and he desires, it is sufficiently evident that when a man is called a king it does not change his nature; so that when he has got power to enable him to take from every man what he pleases, he will take whatever he pleases. To suppose that he will not is to affirm that government is unnecessary and that human beings will abstain from injuring one another of their own accord.

It is very evident that this reasoning extends to every modification of the smaller number. Whenever the powers of government are placed in any hands other than those of the community – whether those of one man, of a few, or of several – those principles of human nature which imply that government is at all necessary imply that those persons will make use of them to defeat the very end for which government exists …

Document 3.12

The *English Chartist Circular* on Popular Republicanism

The following was published by the *English Chartist Circular* in 1841. This journal was a voice of the moderate wing of the Chartist movement. The support for republicanism is qualified by a recognition that it is unlikely to be practical politics in Victorian Britain. Chartism took its name from the People's Charter (1838) which demanded radical parliamentary reform including manhood suffrage.

A monarchy is in itself a state which no one can contemplate with any patience or satisfaction. Live under a monarchy you may, and live under it in peace and submission, because we may consider it as our duty so to conduct ourselves, as not to disturb the peace of the society of which we form a part, but to yield an entire approbation to its institutions: to submit one's capacity to all its follies and its anomalies, that, in our opinion, is not possible for an honest and a sensible man to do.

It would be no very difficult matter to prove that whenever monarchies deviate into republics they always do so to the improvement and elevation of mankind, and to the bettering of the condition of the human beings whom such change concerns. It would not be difficult to prove also the converse of this proposition, which is that whenever republics merge in monarchies, the human race in those monarchies suffer a deterioration, and the people become more wretched and debased. Now we are not arguing in favour of republics, for two reasons. Firstly, because it would ill become us living under a monarchy to hold such opinions. Secondly, because if we were to hold such arguments our readers would not attend to them. No! our opinions are merely speculative, and are rather taken up as amusing objects of meditation than as matters on which we hope to convince. We assert it, aye! and we are ready to maintain the opinion, too, against all, that when monarchies deviate into republics, they render men happy, and when republics deviate into monarchies, they render them wretched. Nay! we will go further than that and assert, that monarchies, are political machines, are the mere commencement of civilization, and that all monarchies must – if the human race advance in improvement – end in republics. These are facts we lay down, and it only remains for us to prove the truth of our opinions. It will be admitted, we presume, that the ancient states of Greece and Rome began in the establishment of pure tyrannies, and afterwards deviated, when the people became more improved, into republics. Republics were then the offspring of improvement in those countries; and if this conclusion be not allowed, we know not what other can.

Document 3.13

Alexis de Tocqueville on the Distinctiveness of the American Federal Constitution

Alexis de Tocqueville (1805–1859), was a magistrate, parliamentarian and writer. He published *Democracy in America* in two parts in 1835 and 1840. He offered one of the most penetrating analyses of the new political order in the USA and of the implications of democracy. Of aristocratic background, he nevertheless reconciled himself to democracy. This book became the classic description of Jacksonian America. Subsequently he was a Deputy, and briefly Foreign Minister in 1849, before retiring from politics after the *coup d'état* of 1851.

The United States of America do not afford either the first or the only instance of confederate States, several of which have existed in modern Europe, not to mention those of antiquity. Switzerland, the Germanic Empire, and the Republic of the United Provinces either have been or still are confederations. In studying the constitutions of these different countries, one is surprised to observe that the powers with which they invested the Federal Government are nearly identical with the privileges awarded by the American Constitution to the government of the United States. They confer upon the central power the same rights of making peace and war, of raising money and troops, and of providing for the general exigencies and the common interests of the nation. Nevertheless the Federal Government of these different peoples has always been as remarkable for its weakness and inefficiency as that of the Union is for its vigorous and enterprising spirit. Again, the first American Confederation perished through the excessive weakness of its Government; and this weak Government was, notwithstanding, in possession of rights even more extensive than those of the Federal Government of the present day. But the more recent Constitution of the United States contains certain principles which exercise a most important influence, although they do not at once strike the observer.

This Constitution, which may at first sight be confounded with the federal constitutions which preceded it, rests upon a novel theory, which may be considered as a great invention in modern political science. In all the confederations which had been formed before the American Constitution of 1789, the allied States agreed to obey the injunctions of a Federal Government; but they reserved to themselves the right of ordaining and enforcing the execution of the laws of the Union. The American States which combined in 1789 agreed that the Federal Government should not only dictate the laws, but that it should execute its own enactments. In both cases the right is the same, but the exercise of the right is different, and this alteration produced the most momentous consequences.

In all the confederations which had been formed before the American Union, the Federal Government demanded its supplies at the hands of the separate Governments; and if the measure it prescribed was onerous to any one of those bodies, means were found to evade its claims. If the State was powerful, it had recourse to arms; if it was weak, it connived at the resistance which the law of the Union, its sovereign, met with, and resorted to inaction under the plea of inability. Under these circumstances one of two alternatives has invariably occurred: either the most preponderant of the allied peoples has assumed the privileges of the Federal authority, and ruled all the other states in its name; or the Federal Government has been abandoned by its natural supporters, anarchy has arisen between the confederates, and the Union has lost all powers of action.

In America, the subjects of the Union are not States, but private citizens: the national Government levies a tax, not upon the State of Massachusetts, but upon each inhabitant of Massachusetts. All former confederate governments presided over communities, but that of the Union rules individuals. Its power is not borrowed, but self-derived. It is served by its own courts of justice. It cannot be doubted that the spirit of the nation, the passions of the multitude, and the provincial prejudices of each State, tend singularly to diminish the authority of a Federal power thus constituted, and to facilitate the means of resistance to its mandates; but the comparative weakness of a restricted sovereignty is an evil inherent in the Federal system. In America, each State has fewer opportunities of resistance, and fewer temptations to non-compliance: nor can such a design be put in execution (if indeed it be entertained) without an open violation of the laws of the Union, a direct interruption of the ordinary course of justice, and a bold declaration of revolt; in a word, without taking a decisive step which men hesitate to adopt. In all former confederations, the privileges of the Union furnished more elements of discord than of power, since they multiplied the claims of the nation without augmenting the means of enforcing them: and in accordance with this fact it may be remarked, that the real weakness of federal governments has almost always been in exact proportion to their nominal power. Such is not the case in the American Union, in which, as in ordinary governments, the Federal government has the means of enforcing all it is empowered to demand ...

Document 3.14

Sir Henry Maine on the US President and Monarchy

The following extract is taken from the English jurist's analysis of the Constitution of the United States in *Popular Government* (1885). He lived between 1822 and 1888 and is best known for his *Ancient Law* and subsequent volumes on legal history.

On the face of the Constitution of the United States, the resemblance of the President of the United States to the European King, and especially to the King of Great Britain, is too obvious for mistake. The President has, in various degrees, a number of powers which those who know something of Kingship in its general history recognise at once as peculiarly associated with it and with no other institution. The whole Executive power is vested in him. He is Commander-in-Chief of the Army and Navy. He makes treaties with the advice and consent of the Senate, and with the same advice and consent he appoints Ambassadors, Ministers, Judges, and all high functionaries. He has a qualified veto on legislation. He convenes Congress, when no special time of meeting has been fixed. It is conceded in the 'Federalist' that the similarity of the new President's office to the functions of the British King was one of the points on which the opponents of the Constitution fastened. Hamilton replies to their arguments, sometimes with great cogency, sometimes, it must be owned, a little captiously. He urges that the only alternative to a President was a plural Executive, or Council, and he insists on the risk of a paralysis of Executive authority produced by party opposition in such a body. But he mainly relies on the points in which the President differs from the King – on the terminability of the office, on the participation of the Senate in the exercise of several of his powers, on the limited nature of his veto on Bills passed by Congress. It is, however, tolerably clear that the mental operation through which the framers of the American Constitution passed was this: they took the King of Great Britain, went through his powers, and restrained them whenever they appeared to be excessive or unsuited to the circumstances of the United States. It is remarkable that the figure they had before them was not a generalised English king nor an abstract Constitutional monarch; it was no anticipation of Queen Victoria, but George III.

Document 3.15

Pierre-Joseph Proudhon on Federalism

Proudhon (1809–65) was a French anarchist thinker who argued that the abolition of exploitation of man by man and the 'abolition of government are one and the same thing'. He set against existing state government the model of a 'mutualist' society in which peace and social cooperation were achieved without coercion by the State. Self-governing producers, financed by free credit, were to be linked by what he described as 'the federal principle'.

To sum up, the federal system is the very reverse of hierarchy or centralized administration and government. Hierarchy is the distinguishing feature common, to an equal degree, to imperial democracy, constitutional monarchy and republics. The basic distinguishing law of a federation is that, as more states join the Confederation, the powers of the central authority become increasingly specialized and restricted in number, range and, so to speak, intensity. On the other hand in a centralized government, in proportion to any increases it reaches further, and becomes more direct – bringing the affairs of provinces, communes, corporations and private individuals under the direct control of the prince. The result of this is that liberty, not only at the communal and provincial level but also at the individual and national level, is completely suppressed.

In a free society the role of the State or Government is essentially one of legislating, initiating, creating, inaugurating and setting up; it should be as little as possible one of executing. In this respect the term executive power, which describes one of the features of sovereign power, has been very misleading. The State does not undertake public works, for this would identify it with industrialists who undertake public contracts.

Whether it decrees, acts or oversees, the State is the instigator and supreme guide of all developments. If it sometimes takes a hand in the work itself, it is in order to set things in motion and give an example. Once a new service has been created, once it has been installed and set up, the State withdraws and leaves the local authority and citizens in charge of operating it. The State is responsible for deciding weights and measures, and it decides the standard, value and units of currency. When the models have been provided and the first issue completed the minting of gold, silver and copper coins ceases to be a public responsibility. It is no longer in the hands of the State or its Ministries, but must be left in the hands of the towns and nothing should prevent it from being entirely free, in the same way as the making of scales, weighing machines, barrels and bottles. The only law that should operate here is that of maintaining the lowest possible price. What are the standards operating in France to decide whether gold and silver coins may be accepted as standard? They are that the coins should be composed of one tenth alloy and nine tenths fine metal. I am all in favor of inspection and control during the minting, but the role of the State, should go no further than this.

My remarks about money are also true of countless services which are wrongly left in government hands, namely, roads, canals, tobacco, the postal and telegraph service, the railways and so on. I quite understand, accept, and if need be, demand the principle of State intervention in these large-scale public services. What I do not see is why they should still be subject to State control once they have been handed over to the public. Centralization of this kind seems to me to indicate excessive power. In 1848 I asked the State to set up national banks, credit institutions, provident funds and insurance organizations, as well as railways. It never occurred to me that the State should from then on be a banker, insurance agent, carrier and so on when once its initial functions had been completed. I do not of course think that the education of the people can be organized without considerable help from the State, but I nevertheless believe firmly in the freedom of education, as I do in the freedom of everything else. I want education to be as separate from the State as is the Church itself …

Is it really necessary that the courts should be dependent on the central authority? I know that it has always been the highest prerogative of the prince to dispense justice. But this prerogative is a relic of the time of divine right and cannot be claimed by a constitutional monarch, let alone by the head of an Empire based on universal suffrage. Once the idea of Law has again become man-made and gained thereby predominance in the political system, then the independence of the magistrature will necessarily follow. To consider Justice as an attribute of the central or federal authority is repugnant, for Justice can never be delegated other than to the municipal or, at the most, to the provincial authority. Justice is the essential characteristic of man, which should never be surrendered up for any reasons of national interest. I do not even allow military affairs to be an exception to this rule. The militia, the munition depots, the fortresses, should only pass into the hands of the federal authorities in the actual event of war and for the particular purpose of that war. Otherwise soldiers and munitions should remain in the hands of the local authorities.

In a well-regulated society everything must be in a continual state of growth; science, industry, labor, wealth, public health, liberty and morality must move forward at the same pace. Activity and life must not be suspended for an instant. The State, which is the principal moving force, is always active, for there are always new demands to be satisfied and new problems to be solved, while its functions as prime mover and overall director never come to an end, this does not imply that it ever repeats itself in what it produces. This is the ultimate expression of progress. Now what happens when – and we see examples of this everywhere and all the time – it retains control of the services it has created and succumbs to the temptation of monopolizing? It changes from being a founder to being a worker. It is no longer the fertile, enriching, guiding spirit of the community, which at the same time imposes no restraint, but is rather a vast limited liability company with six hundred thousand employees and six hundred thousand soldiers entirely at its disposal. Instead of serving citizens and communes, it disinherits and exploits them, and it is not long before corruption, dishonesty and slackness creep into the system. The State is so engrossed in maintaining its position, increasing its prerogatives and services and enlarging its budget, that it loses sight of its true function and degenerates into autocracy and conservatism. Society suffers, and, going against historical law, the nation starts to decay.

Document 3.16

James Bryce on Forms of Democratic Government

First Viscount Bryce (1838–1922) was a jurist, historian, Liberal politician and, from 1907–13, British Ambassador to the US. He included the following analysis in *The American Commonwealth* (1888).

For the sake of making clear what follows, I will venture to recapitulate what was said in an earlier chapter as to the three forms which government has taken in free countries. First came primary assemblies, such as those of the Greek republics of antiquity, or those of the early Teutonic tribes, which have survived in a few Swiss cantons. The whole people met, debated current questions, decided them by its votes, chose those who were to carry out its will. Such a system of direct popular government is possible only in small communities, and in this day of large States has become a matter rather of antiquarian curiosity than of practical moment.

In the second form, power belongs to representative bodies, Parliaments and Chambers. The people in their various local areas elect men, supposed to be their wisest ·or most influential, to deliberate for them, resolve for them, choose their executive servants for them. They give these representatives a tolerably free hand, leaving them in power for a considerable space of time, and allowing them to act unchecked, except in so far as custom, or possibly some fundamental law, limits their discretion. This is done in the faith that the Chamber will feel its responsibility and act for the best interests of the country, carrying out what it believes to be the wishes of the majority, unless it should be convinced that in some particular point it knows better than the majority what the interests of the country require. Such a system has prevailed in England, and the English model has been widely imitated on the continent of Europe and in the British colonies.

The third is something between the other two. It may be regarded either as an attempt to apply the principle of primary assemblies to large countries, or as a modification of the representative system in the direction of direct popular sovereignty. There is still a legislature, but it is elected for so short a time and checked in so many ways that much of its power and dignity has departed. Supremacy is not with it, but with the people, who have fixed limits beyond which it cannot go, and who use it merely as a piece of machinery for carrying out their wishes and settling points of detail for them. The supremacy of their will is expressed in the existence of Constitution placed above the legislature, although capable of alteration by a direct popular vote. The position of the representatives has been altered. They are conceived of, not as wise and strong men chosen to govern, but as delegates under specific orders to be renewed at short intervals.

QUESTIONS FOR DISCUSSION

1. If governments rule in the interest of the majority does it matter if they are monarchies, aristocracies or democracies?
2. Should we rely upon the separation of powers or a system of checks and balances?
3. What are the main strengths and weaknesses of federations?
4. How much discretionary power, if any, do we have to concede to governments?

NOTES

1 Quoted by M.J.C. Vile, *Constitutionalism and the Separation of Powers* (Oxford, Oxford University Press, 1967), p. 22.
2 James M. Blythe, *Ideal Government and the Mixed Constitution in the Middle Ages* (Princeton NJ, Princeton University Press, 1992), p. 302

FURTHER READING

On constitutionalism see Vernon Bogdanor, *Constitutions in Democratic Politics* (Aldershot, Gower, 1988), J. Elsted and R. Slagstad (eds), *Constutionalism and Democracy* (Cambridge, Cambridge University Press, 1988) and Neil MacCormick, 'Consitutionalism and Democracy', in R. Bellamy (ed.), *Theories and Concepts of Politics* (Manchester, Manchester University Press, 1993). Older recommended texts include C.H. McIlwain, *Constitutionalism Ancient and Modern* (New York, Cornell University Press, 1944) and F.D. Wormuth, *The Origins of Modern Constitutionalism* (New York, Harper, 1949). On Aristotle's classification of government see R.G. Mulgan, *Aristotle's Political Theory* (Oxford, Clarendon Press, 1977). On medieval views see James M. Blythe, *Ideal Government and the Mixed Constitution in the Middle Ages* (Princeton NJ, Princeton University Press 1992). Two key authorities on the separation of powers are M.J.C. Vile, *Constitutionalism and the Separation of Powers* (Oxford, Oxford University Press, 1967) and W.B. Gwyn, *The Meaning of the Separation of Powers* (The Hague, Martinus Nijhoff, 1965). There is a very interesting account of monarchy in J.H. Burns, *Lordship, Kingship, and Empire. The idea of Monarchy, 1400–1525* (Oxford, Clarendon Press, 1992). For a recent assessment of the debate on the 'ancient constitution' see Glen Burgess, *The Politics of the Ancient Constitution. An Introduction to English Political Thought 1603–1642* (Houndmills, Macmillan, 1992). For Montesquieu's assessment of the prospects of liberty in different governmental forms see P.T. Mancias, 'Montesquieu and the Eighteenth Century View of the State', *History of Political Thought*, Vol. 2 (1981). For a useful collection of views on the forms of the executive see Arend Lijphart (ed.), *Parliamentary versus Presidential Government* (Oxford, Oxford University Press, 1992). There is no comprehensive survey of the idea of federalism but see S.R. Davis, *The Federal Principle* (Berkeley CA, University of California Press, 1978), P. King, *Federalism and Federation* (London, Croom Helm, 1982), and K. Wheare, *Federal Government* (Oxford, Oxford University Press, 1946). There are some useful contributions in A. Bosco (ed.), *The Federal Idea*, Vol. 1 (London, Lothian Foundation Press, 1991). Murray Forsyth, *Unions of States. The Theory and Practice of Confederations* (Leicester, Leicester University Press, 1981) is essential reading on that subject.

4

THE ORIGIN AND NATURE OF RIGHTS

INTRODUCTION

To a greater extent than at any other time our political, social and economic life is dominated by the language of rights. The language of rights is, however, as varied as it is prevalent. We claim, for example, that we have a right to free speech. In asserting this right we claim that no one else has a right to prevent us from saying whatever it is we wish to say. Alternatively, we may well assert our right to be paid by someone to whom, for example, we have supplied certain goods according to an agreed contract. He is under a duty to pay us and we expect this obligation to be enforced. In another usage of the language of rights we may give our savings to a favoured charity or to a religious body. Here we create new rights in the charity, that is, rights of ownership over the savings. At the same time we may deprive our own relatives of the prospect of inheriting these savings. Furthermore, we may claim a right to silence when accused of a certain crime. Others, witnesses to the supposed crime, can be compelled to answer questions about it, but we assert our own immunity from this obligation.[1]

The use of the language of rights in these diverse ways, to assert our liberty to do something, our claims over things and upon others, our ability to create rights in other people, and our immunity from certain requirements, forms part of the complexity of the idea of rights. The complexity of rights is compounded by other ambiguities. For, it is argued, it is not only individuals who have rights; states, nations, minorities, organizations from limited companies to trade unions, and even animals also have rights. If the subjects of rights, that is who or what holds or has rights, potentially constitute a lengthy list, the list of rights claimed is even longer. Few would dispute that man at least has a right to life itself – save in clearly specified cases of warfare or serious crime – but do we have a right to the most advanced medical treatment?, do we have a right to higher education?, a right to work?, or to strike?, a right to be educated in the language of our parents (if that language is not the dominant one in our state)? In the light of the increasing number of potential right-holders and the ever-expanding range of rights, an old question becomes increasingly important: We may agree that we *have* rights, but where do we get them from?

Although it is now customary to say 'I have a right to ...' this has not always been usual, or even possible. It was not possible for the ancient Greeks. They frequently said, 'It is right to do ...', but they could not speak of having rights. Rights were not treated analogously to possessions. Part of the reason for this was the close connection between the idea of rights and the idea of law. That connection is more strongly preserved in some other languages. The German *Recht*, the French *droit* and the Italian *diritto*, can all mean either law or right. The modern idea of rights, however, whatever language it is expressed in, separated out from notions of law and authority (see document 4.3).

According to the new view, we have rights in the same way that we have a physical body. Men are born with the one as they are born with the other. Nobody has a right to take away anything men rightfully hold, just as nobody has a right to take away men's lives.

Several features of this transformation of the language of rights stand out. Rights are now understood as natural rights. Men receive them by right of birth, and not from any political authority. This is important because rights have been, and still are, said to be derived from the state which grants rights to its citizens.

Asserting that rights arise independently of the state opens up the possibility of resisting political authority in defence of those rights. Secondly, all men have rights and they have the same basic rights. Again, this is contrary to the prevalent medieval view according to which rights were associated with membership of particular groups and varied according to the individual's group membership. Thirdly, the focus of rights is liberty. Rights are not associated primarily with obligations save the general obligation of the right-holder not to interfere with the rights (liberty) of others and their general obligation not to interfere with his rights (liberty).

The potential problems of the new vision were evident from the outset, even to some advocates of the new approach to rights. Thus the seventeenth-century English political philosopher, John Locke, insisted that liberty should not be equated with license. Drawing upon older traditions of natural law, he pointed to a code of behaviour which was ultimately derivable from God. This code prescribed how men might exercise their liberty. Locke sought to cut off what was to become an increasingly prominent criticism of the definition of right primarily in terms of liberty. The accusation was that rights thus defined are corrosive of any sense of community or responsibility for the well-being of fellow citizens. In the words of Karl Marx, men in a society governed by this conception of rights will become selfish and egoistic; society will be seen as, at best, a necessary constraint.

In deriving rights from an abstract nature another potential source of rights was being discounted. In seventeenth-century England, where the Ancient Constitution, that is a supposed set of rights dating back before the Norman

Conquest, was often invoked alongside nature by lawyers and parliamentarians, the novelty of the more radical version was somewhat blurred. With the French Revolution the break with history was clear, explicit and intended. The past as a source of accumulated rights was being rejected. In England this was reflected in the dispute between the conservative Edmund Burke and the radical Thomas Paine. Where Burke cited the past of his country as a source of rights, and obligations, Paine saw only constraints. Where Burke wrote of inheriting rights from his ancestors, Paine denied that contemporary men could be bound by their ancestors.

The dispute between Burke and Paine points to another aspect of the problem of the source of rights (see also documents 1.8 and 1.9). Burke insisted that the rights of Englishmen were, being a product of English history, peculiar to that country. Other peoples, with different historical experiences, would have their own distinct set of rights. But if rights are derived from nature, not histories, then the same rights will apply to all men, whatever their country and its history. Rights are universal. At the end of the eighteenth century the issue of the universality or particularity of rights was very much bound up with advocacy of a new, democratic form of government on the one hand, and the preservation of traditional authority on the other. It has, however, much wider implications.

With the expansion of trade, the development of the European empires across the globe, and subsequently the emergence of international organizations, dominated initially by Europeans and Americans, the issue took on new force. Are not, it is asked, the rights proclaimed as universally valid in fact the product of Western civilization? Are they more natural than, or are they superior to, the rights derived from other cultures? Defenders of cultural relativism complain, for example, that the Western emphasis upon the individual as the right-holder conflicts with the emphasis upon social groups in other cultures, that the emphasis upon (individual) private property conflicts with patterns of communal ownership in other cultures, that references to the family (implying nuclear family) as the basic social unit in international charters is incompatible with the extended family which is prevalent in non-Western societies, and so on.

The founder of utilitarianism, Jeremy Bentham, found other reasons for denigrating natural rights – as 'nonsense upon stilts'. Amidst his invective, he raised two criticisms which were to have lasting appeal. First, he insisted that the only rights were those duly enacted by the state. According to this approach, often designated the legal positivist approach, it only makes sense to speak of rights which are recognized by the state and are, therefore, enforceable. Secondly, he proposed a formula to determine which rights ought to be enacted, namely the extent to which the proposed right would be 'advantageous to society'. This criterion has aroused much dispute. Critics object that, considering what is advantageous to society or, in another common formulation, what is conducive to the greatest happiness of the greatest number, may well lead to the sacrifice of the interests, or even life, of the individual or minority. According to the critics, part of what we understand by rights is precisely that they should override other considerations. They cannot be sacrificed, save perhaps in deference to another, higher, right.

The issue of the relationship between different rights has become more problematic as the range of rights has extended. A significant step on the expansion of the realm of rights occurred with the change from natural rights to human rights. It is the latter term which we more commonly use today. According to one summary of this transition: arguments from natural rights typically proceeded from the idea of self-possession, from a property in oneself that must be defended against others; with *human rights*, however, arguments usually rest on some conception of a human or (perhaps more precisely) a person as a being with needs and interests that must be met if he or she is to live a fully human life. Thus the *right against* others of the natural rights theorist tends to become the *claims upon* others of the human rights theorist.[2]

Although not without precedent, this refocusing of rights gained ground in the nineteenth century. In part, the argument was, and still is, that any society must have some model or ideal of citizenship which defines that society and binds it together. Once acknowledged, as it must be, society is then obliged to ensure that all citizens can move towards this ideal. This argument also reinstates society, as against nature, as central to the existence and definition of rights.

The expansion of rights was also facilitated by the rapid social development of the nineteenth century. Thus the English social reformer, John Rae, explicitly cited changing social expectations and susceptibilities as a dynamic factor in the definition of rights (see document 4.11). Men could acquire rights to something, the lack of which previous generations would have regarded with equanimity. The agenda of rights was also being driven forward by an increasing acceptance of the role of the state in social and economic development (see Chapter 11, The state and the economy). Individuals, or whole groups, might suffer because of policies of the state. Do they then have a right to some form of compensation, or a right to remedial action? Since the late nineteenth century these kinds of argument have been pushed forward into ever-new fields and even on to the international agenda. If members of a society have a right to compensation because the policies of the society have systematically disadvantaged them, can we then, by extension, speak of the right of one country to compensation from another, because, perhaps, it has suffered from a period of colonial exploitation?

The expansion of the agenda of rights has thus affected the subject of rights, the potential right-holders, as well as the type of rights at issue. Nowhere is this clearer than in the case of minorities. The criteria for identifying relevant minorities are varied: language, broader cultural criteria, religion, ethnic identity, and gender. So too are the types of right asserted on their behalf. Often the claim is simply for equality. This was the cause of Catholics in nineteenth-century England, of Jews throughout Europe and America, of the coloured populations of the United States of America and of women in general. Although the basic claim was straightforward enough, its ramifications, as Eleanor Rathbone's argument shows, could be quite far reaching (see document 4.13). Equality has been, as in the case of rights in general, only the first step. Minorities have gone on to assert the right to compensation or remedial action, as for example in the case of claims for positive discrimination. Some minorities have, however, sought not just equality of treatment or even remedial action for their individual members, but rather rights to the continuation of the minority as a minority. Initially these minorities were typically religious, since it was the Church, with the secular authorities acting as its agents, that insisted upon conformity. Thus, in the wake of the Reformation the Edict of Nantes of 1585 secured for the French Huguenots the right to practice their religion.

With the development of nationalism, however, it was the state rather than the Church which sought to enforce homogeneity, usually in the use of language. At first the demand was, as in the case of religious minorities, for toleration, that is, for the liberty to follow their own customs and use their own language. Following the general trend in the development of rights, the claims quickly advanced to claims for resources, especially for schools, to preserve the minority's identity. Moreover, these minorities became the object of international consideration.

The major, if flawed, advance in this respect came with the treaties concluded after the First World War. Here we find another answer to the question about the source of rights: international treaty. From the viewpoint of the minorities, however, the protection they were offered was flawed. The problem lay in the conflict between the prevailing emphasis upon universal human rights, according to which individuals were the proper subject of rights, and the desire of the minorities that the group, the minority as such, be recognized as a legal entity and hence that the rights should be seen as the rights of the minority and not just rights of its members. That tension has still not been resolved. The United Nations and the treaties following the Second World War emphasized human rights, rather than group rights, even more than those concluded at the end of the First World War.

The reason why the idea of rights has proved to be so contentious is evident from the discussion found in Plato. Rights, even where they have been suspected of being formulated in the interests of the strong, that is of élites or even of dominant cultures, have continually been turned against them. Similarly, attempts to set limits to rights, to restrict rights to liberties, to restrict the range of right-holders, have been of limited success. The difficulties found in the idea of rights arise in large part from the very success of the idea of rights.

DOCUMENTS

Document 4.1

Plato, *The Republic*

Plato (427–347 BC) was a member of a powerful Athenian family. He was deeply influenced by an older contemporary, Socrates, who was executed in 399 BC. Most of Plato's work takes the form of dialogues between Socrates and various opponents representing typical Athenian views of politics. This dialogue, from *The Republic*, takes place between Thrasymachus, a sceptic, and Socrates. (For another illustration of the kind of views held by Thrasymachus see the argument of the Athenians in document 12.1.) Thrasymachus speaks first, Socrates replying.

'Each ruling class makes laws that are in its own interest, a democracy democratic laws, a tyranny tyrannical ones and so on; and in making these laws they define as "right" for their subjects what is in the interest of themselves, the rulers, and if anyone breaks their laws he is punished as a "wrong-doer". That is what I mean when I say that "right" is the same thing in all states, namely the interest of the established ruling class; and this ruling class is the "strongest" element in each state, and so if we argue correctly we see that "right" is always the same, the interest of the stronger party.'

'Now,' I said, 'I understand your meaning, and we must try to find out whether you are right or not. Your answer defines "right" as "interest" (though incidentally this is just what you forbade me to do), but adds the qualification "of the stronger party".'

'An insignificant qualification, I suppose you will say.'

'Its significance is not yet clear; what is clear is that we must consider whether your definition is true. For I quite agree that what is right is an "interest"; but you add that it is the interest "of the stronger party", and that's what I don't know about and want to consider.'

'Let us hear you.'

'You shall,' said I. 'You say that obedience to the ruling power is right and just?'

'I do.'

'And are those in power in the various states infallible or not?'

'They are, of course, liable to make mistakes,' he replied.

'When they proceed to make laws, then, they may do the job well or badly.'

'I suppose so.'

'And if they do it well the laws will be in their interest, and if they do it badly they won't, I take it.'

'I agree.'

'But their subjects must obey the laws they make, for to do so is right.'

'Of course.'

'Then according to your argument it is right not only to do what is in the interest of the stronger party but also the opposite.'

'What do you mean?' he asked.

'My meaning is the same as yours, I think. Let us look at it more closely. Did we not agree that when the ruling powers order their subjects to do something they are sometimes mistaken about their own best interest, and yet that it is right for the subject to do what his ruler enjoins?'

'I suppose we did.'

'Then you must admit that it is right to do things that are not in the interest of the rulers, who are the stronger party; that is, when the rulers mistakenly give orders that will harm them and yet (so you say) it is right for their subjects to obey those orders. For surely, my dear Thrasymachus, in those circumstances it follows that it is "right" to do the opposite of what you say is right, in that the weaker are ordered to do what is against the interest of the stronger.'

Document 4.2

De Legibus et Consuetudinibus Angliae

This mid-thirteenth-century text was long thought to be by Henry de Bracton (1210–68), a travelling royal judge. It is now believed that most of the text was written in the 1220s and 1230s and subsequently edited and enlarged by Bracton. The text played an important role in the development of the law in medieval England. The ideas expressed in the extract were reflected in the new coronation oath of 1308 in which Edward II promised 'to uphold the laws and rightful customs which the community of the realm have chosen'.

Moreover, although in nearly all regions the written law is used, England alone uses within her bounds unwritten law and custom. Here indeed right is based upon unwritten law, which use has proven. But it will not be absurd to speak of the English laws, although unwritten, as laws, since whatsoever has been justly defined and approved, with the advice and consent of the magnates and the general guaranty of the commonwealth, with the authority of the king or prince presiding, has the force of law. Also, there are in England many and diverse customs, according to the diversity of places. For the English hold many things by custom which they do not hold by law, as in various counties, cities, towns, and villages, where it must be inquired what the custom of the place is and in what way those who allege custom use the custom ...

Now the English laws and customs by the authority of kings sometimes order, sometimes forbid, sometimes sentence and punish transgressors. And these laws, indeed, when they have been approved by the consent of users and confirmed by the oath of kings, cannot be changed or destroyed without the common consent of all those by whose counsel and consent they were promulgated. Yet, without their consent, the laws can be altered for the better, because what is altered for the better is not destroyed. Moreover, if new and unaccustomed things emerge which were not previously used in the kingdom, they may be judged by similar things, if similar things have occurred, and when there is a good opportunity to proceed from like to like.

Document 4.3

Samuel Pufendorf, *Elementorium Jurisprudentiae Universalis*

Samuel Pufendorf (1632–94) was born in Saxony. After studying theology and philosophy, he became tutor in the service of the Swedish Ambassador to Denmark. Later he held chairs in law at Heidelberg and Lund and was court historian in Stockholm and Berlin. The extract from *Elements of Universal Jurisprudence* (1660) reflects the range and ambiguity of the idea of rights at the time.

1. In addition to those meanings by which the word right (*jus*) is used for law, and for a complex or system of homogenous laws, as also for a judicial sentence … the most frequent use is to employ it for that moral quality by which we properly either command persons, or possess things, or by which things are owed us. Thus under the name of right comes commonly authority over persons as well as things, which are our own or another's; and that authority which regards things is in a special sense called 'the right in the thing'. Concerning these words, however, that authority suggests the actual presence of the aforesaid quality over things or person, but more obscurely connotes, and leaves almost undecided, the manner in which one has acquired these things; while right properly and clearly indicates that this authority has been acquired properly and is now also properly held …

2. Now right is either *perfect* or *imperfect*. He who has infringed upon the former does a wrong which gives the injured party in a human court of law ground for bringing an action against the injurer. To this corresponds the perfect obligation in him from whom that which is owed us is to come. Therefore, I am able to compel him, when he refuses to pay this debt voluntarily, either by directing action against him before a judge, or, where there is no place for that, by force …

3. Now it is an imperfect right, which is called by some an aptitude, when something is owed by some one by another in such wise that, if he should deny it, he would, indeed, be acting unfairly, and yet the injured party would by no means be receiving a wrong which would furnish him with an action against the injurer; nor would he be able to assert for himself that right, except when necesity does not admit of any other means to secure his safety.

Document 4.4

Richard Overton, *An Arrow Against All Tyrants*

Little is known of Richard Overton's (1631–64) early life. He produced numerous pamphlets against Royalism and Catholicism in the early 1640s and on behalf of the Levellers (a radical political movement) in the latter years of the decade. He was imprisoned several times, in 1646–47, 1649 and again in 1659. *An Arrow Against All Tyrants* (10 October 1646) was written as part of a campaign against the imprisonment of another radical, John Lilburne (1615–57), by the House of Lords. It is notable however for its definition of rights.

Sir, To every Individuall in nature, is given an individuall property by nature, not to be invaded or usurped by any: for every one as he is himselfe, so he hath a selfe propriety, else he could not be himselfe, and on this no second may presume to deprive any of, without manifest violation and affront to the very principles of nature, and of the Rule of equity and justice between man and man; mine and thine cannot be, except this be: No man hath power over my rights and liberties and I over no mans; I may be but an Individuall, enjoy *my selfe* and my selfe propriety, and I may write my selfe no more than my selfe, or presume any further; if I doe, I am an encroacher and an invader upon an other mans Right, to which I have no *Right*. For by naturall birth, all men are equally and alike borne to like propriety, liberty and freedome, and as we are delivered of God by the hand of nature into this world, every one with a naturall, innate freedome and propriety (as it were writ in the table of every mans heart, never to be obliterated) even so are we to live, every one equally and alike to enjoy his Birthright and priviledge; even all whereof God by nature hath made him free … And from this fountain or root, all just humain powers take their original; not immediatly from God (as Kings usually plead their prerogative) but mediatly by the hand of nature, as from the represented to the representors; for originally, God hath implanted them in the creature, and from the creature those powers immediatly proceed; and no further: and no more may be communicated than stands for the better being, weale or safety thereof: and this is mans prerogative and no further, so much and no more may be given or received thereof: even so much as is conducent to a better being, more safety and freedome, and no more; he that gives more, sins against his owne self; and he that takes more, is a Theife and Robber to his kind: Every man by nature being a King, Priest and Prophet in his one naturall circuite and compasse, whereof no second may partake, but by deputation, commission, and free consent from him, whose naturall right and freedome it is.

Document 4.5

John Locke on Rights in the State of Nature

This statement of the law of nature by John Locke (see introduction to document 1.5) in his *Two Treatises of Government* is important for its insistence that rights do exist in a state of nature, that is, prior to the establishment of political authority.

But though this be a state of liberty, yet it is not a state of licence, though man in that state have an uncontrollable liberty to dispose of his person or possessions, yet he has not liberty to destroy himself, or so much as any creature in his possession, but where some nobler use, than its bare preservation calls for it. The state of nature has a law of nature to govern it, which obliges every one: and reason, which is that law, teaches all mankind, who will but consult it, that being all equal and independent, no one ought to harm another in his life, health, liberty or possessions; for men being all the workmanship of one omnipotent, and infinitely wise maker; all the servants of one sovereign master, sent into the world by his order and about his business; they are his property, whose workmanship they are, made to last during his, not one anothers pleasure: and being furnished with like faculties, sharing all in one community of nature, there cannot be supposed any such subordination among us, that may authorize us to destroy another, as if we were made for one anothers uses, as the inferior ranks of creatures are for ours. Every one as he is bound to preserve himself, and not to quit his station wilfully, so by the like reason, when his own preservation comes not in competition, ought he, as much as he can, to preserve the rest of mankind, and may not, unless it be to do justice to an offender, take away or impair the life, or what tends to the preservation of the life, liberty, health, limb or goods of another.

And that all men be restrained from invading others rights, and from doing hurt to one another, and the law of nature be observed, which willeth the peace and preservation of all mankind, the execution of the law of nature is, in that state, put into every mans hands, whereby every one has a right to punish the transgressors of that law to such a degree, as may hinder its violation: for the law of nature would, as all other laws that concern men in this world, be in vain, if there were no body that in the state of nature, had a power to execute that law, and thereby preserve the innocent and restrain offenders. And if any one in the state of nature may punish another for any evil he has done, every one may do so: for in that state of perfect equality, where naturally there is no superiority or jurisdiction of one over another, what any may do in prosecution of that law, every one must needs have a right to do.

Document 4.6

Declaration of the Rights of Man and of the Citizen

This document was a product of the French Revolution. It was adopted by the National Assembly on 27 August 1791 after prolonged debate. The text itself was a compromise and a provisional document. Further articles were to be considered after agreement was reached on a constitution. The *Declaration* nevertheless became the reference point for subsequent discussion (see documents 4.8 and 4.10).

The representatives of the people of France, formed into a National Assembly, considering that ignorance, neglect, or contempt of human rights, are the sole causes of public misfortunes and corruptions of Government, have resolved to set forth in a solemn declaration, these natural, imprescriptible, and inalienable rights: that this declaration being constantly present to the minds of the members of the body social, they may for ever kept attentive to their rights and their duties; that the acts of the legislative and executive powers of government, being capable of being every moment compared with the end of political institutions, may be more respected; and also, that the future claims of the citizens, being directed by simple and incontestable principles, may always tend to the maintenance of the Constitution, and the general happiness.

For these reasons, the National Assembly doth recognize and declare, in the presence of the Supreme Being, and with the hope of his blessing and favour, the following sacred rights of men and of citizens:

I Men are born, and always continue, free and equal in respect of their rights. Civil distinctions, therefore, can be founded only on public utility.

II The end of all political associations, is the preservation of the natural and imprescriptible rights of man; and these rights are liberty, property, security, and resistance of oppression.

III The nation is essentially the source of all sovereignty; nor can any individual, or any body of men, be entitled to any authority which is not expressly derived from it.

IV Political liberty consists in the power of doing whatever does not injure another. The exercise of the natural rights of every man, has no other limits than those which are necessary to secure to every other man the free exercise of the same rights; and these limits are determinable only by the law.

V The law ought to prohibit only actions hurtful to society. What is not prohibited by the law, should not be hindered; nor should any one be compelled to that which the law does not require.

VI The law is an expression of the will of the community. All citizens have a right to concur, either personally, or by their representatives, in its formation. It should be the same to all, whether it protects or punishes; and all being equal in its sight, are equally eligible to all honours, places, and employments, according to their different abilities, without any other distinction than that created by their virtues and talents.

VII No man should be accused, arrested, or held in confinement, except in cases determined by the law, and according to the forms which it has prescribed. All who promote, solicit, execute, or cause to be executed, arbitrary orders, ought to be punished, and every citizen called upon, or apprehended by virtue of the law, ought immediately to obey, and renders himself culpable by resistance.

VIII The Law ought to impose no other penalties but such as are absolutely and evidently necessary; and no one ought to be punished, but in virtue of a law promulgated before the offence, and legally applied.

XI Every man being presumed innocent till he has been convicted, whenever his detention becomes indispensable, all rigour to him, more than is necessary to secure his person, ought to be provided against by the law.

X No man ought to be molested on account of his opinions, not even on account of his religious opinions, provided his avowal of them does not disturb the public order established by the law.

XI The unrestrained communication of thoughts and opinions being one of the most precious rights of man, every citizen may speak, write, and publish freely, provided he is responsible for the abuse of this liberty, in cases determined by the law.

XII A public force being necessary to give security to the rights of men and of citizens, that force is instituted for the benefit of the community and not for the particular benefit of the persons to whom it is intrusted.

XIII A common contribution being necessary for the support of the public force, and for defraying the other expenses of government, it ought to be divided equally among the members of the community, according to their abilities.

XIV Every citizen has a right, either by himself or his representative, to a free voice in determining the necessity of public contributions, the appropriation of them, and their amount, mode of assessment, and duration.

XV Every community has had a right to demand of all its agents an account of their conduct.

XVI Every community in which a separation of powers and a security of rights is not provided for, wants a constitution.

XVII The right to property being inviolable and sacred, no one ought to be deprived of it, except in cases of evident public necessity, legally ascertained, and on condition of a previous just indemnity.

Document 4.7

Thomas Paine, *The Rights of Man*

Thomas Paine (1737–1809) (see introduction to document 1.8) was a sympathizer of the French Revolution, becoming a French citizen and member of the Convention. He died in America. He wrote *The Rights of Man* (1790–92) in reply to Edmund Burke's (1728–97) criticism of the Revolution. The immediate stimulus for Burke's *Reflections on the Revolution in France* was the publication of a sermon by the radical preacher Richard Price. In the extract Paine attacks Burke's attempt to construe rights as part of a tradition or inheritance.

Dr. Price had preached a sermon on the 4th of November, 1789, being the anniversary of what is called in England the Revolution, which took place 1688. Mr. Burke, speaking of this sermon, says, 'The political Divine proceeds dogmatically to assert, that by the principles of the Revolution, the people of England have acquired three fundamental rights:

1. To choose their own governors.
2. To cashier them for misconduct.
3. To frame a government for ourselves.'

Dr. Price does not say that the right to do these things exists in this or in that person, or in this or in that description of persons, but that it exists in the whole; that it is a right resident in the Nation. Mr. Burke, on the contrary, denies that such a right exists in the Nation, either in whole or in part, or that it exists anywhere; and, what is still more strange and marvellous, he says, 'that the people of England utterly disclaim such a right, and that they will resist the practical assertion of it with their lives and fortunes.' That men should take up arms and spend their lives and fortunes, not to maintain their rights, but to maintain they have not rights, is an entirely new species of discovery, and suited to the paradoxical genius of Mr. Burke.

The method which Mr. Burke takes to prove that the people of England have no such rights, and that such rights do not now exist in the Nation, either in whole or in part, or anywhere at all, is of the same marvellous and monstrous kind with what he has already said; for his arguments are that the persons, or the generation of persons, in whom they did exist, are dead, and with them the right is dead also. To prove this, he quotes a declaration made by parliament about a hundred years ago, to William and Mary, in these words: 'The Lords Spiritual and Temporal, and Commons, do, in the name of the people aforesaid [meaning the people of England then living], most humbly and faithfully *submit* themselves, their *heirs* and *posterities*, for EVER.' He also quotes a clause of another act of Parliament made in the same reign, the terms of which, he says, 'bind us [meaning the people of that day], our heirs and our posterity, to them, their heirs and posterity, to the end of time ...'

As Mr. Burke occasionally applies the poison drawn from his horrid principles (if it is not prophanation to call them by the name of principles) not only to the English Nation, but to the French Revolution and the National Assembly, and charges that august, illuminated and illuminating body of men with the epithet of *usurpers*, I shall, *sans cérémonie*, place another system of principles in opposition to his.

The English Parliament of 1688 did a certain thing, which, for themselves and their constituents, they had a right to do, and which it appeared right should be done: but, in addition to this right, which they possessed by delegation, *they set up another right by assumption*, that of binding and controlling posterity to the end of time. The case, therefore, divides itself into two parts; the right which they possessed by delegation, and the right which they set up by assumption The first is admitted; but with respect to the second, I reply –

There never did, there never will, and there never can, exist a Parliament, or any description of men, or any generation of men, in any country, possessed of the right or the power of binding and controlling posterity to the 'end of time,' or of commanding for ever how the world shall be governed, or who shall govern it; and therefore all such clauses, acts or declarations by which the makers of them attempt to do what they have neither the right nor the power to do, nor the power to execute, are in themselves null and void. Every age and generation must be as free to act for itself *in all cases* as the ages and generations which preceded it. The vanity and presumption of governing beyond the grave is the most ridiculous and insolent of all tyrannies. Man has no property in man; neither has any generation a property in the generations which are to follow. The Parliament or the people of 1688, or of any other period, had no more right to dispose of the people of the present day, or to bind or to control them *in any shape whatever*, then the Parliament or the people of the present day have to dispose of, bind or control those who are to live a hundred or a thousand years hence. Every generation is, and must be, competent to all the purposes which its occasions require. It is the living, and not the dead, that are to be accommodated. When man ceases to be, his power and his wants cease with him; and having no longer any participation in the concerns of this world, he has no longer any authority in directing who shall be its governors, or how its Government shall be organised, or how administered ...

Those who have quitted the world, and those who are not yet arrived at it, are as remote from each other as the utmost stretch of mortal imagination can conceive. What possible obligation, then, can exist between them; what rule or principle can be laid down that of two non-entities, the one out of existence and the other not in, and who never can meet in this world, the one should control the other to the end of time?

In England it is said that money cannot be taken out of the pockets of the people without their consent. But who authorised, or who could authorise, the Parliament of 1688 to control and take away the freedom of posterity (who were not in existence to give or to withhold their consent), and limit and confine their right of acting in certain cases for ever? ...

Hitherto we have spoken only (and that but in part) of the natural rights of man. We have now to consider the civil rights of man, and to show how the one originates from the other. Man did not enter into society to become *worse* than he was before, not to have fewer rights than he had before, but to have those rights better secured. His natural rights are the foundation of all his civil rights. But in order to pursue this distinction with more precision, it will be necessary to mark the different qualities of natural and civil rights.

A few words will explain this. Natural rights are those which appertain to man in right of his existence. Of this kind are all the intellectual rights, or rights of the mind, and also all those rights of acting as an individual for his own comfort and happiness, which are not injurious to the natural rights of others. Civil rights are those which appertain to man in right of his being a member of society. Every civil right has for its foundation some natural right pre-existing in the individual, but to the enjoyment of which his individual power is not, in all cases, sufficiently competent. Of this kind are all those which relate to security and protection.

From this short view it will be easy to distinguish between that class of natural rights which man retains after entering into society and those which he throws into the common stock as a member of society.

The natural rights which he retains are all those in which the *power* to execute it is as perfect in the individual as the right itself. Among this class, as is before mentioned, are all the intellectual rights, or rights of the mind; consequently religion is one of those rights. The natural rights which are not retained, are all those in which, though the right is perfect in the individual, the power to execute them is defective. They answer not his purpose. A man, by natural right, has a right to judge in his own cause; and so far as the right of the mind is concerned, he never surrenders it. But what availeth it him to judge, if he has not power to redress? He therefore deposits this right in the common stock of society, and takes the arm of society, of which he is a part, in preference and in addition to his own. Society grants him nothing. Every man is a proprietor in society, and draws on the capital as a matter of right.

From these premisses two or three certain conclusions will follow:

First, *That every civil right grows out of a natural right; or, in other words, is a natural right exchanged.*

Secondly, *That civil power properly considered as such is made up of the aggregate of that class of the natural rights of man, which becomes defective in the individual in point of power, and answers not his purpose, but when collected to a focus becomes competent to the purpose of every one.*

Thirdly, *That the power produced from the aggregate of natural rights, imperfect in power in the individual, cannot be applied to invade the natural rights which are retained in the individual, and in which the power to execute is as perfect as the right itself* …

Document 4.8

Jeremy Bentham on Natural Rights

Jeremy Bentham (1748–1832) was the founder of the doctrine of Utilitarianism (see introduction to document 3.10). The extract is from a critique of the 1791 Declaration of Rights. It reflects Bentham's obsession with clarity of thought and language without which, he thought, men would remain slaves to prejudice and delusion.

Article I

Men (all men) are born and remain free, and equal in respect of rights. Social distinctions cannot be founded, but upon common utility.

In this article are contained two distinct sentences grammatically speaking. The first is full of error, the other of ambiguity.

In the first are contained four distinguishable propositions, all of them false – all of them notoriously and undeniably false:

1. That all men are born free.
2. That all men remain free.
3. That all men are born equal in rights.
4. That all men remain (i.e. remain for ever, for the proposition is indefinite and unlimited) equal in rights.

All men are born free? All men remain free? No, not a single man: not a single man that ever was, or is, or will be. All men, on the contrary are born in subjection, and the most absolute subjection – the subjection of a helpless child to the parents on whom he depends every moment for his existence. In this subjection every man is born, in this subjection he continues for years, for a great number of years, and the existence of the individual and of the species depends upon his so doing ...

All men are born free? Absurd and miserable nonsense! When the great complaint, a complaint made perhaps by the very same people at the same time, is that so many men are born slaves ...

All men are born equal in rights. The rights of the heir of the most indigent family equal to the rights of the heir of the most wealthy. In what case is this true? ...

All men (i.e. all human creatures of both sexes) remain equal in rights ... The apprentice, then, is equal in rights to his master; he has as much liberty with relation to his master, as the master has with relation to him; he has as much right to command and punish him, he is as much owner and master of the master's house, as the master himself ...

Sentence 2. Social distinctions can not be founded but upon common utility ...

What is meant by can not be founded but upon common utility? Is it meant to speak of what is established, or of what *ought to be established?* Does it mean that no social distinctions but those which it approves of as having the foundation in question, *are* established anywhere, or simply that none such ought to be established anywhere? Or that, if the establishment or maintenance of such dispositions by the laws is attempted anywhere, such laws ought to be treated as void, and the attempt to execute them to be resisted?

Article II

The end in view of every political association is the preservation of the natural and imprescriptible rights of man …

More confusion – more nonsense, and the nonsense, as usual, dangerous nonsense …

How stands the truth of things? That there are no such things as natural rights, no such things as rights anterior to the establishment of government, no such things as natural rights opposed to, in contradistinction to, legal [rights] …

In proportion to the want of happiness resulting from the want of rights, a reason [exists] for wishing that there were such things as rights. But reasons for wishing there were such things as rights, are not rights; a reason for wishing that a certain right were established is not that right; want is not supply; hunger is not bread.

That which has no existence cannot be destroyed; that which cannot be destroyed cannot require anything to preserve it from being destroyed. Natural rights is simple nonsense: nataural and imprescriptible rights, rhetorical nonsense, nonsense upon stilts …

So much for terrorist language. What is the language of reason and plain sense upon this same subject? That in proportion as it is right and proper, i.e. advantageous to the society in question, that this or that right, a right to this or that effect, should be established and maintained, in that same proportion it is wrong that it should be abrogated; but as there is no right which ought not to be maintained so long as it is upon the whole advantageous to the society that is should be maintained, so there is no right which, when the abolition of it is advantageous to society, should not be abolished.

Document 4.9

William Cobbett on the Rights of an Englishman

William Cobbett (1763–1835) served in the British Army before embarking on a career as a radical, conservative pamphleteer and journalist. He was a severe critic of corruption and the brutality of army life. Criticism of the practice of flogging earned him two years imprisonment. He brought the remains of his old opponent Thomas Paine back to England. His *Rural Rides* (1830), from which the extract is taken, lamented the demise of traditional English country life.

The law may say what it will, but the feelings of mankind will never be in favour of this Code; and whenever it produces putting to death, it will necessarily, excite horror. it is impossible to make men believe that any particular set of individuals should have a permanent property in wild creatures. That the owner of land should have a quiet possesion of it is reasonable and right and necessary; it is also necessary that he should have the power of inflicting pecuniary punishment, in a moderate degree, upon such as trespass upon his lands; but, his right can go no further according to reason. If the law give him ample compensation for every damage that he sustains, in consequence of a trespass on his lands, what right has he to complain?

The law authorizes the King, in case of invasion, or apprehended invasion, to call upon all his people to take up arms in defence of the country. The Militia Law compels every man, in his turn, to become a soldier. And upon what ground is this? There must be some reason for it, or else the law would be tyranny. The reason is, that every man has *rights* in the country to which he belongs; and that, therefore, it is his duty to defend the country. Some rights, too, beyond that of merely living, merely that of breathing the air. And then, I should be glad to know, what rights an Englishman has, if the pursuit of even wild animals is to be the ground of transporting him from his country?

Document 4.10

Karl Marx on Rights and Egoism

Karl Marx (1818–83) was influenced by the ideas of the German philosopher G.W.F. Hegel before turning to the study of political economy which eventually issued in his major, unfinished, work *Capital*. In an early work, *On the Jewish Question* (1844) Marx criticized the ideas of Bruno Bauer who argued that the secularization of the state was the way to guarantee liberty. Marx objected that purely political reform was insufficient, not least because the prevailing ideas of rights were stamped by bourgeois society. The term species-being (*Gattungswesen*) refers to a complex of intellectual capacities and social relationships which define human nature.

Let us discuss for a moment the so-called human rights, human rights in their authentic form, the form they have in the writings of their discoverers, the North Americans and the French! … *Declaration of the Rights of Man* …, Article 2. These rights etc. (natural and imprescriptable) are: equality, liberty, security, property.

What does liberty consist of?

Article 6: 'Liberty is the power that belongs to man to do anything that does not infringe on the right of someone else' …

Thus freedom is the right to do and perform what does not harm others. The limits within which each person can move without harming others, is defined by the law, just as the boundary between two fields is defined by the fence. The freedom in question is that of man as an isolated monad and withdrawn into himself ...

What does the right of property consist in? ...

The right of man to property is the right to enjoy his possessions and dispose of the same arbitrarily, without regard for other men, independently from society, the right of selfishness ...

There still remain the other rights of man, equality and security.

Equality, here in its non-political sense, is simply the counterpart of liberty described above, namely that each man shall without discrimination be treated as a self-sufficient monad ...

Security is the highest concept of civil society, the concept of the police. The whole of society is merely there to guarantee to each of its members the preservation of his person, rights and property ...

Thus none of the so-called rights of man goes beyond egoistic man, man as he is in civil society, namely an individual withdrawn behind his private interests and whims and separated from the community. Far from the rights of man conceiving of man as a species-being, species-life itself, society, appears as a framework exterior to individuals, a limitation of their original self-sufficiency. The only bond that holds them together is natural necessity, need and private interest, the conservation of their property and egoistic person.

Document 4.11

John Rae on Rights and Social Reform

John Rae (1845–1915) was an author and journalist. He was one of a group of liberals who rejected the old *laissez-faire* approach. As part of his attempt to formulate a new liberalism Rae reconsidered the nature and limits of rights. The extract is taken from his 'State Socialism and Social Reform', *The Contemporary Review* (1890).

The State is asked to go in Social Reform only as far as it goes in judicial administration – it is asked to secure for every man as effectively as it can those essentials of all rational and humane living which are really every man's right, because without them he would be something less than a man, his manhood would be wanting, maimed, mutilated, deformed, incapable of fulfilling the ends of its being. Those original requirements of humane existence are dues of the common nature we wear, which we cannot see extinguished in others without an injury to our own self-respect, and the State is bound to provide adequate securities for one of them as much as for the other. The same reason which justified the State at first in protecting person and property against violence, justified it yesterday in abolishing slavery, justifies it to-day in abolishing ignorance, and will justify it to-morrow in abolishing other degrading conditions of life. The public sense of human dignity may grow from age to age and be offended to-morrow by what it tolerates to-day, but the principle of sound intervention is all through the same – that the proposed measure is necessary to enable men to live the true life of a man and fulfil the proper ends of rational beings. A thoughtful French writer defends State intervention for the purpose of social amelioration as being a mere duty of what he calls reparative justice. Popular misery and decadence, he would say, is always very largely the result of bad laws and other bad civil conditions, as we see it plainly to have been in the case of the Irish cottiers, the Scotch crofters, and the rural labourers of England, and when the community has really inflicted the injury, the community is bound in the mearest justice to repair it. And the obligation would not be exhausted with the repeal of bad laws, it would require the positive restoration to the declining populations of the conditions of real prosperity from which they fell. But though this is a specific ground which may occasionally quicken the State's remedial action with something of the energy of remorse, it is no extension of its natural and legitimate sphere of intervention, and the State might properly take every measure necessary for the effectual restoration of a declining section of the population to conditions of real prosperity on the broad and simple principle already laid down, that the measure is necessary to put those people in a position to fulfil their vocation as human beings. Hopeless conditions of labour are as contrary to sound nature, and as fatal to any proper use of man's energies, as slavery itself, and their mere existence constitutes a sufficient cause for the State's intervention, apart from any special responsibility the State may bear for their historical origin. Even the measure of the required intervention is no way less, for if its purpose is to preserve some essential of full normal manhood, its only limit is that of being effectual to serve the purpose. The original natural obligation of the State needs no expansion then from historical responsibilities to cover any effectual form of remedial action against the social decadence of particular classes of the population, whether it be the constitution of a new right like the right to a fair rent, the adoption of administrative measures like the migration of redundant inhabitants, or the provision of wise facilities for the rest by the loan of public money.

Document 4.12

Thomas H. Green,
Lectures on the Principles of Political Obligation

Thomas H. Green (1836–82) was a lecturer and then Professor at Oxford University from 1860 until his early death at the age of 47. Although he published little in his lifetime he exerted considerable influence through his students. The extract is taken from the posthumously published *Lectures on the Principles of Political Obligation*. In it Green rejected the idea of natural rights as too individualistic, insisting that men had rights only as members of a community.

I have tried to show in lectures on morals that the conception expressed by the 'should be' is not identical with the conception of a right possesed by some man or men, but one from which the latter conception is derived. It is, or implies on the part of whoever is capable of it, the conception of an ideal, unattained condition of himself as an absolute end. Without this conception the recognition of a power as a right would be impossible. A power on the part of anyone is so recognised by others, as one which should be exercised, when these others regard it as in some way a means to that ideal good of themselves which they alike conceive: and the possessor of the power comes to regard it as a right through consciousness of its being thus recognised as contributory to a good in which he too is interested. No one therefore can have a right except (1) as a member of a society, and (2) of a society in which some common good is recognised by the members of the society as their own ideal good, as that which should be for each of them … everyone capable of being determined by the conception of a common good as his own ideal good, as that which unconditionally should be (of being in that sense an end to himself), in other words, every moral person, is capable of rights; i.e., of bearing his part in a society in which the free exercise of his powers is secured to each member through the recognition by each of the others as entitled to the same freedom with himself.

Document 4.13

Eleanor Rathbone on the Rights of Women

Eleanor Rathbone (1872–1946) became the first female Justice of the Peace in her native Lancashire before the First World War. She sat on Liverpool City Council from 1909 to 1934 and was an Independent Member of Parliament from 1928 representing the Combined English Universities until her death. In 1917 she founded the Family Endowment Committee to campaign for family allowances, a campaign which finally succeeded with the Government Allowances Bill (1945). The extract is taken from 'The Remuneration of Women's Services' (1917).

Since the State, though it recognizes in theory the rights of wife and children to maintenance, does practically nothing to enforce it; such laws as do embody this right being so imperfect and so badly carried out that they are next door to valueless as a protection. In the normal case, however, the family does receive the benefit of the man's wages, at least up to the point of minimum subsistence level, and the vast majority of wives and of children below fourteen are wholly or mainly maintained out of this source. In other words, the wages of the worker represent not only the value of his services to his employer, and through him to the community, but also the value of his wife's services to him and their children, and through them to the community, and, in addition, the value to the State of the children themselves. His wages, in short, are the channel by which the community, indirectly and only half-consciously, pays for the continuance of its own existence and the rearing of fresh generations. The amount so paid becomes part of the cost of production of the commodities produced or services rendered by the trades or occupations which male workers follow, and comes eventually out of the pockets of the community as consumers.

The wages of women workers are not based on the assumption that 'they have families to keep,' and in so far as these wages are determined by the standard of life of the workers it is a standard based on the cost of individual subsistence, and not on the cost of family subsistence. It is perfectly true that many women workers (according to information obtained by the Fabian Women's Group, above 50 per cent. of them) contribute towards the maintenance of relations, and no doubt that fact, by making them more ambitious and anxious for money, exercises a certain upward pull upon their wages. But it must be remembered that against the influence on wages of the woman who keeps others besides herself must be set the influence of the pocket-money or supplementary wage-earners who do not even keep themselves – the daughters living partly on their fathers, the wives working to supplement their husbands' wages, and the widows who eke out their poor relief. The number of women whose family responsibilities are really equivalent to the normal responsibilities of the average-sized household of man, woman, and three children is, after all, very small. Even the position of the independent widow householder is not really comparable, since the family she works for has lost its most expensive member.

If this view of the facts is correct, it would appear that the difference between the wages of men and women is a much more deep-rooted thing than is commonly supposed. It has its roots in an arrangement which to most people appears a fundamental part of the social structure, the arrangement by which the financial responsibility for the upbringing of the family is thrown on the father. The argument that it is an indisputable principle of justice that if men and women do the same work they shall receive the same pay can be countered by the proposition, apparently equally indisputable, that if men are to pay for the upbringing of the rising generation they must be given some money to do it with. Looked at in this way, the claim of women who do not bear the same domestic burdens to receive the same remuneration seems to involve an ignoring of the still more potent claims of those wives and mothers who are rendering the most essential of all services to the State, who have to be maintained during the performance of those services, and who are at present receiving their maintenance in an indirect fashion through the wages of their husbands.

The line of argument I have been following usually either irritates or depresses all women who have the interests of their own sex at heart, because it seems to point to an impasse. If the wages of men and women are really based upon fundamentally different conditions, and if these conditions cannot be changed, then it would seem that fair competition between them is impossible, and that women are the eternal black-legs, doomed, despite themselves, to injure the prospects of men whenever they are brought into competition with them, and by a sort of irony of fate to undermine just those standards of family life which should be most sacred to them. If that were really so, then it would seem as if men were justified in treating women – as in practice they have treated them – as a kind of industrial lepers, segregated in trades which men have agreed to abandon to them, permitted to occupy themselves in making clothing or in doing domestic services for each other, and in performing those subsidiary processes in the big staple trades, which are so monotonous or unskilled that men do not care to claim them. The result of this treatment has been a marked growth of unrest and discontent, due as much to the consciousness of thwarted powers and undeveloped capacities as to actual suffering through underpayment and unemployment.

Document 4.14

Wesley Newcomb Hohfeld, *Fundamental Legal Conceptions*

Wesley Newcomb Hohfeld (1879–1918) was born in California and practised law before holding a series of academic posts. His early death resulted from a heart condition. The extract is taken from *Fundamental Legal Conceptions. As Applied in Judicial Reasoning and Other Legal Cases* (1920).

A multital right, or claim (right in rem), should not be confused with any co-exisitng privileges or other jural relations that the holder of the multital right or rights may have …

Suppose, for example, that A is fee-simple owner of Blackacre. His 'legal interest' or 'property' relating to the tangible object that we call *land* consists of a complex aggregate of rights (or claims), privileges, powers and immunities. First, A has multital legal, rights, or claims, that *others*, respectively, shall *not* enter on the land, that they shall not cause physical harm to the land, etc., such others being under respective correlative legal duties. Second, A has an indefinite number of legal privileges of entering on the land, using the land, harming the land, etc., that is, within limits fixed by law on grounds of social and economic policy … Third, A has the legal power to alienate his legal interest to another, i.e., to extinguish his complex aggregate of jural relations and create a new and similar aggregate in the other person … also the legal power to create a privilege of entrance in any other person by giving 'leave and license'; and so on indefinitely … Fourth, A has an indefinite number of legal immunities, using the term immunity in the very specific sense of non-liability or non-subjection to a power on the part of another person. Thus A has the immunity that no ordinary person can alienate A's legal interest or aggregate of jural relations to another person; the immunity that no ordinary person can extinguish A's privilege of using the land; the immunity that no ordinary person can extinguish A's right that another person shall not enter on the land or, in other words, create in X a privilege of entering on the land …

Not only as a matter of accurate analysis and exposition, but also as a fact of great practical consequence and economic significance, the property owner's rights, or claims, should be sharply differentiated from his privileges. It is sometimes thought that A's rights, or claims are created by the law for the sole purpose of guarding or protecting A's own physical user or enjoyment of the land, as if such physical user or enjoyment of the land were the only economic factor of importance. A moments reflection, however, shows that this is a very inadequate view. Even though the land be entirely vacant and A have no intention whatever of personally using the land, his rights or claims that others shall not use even temporarily in such ways as would not alter its physical character are, generally of great economic significance as tending to make others compensate A in exchange for the extinguishment of his rights, or claims, or in other words, the creation of privileges of user and enjoyment.

Document 4.15

Treaty between the Principal Allied and Associated Powers and Poland, 28 June 1919

The Treaty was signed at Versailles. Similar provisions concerning minorities were incorporated in treaties with other East European states. No such provisions were incorporated in the Treaty with Germany. The Great Powers rejected pleas for a generalization of the protection of minorities. Despite the apparent strictness of the guarantees, the difficulties of the procedure for lodging complaints and the general mood of the Council of the League of Nations inhibited any serious attempt to enforce the provisions. In September 1934 Poland refused any further cooperation in implementing the minorities provisions until a 'general and uniform system for the protection of minorities' was introduced.

Article 8

Polish nationals who belong to racial, religious or linguistic minorities shall enjoy the same treatment and security in law and in fact as other Polish nationals. In particular they shall have an equal right to establish, manage and control at their own expense charitable, religious and social institutions, schools and other educational establishments, with the right to use their own language and to exercise their religion freely therein.

Article 9

Poland will provide in the public educational system in towns and districts in which a considerable proportion of Polish nationals of other than Polish speech are residents adequate facilitites for ensuring that in the primary schools the instruction shall be given to the children of such Polish nationals through the medium of their own language.

In towns and districts where there is a considerable proportion of Polish nationals belonging to racial, religious or linguistic minorities, these minorities shall be assured an equitable share in the enjoyment and application of the sums which may be provided out of public funds under the State, municipal or other budget, for educational, religious or other charitable purposes …

Article 12

Poland agrees that the stipulations in the foregoing Articles, so far as they affect persons belonging to racial, religious or linguistic minorities, constitute obligations of international concern and shall be placed under the guarantee of the League of Nations. They shall not be modified without the assent of a majority of the Council of the League of Nations …

Poland agrees that any Member of the Council of the League of Nations shall have the right to bring to the attention of the Council any infraction, or any danger of infraction, of any of these obligations, and that the Council may thereupon take such action and give such direction as it may deem proper and effective in the circumstances.

Document 4.16

International Convention on Economic, Social and Cultural Rights

Although the United Nations adopted The Universal Declaration of Human Rights in 1948, this Declaration was intended as a statement of principles. It took another eighteen years before the General Assembly gave approval to two Covenants which would be binding upon those who signed them. These were The International Covenant on Civil and Political Rights and The International Covenant on Economic, Social and Cultural Rights (1966).

Preamble

The States Parties to the present Covenant,

Considering that, in accordance with the principles proclaimed in the Charter of the United Nations, recognition of the inherent dignity and of the equal and inalienable rights of all members of the human family is the foundation of freedom, justice and peace in the world,

Recognizing that these rights derive from the inherent dignity of the human person,

Recognizing that, in accordance with the Universal Declaration of Human Rights, the ideal of free human beings enjoying freedom from fear and want can only be achieved if conditions are created whereby everyone may enjoy his economic, social and cultural rights, as well as his civil and political rights,

Considering the obligation of States under the Charter of the United Nations to promote universal respect for, and observance of, human rights and freedoms,

Realizing that the individual, having duties to other individuals and to the community to which he belongs, is under a responsibility to strive for the promotion and observance of the rights recognized in the present Covenant,

Agree upon the following articles:

Article 1

All peoples have the right of self-determination. By virtue of that right they freely determine their political status and freely pursue their economic, social and cultural development ...

Article 2

Each State Party to the present Covenant undertakes to take steps, individually and through international assistance and co-operation, especially economic and technical, to the maximum of its available resources, with a view to achieving progressively the full realization of the rights recognized in the present Covenant by all appropriate means, including particularly the adoption of legislative measures ...

Article 3

The States Parties to the present Covenant undertake to ensure the equal right of men and women to the enjoyment of all economic, social and cultural rights set forth in the present Covenant ...

Article 6

The States Parties to the present Covenant recognize the right to work, which includes the right of everyone to the opportunity to gain his living by work which he freely chooses or accepts, and will take appropriate steps to safeguard this right ...

Article 7

The States Parties to the present Covenant recognize the right of everyone to the enjoyment of just and favourable conditions of work, which ensure, in particular:

(a) Remuneration which provides all workers, as a minimum with:
   (i)   Fair wages and equal remuneration for work of equal value without distinction

of any kind, in particular women being guaranteed conditions of work not inferior to those enjoyed by men, with equal pay for equal work;

(ii) A decent living for themselves and their families in accordance with the provisions of the present Covenant;

(b) Safe and healthy working conditions;

(c) Equal opportunity for everyone to be promoted in his employment to an appropriate higher level, subject to no considerations other than those of seniority and competence;

(d) Rest, leisure and reasonable limitation of working hours and periodic holidays with pay, as well as remuneration for public holidays.

Article 8

The States Parties to the present Covenant undertake to ensure:

The right of everyone to form trade unions and join the trade union of his choice, subject
 only to the rules of the organization concerned for the promotion and protection of
 his economic and social interests. No restrictions may be placed on the exercise of
 this right other than those prescribed by law and which are necessary in a democratic
 society in the interests of national security or public order or for the protection of the
 rights and freedoms of others …

Article 9

The States Parties to the present Covenant recognize the right of everyone to social security, including social insurance.

Article 10

The States Parties to the present Covenant recognize:

The widest possible protection and assistance should be accorded to the family, which is the natural and fundamental group unit of society, particularly for its establishment and while it is responsible for the care and education of dependent children. Marriage must be entered into with the free consent of the intending spouses …

Article 11

The States Parties to the present Covenant recognize the right of everyone to an adequate standard of living for himself and his family, including adequate food, clothing and housing, and to the continuous improvement of living conditions. The States Parties will take appropriate steps to ensure the realization of this right, recognizing to this effect the essential importance of international co-operation based on free consent …

Article 12

The States Parties to the present Covenant recognize the right of everyone to the enjoyment of the highest attainable standard of physical and mental health ...

Article 13

1. The States Parties to the present Covenant recognize the right of everyone to education. They agree that education shall be directed to the full development of the human personality and the sense of its dignity, and shall strengthen the respect for human rights and fundamental freedoms. They further agree that education shall enable all persons to participate effectively in a free society, promote understanding, tolerance and friendship among all nations and all racial, ethnic or religious groups, and further the activities of the United Nations for the maintenance of peace.
2. The States Parties to the present Covenant recognize that, with a view to achieving the full realization of this right:
(a) Primary education shall be compulsory and available free to all;
(b) Secondary education in its different forms, including technical and vocational secondary education, shall be made generally available and accessible to all by every appropriate means, and in particular by the progressive introduction of free education;
(c) Higher education shall be made equally accessible to all, on the basis of capacity, by every appropriate means, and in particular by the progressive introduction of free education;
(d) Fundamental education shall be encouraged or intensified as far as possible for those persons who have not received or completed the whole period of their primary education;
(e) The development of a system of schools at all levels shall be actively pursued, an adequate fellowship system shall be established, and the material conditions of teaching staff shall be continuously improved ...

Article 15

The States Parties to the present Covenant recognize the right of everyone:
(a) To take part in cultural life;
(b) To enjoy the benefits of scientific progress and its applications;
(c) To benefit from the protection of the moral and material interests resulting from any scientific, literary or artistic production of which he is the author.

QUESTIONS FOR DISCUSSION

1. What is the difference between licence and liberty?
2. Which rights are perfect rights and which are imperfect rights?
3. Do you agree with Bentham's dismissal of natural rights as 'nonsense upon stilts'?
4. What rights should minorities have?
5 Where do we get rights from?

NOTES

1 These examples of different usages of the term rights are taken from Wesley Newcomb Hohfeld, *Fundamental Legal Conceptions. As Applied in Judicial Reasoning and Other Legal Cases* (New Haven, Yale University Press, 1920). Hohfeld's legalistic terminology is explained at length by Richard E. Flathman, *The Practice of Rights* (Cambridge, Cambridge University Press, 1976), pp. 34–61.
2 Richard Dagger, 'Rights', in Terence Ball, James Farr and Russell L. Hanson (eds), *Political Innovation and Conceptual Change* (Cambridge, Cambridge University Press, 1989), p. 305.

FURTHER READING

Most general surveys of the idea of rights are analytical in approach. Among these see L.J. Macfarlane, *The Theory and Practice of Human Rights* (London, Maurice Temple Smith, 1985) and Richard E. Flathman, *The Practice of Rights* (Cambridge, Cambridge University Press, 1976). Michael Freeden, *Rights* (Milton Keynes, Open University Press, 1991) also pays some attention to the historical development of the idea. For a succinct survey of the history of rights see Richard Dagger, 'Rights', in Terence Ball, James Farr and Russell L. Hanson (eds), *Political Innovation and Conceptual Change* (Cambridge, Cambridge University Press, 1989). A selection of substantial extracts is provided by J. Waldron (ed.), *Theories of Rights* (Oxford, Oxford University Press, 1984). A critical account of the liberal approach can be found in Ian Schapiro, *The Evolution of Rights* (Cambridge, Cambridge University Press, 1986). The cultural relativity of human rights is asserted in Adamantia Pollis and Peter Schwab, 'Human Rights: A Western Construct with Limited Applicability', in Adamantia Pollis and Peter Schwab (eds), *Human Rights. Cultural and Ideological Perspectives* (New York, Praeger, 1979), pp. 1–18. Jack Donnelly, *Universal Human Rights in Theory and Practice* (Ithaca, Cornell University

Press, 1989) is a refreshingly vigorous defence of its topic. On the expansion of rights see Michael Freeden, 'Rights, Needs and Community: The Emergence of British Welfare Thought', in Alan Ware and Robert E. Goodin (eds), *Needs and Welfare* (London, Sage, 1990), pp. 54–72. An analytical defence of welfare rights is provided by Raymond Plant, 'Needs, Agency and Rights', in C.J.G. Sampford and D.J. Galligan (eds), *Law, Rights and the Welfare State* (London, Croom Helm, 1986), pp. 23-48. Jay A. Sigler, *Minority Rights. A Comparative Analysis* (Westport, Greenwood, 1983) is comprehensive. Ian Brownlie (ed.), *Basic Documents on Human Rights* (Oxford, Clarendon Press, 1992) includes the major international documents.

5

CONCEPTS OF LIBERTY

INTRODUCTION

The notion of liberty, or freedom, has attracted an extremely wide range of interpretations and found an equally wide range of applications. We speak of the freedom of religion, speech, writing, association and of participation in the political process (see documents 5.6 and 5.8). The idea has been extended to cover demands for economic liberty, freedom from want and even national self-determination (see document 5.5). It was precisely this prevalence of the words 'liberty' and 'freedom' that led the political theorist Bernard Crick to observe that 'So important, indeed, is the concept of liberty that we are all reluctant to define it too closely, wanting to apply it to everything we value'.[1]

The roots of liberty have often been sought in the Greek city-states and the Roman Republic. Although, as one modern admirer of ancient liberty noted, with approval, the liberty of these states was associated with policies of imperial conquest. Liberty meant the freedom of one's own state and was seen as quite compatible with denying liberty of other states (see document 5.1). Liberty also meant not being subject to despotic power, which was the kind of power a master exercised over a slave. The comparison with despotic power is an important one in understanding ancient concepts of liberty for liberty was, above all, a matter of status. The free man was defined in contrast to the slave. Being free meant that one had a series of abilities, including the capacity to own slaves. It meant that one could, and indeed ought to, participate in the political process.

The intensely political aspect of liberty in the ancient world contrasts sharply with contemporary emphasis upon the freedom of the individual from political control and interference. For the Greeks, liberty was seen as being compatible with the authority of the community over the individual, so long as this authority was exercised according to law rather than according to the will of a despot. Similarly, liberty was justified in terms of its advantages for the community rather than in terms of its importance to the individual. It was this distinction between ancient and modern conceptions which led the French defender of liberty, Benjamin Constant to warn against any attempt to revive the ancient conception. Such an attempt had in fact been made, during the French Revolution, with dire consequences.

To find a sense of personal liberty set against the liberty of the community in the ancient world one would have to turn to the Cynics who advocated self-sufficiency and disparaged social life. A much more radical divorce between political liberty and personal liberty was to be made by Christianity. The freedom, here, which St Augustine emphasized, was the freedom of the will. This interpretation was important in that it linked freedom with the individual person, or rather with the soul. But it was a limited freedom. For, although the freedom of the will was later to be given a radical interpretation, it was held by some Christians to be quite compatible with physical restriction. The soul could be free even while the body was in chains. Freedom of the will and equality before God went hand in hand with the necessity of political authority to rule over sinful men.

The pre-eminence of Christianity in medieval Europe did not, however, prevent the development of complex and vibrant ideas about liberty. It was these liberties which English monarchs promised to uphold in their coronation oaths. The liberties were privileges and exemptions granted to ecclesiastical institutions, feudal lords and later urban communities. They included both exemptions from various kinds of taxation but also positive powers of adjudication. Rather confusingly, for modern readers, the noble's 'liberty' or 'franchise' could mean not only his power to judge, but also the territory over which he exercised that power. Although liberty was first and foremost a 'quality of lordship' it is also true that by the end of the thirteenth century it is possible to identify an emergent 'opposition between the liberties of the whole community and the license of the magnates'.

It was only in the sixteenth and seventeenth centuries that the idea of liberty and freedom came to be seen as a general condition shared equally among all citizens. This expansion of the idea of liberty was concurrent with the growth of the modern state and was, in part, a reaction to the centralization of power. It was also linked to the new interpretation of rights which pervaded political discourse. Symptomatic of the association was the proclamation in the American Declaration of Independence that all men were 'endowed by their Creator with certain inalienable rights', among which was liberty (document 5.5).

As the claims made for liberty and freedom became more general and more expansive, so the need to set limits to the exercise of liberty became more pressing. The difficulty lies in finding a means of allowing for liberty without letting it degenerate into license. For the German philosopher Immanuel Kant one solution lay in morality. For Kant, freedom was essentially a matter of autonomy, that is of self-determination, of being a self-governing agent. Being self-governing did not mean acting as one happens to wish. It meant laying down laws for oneself. The law which Kant recommended was that the rules which one prescribed for oneself ought to be rules which one would wish to see all other agents following.

The English utilitarian James Stuart. Mill emphasized a different, but equally influential, strategy. He distinguished between 'self-regarding' and 'other-regarding' actions. As far as the former are concerned, liberty ought not to be constrained, even if they are harmful to oneself. It was only actions which harmed others which warranted a restriction of liberty. According to this distinction, society had no business forbidding people from drinking to excess, still less from imposing prohibition. It could rightly impose penalties for illegal acts a man might commit while intoxicated, but only because those acts are illegal, not because he is intoxicated. In making this distinction Mill was concerned to set limits to a new kind of tyranny, the tyranny of public opinion which wanted to enforce conformity in all manner of behaviour.

Other commentators were concerned with yet another form of tyranny which they ascribed to an inflation of the concept of liberty. The roots of this inflation lay in the connection between liberty and equality. It was expressed with vigour by the seventeenth-century English agrarian radical, Gerrard Winstanley (see document 5.2). For Winstanley, oppression was rooted in a distribution of land which denied some men access to the very means of subsistence. His basic point was to be developed by socialist critics of 'bourgeois' political rights. What was the use, they asked, of political and civil liberties when the majority of the population lacked the economic resources to exercise them. Marxists have, accordingly, denigrated the economic and civic freedoms of liberal capitalist societies, denouncing them as merely 'formal' freedoms.

It was not necessary to be a Marxist to argue that liberty and social justice were linked, that economic deprivation could be so severe as to deny people the capacity to exercise their freedom. Such criticism was linked with a slow but gradual expansion of the role of the state. It was justified in part by the need to alleviate absolute poverty, but also by a more expansive concept of freedom. Here freedom was associated with self-development and maximization of one's potential. It was this that encouraged critics of the growth of state involvement to claim that the only permissible definition of liberty is as negative liberty, that is, liberty is achieved where men are free 'from' restraint. Liberty is maximized, according to this conception, by keeping the interference of the state and others in our lives to the minimum. For some of these critics this amounts, in practice, to restricting government to the maintenance of law and order so as to secure our person and property. Anything else is condemned as an infringement of liberty.

The relation between the state and liberty has developed into one of the central dilemmas of the modern conception of liberty and freedom. On the one hand, the state appears as a threat to liberty: it is the actions of the state which are the usual target when people call for the defence of our civil liberties. On the other hand, the state also appears as a guarantor of liberty. It is not necessary here to draw upon the distinction between freedom *from* something (negative liberty) and freedom *to* something (positive liberty) and say that we need the state's help to enable us to do something. There is a much simpler sense in which the state is needed. This occurs in the case of freedom of speech. Freedom of speech occurs in practically all catalogues of modern liberties and is often given a fairly high rank within them. Yet at the same time freedom of speech has been limited in many modern societies to prevent virulent attacks upon racial minorities.

The distinction between 'negative' and 'positive' liberty was taken up by I. Berlin in a lecture, 'Two Concepts of Liberty', which has exercised considerable influence over the subsequent debate. The core of his argument concerned the concept of positive liberty. This, he said, arose from the desire to be one's own master, to govern oneself. The danger arose, he continued, because being one's own master was taken as involving mastering one's own baser desires and inclinations. This notion had in fact been familiar to, indeed commonplace, among the Greeks. It involved positing some higher self or norm of behaviour to which one should aspire. It is then but a small step, Berlin warned, to the argument that a man may be coerced for his own good, that a man may be forced to be free.

Such arguments have taken different forms, depending upon the assumptions made about the underlying causes of the unfreedom from which men are to be liberated and about human nature. An essentially optimistic view of human nature, according to which men will naturally and voluntarily do good unless they have in some way been corrupted, led to the dictum of the Jacobin Club during the French Revolution: 'No man is free doing evil. To prevent him is to set him free.' A more contemporary argument, although one with an equally long pedigree, focuses upon the causes of the lack of freedom. Here, the deplored state is ascribed to the manipulation of oppressors, to the malign effect of modern propaganda apparatuses under the control of totalitarian states or to seduction by trivial luxuries and fashions. The prescription has been that men must be dragged away from their dependence upon false doctrines and ideologies or superfluous, if addictive, dependencies. Once more, they must be forced to be free.

Most citizens of contemporary liberal societies would probably reject such arguments. The concept of liberty, like the idea of rights, is one of the great success stories of the history of political thought. It has been, however, the success of a distinctly modern conception of liberty. Yet the modern conception of liberty has never entirely supplanted the ancient conception. As Benjamin Constant proclaimed the triumph of modern liberty he also warned that, 'The danger of modern liberty is that, absorbed in the enjoyment of our private independence, and in the pursuit of our particular interests, we should surrender our right to share in political power too easily'.[3]

DOCUMENTS

Document 5.1

Niccolò Machiavelli on The Ancient Love of Liberty

Machiavelli (1496–1527), diplomat, historian and political thinker (see document 8.1), included the following observations in *The Discourses on the First Ten Books of Titus Livy* (1513–17). His admiration for the Roman Republic of antiquity provoked him to make this contrast, and reflect on the causes of the weakness and corruption of contemporary Italy. As secretary of the Florentine Republic between 1498 and 1512, he had first-hand experience of this weakness and corruption.

If one asks oneself how it comes about that peoples of old were more fond of liberty than they are today, I think the answer is that it is due to the same cause that makes men today less bold than they used to be; and this is due, I think, to the difference between our education and that of bygone times, which is based on the difference between our religion and the religion of those days. For our religion, having taught us the truth and the true way of life, leads us to ascribe less esteem to worldly honour. Hence the gentiles, who held it in high esteem and looked upon it as their highest good, displayed in their actions more ferocity than we do. This is evidenced by many of their institutions. To begin with, compare the magnificence of their sacrifices with the humility that characterizes ours. The ceremonial in ours is delicate rather than imposing, and there is no display of ferocity or courage. Their ceremonies lacked neither pomp nor magnificence, but, conjoined with this, were sacrificial acts in which there was much shedding of blood and much ferocity; and in them great numbers of animals were killed. Such spectacles, because terrible, caused men to become like them. Besides, the old religion did not beatify men unless they were replete with worldly glory: army commanders, for instance, and rulers of republics. Our religion has glorified humble and contemplative men, rather than men of action. It has assigned as man's highest good humility, abnegation, and contempt for mundane things, whereas the other identified it with magnanimity, bodily strength, and everything else that conduces to make men very bold. And, if our religion demands that in you there be strength, what it asks for is strength to suffer rather than strength to do bold things.

This pattern of life, therefore, appears to have made the world weak, and to have handed it over as a prey to the wicked, who run it successfully and securely since they are well aware that the generality of men, with paradise for their goal, consider how best to bear, rather than how best to avenge, their injuries. But, though it looks as if the world were become effeminate and as if heaven were powerless, this undoubtedly is due rather to the pusillanimity of those who have interpreted our religion in terms of *laissez faire*, not in terms of *virtù*. For, had they borne in mind that religion permits us to exalt and defend the fatherland, they would have seen that it also wishes us to love and honour it, and to train ourselves to be such that we may defend it.

This kind of education, then, and these grave misinterpretations account for the fact that we see in the world fewer republics than there used to be of old, and that, consequently, in peoples we do not find the same love of liberty as there then was. Yet I can well believe that it was rather the Roman empire, which, with its armed forces and its grandiose ideas, wiped out all republics and all their civic institutions, that was the cause of this. And though, later on, Rome's empire disintegrated, its cities have never been able to pull themselves together nor to set up again a constitutional regime, save in one or two parts of that empire.

Document 5.2

Gerrard Winstanley on The Law of Freedom

Gerrard Winstanley (c.1609–76) was leader of the short-lived Digger Movement and one of the most radical thinkers of the English Civil War. His vision of a just order was proclaimed in *The New Law of Righteousness* (1649). Men could be free only when private property in land was abolished, when all men had access to the land, worked in common and no man worked for wages. *The Law of Freedom in a Platform* (1652), from which the following extract is taken, was dedicated to Oliver Cromwell. This pamphlet described a communal agrarian society in which all buying and selling are abolished. The fundamental freedom is freedom from economic insecurity.

True Commonwealth's Freedom Lies in the Free Enjoyment of the Earth.

True Freedom lies where a man receives his nourishment and preservation, and that is in the use of the Earth ... All that a man labours for, saith Solomon, is this, That he may enjoy the free use of the Earth with the fruits thereof (Eccles. 2:24). Do not the Ministers preach for maintenance in the Earth? Doth not the Soldier fight for the Earth? And doth not the Land Lord require Rent that he may live in the fullness of the Earth by the labour of his Tenants? And so from the Thief upon the Highway to the King who sits upon the Throne, does not everyone strive, either by force of Arms or secret Cheats, to get the possessions of the Earth one from another, because they see their Freedom lies in plenty, and their Bondage lies in Poverty?

Surely, then, oppressing Lords of Manors, exacting Landlords and Tythetakers, may as well say their Bretheren shall not breathe in the air, nor enjoy warmth in their bodies, nor have the moist waters to fall upon them in showers, unless they will pay them rent for it, as to say their Brethren shall not work upon Earth, nor eat the fruits thereof, unless they will hire that liberty of them. For he that takes upon him to restrain his Brother from the liberty of the one, may upon the same ground restrain him from the liberty of all four viz, Fire, Water, Earth and Air.

A Man had better to have had no body than to have no food for it.

Therefore this restraining of the Earth from Brethren by Brethren is oppression and bondage; but the free enjoyment thereof is true Freedom.

Inward and Outward Bondage

I speak now in relation between the Oppressor and the Oppressed, the Inward Bondages I meddle not with in this place, though I am assured that if it be rightly searched into, the inward bondages of the mind, as covetousness, pride, hypocrisy, envy, sorrow, fears, desperation and madness, are all occasioned by the outward bondage that one sort of people lay upon another. And thus far natural experience makes it good, THAT TRUE FREEDOM LIES IN THE FREE ENJOYMENT OF THE EARTH.

What is Government in General?

Government is a wise and free ordering of the Earth and of the Manners of Mankind by observation of particular Laws or Rules, so that all the inhabitants may live peaceably in plenty and freedom in the Land where they are born and bred.

What is Kingly Government?

There is a twofold Government: a Kingly Government and a Commonwealth's Government.

Kingly Government governs the Earth by that cheating art of buying and selling, and thereby becomes a man of contention, his hand is against every man, and every man's hand against him … and if it had not a Club Law to support it, there would be no order in it, because it is but the covetous and proud will of a Conqueror enslaving a conquered people … Indeed, this Government may well be called the Government of Highwaymen, who hath stolen the Earth from the Younger Brethren by force and holds it from them by force … The great Lawgiver of this Kingly Government is Covetousness, ruling in the hearts of mankind, making one Brother to covet a full possession of the Earth, and a Lordly Rule over another Brother …. The Rise of Kingly Government is attributable to a politic wit in drawing the people out of Common Freedom into a way of Common Bondage: FOR SO LONG AS THE EARTH IS A COMMON TREASURY TO ALL MEN, KINGLY COVETOUSNESS CAN NEVER REIGN AS KING.

What is Commonwealth's Government?

Commonwealth's Government governs the Earth without buying and selling, and thereby becomes a man of peace, and the Restorer of Ancient Peace and Freedom. He makes provision for the oppressed, the weak and the simple, as well as for the rich, the wise and the strong … All slavery and Oppressions … are cast out by this government, if it be right in power as well as in name … IF ONCE COMMONWEALTH'S GOVERNMENT BE SET UPON THE THRONE, THEN NO TYRANNY OR OPPRESSION CAN LOOK HIM IN THE FACE AND LIVE.

Document 5.3

Thomas Hobbes on Liberty

Thomas Hobbes (1588–1679) (see introduction to document 1.3) was much concerned by what he regarded as the abuse and misunderstanding of liberty by his contemporaries in the English Civil War period. The following discussion of liberty is taken from *Leviathan*. Although Hobbes' political theory was primarily a defence of authority and undivided sovereignty, he allows that the individual retains, even against the sovereign, the right of self-preservation. He uses the concept of liberty in a variety of ways, as freedom to choose between alternative courses of action, freedom from obligation, absence of compulsion and of external impediment.

LIBERTY, or FREEDOM, signifies properly the absence of opposition – by opposition I mean external impediments of motion – and may be applied no less to irrational and inanimate creatures than to rational. For whatsoever is so tied or environed as it cannot move but within a certain space, which space is determined by the opposition of some external body, we say it has not liberty to go farther. And so of all living creatures while they are imprisoned or restrained with walls or chains, and of the water while it is kept by banks or vessels that otherwise would spread itself into a larger space, we use to say that they are not at liberty to move in such manner as without those external impediments they would. But when the impediment of motion is in the constitution of the thing itself, we use not to say it wants the liberty but the power to move as when a stone lies still or a man is fastened to his bed by sickness.

And according to this proper and generally received meaning of the word, a FREEMAN is he that in those things which by his strength and wit he is able to do is not hindered to do what he has a will to. But when the words free and liberty are applied to anything but bodies, they are abused, for that which is not subject to motion is not subject to impediment; and therefore, when it is said for example, the way is free, no liberty of the way is signified but of those that walk in it without stop. And when we say a gift is free, there is not meant any liberty of the gift but of the giver, that was not bound by any law or covenant to give it. So when we speak freely, it is not the liberty of voice or pronunciation but the man, whom no law has obliged to speak otherwise than he did. Lastly, from the use of the word free will no liberty can be inferred of the will, desire, or inclination but the liberty of the man, which consists in this: that he finds no stop in doing what he has the will, desire, or inclination to do.

Fear and liberty are consistent, as when a man throws his goods into the sea for fear the ship should sink, he does it nevertheless very willingly, and may refuse to do it if he will: it is therefore the action of one that was free; so a man sometimes pays his debt only for fear of imprisonment, which, because nobody hindered him from detaining, was the action of a man at liberty. And generally all actions which men do in commonwealths for fear of the law are actions which the doers had liberty to omit.

Liberty and necessity are consistent, as in the water that has not only Liberty but a necessity of descending by the channel; so likewise in the actions which men voluntarily do, which, because they proceed from their will, proceed from liberty, and yet – because every act of man's will and every desire and inclination proceeds from some cause, and that from another cause, in a continual chain whose first link is in the hand of God, the first of all causes – proceed from necessity. So that to him that could see the connection of those causes the necessity of all men's voluntary actions would appear manifest. And therefore God, that sees and disposes all things, sees also that the liberty of man in doing what he will is accompanied with the necessity of doing that which God will, and no more nor less. For though men may do many things which God does not command, nor is therefore author of them, yet they can have no passion nor appetite to anything of which appetite God's will is not the cause. And did not His will assure the necessity of man's will depends, the liberty of men would be a contradiction and impediment to the omnipotence and liberty of God. And this shall suffice, as to the matter in hand, of that natural liberty which only is properly called liberty.

But as men, for the attaining of peace and conservation of themselves thereby, have made an artificial man, which we call a commonwealth, so also have they made artificial chains, called civil laws which they themselves by mutual covenants, have fastened at one end to the lips of that man or assembly to whom they have given the sovereign power, and at the other end of their own ears. These bonds, in their own nature but weak, may nevertheless be made to hold by the danger, though not by the difficulty, of breaking them.

In relation to these bonds only it is that I am to speak now of the liberty of subjects. For seeing there is no commonwealth in the world wherein there be rules enough set down for the regulating of all the actions and words of men, as being a thing impossible, it follows necessarily that in all kinds of actions by the laws permitted men have the liberty of doing what their own reasons shall suggest for the most profitable to themselves. For if we take liberty in the proper sense for corporal liberty – that is to say, freedom from chains and prison – it were very absurd for men to clamour as they do for the liberty they so manifestly enjoy. Again, if we take liberty for an exemption from laws, it is no less absurd for men to demand as they do that liberty by which all other men may be masters of their lives. And yet, as absurd as it is, this is it they demand, not knowing that the laws are of no power to protect them without a sword in the hands of a man or men to cause those laws to be put in execution. The liberty of a subject lies, therefore, only in those things which, in regulating their actions, the sovereign has permitted: such as is the liberty to buy and sell and otherwise contract with one another; to choose their own abode, their own diet, their own trade of life, and institute their children as they themselves think fit; and the like.

Document 5.4

Montesquieu, *The Spirit of the Laws*

Charles Louis de Secondat, Baron de Montesquieu (1689–1755), published *The Spirit of the Laws,* from which the extract below is taken, in 1748. He asserted that political liberty presupposed freedom of thought and expression and that freedom depended on the exercise of political power being moderated or checked. The object of his criticism was despotism which he contrasted with 'monarchy'. His thought exercised enormous influence on the development of constitutional liberalism. (See also document 3.5.)

Different Significations of the Word Liberty

There is no word that admits of more various significations, and has made more different impressions on the human mind, than that of Liberty. Some have taken it for a facility of deposing a person on whom they had conferred a tyrannical authority; others for the power of choosing a superior whom they are obliged to obey; others for the right of bearing arms, and of being thereby enabled to use violence; others, in fine, for the privilege of being governmed by a native of their own country, or by their own laws … Some have annexed this name to one form of government exclusive of others: those who had a republican taste, applied it to this species of polity; those who liked a monarchical state, gave it to monarchy. Thus they have all applied the name of Liberty to the government most suitable to their own customs and inclinations: and as in republics, the people have not so constant and so present a view of the causes of their misery, and as the magistrates seem to act only in conformity to the laws, hence liberty is generally said to reside in republics, and to be banished from monarchies. In fine, as in democracies the people seem to act almost as they please; this sort of government has been deemed the most free; and the power of the people has been confounded with their liberty.

In What Liberty Consists

It is true, that in democracies the people seem to act as they please; but political liberty does not consist in an unlimited freedom. In governments, that is, in societies directed by laws, liberty can consist only in the power of doing what we ought to will, and in not being constrained to do, what we ought not to will.

We must have continually present to our minds the difference between independence and liberty. Liberty is a right of doing whatever the laws permit; and if a citizen could do what they forbid, he would be no longer possessed of liberty, because all his fellow citizens would have the same power.

Democratic and aristocratic states are not in their own nature free. Political liberty is to be found only in moderate governments: and even in these, it is not always found. It is there only when there is no abuse of power; but constant experience shows us, that every man invested with power is apt to abuse it; and to carry his authority as far as it will go. Is it not strange, though true, that virtue itself has need of limits?

To prevent this abuse, it is necessary from the very nature of things, power should be a check to power. A government may be so constituted, as no man shall be compelled to do things to which the law does not oblige him, nor forced to abstain from things which the law permits.

Document 5.5

The American Declaration of Independence, 4 July 1776

This was the fundamental constitutional document adopted by the United States of America in Congress. When independence was declared, any appeal to the traditions of the British Government became irrelevant. The liberties claimed here were, it was argued, based on natural law and justified by reason, not by historical custom. There was a higher law to which every human law was answerable. Both the Declaration and the US Constitution rested on the natural right of the people to alter or dislodge their government and institute such forms as they saw fit.

When, in the course of human events, it becomes necessary for one people to dissolve the political bonds which have connected them with another, and to assume, among the powers of the earth, the separate and equal station to which the laws of nature and of nature's God entitle them, a decent respect to the opinions of mankind requires that they should declare the causes which impel them to the separation.

We hold these truths to be self-evident, that all men are created equal; that they are endowed by their Creator with certain unalienable rights; that among these are life, liberty, and the pursuit of happiness. That, to secure these rights, governments are instituted among men, deriving their just powers from the consent of the governed; that, whenever any form of government becomes destructive of these ends, it is the right of the people to alter or to abolish it, and to institute a new government, laying its foundation on such principles, and organizing its powers in such form, as to them shall seem most likely to effect their safety and happiness. Prudence, indeed, will dictate that governments long established should not be changed for light and transient causes; and, accordingly, all experience hath shown, that mankind are more disposed to suffer, while evils are sufferable, than to right themselves by abolishing the forms to which they are accustomed. But, when a long train of abuses and usurpations, pursuing invariably the same object, evinces a design to reduce them under absolute despotism, it is their right, it is their duty, to throw off such government, and to provide new guards for their future security. Such has been the patient sufferance of these colonies, and such is now the necessity which constrains them to alter their former systems of government. The history of the present King of Great Britain is a history of repeated injuries and usurpations, all having, in direct object, the establishment of an absolute tyranny over these states. To prove this, let facts be submitted to a candid world:

He has refused his assent to laws the most wholesome and necessary for the public good.

He has forbidden his governors to pass laws of immediate and pressing importance, unless suspended in their operation till his assent should be obtained; and, when so suspended, he has utterly neglected to attend to them.

He has refused to pass other laws for the accommodation of large districts of people, unless those people would relinquish the right of representation in the legislature; a right inestimable to them, and formidable to tyrants only.

He has called together legislative bodies at places unusual, uncomfortable, and distant from the depository of their public records, for the sole purpose of fatiguing them into compliance with his measures.

He has dissolved representative houses repeatedly, for opposing, with manly firmness, his invasions on the rights of the people.

He has refused, for a long time after such dissolutions, to cause others to be elected; whereby the legislative powers, incapable of annihilation, have returned to the people at large for their exercise; the state remaining, in the meantime, exposed to all the danger of invasion from without, and convulsions within.

He has endeavored to prevent the population of these States; for that purpose, obstructing the laws for naturalization of foreigners, refusing to pass others to encourage their migration hither, and raising the conditions of new appropriations of lands.

He has obstructed the administration of justice, by refusing his assent to laws for establishing judiciary powers.

He has made judges dependent on his will alone, for the tenure of their offices, and the amount and payment of their salaries.

He has erected a multitude of new offices, and sent hither swarms of officers to harass our people, and eat out their substance.

He has kept among us, in time of peace, standing armies, without the consent of our legislatures.

He has affected to render the military independent of, and superior to, the civil power.

He has combined, with others to subject us to a jurisdiction foreign to our

Constitution, and unacknowledged by our laws; giving his assent to their acts of pretended legislation:

For quartering large bodies of armed troops among us:

For protecting them by a mock trial, from punishment, for any murders which they should commit on the inhabitants of these States:

For cutting off our trade with all parts of the world:

For imposing taxes on us without our consent:

For depriving us, in many cases, of the benefit of trial by jury:

For transporting us beyond seas to be tried for pretended offenses:

For abolishing the free system of English laws in a neighboring province, establishing therein an arbitrary government, and enlarging its boundaries, so as to render it at once an example and fit instrument for introducing the same abolute rule into these colonies:

For taking away our charters, abolishing our most valuable laws, and altering fundamentally the forms of our governments:

For suspending our own legislatures, and declaring themselves invested with power to legislate for us in all cases whatsoever.

He has abdicated government here, by declaring us out of his protection, and waging war against us.

He has plundered our seas ravaged our coasts, burnt our towns, and destroyed the lives of our people.

He is, at this time, transporting large armies of foreign mercenaries to complete the works of death, desolation, and tyranny, already begun, with circumstances of cruelty and perfidy scarcely paralleled in the most barbarous ages, and totally unworthy the head of a civilized nation.

He has constrained our fellow-citizens, taken captive on the high seas, to bear arms against their country, to become the executioners of their friends and brethren, or to fall themselves by their hands.

He has excited domestic insurrections amongst us,and has endeavored to bring on the inhabitants of our frontiers, the merciless Indian savages, whose known rule of warfare is an undistinguished destruction of all ages, sexes, and conditions.

In every state of these oppressions, we have petitioned for redress, in the most humble terms; our repeated petitions have been answered only by repeated injury. A prince, whose character is thus marked by every act which may define a tyrant, is unfit to be the ruler of a free people.

Nor have we been wanting in attention to our British brethren. We have warned them, from time to time, of attempts by their legislature to extend an unwarrantable jurisdiction over us. We have reminded them of the circumstances of our emigration and settlement here. We have appealed to their native justice and magnanimity, and we have conjured them, by the ties of our common kindred, to disavow these usurpations, which would inevitably interrupt our connections and correspondence. They, too, have been deaf to the voice of justice and consanguinity. We must, therefore, acquiesce in the necessity which denounces our separation, and hold them, as we hold the rest of mankind, enemies in war, in peace, friends.

We, therefore, the representatives of the United States of America, in general Congress assembled, appealing to the Supreme Judge of the world for the rectitude of our intentions, do, in the name, and by the authority of the good people of these colonies, solemnly publish and declare, that these united colonies are, and of right ought to be, free and independent states; that they are absolved from all allegiance to the British Crown, and that all political connection between them and the state of Great Britain is, and ought to be, totally dissolved; and that, as free and independent states, they have full power to levy war, conclude peace, contract alliances, establish commerce, and to do all other acts and things which independent states may of right do. And, for the support of this declaration, with a firm reliance on the protection of Divine Providence, we mutually pledge to each other our lives, our fortunes, and our sacred honour.

Document 5.6

David Hume on the Liberty of the Press

David Hume (1711–76), Scottish philosopher and historian, published the essay, from which this is an extract, in *Essays Moral and Political* (1741). After explaining why such an unusual liberty of the press existed, as it did in eighteenth-century England (something which he attributed to its mixed constitution), he went on to ask whether such freedom was beneficial or not.

These principles account for the great liberty of the press in these kingdoms, beyond what is indulged in any other government. It is apprehended that arbitrary power would steal in upon us, were we not careful to prevent its progress, and were there not an easy method of conveying the alarm from one end of the kingdom to the other. The spirit of the people must frequently be roused, in order to curb the ambition of the court; and the dread of rousing this spirit must be employed to prevent that ambition. Nothing so effectual to this purpose as the liberty of the press, by which all the learning, wit, and genius of the nation may be employed on the side of freedom, and every one be animated to its defence. As long, therefore, as the republican part of our government can maintain itself against the monarchical, it will naturally be careful to keep the press open, as of importance to its own preservation.

Since therefore that liberty is so essential to the support of our mixed government, this sufficiently decides the second question, Whether such a liberty be advantageous or prejudicial; there being nothing of greater importance in every state than the preservation of the ancient government, especially if it be a free one. But I would fain go a step farther, and assert that this liberty is attended with so few inconveniences, that it may be claimed as the common right of mankind, and ought to be indulged them almost in every government, except the ecclesiastical, to which indeed it would prove fatal. We need not dread from this liberty any such ill consequences as followed from the harangues of the popular demagogues of Athens and tribunes of Rome. A man reads a book or pamphlet alone and coolly. There is none present from whom he can catch the passion by contagion. He is not hurried away by the force and energy of action. And should he be wrought up to ever so seditious a humour, there is no violent resolution presented to him, by which he can immediately vent his passion. The liberty of the press, therefore, however abused, can scarce ever excite popular tumults or rebellion. And as to those murmurs or secret discontents it may occasion, it is better they should get vent in words, that they may come to the knowledge of the magistrate before it be too late in order to his providing a remedy against them. Mankind, it is true, have always a greater propensity to believe what is said to the disadvantage of their governors, than the contrary; but this inclination is inseparable from them, whether they have liberty or not. A whisper may fly as quick, and be as pernicious as a pamphlet. Nay, it will be more pernicious, where men are not accustomed to think freely, or distinguish between truth and falsehood.

It has also been found as the experience of mankind increases, that the people are no such dangerous monster as they have been represented, and that it is in every respect better to guide them like rational creatures, than to lead or drive them like brute beasts. Before the United Provinces set the example, toleration was deemed incompatible with good government and it was thought impossible that a number of religious sects could live together in harmony and peace, and have all of them an equal affection to their common country, and to each other. England has set a like example of civil liberty; and though this liberty seems to occasion some small ferment at present, it has not as yet produced any pernicious effects; and it is to be hoped that men, being every day more accustomed to the free discussion of public affairs, will improve in the judgment of them, and be with greater difficulty seduced by every idle rumour and popular clamour.

It is a very comfortable reflection to the lovers of liberty, that this peculiar privilege of Britain is of a kind that cannot easily be wrested from us, but must last as long as our government remains, in any degree, free and independent. It is seldom that liberty of any kind is lost all at once. Slavery has so frightful an aspect to men accustomed to freedom, that it must steal upon them by degrees, and must disguise itself in a thousand shapes, in order to be received. But, if the liberty of the press ever be lost, it must be lost at once. The general laws against sedition and libelling are at present as strong as they possibly can be made. Nothing can impose a further restraint, but either the clapping an Imprimatur upon the press, or the giving to the court very large discretionary powers to punish whatever displeases them. But these concessions would be such a bare-faced violation of liberty, that they will probably be the last efforts of a despotic government. We may conclude that the liberty of Britain is gone forever when these attempts shall succeed.

Document 5.7

John Stuart Mill, *On Liberty*

John Stuart Mill (1806–73) was brought up under the strict supervision of his father James Mill and Jeremy Bentham to be a future leader of the utilitarian cause. After a period of severe depression – caused in part by the rigours of his education – he adopted a more flexible form of utilitarianism. Mill worked for the East India Company from 1823 until it was taken over by the government in 1858 and was briefly a Member of Parliament (1865–68). The following extract is from Mill's celebrated essay *On Liberty* (1859). This defended freedom and toleration as human values and as essential to the full development of moral personality. The threat to liberty which he feared most was that of the intolerant majority.

The struggle between Liberty and Authority is the most conspicuous feature in the portions of history with which we are earliest familiar, particularly in that of Greece, Rome, and England. But in old times this contest was between subjects, or some classes of subjects, and the government. By liberty was meant protection against the tyranny of the political rulers ... The aim, therefore, of patriots was to set limits to the power which the ruler should be suffered to exercise over the community; and this limitation was what they meant by liberty. It was attempted in two ways. First, by obtaining a recognition of certain immunities, called political liberties or rights, which it was to be regarded as a breach of duty in the ruler to infringe, and which, if he did infringe, specific resistance, or general rebellion, was felt to be justifiable. A second, and generally a later expedient, was the establishment of constitutional checks; by which the consent of the community, or of a body of some sort supposed to represent its interests, was made a necessary condition to some of the more important acts of the governing power ...

A time, however, came, in the progress of human affairs, when men ceased to think it a necessity of nature that their governors should be an independent power, opposed in interest to themselves. It appeared to them much better that the various magistrates of the State should be their tenants or delegates, revocable at their pleasure. In that way alone it seemed, could they have complete security that the power of government would never be abused to their disadvantage. By degrees, this new demand for elective and temporary rulers became the prominent object of the exertions of the popular party wherever any such party existed; and superseded, to a considerable extent, the previous efforts to limit the power of rulers ...

It was now perceived that such phrases as 'self-government,' and 'power of the people over themselves,' do not express the true state of the case. The 'people' who exercise the power are not always the same people with those over whom it is exercised; and the 'self government' spoken of is not the government of each by himself, but of each by all the rest. The will of the people, moreover, practically means the will of the most numerous or the most active part of the people; the majority, or those who succeed in making themselves accepted as the majority: the people consequently, may desire to oppress a part of their number; and precautions are as much needed against this, as against any other abuse of power. The limitation, therefore, of the power of government over individuals loses none of its importance when the holders of power are regularly accountable to the community, that is, to the strongest party therein … There is a limit to the legitimate interference of collective opinion with individual independence; and to find that limit, and maintain it against encroachment, is as indispensable to a good condition of human affairs, as protection against political despotism …

The only part of the conduct of any one, for which he is amenable to society, is that which concerns others. In the part which merely concerns himself, his independence is, of right, absolute. Over himself, over his own body and mind, the individual is sovereign …

This, then, is the appropriate region of human liberty. It comprises, first, the inward domain of consciousness; demanding liberty of conscience, in the most comprehensive sense; liberty of thought and feeling; absolute freedom of opinion and sentiment on all subjects, practical or speculative, scientific, moral, or theological. The liberty of expressing and publishing opinions may seem to fall under a different principle, since it belongs to that part of the conduct of an individual which concerns other people; but, being almost of as much importance as the liberty or thought itself, and resting in great part on the same reasons, is practically inseparable from it. Secondly, the principle requires liberty of tastes and pursuits; of framing the plan of our life to suit our own character; of doing as we like, subject to such consequences as may follow; without impediment from our fellow creatures, so long as what we do does not harm them, even though they should think our conduct foolish, perverse, or wrong. Thirdly, from this liberty of each individual follows the liberty, within the same limits, of combination among individuals; freedom to unite, for any purpose not involving harm to others; the persons combining being supposed to be of full age, and not forced or deceived.

No society in which these liberties are not, on the whole, respected is free, whatever may be its form of government; and none is completely free in which they do not exist absolute and unqualified.

Document 5.8

Pope Leo XIII, *Libertas*

Leo XIII (Gioacchino Pecci) (1810–1903) was Pope from 1878. The Encyclical *Libertas* was one of a series on the organization of society and relations between Church and State which reaffirmed the condemnation of the principles of

Liberalism by his immediate predecessors. He emphasizes the contrast between 'legitimate and honest liberty' and 'licence'. While he stressed the divine origin of authority, he at the same time was to state that democracy was as acceptable as other forms of government, embrace the workers' movement and labour rights (*Rerum Novarum*) (1891).

15. What naturalists or rationalists aim at in philosophy, that the supporters of liberalism, carrying out principles laid down by naturalism, are attempting in the domain of morality and politics. The fundamental doctrine of rationalism is the supremacy of the human reason, which, refusing due submission to the divine and eternal reason, proclaims its own independence, and constitutes itself the supreme principle and source and judge of truth. Hence, these followers of liberalism deny the existence of any divine authority to which obedience is due, and proclaim that every man is the law to himself; from which arises that ethical system which they style independent morality, and which, under the guise of liberty, exonerates man from any obedience to the commands of God, and substitutes a boundless license. The end of all this is not difficult to foresee, especially when society is in question. For, when once man is firmly persuaded that he is subject to no one, it follows that the efficient cause of the unity of civil society is not to be sought in any principle external to man, or superior to him, but simply in the free will of individuals; that the authority in the State comes from the people only; and that, just as every man's individual reason is his only rule of life, so the collective reason of the community should be the supreme guide in the management of all public affairs. Hence the doctrine of the supremacy of the greater number, and that all right and all duty reside in the majority. But, from what has been said, it is clear that all this is in contradiction to reason. To refuse any bond of union between man and civil society, on the one hand, and God the Creator and consequently the supreme Law-giver, on the other hand, is plainly repugnant to the nature, not only of man, but of all created things; for, of necessity, all effects must in some proper way be connected with their cause; and it belongs to the perfection of every nature to contain itself within that sphere and grade which the order of nature has assigned to it, namely, that the lower should be subject and obedient to the higher.

18 There are others, somewhat more moderate though not more consistent, who affirm that the morality of individuals is to be guided by the divine law, but not the morality of the State, so that in public affairs the commands of God may be passed over, and may be entirely disregarded in the framing of laws. Hence follows the fatal theory of the need of separation between Church and State. But the absurdity of such a position is manifest. Nature herself proclaims the necessity of the State providing means and opportunities whereby the community may be enabled to live properly, that is to say, according to the laws of God. For, since God is the source of all goodness and justice, it is absolutely ridiculous that the State should pay no attention to these laws or render them abortive by contrary enactments. Besides, those who are in authority owe it to the commonwealth not only to provide for its external well-being and the conveniences of

life, but still more to consult the welfare of men's souls in the wisdom of their legislation. But, for the increase of such benefits, nothing more suitable can be conceived than the laws which have God for their author; and, therefore, they who in their government of the State take no account of these laws abuse political power by causing it to deviate from its proper end and from what nature itself prescribes. And, what is still more important, and what We have more than once pointed out, although the civil authority has not the same proximate end as the spiritual, nor proceeds on the same lines, nevertheless in the exercise of their separate powers they must occasionally meet. For their subjects are the same, and not infrequently they deal with the same objects, though in different ways. Whenever this occurs, since a state of conflict is absurd and manifestly repugnant to the most wise ordinance of God, there must necessarily exist some order or mode or procedure to remove the occasions of difference and contention, and to secure harmony in all things. This harmony has been not inaptly compared to that which exists between the body and the soul for the well-being of both one and the other, the separation of which brings irremediable harm to the body, since it extinguishes its very life.

23. We must now consider briefly liberty of speech, and liberty of the press. It is hardly necessary to say that there can be no such right as this, if it be not used in moderation, and if it pass beyond the bounds and end of all true liberty. For right is a moral power which – as We have before said and must again and again repeat – it is absurd to suppose that nature has accorded indifferently to truth and falsehood, to justice and injustice. Men have a right freely and prudently to propagate throughout the state what things soever are true and honourable, so that as many as possible may possess them; but lying opinions, than which no mental plague is greater, and vices which corrupt the heart and moral life, should be diligently repressed by public authority, lest they insidiously work the ruin of the State. The excesses of an unbridled intellect, which unfailingly end in the oppression of the untutored multitude, are no less rightly controlled by the authority of the law than are the injuries inflicted by violence upon the weak. And this all the more surely, because by far the greater part of the community is either absolutely unable or able only with great difficulty, to escape from illusions and deceitful subtleties, especially such as flatter the passions. If unbridled license of speech and of writing be granted to all, nothing will remain sacred and inviolate; even the highest and truest mandates of natures, justly held to be the common and noblest heritage of the human race, will not be spared. Thus, truth being gradually obscured by darkness, pernicious and manifold error, as too often happens, will easily prevail. Thus, too, license will gain what liberty loses; for liberty will ever be more free and secure in proportion as license is kept in fuller restraint. In regard, however, to all matters of opinion which God leaves to man's free discussion, full liberty of thought and of speech is naturally within the right of every one; for such liberty never leads men to suppress the truth, but often to discover it and make it known.

24. A like judgment must be passed upon what is called liberty of teaching. There can be no doubt that truth alone should imbue the minds of men, for in it are found the well-

being, the end, and the perfection of every intelligent nature; and therefore nothing but truth should be taught both to the ignorant and to the educated, so as to bring knowledge to those who have it not, and to preserve it in those who possess it. For this reason it is plainly the duty of all who teach to banish error from the mind, and by sure safeguard to close the entry to all false convictions. From this it follows, as is evident, that the liberty of which We have been speaking is greatly opposed to reason, and tends absolutely to pervert men's minds, in as much as it claims for itself the right of teaching whatever it pleases as liberty which the State cannot grant without failing in its duty. And the more so because the authority of teachers has great weight with their hearers, who can rarely decide for themselves as to the truth or falsehood of the instruction given to them.

Document 5.9

Alfredo Rocco, on the Fascist Concept of Liberty

Alfredo Rocco (1875–1935) was a leading Italian nationalist and Fascist, a theorist and Minister of Justice. He was highly critical of the Liberal state. He believed that only a select few could transcend their immediate personal concerns and grasp the nation's long-term interest. The challenges of the industrial age could only be met if the state extended its sovereignty, mobilized people more fully and became totalitarian.

There is a Liberal theory of freedom, and there is a Fascist concept of liberty. For we, too, maintain the necessity of safeguarding the conditions that make for the free development of the individual; we, too, believe that the oppression of individual personality can find no place in the modern state. We do not, however, accept a bill of rights which tends to make the individual superior to the state and to empower him to act in opposition to society. Our concept of liberty is that the individual must be allowed to develop his personality on behalf of the state, for these ephemeral and infinitesimal elements of the complex and permanent life of society determine by their normal growth the development of the state. But this individual growth must be normal. A huge and disproportionate development of the individual of classes, would prove as fatal to society as abnormal growths are to living organisms. Freedom therefore is due to the citizen and to classes on condition that they exercise it in the interest of society as a whole and within the limits set by social exigencies, liberty being, like any other individual right, a concession of the state. What I say concerning civil liberties applies to economic freedom as well. Fascism does not look upon the doctrine of economic liberty as an absolute dogma. It does not refer economic problems to individual needs, to individual interest, to individual solutions. On the contrary it considers the economic development, and especially the production of wealth, as an eminently social concern, wealth being for society an essential element of power and prosperity. But Fascism maintains that in the ordinary run of events economic liberty serves the social purposes best; that it is profitable to entrust to individual initiative the task of economic development both as to production and as to distribution; that in the economic world individual ambition is the most effective means for obtaining the best social results with the least effort. Therefore, on the question also of economic liberty the Fascists differ fundamentally from the Liberals; the latter see in liberty a principle, the Fascists accept it as a method. By the Liberals, freedom is recognized in the interest of the citizens; the Fascists grant it in the interest of society. In other terms, Fascists make of the individual an economic instrument for the advancement of society, an instrument which they use so long as it functions and which they subordinate when no longer serviceable. In this guise Fascism solves the eternal problem of economic freedom and of state interference, considering both as mere methods which may or may not be employed in accordance with the social needs of the moment.

Document 5.10

Lord Hailsham, A Conservative View of Freedom

Lord Hailsham (Quintin Hogg) (born 1907) Tory politician and subsequently Lord Chancellor, published the following in his polemical tract *The Case for Conservatism* in 1947. At the time the Conservative Party was in opposition to a Labour government.

Political liberty is nothing else but the diffusion of power. All power tends to corrupt, absolute power to corrupt absolutely. It follows that political liberty is impossible to the extent that power is concentrated in the hands of a few men. It does not matter whether these be popularly elected or no. Give men power and they will misuse it. Give them absolute power, that is, concentrate in their hands all the various kinds and degrees of power, and they will abuse it absolutely. If power is not to be abused it must be spread as widely as possible throughout the community.

Thus, although Conservatives have always supported a strong central authority when the danger to order has consisted in too much decentralisation, today they believe that it would be an evil day for Britain, and for freedom, if all power fell into the hands of the Cabinet. For since political liberty is nothing else than the diffusion of power, the splitting up of political and legal power into different parcels is the essential means of securing it.

Conservatives see no inconsistency in having opposed Liberals and Whigs in the name of authority, Socialists in the name of freedom. The ground is the same, but it is being attacked from a different direction. The great heresy of the nineteenth century was self-interest. But today the boot is on the other foot. When the predominant left wing philosophy was Liberalism, the danger was too much liberty – in the political sphere creating chaos, in the economic sphere producing alternate boom and slump, and creating mass unemployment.

But today the predominant theory of the left is Socialism, and the danger is not too much but too little freedom. The great heresy of our age is no longer self-interest, it is State Worship, and instead of the altars being ablaze in honour of Mammon, we make our children pass through the fire to Moloch.

In each fight Conservatives have taken the same stand. Abused and traduced as reactionaries and out of touch with the times, they opposed the excessive individualism of the Liberals in the name of the same principle as that in defence of which they now oppose Socialism – the Rule of Law, the enemy alike of dictatorship and anarchy, the friend by whose good offices authority and liberty can alone be reconciled.

There are some who tend to deny the value of freedom. What is freedom, they ask, under Capitalism but freedom to starve? It is not enough to enjoy a political democracy; it is necessary to have an economic democracy as well.

In a sense, these critics are right.

But what is meant by economic freedom or economic democracy? Conservatives are tempted to reply in a single sentence.

Just as political democracy and political freedom mean the diffusion, the sharing of political power, so economic democracy, economic freedom, means the sharing, the diffusion, of economic power, that is property, as widely as possible throughout the community. This diffusion Conservatives regard as the very antithesis of Socialism.

Conservatives therefore wish to see economic democracy, but they can find no meaning in the phrase unless it implies the sharing of property as widely as possible. Economic democracy is, and is nothing else than, the 'property-owning democracy' called for by Mr Anthony Eden. Such a property-owning democracy, although it is inconsistent with the co-existence of great wealth coupled with great poverty, is not inconsistent with the existence of large independent fortunes held either by Corporations or by individuals. Such independent fortunes, properly controlled by law, form, in our view, a valuable, indeed an indispensable, counterpoise to the vast complex of economic power controlled by the modern state.

Conservatives therefore consider it an essential part of economic democracy to see wealth shared as widely as possible by individuals. They desire to see wealth also shared by groups. They rejoice to see it shared by great Trade Unions so long as these are neither subservient to the interests of a single political party nor ambitious to control the political machinery of the state. Conservatives also wish property to be shared by traders and trading companies and by local authorities. But, above all, they want to see property in the family, and the family itself an independent centre of power enjoying its own franchises and prerogatives and occupying its true position as the foundation of civilised society.

In all this the Conservatives find an unanswerable case against Socialism, under which name they include all forms of state worship, in all the forms in which it has been present, Leninist, Marxist, Fascist, or Transport House (and each of these can by this test be regarded as Socialist, though not all are equally evil). Socialism aims at the concentration of power, political and economic, in the hands of a few political chiefs. The arguments for it are the arguments which have been used for dictatorship from the time immemorial – efficiency, national crisis, the protection of the multitude of 'common men' against the power of the wealthy or influential, the efficient redistribution of wealth or the like.

The Socialist is not content with control. He must have ownership. That is to say, he is not satisfied with preventing wrongful action by the owners of industry; he demands to use industry as he desires himself in despite of those from whom he proposes to take it by force, and notwithstanding that their own use of it may be proved to be legitimate.

Document 5.11

R.H. Tawney on Economic Liberty

Richard Henry Tawney (1880–1962) exercised a major influence on the development of English Socialist thought. Inspired by Christian moralism, he argued that a society based on possessive individualism was morally deficient. As a social philosopher and economic historian he emphasized that the organization of society was 'a common enterprise, which is the concern of all'. The extract below is taken from his major work, *Equality* (1931), in which, among other things, he criticised a society in which, as he saw it, industry and property had become detached from any principle of function and purpose.

Political principles resemble military tactics; they are usually designed for a war which is over. Freedom is commonly interpreted in England in political terms, because it was in the political arena that the most resounding of its recent victories were won. It is regarded as belonging to human beings as citizens, rather than citizens as human beings; so that it is possible for the nation, the majority of whose members have as little influence on the decisions that determine their economic certainties as on the motions of the planets, to applaud the idea with self-congratulatory gestures of decorous enthusiasm, as though history were of the past, but not of the present. If the attitude of the ages from which it inherits a belief in liberty had been equally ladylike, there would have been, it is probable, little liberty to applaud.

For freedom is always relative to power, and the kind of freedom which at any moment it is most urgent to affirm depends on the nature of the power which is relevant and established. Since political arrangements may be such as they check excesses of power, while economic arrangements permit or encourage them, a society, or a large part of it, may be both politically free and economically the opposite. It may be protected against arbitrary action by the agents of government, and be without the security against economic oppression which corresponds to civil liberty. It may possess the political institutions of an advanced democracy, and lack the will and ability that control the conduct of those powerful in its economic affairs, which is the economic analogy of political freedom.

The extension of liberty from the political to the economic sphere is evidently among the most urgent tasks of industrial societies. It is evident also, however, that, in so far as this extension takes place, the traditional antithesis between liberty and equality will no longer be valid. As long as liberty is interpreted as consisting exclusively in security against oppression by the agents of the state, or as a share in its government, it is plausible, perhaps, to dissociate it from equality; for, though experience suggests that, even in this meagre and restricted sense, it is not easily maintained in the presence of extreme disparities of wealth and influence, it is possible for it to be enjoyed, in form at least, by pauper and millionaire. Such disparities, however, though they do not enable one group to become the political master of another, necessarily cause it to exercise a preponderant influence on the economic life of the rest of society.

Hence, when liberty is construed, realistically, or implying, not merely the minimum of civil and political rights, but securities that the economically weak will not be at the mercy of the economically strong, and that the control of those aspects of economic life by which all are affected will be amenable in the last resort, to the will of all, a large measure of equality, so far from being inimical to liberty, is essential to it. In conditions which impose co-operative, rather than merely individual effort, liberty is, in fact, equality in action, in the sense, not that all men perform identical functions or wield the same degree of power, but that all men are equally protected against the abuse of power and equally entitled to insist that power shall be used, not for personal ends, but for the general advantage. Civil and political liberty obviously imply, not that all men shall be members of parliament, cabinet ministers, or civil servants, but the absence of such civil and political inequalities as enable one class to impose its will on another by legal coercion. It should be not less obvious that economic liberty implies, not that all men shall initiate, plan, direct, manage, or administer, but the absence of such economic inequalities as can be used as means of economic constraint.

The danger to liberty which is caused by inequality varies with difference in economic organisation and public policy. When the mass of the population are independent producers, or when, if they are dependent on great undertakings, the latter are subject to strict public control, it may be absent or remote. It is seen at its height when important departments of economic activity and the province of large organisations, which, if they do not themselves, sometimes occurs, control the state, are sufficiently powerful to resist control by it. Among the numerous interesting phenomena which impress the foreign observer of American economic life, not the least interesting is the occasional emergence of industrial enterprises which appear to him, and, indeed, to some Americans, to have developed the characteristics, not merely of an economic undertaking, but of a kind of polity. Their rule may be a mild and benevolent paternalism, lavishing rest-rooms, schools, gymnasia, and guarantees for constitutional behaviour on care-free employees; or it may be a harsh and suspicious tyranny. But, whether as amiable as Solon, or as ferocious as Lycurgus, their features are cast in a heroic mould. Their gestures are those of the sovereigns of little commonwealths rather than of mere mundane employers.

American official documents have, on occasion, called attention to the tendency of the bare stem of business to burgeon, in a favourable environment, with almost tropical exuberance, so that it clothes itself with functions that elsewhere are regarded as belonging to political authorities. The corporations controlled by six financial groups, stated the Report of the United States Commission on Industrial Relations some twenty years ago, employ 2,651,684 wage earners, or 440,000 per group. Some of these companies own, not merely the plant and equipment of industry, but the homes of the workers, the streets through which they pass to work, and the halls in which, if they are allowed to meet, their meetings must be held. They employ private spies and detectives, private police and, sometimes, it appears, private troops, and engage, when they deem it expedient, in private war. While organised themselves, they forbid organisation among their employees, and enforce their will by evicting malcontents from their homes, and even, on occasion, by the use of armed force. In such conditions business may continue in its modesty, since its object is money, to describe itself as business; but, in fact, it is a tyranny. The main objection to the large corporation, remarks Mr Justice Brandeis, who, as a judge of the Supreme Court, should know the facts, is that it makes possible – and in many cases makes inevitable – the exercise of industrial absolutism. Property in capital, thus inflated and emancipated, acquires attributes analogous to those of property in land in a feudal society. It carries with it the disposal, in fact, if not in law, of an authority which is quasi-governmental. Its owners possess what would have been called in the ages of darkness a private jurisdiction, and their relations to their dependents, though contractual in form, resemble rather those of ruler and subject than of equal parties to a commercial venture. The liberty which they defend against the encroachments of trade unionism and the state is most properly to be regarded, not as freedom, but as a franchise.

The conventional assertion that inequality is inseparable from liberty is obviously, in such circumstances, unreal and unconvincing; for the existence of the former is a menace to the latter, and the latter is most likely to be secured by curtailing the former. It is true that in England, where three generations of trade unionism and state intervention have done something to tame it, the exercise of economic power is, at ordinary times, less tyrannical than it once was. It still remains, nevertheless, a formidable menace to the freedom of the common man.

Document 5.12

Hannah Arendt, 'What is Freedom?'

Hannah Arendt (1906–75), born in Germany of a Jewish family, subsequently emigrated to the United States of America and established her reputation as a theorist with *The Origins of Totalitarianism.* (1951). Her most significant philosophical work was *The Human Condition* (1958) in which she contrasted freedom in the modern state with that in the Greek *polis*. In the latter, freedom was enjoyed and exercised the company of other men and consisted of the freedom to appear in the public realm, debate and decide collective affairs in cooperation with one's fellow citizens. Latterly, though, she argued it had come to mean the non-interference by others in one's private concerns. The proper worth of public human activities had come to be obscured and freedom had come to be defined in negative and isolationist terms.

Obviously not every form of human intercourse and not every kind of community is characterized by freedom. Where men live together but do not form a body politic – as, for example, in tribal societies or in the privacy of the household – the factors ruling their actions and conduct are not freedom but the necessities of life and concern for its preservation. Moreover, wherever the man-made world does not become the scene for action and speech – as in despotically ruled communities which banish their subjects into the narrowness of the home and thus prevent the rise of a public realm – freedom has no worldly reality. Without a politically guaranteed public realm, freedom lacks the worldly space to make its appearance. To be sure it may still dwell in men's hearts as desire or will or hope or yearning; but the human heart, as we all know, is a very dark place, and whatever goes on in its obscurity can hardly be called a demonstrable fact. Freedom as a demonstrable fact and politics coincide and are related to each other like two sides of the same matter.

Yet it is precisely this coincidence of politics and freedom which we cannot take for granted in the light of our present political experience. The rise of totalitarianism, its claim to having subordinated all spheres of life to the demands of politics and its consistent non-recognition of civil rights, above all the rights of privacy and the right to freedom from politics, makes us doubt not only the coincidence of politics and freedom but their very compatibility. We are inclined to believe that freedom begins where politics ends, because we have seen that freedom has disappeared when so-called political considerations overruled everything else. Was not the liberal credo, 'The less politics the more freedom', right after all? Is it not true that the smaller the space occupied by the political, the larger the domain left to freedom? Indeed, do we not rightly measure the extent of freedom in any given community by the free scope it grants to apparently nonpolitical activities, free economic enterprise or freedom of teaching, of religion, of cultural and intellectual activities? Is it not true, as we all somehow believe, that politics is compatible with freedom only because and insofar as it guarantees a possible freedom from politics?

This definition of political liberty as a potential freedom from politics is not urged upon us merely by our most recent experiences; it has played a large part in the history of political theory. We need go no farther than the political thinkers of the seventeenth and eighteenth centuries, who more often than not simply identified political freedom with security. The highest purpose of politics, 'the end of government', was the guaranty of security; security, in turn, made freedom possible, and the word 'freedom' designated a quintessence of activities which occurred outside the political realm.

Even Montesquieu, though he had not only a different but a much higher opinion of the essence of politics than Hobbes or Spinoza, could still occasionally equate political freedom with security. The rise of the political and social sciences in the nineteenth and twentieth centuries has even widened the breach between freedom and politics; for government, which since the beginning of the modern age had been identified with the total domain of the political, was now considered to be the appointed protector not so much of freedom as of the life process, the interests of society and its individuals. Security remained the decisive criterion, but not the individual's security against 'violent death,' as in Hobbes (where the condition of all liberty is freedom from fear), but a security which should permit an undisturbed development of the life process of society as a whole. This life process is not bound up with freedom but follows its own inherent necessity; and it can be called free only in the sense that we speak of a freely flowing stream. Here freedom is not even the nonpolitical aim of politics, but a marginal phenomenon – which somehow forms the boundary government should not overstep unless life itself and its immediate interests and necessities are at stake.

Thus not only we, who have reasons of our own to distrust politics for the sake of freedom, but the entire modern age has separated freedom and politics. I could descend even deeper into the past and evoke older memories and traditions. The pre-modern secular concept of freedom certainly was emphatic in its insistence on separating the subjects' freedom from any direct share in government; the people's 'liberty and freedom consisted in having the government of those laws by which their life and their goods may be most their own: 'tis not for having share in government, that is nothing pertaining to them' – as Charles I summed it up in his speech from the scaffold. It was not out of a desire for freedom that people eventually demanded their share in government or admission to the political realm, but out of mistrust in those who held power over their life and goods. The Christian concept of political freedom, moreover, arose out of the early Christians' suspicion of and hostility against the public realm as such, from whose concerns they demanded to be absolved in order to be free. And this Christian freedom for the sake of salvation had been preceded, as we saw before, by the philosophers' absention from politics as a prerequisite for the highest and freest way of life, the *vita contemplativa.*

Despite the enormous weight of this tradition and despite the perhaps even more telling urgency of our own experiences, both pressing into the same direction of a divorce of freedom from politics, I think the reader may believe he has read only an old truism when I said that the *raison d'être* of politics is freedom and that this freedom is primarily experienced in action.

Document 5.13

The Declaration of Black Independence, July 4 1970

The extract below is from a declaration issued by the American National Committee of Black Churchmen. The background to this was the Civil Rights Movement of the 1960s. There are obvious echoes in it of the original American Declaration of Independence and Liberian Declaration of Independence of 1847. In the latter case, black leaders had advocated liberation from inequality and discrimination by migration, and the foundation of the free black state of Liberia. In the 1970 declaration the demand is for freedom and independence within American society.

When in the course of Human Events, it becomes necessary for a People who were stolen from the lands of their Fathers, transported under the most ruthless and brutal circumstances 5,000 miles to a strange land, sold into dehumanizing slavery, emasculated, subjugated, exploited and discriminated against for 351 years, to call, with finality, a halt to such indignities and genocidal practices – by virtue of the Laws of Nations and of Nature's God, a decent respect to the Opinions of mankind requires that they should declare their just grievances and the urgent and necessary redress thereof.

We hold these truths to be self-evident, that all Men are not only created equal and endowed by their Creator with certain unalienable rights among which are Life, Liberty, and the Pursuit of Happiness, but that when this equality and these rights are deliberately and consistently refused, withheld or abnegated, men are bound by self-respect and honor to rise up in righteous indignation to secure them. Whenever any Form of Government, or any variety of established traditions and systems of Majority becomes destructive of Freedom and of legitimate Human Rights, it is the Right of the Minorities to use every necessary and accessible means to protest and to disrupt the machinery of Oppression, and so to bring such general distress and discomfort upon the oppressor as to the offended Minorities shall seem most appropriate and most likely to effect a proper adjustment of the society.

Prudence, indeed, will dictate that such bold tactics should not be initiated for light and transient Causes; and, accordingly, the Experience of White America has been that the descendants of the African citizens transported to the shores of the Caribbean Islands, as slaves, have been patient long past what can be expected of any human beings so affronted. But when a long train of Abuses and Violence, pursuing invariably the same Object, manifests a Design to reduce them under Absolute Racist Domination and Injustice, it is their Duty radically to confront such Government or system of traditions, and to provide, under the aegis of Legitimate Minority Power and Self Determination, for their present Relief and future Security ...

We, therefore, the Black People of the United States of America, in all parts of this

Nation, …. Solemnly Publish and Declare that we shall be, and of Right ought to be, FREE AND INDEPENDENT FROM THE INJUSTICE, EXPLOITATIVE CONTROL, INSTITUTIONALIZED VIOLENCE AND RACISM OF WHITE AMERICA, that unless we receive full Redress and Relief from these Inhumanities we will move to renounce all Allegiance to this Nation, and will refuse, in every way, to cooperate with the Evil which is perpetrated upon ourselves and our Communities. And for the support of the Declaration, with a firm Reliance on the Protection of divine Providence, we mutually pledge to each other our Lives, our Fortunes, and our Sacred Honor.

QUESTIONS FOR DISCUSSION

1. In what sense can the economically underprivileged or the 'propertyless' be free in an unequal society?
2. Do you agree with Arendt's claim that freedom is to be found in the public arena?
3. What is the difference between positive and negative freedom?
4. How can we reconcile the demands of the law and the claims of liberty?
5. How important is the liberty of the press?

NOTES

1   Bernard Crick, *Political Theory and Practice* (London, Penguin, 1971), p.37.
2   Alan Harding, 'Political Liberty in the Middle Ages', *Speculum*, Vol. 55 (1980),pp. 441–2.
3   B. Fontana (ed.), *Benjamin Constant. Political Writings* (Cambridge, 1988), p. 326.

FURTHER READING

For a general historical survey see A.J. Carlyle, *Political Liberty. A History of the Conception in the Middle Ages and Modern Times* (Oxford, 1941). J. Gray and Z. Pelczynski (eds), *Conceptions of Liberty in Political Philosophy* (London, Athlone Press, 1984) includes a number of useful articles; see especially R. Mulgan, 'Liberty in Ancient Greece'. A sense of the complexity of medieval conceptions can be gained from Alan Harding, 'Political Liberty in the Middle Ages', *Speculum*, Vol. 55 (1980). There are two interesting accounts of eighteenth-century conceptions in E. Hellmuth, *The Transformation of Political Culture. England and Germany in the Late Eighteenth Century* (Oxford, 1990): D. Klippel, 'The True Concept of Liberty: Political Theory in Germany in the Second Half of the Eighteenth Century' and E. Hellmuth, '"The Palladium of all other English Liberties": Reflections on the Liberty of the Press in England during the 1760s and 1780s'. There are a number of useful general accounts, including D. Miller (ed.), *Liberty* (Oxford, Oxford University Press, 1991), S.I. Benn, *A Theory of Freedom* (Cambridge, Cambridge University Press, 1988), and A. Ryan (ed.), *The Idea of Freedom: Essays in Honour of Isaiah Berlin* (Oxford, Oxford University Press, 1979). For Berlin's lecture see his *Four Essays on Liberty* (Oxford, Oxford University Press, 1969). On the subject of liberty and justice see J.P. Day, *Liberty and Justice* (London, Croom Helm, 1987) and D.D. Raphael, *Justice and Liberty* (London, Athlone Press, 1980)

6

JUSTICE AND EQUALITY

INTRODUCTION

From at least the time of Plato's *Republic,* the idea of justice has been central to political thought. It is, therefore, no surprise that the idea has been applied to a variety of situations. We readily speak about a lack of justice in a particular trial, where we believe someone has been wrongly convicted, or acquitted, about the injustice of a particular state, usually meaning that it ignores basic rights, about the injustice of the distribution of wealth within a country, or even about the injustice of the consumption of the earth's finite resources by the industrialized world. On a smaller scale we might call the appointment of one person rather than another to some office or position of employment unjust, though the term 'unfair' would probably be used more frequently. Similarly, the meteoric rise to wealth and fame of someone we judge to be of little talent brings forth the charge of injustice: 'he doesn't deserve it'. We might even extend the latter idea to the case of someone with whom we do sympathize, who has been cut down in the prime of life, perhaps by some incurable, genetically inherited disease.

The elasticity of the idea has given concern to several theorists, including James Stuart Mill who listed six frequent usages and then set out to determine the common element in them (see document 6.6). Much earlier, Aristotle had responded to the same dilemma by suggesting that we distinguish between different kinds of justice. In doing so he was criticizing Plato who, he held, had conflated justice with virtue in general. There is some dispute as to whether the Greeks had a distinct concept of justice. In medieval political theory, too, the idea of justice was used more liberally than is customary now. Justice was associated with order and maintaining everything in its proper place. The realms of religion, psychology or virtue in general had not been fully separated out from justice as a judgement upon the conflicting acts and claims of men. Yet within these broader conceptions we find familiar distinctions and dilemmas.

Aristotle agreed that justice in the widest sense was equivalent to virtue. But this was not his main concern. Aristotle was interested in a more limited meaning of justice, that is the justice or injustice concerning 'honours, money, security'. Within this more limited conception he distinguished between distributive justice, that is how much of a good each individual should get, and corrective justice under which he incorporated commercial transactions and crimes against persons and property. There are here two broad categories: social justice and legal justice. In discussions of justice in political theory it is social justice which is usually the focus of dispute. Nevertheless, the interaction between the two is important. Many of the characteristics which we associate with justice have clear legal parallels. The idea, for example, that the distribution of a good should not be decided by an interested party is connected with the idea that people cannot be trusted to be 'judges' in their own case. Justice, whether legal or social, is expected to be impartial. An alternative to finding an impartial, disinterested, judge is to find some procedure which will automatically foil the self-interest and partiality of the parties, as theorists as diverse as Harrington (see document 6.2) and Rawls have done .

The seventeenth-century political theorist, Hobbes, took up another element of Aristotle's distinction. Justice for Hobbes was whatever free, rational and equal individuals agreed to. The commercial model, according to which arrangements to which both parties consented were *ipso facto* just, predominated to the extent that it supplanted all others. The significance of this was twofold. First, it cut out the plethora of acquired or inherited distinctions of status which had long been taken into account in determining what was just. Secondly, Hobbes said little about what a just distribution of goods would look like. A prime concern of later generations, who gets what, what is the difference between the most and the least which individuals receive, did not figure in his account. So long as the distribution was the result of a freely entered agreement the outcome was just.

Equality, the most contentious word in the vocabulary of justice, applied only in a very specific sense to Hobbes' theory. Men were equal in the sense that each posed a threat to another. Each was vulnerable. The resultant danger provided the motive for entering into agreements to institute a political order within which, in turn, the sanctity of agreements would be enforced by political authority. Hobbes carried this equality over into his approach to justice. Whether men were equal in other respects was irrelevant. If they were, the fact should be acknowledged in the idea of justice. If they were not, it made no difference for men would not enter into a political arrangement on any other terms than those of equality.

For many subsequent theories the presumption of equality came to be a step in an argument for equality in outcomes; either absolute equality or at least less inequality than currently exists. The case for equality was put with vigour by the Frenchman Gracchus Babeuf (see document 6.5). For Babeuf and his followers equality of political and legal rights was insufficient. The heart of the problem lay in economic inequality. Moreover, it was not merely the absolute poverty of some citizens that Babeuf and his egalitarians found reprehensible. It was also the distinctions which arose between those who had more and those who had less. Inequality in outcomes was destructive of social harmony. Justice lay in equality and simplicity. Since then the advocates and critics alike of equality have complained that the other side has the benefit of customary prejudice, that the doctrine of equality has become the benchmark or that the doctrine of inequality has attained, in Tawney's words, the status of a religion (see document 6.8).[1] The case for equality itself has been reformulated on innumerable occasions, with varying degrees of equality being asserted for different aspects of individual and social life. The inherent complexities are evident from the response of Karl Marx (see document 6.7). Despite being the most prominent representative of the socialist tradition, a tradition deeply influenced by egalitarianism, Marx ultimately turned his back on equality as a determinant of justice.

The arguments which associate justice with equality, however defined, stand, of course, in stark contrast to the persistence of often gross inequalities in most societies. The fact is reflected in the claim by a leading contemporary theorist, Brian Barry, that, 'In Plato's time as in ours, the central issue in any theory of justice is the defensibility of unequal relations between people'.[2] But if it is decided that some inequalities are defensible, the question then becomes one of which criterion is to determine the unequal distribution. The conservative response has been to defend existing claims. Echoing the Roman precept that justice entailed rendering to each his own, conservatives have argued that where someone has acquired just title to something, he should keep it. But this requires at the least that it was acquired justly, and usually that it was transferred (or inherited) justly and that unjust acquisition and transfer can be rectified.[3]

Critics of entitlement theories of justice will often point to the extent to which property or other resources, including status, have been acquired by fraud, violence, or the preferment of tyrannical regimes. They are also likely to look, if they are not strict egalitarians, to some criterion which will relate distribution to characteristics of individuals or to their behaviour. There are two criteria which do this, both referred to as attempts to relate distribution to merit. One relates distribution to the individual's behaviour or performance. The more industrious, intelligent or skilful, should, on this account, receive more than the less industrious, intelligent or skilful. This theory of desert need not, as Marx pointed out, produce the same outcome as the second. According to the second, distribution should be related to need. Both ideas would, if we knew sufficient about individuals' performance or needs and could agree on how to assess them, tell us exactly who would get what. The results would, however, be different. The most productive member of a society might very well be in good physical health, might have no dependents, and might even be ascetic. On the other hand, the needs of someone suffering from a terminal illness or born into a community suffering from endemic malnutrition are likely to be as extensive as his performance is limited.

Since Plato, a prime concern of any theory of justice has been to explain why men should be just. Among the theories which Plato sought to counter the one introduced by Glaucon (see document 6.1) has persisted ever since. According to this theory men behave justly because it is in their own interest to do so, and for no other reason. The point was repeated by, amongst others, Hobbes and Hume. Hume, however, added new dimensions to the discussion of justice. He sought to explain why men might adhere to justice by arguing that justice was socially useful. He made the important point that individual acts which are in accordance with the rules of justice still might be contrary to society's interests. What matters though is the utility of a system of justice as a whole (see document 6.4) But utility was not the whole story. Why, Hume asked, should we be interested in cases of injustice which do not directly affect our own interests or which do not seem important enough to pose a threat to the entire system of justice? His answer involved an appeal to our sentiments rather than to our calculations of interest, either our own immediate interest or the wider, social interest. Utility would explain why the idea of justice had arisen in the first place, but emotion and sentiment were needed to explain why we customarily behave justly.[4]

That justice contained an emotive element was agreed by J.S. Mill, although the sentiment he emphasized, the desire for retribution, was less attractive. Mill, like other utilitarians, ultimately downgraded the idea of justice. From the existence of different and competing criteria of justice, the claims of equality and the claims of merit, he drew the conclusion that only the standard of social utility could decide. The danger, as critics have never ceased to point out, was that once social utility was elevated to the ultimate criterion it could be argued that the interests or rights of one individual might be sacrificed for the greater good of others. This is the objection raised by Rawls (see document 6.9).[5]

As with the idea of rights, the idea, or rather ideas, of justice have been extended to ever more areas of social and political life during the twentieth century. Meeting these demands of justice, or, as frequently, having to deal with the dissent induced by failing to meet them, imposes greater and greater demands upon the modern polity and society. The recent responses to this have been threefold. One, exemplified by Nozick, is to reduce radically the demands by ruling out of court the two most expansive criteria of justice: desert and need. Entitlement is privileged and consequently, as with Hobbes, outcomes cease to be the determining factor. A second response, exemplified by Rawls, is to seek to reconcile the claims of divergent conceptions of justice by linking them through a formula which makes increased rewards for those who benefit most dependent upon improving the position of those who benefit least. The third approach, that of Walzer, is to accept the diversity of approaches to justice and argue that the problem lies in attempts to subordinate all aspects of life to one criterion.

The idea of justice has been a constant theme throughout the history of political thought. It is also an idea which is almost universally affirmed. Even societies which have, for example, denied that some people, slaves or women, have rights have nevertheless sought to defend the justice of their political order. It has been argued that it pays to be unjust, or that men have no distinct love of justice, that they act justly only if it pays. Few have upheld injustice as a positive virtue. But behind this consensus lies the problem of what justice consists of, what the criteria of justice are. The difficulty this poses has led some, in different degrees Marx and Mill, to turn their back on the question and seek an answer elsewhere, in a future society or in the principle of utility. Yet the attraction of the question has played a role in the major texts of recent political theory; in the works of John Rawls, Robert Nozick and Brian Barry. Modern political theory is, in large part, a renewed attempt to answer Plato's question: what is justice?

DOCUMENTS

Document 6.1

Plato on Justice

The extract is taken from Plato's *The Republic* (see introduction to document 2.1). Glaucon was one of Plato's brothers.

'Splendid' said Glaucon. 'And now for my first heading, the nature and origin of justice. What they say is that our natural instinct is to inflict wrong or injury, and to avoid suffering it, but that the disadvantages of suffering it exceed the advantages of inflicting it; after a taste of both, therefore, men decide that, as they can't have the ha'pence without the kicks, they had better make a compact with each other and avoid both. They accordingly proceed to make laws and mutual agreements, and what the laws lay down they call lawful and right. This is the origin and nature of justice. It lies between what is most desirable, to do wrong and avoid punishment, and what is most undesirable, to suffer wrong without redress; justice and right lie between these two and are accepted not as being good in themselves, but as having relative value due to our inability to do wrong. For anyone who had the power to do wrong and called himself a man would never make any such agreement with anyone– he would be mad if he did.'

Document 6.2

James Harrington on Justice and Self-Interest

James Harrington (1611–77) avoided taking sides in the Civil War, though he did become an attendant to Charles I in 1647. Harrington, like Machiavelli, was an admirer of the Roman republic and argued for a return to ancient principles of government in his major work, *Oceana* (1656). The mechanism for ensuring a just distribution, described below, also had constitutional implications. Harrington suggested a bicameral parliament with one chamber formulating proposals and the second chamber voting upon them without debate.

But it may be said that the difficulty remains yet; for be the interest of popular government right reason, a man doth not look upon reason as it is right or wrong in itself, but as it makes for him or against him; wherefore unless you can show such orders of a government as, like those of God in nature, shall be able to constrain this or that creature to shake of that inclination which is more peculiar unto it, and take up that which regards the common good or interest, all this is to no more end than to persuade every man in a popular government not to carve himself of that which he desires, but to be mannerly at the public table, and give the best from himself unto decency and the common interest. But that such orders may be established as may, nay must, give the upper hand in all cases unto common right or interest, notwithstanding the nearness of that which sticks unto every man in private, and this in a way of equal certainty and facility, is known even unto girls, being no other than those that are common with them in divers cases. For example, two of them have a cake as yet undivided, which was given between them. That each of them therefore may have that which is due, 'Divide', says one unto the other, 'and I will chose; or let me divide, and you shall choose.' If this be but once agreed upon, it is enough; for the divident dividing unequally loses, in regard that the other takes the better half; wherefore she divides equally, and so both have right ... that which great philosophers are disputing upon in vain is brought unto light by two silly girls: even the whole mystery of a commonwealth, which lies only in dividing and choosing.

Document 6.3

Thomas Hobbes on Covenants

In this extract from *Leviathan* Hobbes (see introduction to document 1.3) subsumes distributive justice under commutative justice.

From that law of Nature, by which we are obliged to transferre to another, such Rights, as being retained, hinder the peace of Mankind, there followeth a Third; which is this, *That men performe their Covenants made:* without which, Covenants are in vain, and but Empty words; and the Right of all men to all things remaining, wee are still in the condition of Warre.

And in this law of Nature, consisteth the Fountain and Originall of JUSTICE. For where no Covenant hath preceded, there hath no Right been transferred, and every man has right to every thing; and consequently, no action can be *Unjust.* But when a Covenant is made, then to break it is Unjust: And the definition of INJUSTICE, is no other than the *not Performance of Covenant.* And whatsoever is not Unjust, is *Just.*

But because Covenants of mutuall trust, where there is a feare of not performance on either part, (as hath been said in the former Chapter,) are invalid; though the Originall of Justice be the making of Covenants; yet Injustice actually there can be none, till the cause of such feare be taken away; which while men are in the naturall condition of Warre, cannot be done. Therefore before the names of Just, and Unjust can have place, there must be some coercive Power, to compell men equally to the performance of their Covenants, by the terrour of some punishment, greater than the benefit they expect by the breach of their Covenant; and to make good that Propriety, which by mutuall Contract men acquire, in recompence of the universall Right they abandon: and such power there is none before the erection of a Common-wealth. And this is also to be gathered out of the ordinary definition of *Justice is the constant Will of giving to every man his own*. And therefore where there is no Own, that is, no Propriety, there is no Injustice; and where there is no coerceive Power erected, that is, where there is no Common-wealth, there is no Propriety; all men having Right to all things: Therefore where there is no Common-wealth, there nothing is Unjust. So that the nature of Justice, consisteth in keeping of valid Covenants: but the Validity of Covenants begins not but with the Constitution of a Civill Power, sufficient to compell men to keep them: And then it is also that Propriety begins …

Justice of Actions, is by Writers divided into *Commutative*, and *Distributive*: and the former they say consisteth in proportion Arithmeticall; the later in proportion Geometricall. Commutative therefore, they place in the equality of value of the things contracted for; And Distributive, in the distribution of equall benefit, to men of equall merit. As if it were Injustice to sell dearer than we buy; or to give more to a man than he merits. The value of all things contracted for, is measured by the Appetite of the Contractors: and therefore the just value, is that which they be contented to give. And Merit (besides that which is by Covenant, where the performance on one part, meriteth the performance of the other part, and falls under Justice Commutative, not Distributive,) is not due by Justice; but is rewarded to Grace onely. And therefore this distinction, in the sense wherein it useth to be expounded, is not right. To speak properly, Commutative Justice, is the Justice of a Contractor; that is, a Performance of Covenant, in Buying, and Selling; Hiring, and Letting to Hire; Lending, and Borrowing; Exchanging, Bartering, and other acts of Contract. And Distributive Justice, the Justice of an Arbitrator; that is to say, the act of defining what is Just. Wherein, (being trusted by them that make him Arbitrator,) if he performe his Trust, he is said to distribute to every man his own: and this is indeed Just Distribution, and may be called (though improperly) Distributive Justice; but more properly Equity; which also is a Law of Nature, as shall be shewn in due place …

The question who is the better man, has no place in the condition of meer Nature; where, (as has been shewn before,) all men are equall. The inequallity that now is, has bin introduced by the Lawes civill. I know that *Aristotle* in the first booke of his Politiques, for a foundation of his doctrine, maketh men by Nature, some more worthy to Command, meaning the wiser sort (such as he thought himselfe to be for his Philosophy;) othere to Serve, (meaning those that had strong bodies, but were not Philosophers as he;) as if Master and Servant were not introduced by consent of men, but by difference of Wit: which is not only against reason; but also against experience. For there are very few so foolish, that had not rather governe themselves, than be governed by others: Nor when the wise in their own conceit, contend by force, with them who distrust their owne wisdome, do they alwaies, or often, or almost at any time, get the Victory. If Nature therefore have made men equall, that equalitie is to be acknowledged: or if Nature have made men unequall; yet because men that think themselves equall, will not enter into conditions of Peace, but upon Equall termes, such equalitie must be admitted. And therefore for the ninth law of Nature, I put this, *That every man acknowledge other for his*

Equall by Nature. The breach of this Precept is *Pride*.

On this law, dependeth another, *That at the entrance into conditions of Peace, no man require to reserve to himselfe any Right, which he is not content should be reserved to every one of the rest.* As it is necessary for all men that seek peace, to lay down certaine Rights of Nature; that is to say, not to have libertie to do all they list: so is it necessarie for mans life, to retaine some; as right to governe their owne bodies; enjoy aire, water, motion, waies to go from place to place; and all things else without which a man cannot live, or not live well. If in this case, at the making of Peace, men require for themselves, that which they would not have to be granted to others, they do contrary to the precedent law, that commandeth the acknowledgment of naturall equalitie, and therefore also against the law of Nature. The observers of this law, are those we call *Modest*, and the breakers *Arrogant* men. The Greeks call the violation of this law πλεονεξια that is, a desire of more than their share.

Also if *a man be trusted to judge between man and man*, it is a precept of the Law of Nature, *that he deale Equally between them*. For without that, the Controversies of men cannot be determined but by Warre. He therefore that is partiall in judgment, doth what in him lies, to deterre men from the use of Judges, and Arbitrators; and consequently, (against the fundamentall Lawe of Nature) is the cause of Warre.

The observance of this law, from the equall distribution to each man, of that which in reason belongeth to him, is called EQUITY, and (as I have sayd before) distributive Justice: the violation, *Acception of persons*, ...

Document 6.4

David Hume, Treatise of Human Nature

The account of justice offered by David Hume (see introduction to document 1.6) in his *Treatise of Human Nature* is developed entirely with reference to the security of property and took no account of political justice. It is notable for insisting on the benefits of a system of justice and acknowledging that particular just acts can be contrary to the public good.

I have already observed that justice takes its rise from human conventions, and that these are intended as a remedy to some inconveniences which proceed from the concurrence of certain *qualities* of the human mind with the *situation* of external objects. The qualities of the mind are *selfishness* and *limited generosity*; and the situation of external objects is their *easy change*, joined to their *scarcity* in comparison of the wants and desires of men. But however philosophers may have been bewildered in those speculations, poets have been guided more infallibly by a certain taste or common instinct which, in most kinds of reasoning, goes further than any of that art and philosophy with which we have been yet acquainted. They easily perceived, if every man had a tender regard for another, or if nature supplied abundantly all our wants and desires, that the jealousy of interest, which justice supposes, could no longer have place; nor would there by any occasion for those distinctions and limits of property and possession which at present are in use among mankind. Increase to a sufficient degree the benevolence of men, or the bounty of nature, and you render justice useless by supplying its place with much nobler virtues and more valuable blessings. The selfishness of men is animated by the few possessions we have in proportion to our wants; and it is to restrain this selfishness that men have been obliged to separate themselves from the community, and to distinguish betwixt their own goods and those of others …

Here then is a proposition which, I think, may be regarded as certain, *that it is only from the selfishness and confined generosity of man, along with the scanty provision nature has made for his wants that justice derives its origin.* If we look backward we shall find that this proposition bestows an additional force on some of those observations which we have already made on this subject.

First, we may conclude from it that a regard to public interest, or a strong extensive benevolence, is not our first and original motive for the observation of the rules of justice, since it is allowed that if men were endowed with such a benevolence, these rules would never have been dreamed of.

Secondly, we may conclude from the same principle that the sense of justice is not founded on reason, or on the discovery of certain connections and relations of ideas which are eternal, immutable, and universally obligatory. For since it is confessed that such an alteration as that above mentioned, in the temper and circumstances of mankind, would entirely alter our duties and obligations, it is necessary upon the common system *that the sense of virtue is derived from reason*, to show the change which this must produce in the relations and ideas. But it is evident that the only cause why the extensive generosity of man and the perfect abundance of everything would destroy the very idea of justice is because they render it useless; and that, on the other hand, his confined benevolence and his necessitous condition give rise to that virtue only by making it requisite to the public interest and to that of every individual. It was therefore a concern for our own and the public interest which made us establish the laws of justice; and nothing can be more certain than that it is not any relation of ideas which gives us this concern, but our impressions and sentiments, without which everything in nature is perfectly indifferent to us, and can never in the least affect us. The sense of justice, therefore, is not founded on our ideas but on our impressions.

Thirdly, we may further confirm the foregoing proposition *that those impressions, which give rise to this sense of justice, are not natural to the mind of man, but arise from artifice and human conventions.* For since any considerable alteration of temper and circumstances destroys equally justice and injustice, and since such an alteration has an effect only by changing our own and the public interest, it follows that the first establishment of the rules of justice depends on these different interests. But if men pursued the public interest naturally, and with a hearty affection, they would have never dreamed of restraining each other by these rules; and if they pursued their own interest, without any precaution, they would run headlong into every kind of injustice and violence. These rules, therefore, are artificial and seek their end in an oblique and indirect manner; nor is the interest which gives rise to them of a kind that could be pursued by the natural and inartificial passions of men.

To make this more evident, consider that, though the rules of justice are established merely by interest, their connection with interest is somewhat singular, and is different from what may be observed on other occasions. A single act of justice is frequently contrary to *public interest*; and were it to stand alone, without being followed by other acts, may in itself be very prejudicial to society. When a man of merit, of a beneficent disposition, restores a great fortune to a miser or a seditious bigot, he has acted justly and laudably; but the public is a real sufferer. Nor is every single act of justice, considered apart, more conducive to private interest than to public; and it is easily conceived how a man may impoverish himself by a single instance of integrity, and have reason to wish that, with regard to that single act, the laws of justice were for a moment suspended in the universe. But however single acts of justice may be contrary either to public or private interest, it is certain that the whole plan or scheme is highly conducive, or indeed absolutely requisite, both to the support of society and the well-being of every individual. It is impossible to separate the good from the ill. Property must be stable, and must be fixed by general rules. Though in one instance the public be a sufferer, this momentary ill is amply compensated by the steady prosecution of the rule and by the peace and order which it establishes in society. And even every individual person must find himself a gainer on balancing the account; since without justice society must immediately dissolve, and every one must fall into that savage and solitary condition which is infinitely worse than the worst situation that can possibly be supposed in society. When, therefore, men have had experience enough to observe that, whatever may be the consequence of any single act of justice performed by a single person, yet the whole system of actions concurred in by the whole society is infinitely advantageous to the whole and to every part, it is not long before justice and property take place. Every member of society is sensible of this interest; every one expresses this sense to his fellows along with the resolution he has taken of squaring his actions by it, on condition that others will do the same. No more is requisite to induce any one of them to perform an act of justice, who has the first opportunity. This becomes an example to others; and thus justice establishes itself by a kind of convention or agreement, that is, by a sense of interest, supposed to be common to all, and where every single act is performed in expectation that others are to perform the like. Without such a convention no one would ever have dreamed that there was such a virtue as justice, or have been induced to conform his actions to it. Taking any single act, my justice may be pernicious in every respect; and it is only upon the supposition that others are to imitate my example that I can be induced to embrace that virtue; since nothing but this combination can render justice advantageous, or afford me any motives to confirm myself to its rules.

We come now to the second question we proposed, viz., *Why we annex the idea of virtue to justice, and of vice to injustice.* This question will not detain us long after the principles which we have already established. All we can say of it at present will be dispatched in a few words; and for further satisfaction the reader must wait till we come to the third part of this book. The *natural* obligation to justice, viz., interest, has been fully explained; but as to the *moral* obligation, or the sentiment of right and wrong, it will first be requisite to examine the natural virtues before we can give a full and satisfactory account of it.

After men have found by experience that their selfishness and confined generosity, acting at their liberty, totally incapacitate them for society, and at the same time have observed that society is necessary to the satisfaction of those very passions, they are naturally induced to lay themselves under the restraint of such rules as may render their commerce more safe and commodious. To the imposition, then, and observance of these rules, both in general and in every particular instance, they are at first induced only by a regard to interest; and this motive, on the first formation of society, is sufficiently strong and forcible. But when society has become numerous and has increased to a tribe or nation, this interest is more remote; nor do men so readily perceive that disorder and confusion follow upon every breach of these rules, as in a more narrow and contracted society. But though in our own actions we may frequently lose sight of that interest which we have in maintaining order, and may follow a lesser and more present interest, we never fail to observe the prejudice we receive either mediately or immediately from the injustice of others, as not being in that case either blinded by passion or biassed by any contrary temptation. Nay, when the injustice is so distant from us as no way to affect our interest, it still displeases us, because we consider it as prejudicial to human society and pernicious to every one that approaches the person guilty of it. We partake of their uneasiness by sympathy; and as everything which gives uneasiness in human actions, upon the general survey, is called *vice*, and whatever produces satisfaction, in the same manner, is denominated *virtue*, this is the reason why the sense of moral good and evil follows upon justice and injustice. And though this sense in the present case be derived only from contemplating the actions of others, yet we fail not to extend it even to our own actions. The *general rule* reaches beyond those instances from which it arose; while at the same time we naturally *sympathize* with others in the sentiments they entertain of us.

Document 6.5

Gracchus Babeuf on Justice and Equality

The 'Analysis' was the product of a group of radical conspirators led by François Noël Babeuf (1760–97) shortly before they were betrayed and arrested on 10 May 1796. Babeuf was executed on 27 May 1797. Others survived, including Filippo Michele Buonarotti (1761–1830) who published an account of the conspiracy, *Babeuf's Conspiracy for Equality* (1828). The Directory referred to was a group of five who had seized power with the aid of Napoleon Bonaparte's soldiers in the autumn of 1795.

ANALYSIS OF THE DOCTRINE OF BABEUF

PROSCRIBED BY THE EXECUTIVE DIRECTORY FOR
HAVING TOLD THE TRUTH!

ARTICLE I

Nature has given to each individual an equal right to the enjoyment of all the goods of life.

PROOFS

Drawn from the discussion to which this piece gave rise.

1. Previously to their first coming together, or forming societies, all men were equally masters of the productions which nature spread with profusion around them.

2. Finding themselves together upon an uncultivated land, what could have established amongst them the inequality of this right? Is it their natural difference? But they have all the same organs and the same wants. Is it the dependence of some upon others? But no one was sufficiently strong to make servants of the rest, who might disperse on the slightest occasion for discontent; and the advantage of mutual succours, and of co-operative benevolence, rendered it necessary for all to respect in others, the rights with which they felt themselves invested by nature. Is it the ferocity of their hearts? But compassion is the immediate consequence of their organization, and ferocity springs only from the exasperation of the passions. Is it an inborn penchant for humiliation and servitude? But the sight of distinctions is even for the most savage beings a painful sensation – a source of jealousy and hatred.

3. The forgetfulness of this equality has introduced amongst mankind –
    False ideas of happiness;
    Perversion of the passions;
    Deterioration and decay of the species;
    Violences, troubles, wars;
    The tyranny of some, and the oppression of others;
Institutions, civil, political, and religious, which, by consecrating injustice, end with dissolving societies, after having for a long time distracted and torn them to pieces.

The sight of distinctions, of pomp, and of pleasures enjoyed only by a few, was, and ever will be, an inexhaustible source of torments and uneasiness to the mass. It is given to only a few philosophers to preserve themselves from corruption, and moderation is a blessing which the vulgar can no longer appreciate, when once their thoughts have been weaned from it. Do certain citizens create to themselves new factitious wants, and introduce into their enjoyments refinements unknown to the multitude? Simplicity is no longer loved, happiness ceases to consist in an active life and tranquil soul, distinctions and pleasures become the supreme of goods, nobody is content with his station, and all seek in vain for that happiness, the entrance of which into society is debarred by inequality ...

If equality of goods be a consequence of that of our organs and wants – if public and private calamities – if the ruin of societies – are inevitable effects of all criminal attempts against it, this equality is, therefore, a *natural right*.

ARTICLE II

The end of society is to defend this equality, often assailed by the strong and wicked in the state of nature; and to augment, by the co-operation of all, the common enjoyments of all ...

ARTICLE III

Nature has imposed on each person the obligation to work; nobody could, without crime, evade his share of the common labour.

PROOFS

Labour is for each a precept of nature.
    1.   Because man, isolated in the deserts, could not, without some kind of labour, procure himself subsistence.
    2.   Because the activity which moderate labour occasions, is for man a source of health and amusement.
    This obligation could not be weakened by society, either for all or for each of its members.
    1.   Because the preservation of society depends upon it.
    2.   Because the labour of each is the least possible only when all participate of it.

ARTICLE IV

Labour and enjoyments ought to be common.

EXPLANATION

That is to say, all ought to bear an equal portion of labour, and derive from it an equal quantity of enjoyments ...

But it may be objected – What will become of those productions of industry, which are the fruits of time and genius? Is it not to be feared that, being no longer better recompensed than other descriptions of work, they will be altogether extinguished to the injury of society? Sophism! It is to the love of glory, not to the thirst for riches, that we have been at all times indebted for the efforts of genius. Every day do millions of poor soldiers devote themselves to death for the honour of serving the caprices of a cruel master; and shall we doubt of the prodigies that might be operated on the human heart by the sentiment of happiness, the love of equality and country, and by the noble incentives of a wise policy? ...

ARTICLE V

There is oppression wherever one part of society is exhausted by labour, and in want of everything, whilst the other part wallows in abundance, without doing any work at all ...

PROOFS

To oppress signifies either to restrain the faculties of a person, or to unjustly augment his burdens; that is precisely what inequality does, by diminishing the enjoyments of him whose duties it aggravates.

ARTICLE VI

Nobody could, without crime, exclusively appropriate to himself the goods of the earth or of industry.

EXPLANATION AND PROOFS

If we demonstrate that inequality has no other cause than this exclusive appropriation, we shall have demonstrated the crime of those who introduce the distinction of *mine* and *thine* (*meum* and *tuum*).

From the moment lands were divided arose the exclusive right of property. Then each person became absolute master of all he could derive from the fields which had devolved to him, and from whatever industry he could exercise. It is probable that men, devoted to the arts of first necessity, were at the same time excluded from all territorial possession, which they had not time to cultivate. Thus one portion of the people remained masters of the things necessary to existence, whilst the rest had only a right to such salaries, or wages, as the former chose to pay them. Nevertheless, this change did not involve a very sensible one in the distribution of enjoyments, so long as the number of those receiving wages did not exceed that of the possessors of the soil. But as soon as natural accidents, acting conjointly with the economy or address of some, with the prodigality or incapacity of others, had concentrated the territorial properties in a small number of families, the men of wages became vastly more numerous than the proprietors, and, as a natural consequence, were utterly at their mercy. The possessors, proud of their opulence, soon reduced the labourers to a life of privations.

From this revolution date the sinister effects of inequality, developed in the first Article.

Docment 6.6

John Stuart Mill on the Meanings of Justice

John Stuart Mill (1806–73) (see introduction to document 5.7) sought to acknowledge the role played by sentiment but also to set limits to it. The extract is taken from his *Utilitarianism* (1861).

Let us … advert successively to the various modes of action, the arrangements of human affairs, which are classed, by universal or widely spread opinion, as Just or as Unjust …

In the first place, it is mostly considered unjust to deprive any one of his personal liberty, his property or any other thing which belongs to him by law …

Secondly, the legal rights of which he is deprived, may be rights which *ought* not to have belonged to him; in other words the law which confers on him these rights, may be a bad law. When it is so, or when … it is supposed to be so, opinions will differ as to the justice of infringing it …

Thirdly, it is universally considered just that each person should obtain that (whether good or evil) which he *deserves* …

Fourthly, it is confessedly unjust to *break faith* with any one …

Fifthly, it is, by universal admission, inconsistent with justice to be *partial*; to show favour or preference to one person over another, in matters to which favour and preference do not properly apply …

Among so many diverse applications of the term Justice, which yet is not regarded as ambiguous, it is a matter of some difficulty to seize the mental link that holds them together, and on which the moral sentiment adhering to the term depends …

When we think that a person is bound in justice to do a thing, it is an ordinary form of language to say, that he ought to be compelled to do it. We should be gratified to see the obligation enforced by anybody who had the power. If we see that its enforcement by law would be inexpedient, we lament the impossibility, we consider the impunity given to injustice as an evil, and strive to make amends for it by bringing a strong expression of our own and the public disapprobation to bear on the offender.

Thus the idea of legal constraint is still the generating idea of the notion of justice …

This, therefore, being the characteristic difference which marks off, not justice, but morality in general, from the remaining provinces of Expediency and Worthiness; the character is still to be sought which distinguishes justice from other branches of morality. Now it is known that ethical writers divide moral duties into two classes, denoted by the ill-chosen expressions, duties of perfect and imperfect obligation; the latter being those in which, though the act is obligatory, the particular occasions of performing it are left to our choice; as in the case of charity or beneficence, which we are indeed bound to practise, but not towards any definite person, nor at any prescribed time. In the more precise language of philosophic jurists, duties of perfect obligation are those duties in virtue of which a correlative *right* resides in some person or persons; duties of imperfect obligation are those moral obligations which do not give birth to any right … It seems to me that this feature in the case – a right in some person, correlative to the moral obligation – constitutes the specific difference between justice, and generosity or beneficence. Justice implies something which it is not only right to do, and wrong not to do, but which some individual person can claim from us as his moral right …

Having thus endeavoured to determine the distinctive elements which enter into the composition of the idea of justice, we are ready to enter on the inquiry, whether the feeling, which accompanies the idea, is attached to it by a special dispensation of nature, or whether it could have grown up, by any known laws, out of the idea itself; and in particular, whether it can have originated in considerations of general expediency.

I conceive that the sentiment itself does not arise from anything which would commonly, or correctly, be termed an idea of expediency; but that though the sentiment does not, whatever is moral in it does …

The sentiment of justice, in that one of its elements which consist of the desire to punish, is thus, I conceive, the natural feeling of retaliation or vengeance, rendered by intellect and sympathy applicable to those injuries, that is, to those hurts, which wound us through, or in common with, society at large …

To recapitulate: the idea of justice supposes two things; a rule of conduct, and a sentiment which sanctions the rule. The first must be supposed common to all mankind, and intended for their good. The other (the sentiment) is a desire that punishment be suffered by those who infringe the rule. There is involved, in addition, the conception of some definite person who suffers by the infringement; whose rights … are violated by it.

Karl Marx, *Critique of the Gotha Programme*

In the *Critique of the Gotha Programme* (1875) Marx attacked the doctrinal basis for the unification of two German socialist parties, the General Association of German Workers (ADAV) and the Social-Democratic Workers' Party (SDAP) which took place in the town of Gotha. Ferdinand Lasalle (1825–64) had founded the ADAV in 1863. Although killed in a duel in the following year, his ideas continued to be influential. In the extract Marx ridiculed Lasalle's economic ideas and, typically, denied that bourgeois society could realize its own ideals.

Labour is the source of all wealth and culture, and since useful labour can only be performed in and through society, all members of society have an equal right to the undiminished proceeds of labour ...

What is 'just' distribution?

Does not the bourgeoisie claim that the present system of distribution is 'just'? And given the present mode of production is it not, in fact, the only 'just' system of distribution? Are economic relations regulated by legal concepts of right or is the opposite not the case, that legal relations spring from economic ones? Do not the socialist sectarians themselves have the most varied notions of 'just' distribution?

To discover what we are meant to understand by the phrase 'just distribution' as used here we must take the opening paragraph and this one together. The latter presupposes a society in which 'the instruments of labour are common property and the whole of labour is regulated on a cooperative basis' and from the opening paragraph we learn that 'all members of society have an equal right to the undiminished proceeds of labour'.

'All members of society'? Including people who do not work? Then what remains of the 'undiminished proceeds of labour'? Only the working members of society? Then what remains of the 'equal right' of all members of society?

'All members of society' and 'equal right', however, are obviously mere phrases. The heart of the matter is that in this communist society every worker is supposed to receive the 'undiminished' Lassallean 'proceeds of labour'.

If we start by taking 'proceeds of labour' to mean the product of labour, then the cooperative proceeds of labour are the *total social product*.

From this the following must now be deducted:

Firstly: cover to replace the means of production used up.

Secondly: an additional portion for the expansion of production.

Thirdly: a reserve or insurance fund in case of accidents, disruption caused by natural calamities, etc.

These deductions from the 'undiminished proceeds of labour' are an economic necessity and their magnitude will be determined by the means and forces available. They can partly be calculated by reference to probability, but on no account by reference to justice.

There remains the other part of the total product, designed to serve as means of consumption.

But before this is distributed to individuals the following further deductions must be made:

Firstly: the general costs of all administration not directly appertaining to production.

This part will, from the outset, be very significantly limited in comparison with the present society. It will diminish commensurately with the development of the new society.

Secondly: the amount set aside for needs communally satisfied, such as schools, health services, etc.

This part will, from the outset, be significantly greater than in the present society. It will grow commensurately with the development of the new society.

Thirdly: a fund for people unable to work, etc., in short, for what today comes under so-called official poor relief.

Only now do we come to that 'distribution' which, under the influence of the Lassalleans, is the only thing considered by this narrow-minded programme, namely that part of the means of consumption which is distributed among the individual producers within the cooperative.

The 'undiminished proceeds of labour' have meanwhile already been quietly 'diminished', although as a member of society the producer still receives, directly or indirectly, what is withheld from him as a private individual.

Just as the phrase 'undiminished proceeds of labour' has vanished, the phrase 'proceeds of labour' now disappears altogether.

Within the cooperative society based on common ownership of the means of production the producers do not exchange their products; similarly, the labour spent on the products no longer appears *as the value* of these products, possessed by them as a material characteristic, for now, in contrast to capitalist society, individual pieces of labour are no longer merely indirectly, but directly, a component part of the total labour. The phrase 'proceeds of labour', which even today is too ambiguous to be of any value, thus loses any meaning whatsoever.

We are dealing here with a communist society, not as it has *developed* on its own foundations, but on the contrary, just as it *emerges* from capitalist society. In every respect, economically, morally, intellectually, it is thus still stamped with the birth-marks of the old society from whose womb it has emerged. Accordingly, the individual producer gets back from society – after the deductions – exactly what he has given it. What he has given it is his individual quantum of labour. For instance, the social working day consists of the sum of the individual hours of work. The individual labour time of the individual producer thus constitutes his contribution to the social working day, his share of it.

Society gives him a certificate stating that he has done such and such an amount of work (after the labour done for the communal fund has been deducted), and with this certificate he can withdraw from the social supply of means of consumption as much as costs an equivalent amount of labour. The same amount of labour he has given to society in one form, he receives back in another.

Clearly, the same principle is at work here as that which regulates the exchange of commodities as far as this is an exchange of equal values. Content and form have changed because under the new conditions no one can contribute anything except his labour and conversely nothing can pass into the ownership of individuals except individual means of consumption. The latter's distribution among individual producers, however, is governed by the same principle as the exchange of commodity equivalents: a given amount of labour in one form is exchanged for the same amount in another.

Hence *equal right* is here still – in principle – a *bourgeois right*, although principle and practice are no longer at loggerheads, while the exchange of equivalents in commodity exchange only exists *on the average* and not in the individual case.

In spite of such progress this *equal right* still constantly suffers a bourgeois limitation. The right of the producers is *proportional* to the labour they do; the equality consists in the fact that measurement is *by the same standard*, labour. One person, however, may be physically and intellectually superior to another and thus be able to do more labour in the same space of time or work for a longer period. To serve as a measure labour must therefore be determined by duration or intensity, otherwise it ceases to be a standard. This *equal* right is an unequal right for unequal labour. It does not acknowledge any class distinctions, because everyone is just a worker like everyone else, but it gives tacit recognition to a worker's individual endowment and hence productive capacity as natural privileges. *This right is thus in its content one of inequality, just like any other right.* A right can by its nature only consist in the application of an equal standard, but unequal individuals (and they would not be different individuals if they were not unequal) can only be measured by the same standard if they are looked at from the same aspect, if they are grasped from one *particular* side, e.g., if in the present case they are regarded *only as workers* and nothing else is seen in them, everything else is ignored. Further: one worker is married, another is not; one has more children than another, etc., etc. Thus, with the same work performance and hence the same share of the social consumption fund, one will in fact be receiving more than another, one will be richer than another, etc. If all these defects were to be avoided rights would have to be unequal rather than equal.

Such defects, however, are inevitable in the first phase of communist society, given the specific form in which it has emerged after prolonged birth-pangs from capitalist society. Right can never rise above the economic structure of a society and its contingent cultural development.

In a more advanced phase of communist society, when the enslaving subjugation of individuals to the division of labour, and thereby the antithesis between intellectual and physical labour, have disappeared; when labour is no longer just a means of keeping alive but has itself become a vital need; when the all-round development of individuals has also increased their productive powers and all the springs of cooperative wealth flow more abundantly – only then can society wholly cross the narrow horizon of bourgeois right and inscribe on its banner: From each according to his abilities, to each according to his needs!

Document 6.8

R.H. Tawney, *Equality*

Richard Henry Tawney (1880–1962) was a journalist and academic. He joined the London School of Economics in 1920 and remained there until his retirement. Tawney wrote several works on economic history, including *Religion and the Rise of Capitalism* (1926). The extract is from his book *Equality* which went through several editions. In it he put forward a broad view of social justice, emphasizing a range of factors in addition to the simple distribution of material goods.

It is obvious, indeed, that, as things are to-day, no redistribution of wealth would bring general affluence, and that statisticians are within their rights in making merry with the idea that the equalization of incomes would make everyone rich. But, though riches are a good, they are not, nevertheless, the only good; and because greater production, which is concerned with the commodities to be consumed, is clearly important, it does not follow that greater equality, which is concerned with the relations between the human beings who consume them, is not important also. It is obvious, again, that the word 'Equality' possesses more than one meaning, and that the controversies surrounding it arise partly, at least, because the same term is employed with different connotations. Thus it may either purport to state a fact, or convey the expression of an ethical judgment. On the one hand, it may affirm that men are, on the whole, very similar in their natural endowments of character and intelligence. On the other hand, it may assert that, while they differ profoundly as individuals in capacity and character, they are equally entitled as human beings to consideration and respect, and that the well-being of a society is likely to be increased if it so plans its organization that, whether their powers are great or small, all its members may be equally enabled to make the best of such powers as they possess.

If made in the first sense, the assertion of human equality is clearly untenable. It is a piece of mythology against which irresistible evidence has been accumulated by biologists and psychologists.

The acceptance of that conclusion, nevertheless, makes a smaller breach in equalitarian doctrines than is sometimes supposed, for such doctrines have rarely been based on a denial of it …

When Arnold, who was an inspector of schools as well as a poet, and who, whatever his failings, was not prone to demagogy, wrote 'choose equality', he did not suggest, it may be suspected, that all children appeared to him to be equally clever, but that a nation acts unwisely in stressing heavily distinctions based on birth or money.

Few men have been more acutely sensitive than Mill to the importance of encouraging the widest possible diversities of mind and taste. In arguing that 'the best state for human nature is that in which, while no one is poor, no one desires to be richer', and urging that social policy should be directed to increasing equality, he did not intend to convey that it should suppress varieties of individual genius and character, but that it was only in a society marked by a large measure of economic equality that such varieties were likely to find their full expression and due need of appreciation ...

The equality which all these thinkers emphasize as desirable is not equality of capacity or attainment, but of circumstances, institutions, and manner of life. The inequality which they deplore is not inequality of personal gifts, but of the social and economic environment. They are concerned, not with a biological phenomenon, but with a spiritual relation and the conduct to be based on it. Their view, in short, is that, because men are men, social institutions – property rights, and the organization of industry, and the system of public health and education – should be planned, as far as is possible, to emphasize and strengthen, not the class differences which divide, but the common humanity which unites, them ...

It is true, again, that human beings have, except as regards certain elementary, though still sadly neglected, matters of health and development, different requirements, and that these different requirements can be met satisfactorily only by varying forms of provision. But equality of provision is not identity of provision. It is to be achieved, not by treating different needs in the same way, but by devoting equal care to ensuring that they are met in the different ways most appropriate to them, as is done by a doctor who prescribes different regimens for different constitutions, or a teacher who develops different types of intelligence by different curricula. The more anxiously, indeed, a society endeavours to secure equality of consideration for all its members, the greater will be the differentiation of treatment which, when once their common human needs have been met, it accords to the special needs of different groups and individuals among them.

It is true, finally, that some men are inferior to others in respect of their intellectual endowments, and it is possible – though the truth of the possibility has not yet been satisfactorily established – that the same is true of certain classes. It does not, however, follow from this fact that such individuals or classes should receive less consideration than others, or should be treated as inferior in respect of such matters as legal status, or health, or economic arrangements, which are within the control of the community ...

It is the confusion of a judgment of fact with a judgment of value – a confusion like that which was satirized by Montesquieu when he wrote, in his ironical defence of slavery: 'The creatures in question are black from head to foot, and their noses are so flat that it is almost impossible to pity them. It is not to be supposed that God, an all-wise Being, can have lodged a soul – still less a good soul – in a body completely black'.

Everyone recognizes the absurdity of such an argument when it is applied to matters within his personal knowledge and professional competence. Everyone realizes that, in order to justify inequalities of circumstance or opportunity by reference to differences of personal quality, it is necessary, as Professor Ginsberg observes, to show that the differences in question are relevant to the inequalities. Everyone now sees, for example, that it is not a valid argument against women's suffrage to urge, as used to be urged not so long ago, that women are physically weaker than men, since physical strength is not relevant to the question of the ability to exercise the franchise, or a valid argument in favour of slavery that some men are less intelligent than others, since it is not certain that slavery is the most suitable penalty for lack of intelligence.

Not everyone, however, is so quick to detect the fallacy when it is expressed in general terms. It is still possible, for example, for one eminent statesman to ridicule the demand for a diminution of economic inequalities on the ground that every mother knows that her children are not equal, without reflecting whether it is the habit of mothers to lavish care on the strong and neglect the delicate; and for another to dismiss the suggestion that greater economic equality is desirable, for the reason, apparently, that men are naturally unequal. It is probable, however, that the first does not think that the fact that some children are born with good digestions, and others with bad, is a reason for supplying good food to the former and bad food to the latter, rather than for giving to both food which is equal in quality but different in kind, and that the second does not suppose that the natural inequality of man makes legal equality of contemptible principle
...

It is the fact that, in spite of their varying characters and capacities, men possess in their common humanity a quality which is worth cultivating, and that a community is most likely to make the most of that quality if it takes it into account in planning its economic organization and social institutions – if it stresses lightly differences of wealth and birth and social position, and establishes on firm foundations institutions which meet common needs, and are a source of common enlightenment and common enjoyment. The individual differences of which so much is made, they would have said, will always survive, and they are to be welcomed, not regretted. But their existence is no reason for not seeking to establish the largest possible measure of equality of environment, and circumstance, and opportunity. On the contrary, it is a reason for redoubling our efforts to establish it, in order to ensure that these diversities of gifts may come to fruition.

It is true, indeed, that even such equality, though the conditions on which it depends are largely within human control, will continue to elude us. The important thing, however, is not that it should be completely attained, but that it should be sincerely sought. What matters to the health of society is the objective towards which its face is set, and to suggest that it is immaterial in which direction it moves, because, whatever the direction, the goal must always elude it, is not scientific, but irrational. It is like using the impossibility of absolute cleanliness as a pretext for rolling in a manure heap, or denying the importance of honesty because no one can be wholly honest.

Document 6.9

John Rawls on Two Principles of Justice

John Rawls (b. 1921) is an American political philosopher. His *Theory of Justice* (1971) marked a turning point in postwar political philosophy. Many of the major texts of the past two decades have been, in part at least, attempts to develop alternatives to Rawls' conception. The extract is taken from 'Distributive Justice' (1967).

We arrive at the principle of utility in a natural way: by this principle a society is rightly ordered, and hence just, when its institutions are arranged so as to realize the greatest sum of satisfactions.

The striking feature of this principle of utility is that it does not matter, except indirectly, how this sum of satisfactions is distributed among individuals ... The precepts of justice are derivative from the one end of attaining the greatest net balance of satisfactions. There is no reason why the greater gains of some should not compensate for the lesser losses of others; or why the violation of the liberty of a few might not be made right by a greater good shared by many. It simply happens, at least under most conditions, that the greatest sum of advantages is not generally achieved in this way. From the standpoint of utility the strictness of common-sense notions of justice has a certain usefulness, but as a philosophical doctrine it is irrational.

If, then, we believe that as a matter of principle each member of society has an inviolability founded on justice which even the welfare of everyone else cannot over-ride, and that a loss of freedom for some is not made right by a greater sum of satisfactions enjoyed by many, we shall have to look to another account of the principles of justice ...

The two principles of justice which we shall discuss may be formulated as follows: first, each person engaged in an institution or affected by it has an equal right to the most extensive liberty compatible with a like liberty for all; and second, inequalities as defined by the institutional structure or fostered by it are arbitrary unless it is reasonable to expect that they will work out to everyone's advantage and provided that the positions and offices to which they attach or from which they may be gained are open to all ...

Thus consider the chief problem of distributive justice, that concerning the distribution of wealth as it affects the life-prospects of those starting out in the various income groups. The income classes define the relevant representative men from which the social system is to be judged. Now, a son of a member of the entrepreneurial class (in a capitalist society) has a better prospect than a son of an unskilled labourer. This will be true, it seems, even when the social inequalities which presently exist are removed and the two men are of equal talent and ability; the inequality cannot be done away with as long as something like the family is maintained. What, then, can justify this inequality in life-prospects? According to the second principle it is justified only if it is to the advantage of the representative man who is worst off, in this case the representative unskilled labourer.

Robert Nozick, *Anarchy, State and Utopia*

Robert Nozick is an American political philosopher whose ideas have been widely cited by critics of the welfare state. The extract is from his major work, *Anarchy, State and Utopia* (1974).

When end-result principles of distributive justice are built into the legal structure of a society, they (as do most patterned principles) give each citizen an enforceable claim to some portion of the total social product; that is, to some portion of the sum total of the individually and jointly made products. This total product is produced by individuals labouring, using means of production others have saved to bring into existence, by people organizing production or creating means to produce new things or things in a new way. It is on this batch of individual activities that patterned distributional principles give each individual an enforceable claim. Each person has a claim to the activities and the products of other persons, independently of whether the other persons enter into particular relationships that give rise to these claims, and independently of whether they voluntarily take these claims upon themselves, in charity or in exchange for something.

Whether it is done through taxation on wages over a certain amount, or through the seizure of profits, or through there being a big *social pot* so that it's not clear what's coming from where and what's going where, patterned principles of distributive justice involve appropriating the actions of others. Seizing the results of someone's labour is equivalent to seizing hours from him and directing him to carry on various activities. If people force you to do certain work, or unrewarded work, for a certain period of time, they decide what you are to do and what purposes your work is to serve apart from your decisions. This process whereby they take this decision from you makes them a *part-owner* of you; it gives them a property right in you. Just as having such partial control and power of decisions, by right, over an animal or inanimate object would be to have a property right in it.

End-state and most patterned principles of distributive justice institute (partial) ownership by others of people and their actions. These principles involve a shift from the classical liberals' notion of self-ownership to a notion of (partial) property rights in *other* people ...

The major objection to speaking of everyone's having a right to various things such as equality of opportunity, life, and so on, and enforcing this right, is that these 'rights' require a substructure of things and materials and actions; and *other* people may have rights and entitlements over these. No one has a right to something whose realization requires certain uses of things and activities that other people have rights and entitlements over. Other people's rights and entitlements to *particular things* (*that* pencil, *their* body, and so on) and how they choose to exercise these rights and entitlements fix the external environment of any given individual and the means that will be available to him …

There are particular rights over particular things held by particular persons, and particular rights to reach agreements with others, *if* you and they together can acquire the means to reach an agreement. (No one has to supply you with a telephone so that you may reach an agreement with another.) No rights exist in conflict with this substructure of particular rights … .The particular rights over things fill the space of rights, leaving no room for general rights to be in a certain material condition.

Document 6.11

Michael Walzer, *Spheres of Justice*

Michael Walzer (born 1935) is an American political theorist and editor of *Dissent*. Walzer has written on several topics, including *Just and Unjust Wars*. The extract is from his *Spheres of Justice* (1983). His denial that there is a single standard of justice explicitly contradicts Rawls' account.

There is no single standard. But there are standards, (roughly knowable even when they are also controversial) for every social good and every distributive sphere in every particular society; and these standards are often violated …

In fact the violations are systematic … For all the complexity of their distributive arrangements, most societies are organized on what we might think of as a social gold standard: one good or one set of goods is dominant and determinative of value in all the spheres of distribution. And that good or set of goods is commonly monopolized whenever a single man or woman, a monarch in the world of value – or a group of men and women, oligarchs – successfully hold it against all rivals. Dominance describes a way of using social goods that isn't limited by their intrinsic meanings or that shapes those meanings in its own image. Monopoly describes a way of owning or controlling social goods in order to exploit their dominance … Physical strength, familial reputation, religious or political office, landed wealth, capital, technical knowledge: each of these, in different historical periods, has been dominant; and each of them has been monopolized by some group of men and women. And then all good things come to those who have the one best thing. Possess that one, and the others come in train. Or, to change the metaphor, a dominant good is converted into another good, into many others, in accordance with what often appears to be a natural process but is in fact magical, a kind of social alchemy …

History reveals no single dominant good and no naturally dominant good, but only different kinds of magic and competing bands of magicians …

To convert one good into another, when there is no intrinsic connection between the two, is to invade the sphere where another company of men and women properly rules. Monopoly is not inappropriate within the spheres. There is nothing wrong, for example, with the grip that persuasive and helpful men and women (politicians) establish on political power. But the use of political power to gain access to other goods is a tyrannical use. Thus an old description of tyranny is generalized: princes become tyrants, according to medieval writers, when they seize the property or invade the family of their subjects. In political life – but more widely too – the dominance of goods makes for the domination of people.

The regime of complex equality is the opposite of tyranny. It establishes a set of relationships such that domination is impossible. In formal terms, complex equality means that no citizen's standing in one sphere or with regard to one social good can be undercut by his standing in some other sphere, with regard to some other good. Thus, citizen X may be chosen over citizen Y for political office, and then the two of them will be unequal in the sphere of politics. But they will not be unequal generally so long as X's office gives him no advantages over Y in any other sphere – superior medical care, access to better schools for his children, entrepreneurial opportunities, and so on. So long as office is not a dominant good, is not generally convertible, office holders will stand, or at least can stand in a relation of equality to the men and women they govern ...

The critique of dominance and domination points toward an open-ended distributive principle. *No social good X should be distributed to men and women who possess some other good Y merely because they possess Y and without regard to the meaning of X.*

QUESTIONS FOR DISCUSSION

1. Is merit or need the best guide to justice?
2. What is the relationship between justice and equality?
3. Why do people act justly?
4. Should the search for justice be guided by considerations of utility?
5. Do you agree with Walzer's approach to justice?

NOTES

1 For a response to the advocates of equality see William Letwin (ed.), *Against Equality* (London, Macmillan, 1983).
2 Brian Barry, *Theories of Justice* (London, Harvester-Wheatsheaf, 1989), p. 3.
3 Nozick attempts to solve these problems. For a criticism of his efforts see M.M. Goldsmith, 'The Entitlement Theory of Justice Considered', *Political Studies*, Vol. 27(1979), pp. 578–93.
4 From this Barry argues that what matters is the element of impartiality involved. See his *Theories of Justice*, pp. 163–8.
5 A different objection is put by David Miller who claims that Utilitarianism is an aggregative not a distributional principle. The former 'refers to the total amount of good enjoyed by a particular group, whereas a distributive principle refers to the share of that good which different members of the group have for themselves'. *Social Justice* (Oxford, Clarendon Press, 1976), p. 19.

FURTHER READING

The chapter on 'Social Justice and Equality' in Barbara Goodwin, *Using Political ideas* (Chichester, Wiley and Sons, 1987: 2nd edition) offers a good starting point. Giorgio del Vecchio, *Justice. An Historical and Philosophical Essay* (Edinburgh, Edinburgh University Press, 1952) emphasizes the transition from ancient to modern conceptions. Hugo M. Bredlau (ed.), *Justice and Equality* (Englewood Cliffs NJ, Prentice Hall, 1971) has a useful introduction and extensive extracts. David Miller, *Social Justice* (Oxford, Clarendon Press, 1976) provides a more analytical approach. Julia Annas, *An Introduction to Plato's Republic* (Oxford, Clarendon Press, 1981) gives a systematic account of the *Republic* as a work on justice. Brian Barry, *Theories of Justice* (London, Harvester Wheatsheaf, 1989) argues for the centrality of Hume's insight. For socialism and equality see Chapter 8 of R.N. Berki, *Socialism* (London, Dent, 1975). More specialized accounts of Marx and justice are provided by the contributions of Allen W. Wood and Ziyad I. Husami to Marshall Cohen, Thomas Nagel and Thomas Scanlon (eds), *Marx, Justice and History* (Princeton

NJ, Princeton University Press, 1980). The three recent texts which have acquired the status of classic works are John Rawls, *A Theory of Justice* (Cambridge MA, Harvard University Press, 1971), Robert Nozick, *Anarchy, State and Utopia* (Oxford, Basil Blackwell, 1974) and Michael Walzer, *Spheres of Justice* (Oxford, Blackwell, 1983). See also Alastair MacIntyre, *Whose Justice? Which Rationality?* (London, Duckworth, 1988).

7

PROPERTY

INTRODUCTION

The question of property is one which has attracted very wide debate in political thought. Thinkers who approach it from completely different viewpoints have assumed that it is one of the most significant determinants of the conditions of life, liberty and the pursuit of happiness At one end of the spectrum of political and economic interpretation it has been regarded as one of the most basic 'natural rights', essential to human dignity and freedom (see document 7.5). At the other, it has been condemned as an evil, as the most important single instrument of the oppression of the many by the few. For thinkers such as the seventeenth-century English agrarian communist Gerrard Winstanley (see document 5.2), it is the common cultivation of the land and common use of goods which are the natural human condition. A key question in political thought and analysis is this relationship between property and political power (see in particular the extracts from Harrington, document 7.4, Rousseau, document 7.6, and the observations from a conservative viewpoint by Edmund Burke, document 7.7, and Sir Walter Scott, document 7.8. Consider, too, the comments in Daniel Webster's speech, document 7.9).

The political significance of property is unequivocally evident in ancient Greece and Rome. It could hardly be otherwise in slave-owning societies. The most striking development of the concept of property occurred in Roman law where property owners had unlimited right to use and abuse their property. Ironically, this right was so unrestricted that many issues which are considered as matters of property law in contemporary societies, for example the relationship between owner and tenant, had to be dealt with in terms of other concepts, in this case, in terms of obligation.[1]

Medieval conceptions of property were heavily marked by the idea that men were not the absolute, unrestricted owners of the earth but stewards responsible to God. Equally important was the idea that private property, although justifiable, was the product of man's sin. The earth had, according to this conception, originally been held in common with all men having a right to use the fruits of the earth. It was only the avaricious nature of men that necessitated the institution of private property. Medieval conceptions were further complicated by the fact that property rights were embedded in a mosaic of social and political relationships. Typical of this outlook was the use of one word, *dominium*, to refer to both property and political authority, whereas our contemporary usage restricts dominion to political authority.

The absence of any absolute right of ownership combined with the idea that common ownership was the natural condition meant that property rights did not necessarily take priority. Hence, Aquinas concluded that in times of famine the starving had a right to take the goods, whether openly or secretly. This did not constitute theft. This conception lasted well into the modern era and was only gradually transformed. Whereas the medieval conception granted the poor a right to the means of subsistence, the modern conception recognized the need of the poor but sought to meet it in a different way. The rich it was claimed had a moral obligation to act charitably in times of famine. The claim of the poor was transformed into the unenforceable obligation of the rich.

The transition from the original feudal conception of property was, of course, a prolonged process. It is now increasingly argued that this transition occurred earlier than was previously thought and is identifiable, in some respects, at the end of the thirteenth century. In parts of Europe at least people who were previously thought to be mere tenants had acquired rights to alienate (sell) land and to bequeath it as they saw fit. They had acquired two key rights which we now associate with the idea of property.

It is, however, the sixteenth and seventeenth centuries which usually form the reference point for modern debates about property. A key figure here is John Locke. Locke's justification of property formed part of his broader argument that men had rights prior to the formation of governments and that government was instituted in order to protect these rights. Locke's argument was that men acquired property by mixing their labour with it. He did understand this broadly since 'the Grass my Horse has bit; the Turfs my Servant has cut' are also mine.

The importance of Locke's argument arises in part from the fact that he clearly ruled out two alternative justifications of property. The first of these is that property titles are derived from political society. Property, according to this conception, is entirely artificial. The second is the idea that private property is justified only by the consent of others. Advocates of this view usually started from the assumption that the earth had originally been held in common and men had agreed to divide it up.

The discussion of the origins of property played a small, if important, part in Locke's overall argument. The idea that one owned what one had created by working upon the natural world was, however, an attractive one. It was to be used by both defenders and critics of established property relationships. Socialists agreed that one had a right to what one had produced and then went on to claim that capitalists and landlords produced nothing. The conclusion was that the capitalist's profit and the landlord's rent ultimately consisted of things that labourers had produced.

The socialists, of course, were not motivated by the intricacies of the justification of property but by the vast disparities in wealth. Historically, perhaps, the most powerful and practically influential justification of private property has been a religious philosophy which not only accepts the inequalities of property but which regards them as divinely sanctioned. John Calvin, for instance, saw the accumulation of wealth as a sign of the grace of God. But the Christian tradition has embraced radical as well as conservative accounts of property (see, for instance the extract from Acts Chapter 4 which has been taken by some as an endorsement of Christian communism (document 7.2).

Political philosophies demanding the complete equalization or abolition of private property have been formulated from the early stages of Greek civilization, through Sir Thomas More to the socialist and communist ideas of the nineteenth and twentieth centuries. Marxist Communism has been among the most radical of the anti-property theories, postulating the abolition of private property as a consequence of dialectical historical necessity.

Even those who have not seen the abolition of private property as desirable, have recognized the link between property and the political system. The link has been asserted by figures as diverse as the seventeenth-century republican James Harrington and the eighteenth-century conservative Edmund Burke (see documents 7.4 and 7.7). In traditional conservative ideology, an essential link between property, family and inheritance has recurrently been emphasized. Property has been construed as an indispensable element in social order.

The link between property and political power is strikingly evident in arguments about the extent of the franchise. On the one hand, it has been argued that only those with property have a stake in the country and can be trusted to act responsibly. Only the propertied, therefore, should have the vote. On the other hand, it has been argued that precisely because the propertyless will be tempted to violate the property rights of the wealthy, political stability requires that either the majority or all should be property owners. The underlying logic is the same in both cases. Property and full citizenship are linked. The conclusions, however, differ. According to one conception the propertyless are simply excluded from political power. According to the other conception the distribution of property has to be adjusted in the interests of the political order.

The link between citizenship and property is not the only one that has been made. From the standard liberal perspective private property is indissolubly bound up with liberty and is seen as an essential element in the freedom of individual lives from state control. Yet classical liberals have not always been staunch defenders of private property. John Stuart Mill, for example, advocated severe restrictions upon the right of inheritance and expressed sympathy for some socialist experiments. One of the characteristics of his own society to which Mill took exception, was the discrepancy between work and property, effort and reward. Property and inequality were justified by merit. Where people did not deserve the wealth they possessed their title was seen as suspect.

An alternative strategy has been to argue that property is justified in the interests of the development of the individual. This conception has been more influential in continental Europe than in the Anglo-Saxon world. The key to it is the belief that there is 'something intrinsically satisfying about *work*; work is a characteristic form of human self-expression, and its reward is not to be found only or primarily in the things it makes available for consumption, but in the nature of the activity itself.'[2] To take away the products of someone's work then becomes more than just robbing them of possessions. It amounts, it is argued, to robbing them of their identity as human beings. Again, this basic argument has been used to defend both private property, by, for example the German philosopher G.W.F. Hegel, and to argue for its abolition, by Karl Marx.

For much of the last century the argument about private property has been conducted predominately in terms of its efficiency. Defenders of private property have argued that the capitalist economic system is superior to all others in terms of generating wealth. They have added, by way of reassurance, that this wealth may, and indeed should, be unequally distributed, but the poorer members of society will still get more than they would under any other system. Critics of private property have pointed to the waste of capitalist systems, to economic crises and unemployment to argue for the abolition or restriction of private property.

The number of people calling for the wholesale abolition of private property has been rather small, at least outside societies dominated by Communist parties. A more typical standpoint has been the argument for the extension of state control over the economy, that is for nationalization. Yet, as C.B. Macpherson (document 7.15) argues, state ownership and private ownership have a striking similarity. Both entail the right to exclude people from the use of the resources which are owned by the private individual or the state corporation.

Against this right of exclusion Macpherson sets a right of inclusion which he sees as the defining characteristic of common property. Where property is common we all have a right to use the resources defined as common property. This is, of course, not a new conception. Macpherson's argument is a reformulation of the rights and rules which political thinkers ascribed to the stage when the earth was held in common.

Macpherson's reference to rights of exclusion and inclusion points to the breadth of relationships inherent in ownership. Property is more than a relationship to things or 'possessions'. Property is an essentially social and political concept. This is also the conclusion of R. Schlatter's *Private Property* –

the History of an Idea: 'Property rights can no longer be defined as a relation between the individual and the material objects which he has created; they must be defined as social rights which determine the relations of the various groups of owners and non-owners to the system of production, and prescribe what each groups' share of the social product shall be'.[3]

This is brought out in a different way by Charles Lindblom. According to Lindblom (document 7.14), property can be considered as a specific form of authority. His point is that in relation to private property authority is not subject to the kinds of restraints which we customarily impose upon other forms of authority. It is essentially an irresponsible authority.

DOCUMENTS

Document 7.1

Aristotle on Slavery

Aristotle (384–321 BC) (see introduction to document 1.1) argued that the condition of slavery, common throughout the ancient world, should be advantageous to the slave – in cases where it was not, he considered it unnatural and unjust. Between natural slaves and their masters, he argued, there was a genuine mutual interest. Those who lacked rational powers and initiative (although they could follow orders and even advice) ought in their own interest to be slaves.

Let us first speak of master and slave, looking to the needs of practical life and also seeking to attain some better theory of their relation than exists at present. For some are of opinion that the rule of a master is a science, and that the management of a household, and the mastership of slaves, and the political and royal rule, as I was saying at the outset, are all the same. Others affirm that the rule of a master over slaves is contrary to nature, and that the distinction between slave and freeman exists by law only, and not by nature; and being an interference with nature is therefore unjust.

Property is a part of the household, and therefore the art of acquiring property is a part of the art of managing the household; for no man can live well, or indeed live at all, unless he be provided with necessaries. And as in the arts which have a definite sphere the workers must have their own proper instruments for the accomplishment of their work, so it is in the management of a household. Now, instruments are of various sorts; some are living, others lifeless; in the rudder, the pilot of a ship has a lifeless, in the look-out man, a living instrument; for in the arts the servant is a kind of instrument. Thus, too, a possession is an instrument for maintaining life. And so, in the arrangement of the family, a slave is a living possession, and property a number of such instruments; and the servant is himself an instrument, which takes precedence of all other instruments … The master is only the master of the slave; he does not belong to him, whereas the slave is not only the slave of his master, but wholly belongs to him. Hence we see what is the nature and office of a slave; he who is by nature not his own but another's and yet a man, is by nature a slave; and he may be said to belong to another who, being a human being, is also a possession. And a possession may be defined as an instrument of action, separable from the possessor.

But is there any one thus intended by nature to be a slave, and for whom such a condition is expedient and right, or rather is not all slavery a violation of nature? …

First then we may observe in living creatures both a despotical and a constitutional rule; for the soul rules the body with a despotical rule, whereas the intellect rules the appetites with a constitutional and royal rule. And it is clear that the rule of the soul over the body, and of the mind and the rational element over the passionate is natural and expedient; whereas the equality of the two or the rule of the inferior is always hurtful. The same holds good of animals as well as of men; for tame animals have a better nature than wild, and all tame animals are better off when they are ruled by man; for then they are all preserved. Again, the male is by nature superior, and the female inferior; and the one rules, and the other is ruled; this principle, of necessity, extends to all mankind. Where then there is such a difference as that between soul and body, or between men and animals (as in the case of those whose business is to use their body, and who can do nothing better), the lower sort are by nature slaves, and it is better for them as for all inferiors that they should be under the rule of a master. For he who can be, and therefore is another's, and he who participates in reason enough to apprehend, but not to have, reason, is a slave by nature. Whereas the lower animals cannot even apprehend reason; they obey their instincts. And indeed the use made of slaves and of tame animals is not very different; for both with their bodies minister to the needs of life. Nature would like to distinguish between the bodies of freemen and slaves, making the one strong for servile labour, the other upright, and although useless for such services, useful for political life in the arts both of war and peace. But this does not hold universally: for some slaves have the soul and others have the bodies of freemen. And doubtless if men differed from one another in the mere forms of their bodies as much as the statues of the Gods do from men, all would acknowledge that the inferior class should be slaves of the superior. And if there is a difference in the body, how much more in the soul? But the beauty of the body is seen, whereas the beauty of the soul is not seen. It is clear, then, that some men are by nature free, and others slaves, and that for these latter slavery is both expedient and right.

Document 7.2

The New Testament on Property

The New Testament statements on property, some of which are quoted below (in the Authorized Version), have encouraged various interpretations. Throughout the New Testament there is a distrust of riches and an emphasis on the spiritual advantages of poverty. At various times some Christian groups have derived a communistic vision from the teachings of the Early Church, but the main emphasis throughout history has been the need for Christian charity and responsible stewardship of wealth.

(i) St Luke, Chapter 10

18 And a certain ruler asked him, saying, Good Master, what shall I do to inherit eternal

life? 19 And Jesus said unto him, Why callest thou me good? none is good, save one, that is, God. 20 Thou knowest the commandments, Do not commit adultery, Do not kill, Do not steal, Do not bear false witness, Honour thy father and thy mother. 21 And he said, All these have I kept from my youth up. 22 Now when Jesus heard these things, he said unto him, Yet lackest thou one thing: sell all that thou hast, and distribute unto the poor, and thou shalt have treasure in heaven: and come, follow me. 23 And when he heard this, he was very sorrowful: for he was very rich. 24 And when Jesus saw that he was very sorrowful, he said How hardly shall they that have riches enter into the kingdom of God! 25 For it is easier for a camel to go through a needle's eye, than for a rich man to enter into the kingdom of God. 26 And they that heard it said, Who then can be saved? 27 And he said, The things which are impossible with men are possible with God. 28 Then Peter said, Lo, we have left all, and followed thee. 29 And he said unto them, Verily I say unto you There is no man that hath left house, or parents, or brethren, or wife, or children, for the kingdom of God's sake, 30 Who shall not receive manifold more in this present time, and in the world to come life everlasting.

(ii) Acts Chapter 4
32 And the multitude of them that believed were of one heart and of one soul: neither said any of them that ought of the things which he possessed was his own; but they had all things common. 33 And with great power gave the apostles witness of the resurrection of the Lord Jesus: and great grace was upon all. 34 Neither was there any among them that lacked: for as many as were possessors of lands of houses sold them, and brought the prices of the things that were sold, 35 And laid them down at the apostles' feet: and distribution was made unto every man according as he had need. 36 And Joses, who by the apostles was surnamed Barnabas, (which is, being interpreted, The son of consolation,) a Levite, and of the country of Cyrus. 37 Having land, sold it, and brought the money and laid it at the apostles' feet.

Acts Chapter 5
But a certain man named Ananias, with Sapphira his wife, sold a possession, 2 And kept back part of the price, his wife also being privy to it, and brought a certain part, and laid it at the apostles' feet. 3 But Peter said, Ananias, why hath Satan filled thine heart to lie to the Holy Ghost, and to keep back part of the price of the land? 4 Whiles it remained, was it not thine own? and after it was sold, was it not in thine own power? why hast thou conceived this thing in thine heart? thou has not lied unto men, but unto God. 5 And Ananias hearing these words fell down, and gave up the ghost: and great fear came on all them that heard these things. 6 And the young men arose, wound him up, and carried him out, and buried him.

(iii) James, Chapter 2
My brethren, have not the faith of our Lord Jesus Christ, the Lord of glory, with respect

of persons. 2 For if there come unto your assembly a man with a gold ring, in goodly apparel, and there come in also a poor man in vile raiment; 3 And ye have respect to him that weareth the gay clothing, and say unto him, Sit thou here in a good place; and say to the poor, Stand though there, or sit here under my footstool: 4 Are ye not then partial in yourselves, and are become judges of evil thoughts? 5 Hearken, my beloved brethren, Hath not God chosen the poor of this world rich in faith, and heirs of the kingdom which he hath promised to them that love him? 6 But ye have despised the poor. Do not rich men oppress you, and draw you before the judgment seats? 7 Do not they blaspheme that worthy name by the which ye are called? 8 If ye fulfil the royal law according to the scripture, Thou shalt love thy neighbour as thyself, ye do well; 9 But if ye have respect to persons, ye commit sin, and are convinced of the law as transgressors.

Document 7.3

St Thomas Aquinas on Private Property

St Thomas Aquinas (1225–74) argued that the distribution of material possessions was the result of human conventions, not divinely ordained. The following extract is from his *Summa Theologica*, written between 1266 and 1273, and is related to his review of the forms of human sinfulness. According to the Church Fathers, property was both the consequence and the social remedy for the sin of covetousness.

2 Is Private Property Legitimate?

Man has two capacities in regard to external things. First, he has the power to care for and dispose of them. To do this it is legitimate for a man to possess private property; indeed it is necessary for human life for three reasons. First, everyone is more concerned to take care of something that belongs only to him than of something that belongs to everyone or to many people, since in the case of common property he avoids effort by leaving its care to others, as occurs when one has a large number of servants. Secondly, human affairs are more efficiently organized if the proper care of each thing is an individual responsibility. There would only be confusion if everyone took care of everything in a disorganized fashion. Third, peace is better preserved among men if each one is content with his property. So we see that quarrels frequently arise among those who hold a thing in common and undivided.

Man is also capable of making use of external things. In regard to this a man should not possess external things as his alone but for the community, so that he is ready to share them with others in cases of necessity. Thus the Apostle Paul says in 1 Timothy, 'Command the rich of this world to be ready to share and to give.'

Community of goods is said to be part of the natural law not because the natural law decrees that all things are to be possessed in common and nothing held privately, but because the distribution of property is not a matter of natural law but of human agreement which pertains to the positive law, as we have said. Therefore private property is not against natural law but it has been added to natural law by the inventiveness of human reason.

7 Is Stealing Allowed in a Case of Necessity?
In cases of necessity everything is common property and thus it is not a sin for someone to take the property of another that has become common property through necessity ... Human law cannot violate natural or divine law. The natural order established by Divine Providence is such that lower ranking things are meant to supply the necessities of men. Therefore the division and appropriation of property by human law does not prevent its being used for the needs of man. Thus the things that anyone has in superabundance ought to be used to support the poor ... However, since the needy are many and they cannot all be supplied from the same source, the decision is left to each individual as to how to manage his property so as to supply the requirements of those in need. But if there is an urgent and clear need, so urgent and clear that it is evident that an immediate response must be made on the basis of what is available, such as when a person is in imminent danger and cannot be helped in any other way – then a person may legitimately supply his need from the property of someone else, whether openly or secretly. Strictly speaking such a case is not theft or robbery.

Document 7.4

James Harrington on the Relation of Political and Economic Power

James Harrington (1611–77) (see also document 6.2), author of *The Commonwealth of Oceana* (1656) was one of the leading republican thinkers of the seventeenth century and subsequently a strong influence on American political and constitutional thought. He advanced the view that power followed property – the distribution of land determined the distribution of independence and dependence. Writing against the background of the English Civil War, he argued that now that the gentry and yeomanry had become independent proprietors, monarchy and aristocracy in their feudal and hereditary form in England had now become impossible. A republican form of government was now inescapable.

Empire is of two kinds: domestic and national or foreign and provincial

Domestic empire is founded upon dominion. Dominion is property, real or personal: that is to say, in lands or in money and goods. Lands, or the parts and parcels of a territory, are held by the proprietor or proprietors, lord or lords of it, in some proportion and such (except it be in a city that has little or no land and whose revenue is in trade) as is the proportion or balance of dominion or property in land, such is the nature of the empire.

If one man be sole landlord of a territory, or overbalance the people, for example, three parts in four, he is Grand Signior: for so the Turk is called from his property; and his empire is absolute monarchy.

If the few or a nobility, or a nobility with the clergy be landlords, or overbalance the people unto the like proportion, it makes the Gothic balance (to be shown at large in the second part of this Discourse), and the empire is mixed monarchy, as that of Spain, Poland, and late of Oceana.

And if the whole people be landlords, or hold the lands so divided among them that no one man or number of men within the compass of the few or aristocracy overbalance them, the empire (without the interposition of force) is a commonwealth.

If force be interposed in any of these three cases, it must either frame the government to the foundation, or the foundation to the government; or, holding the government not according to the balance, it is not natural but violent; and therefore, if it be at the devotion of a prince, it is tyranny; if at the devotion of the few, oligarchy; or if in the power of the people, anarchy. Each of which confusions, the balance standing otherwise, is but of short continuance, because against the nature of the balance which, not destroyed, destroys that which opposes it.

But there be certain other confusions which, being rooted in the balance, are of longer continuance and of greater horror. As first, where a nobility holds half the property, or about that proportion, and the people the other half; in which case, without altering the balance, there is no remedy but the one must eat out the other, as the people did the nobility in Athens, and the nobility the people in Rome. Secondly, when a prince holds about half the dominion and the people the other half, which was the case of the Roman emperors, planted partly upon their military colonies and partly upon the Senate and the people, the government becomes a very shambles both of the princes and the people. Somewhat of this nature are certain governments at this day which are said to subsist by confusion. In this case, to fix the balance is to entail misery; but, in the three former, not to fix it is to lose the government.

The Agrarian Laws

Wherefore the fundamental laws of Oceana, or the centre of this commonwealth, are the Agrarian and the ballot: the Agrarian by the balance of dominion preserving equality in the root: and the ballot by an equal rotation conveying it into the branch, or exercise of sovereign power, as, to being with the former, appears by the thirteenth order, 'Constituting the Agrarian laws of Oceana, Marpesia, and Panopea, whereby it is ordained, first, for all such lands as are lying and being within the proper territories of

Oceana, that every man who is at present possessed, or shall hereafter be possessed, of an estate in land exceeding the revenue of £2000 a year, and having more than one son, shall leave his lands either equally divided among them, in case the lands amount to above £2000 a year to each, or so near equally in case they come under, that the greater part or portion of the same remaining to the eldest exceed not the value of £2000 revenue. And no man, not in present possession of lands above the value of £2000 by the year, shall receive, enjoy (except by lawful inheritance), acquire, or purchase to himself lands within the said territories, amounting, with those already in his possession, above the said revenue. And if a man has a daughter, or daughters, except she be an heiress, or they be heiresses, he shall not leave or give to any one of them in marriage, or otherwise, for her portion, above the value of £1500 in lands, goods, and moneys. Nor shall any friend, kinsman, or kinswoman, add to her or their portion or portions that are so provided for, to make any one of them greater. Nor shall any man demand or have more in marriage with any woman. Nevertheless an heiress shall enjoy her lawful inheritance, and a widow, whatsoever the bounty or affection of her husband shall bequeath to her, to be divided in the first generation, wherein it is divisible according as has been shown.

'Secondly, For lands lying and being within the territories of Marpesia, the Agrarian shall hold in all parts as it is established in Oceana, except only in the standard or proportion of estates in land, which shall be set for Marpesia, at five hundred pounds. And,

'Thirdly, For Panopea, the Agrarian shall hold in all parts as in Oceana. And whosoever possessing above the proportion allowed by these laws, shall be lawfully convicted of the same, shall forfeit the overplus to the use of the State.'

Document 7.5

John Locke on the Origins of Property

John Locke (1632–1704) posed the question in Chapter 2 of his *Second Treatise of Civil Government*, from which the following is an extract – how can one justify private appropriation of commonly available goods when God has given the earth to mankind in common? He argued that labour created property rights by removing the fruits of the earth from the common state. Private possessions did not depend on the consent of society and property rights existed in the original state of nature. In his view, one of the main purposes of civil society and government was the defence of private property.

26. God, who hath given the world to men in common, hath also given them reason to make use of it to the best advantage of life and convenience. The earth and all that is therein is given to men for the support and comfort of their being. And though all the fruits it naturally produces, and beasts it feeds, belong to mankind in common, as they

are thus in their natural state; yet being given for the use of men, there must of necessity be a means to appropriate them some way or other before they can be of any use or at all beneficial to any particular man ...

27. Though the earth and all inferior creatures be common to all men, yet every man has a property in his own person; this nobody has any right to but himself. The labour of his body and the work of his hands we may say are properly his. Whatsoever, then, he removes out of the state that nature hath provided and left it in, he hath mixed his labour with, and joined to it something that is his own, and thereby makes it his property. It being by him removed from the common state nature placed it in, it hath by this labour something annexed to it that excludes the common right of other men. For this labour being the unquestionable property of the labourer, no man but he can have a right to what that is once joined to, at least where there is enough and as good left in common for others ...

31. It will perhaps be objected to this, that if gathering the acorns or other fruits of the earth, etc., makes a right to them, then any one may engross as much as he will. To which I answer, Not so. The same law of nature that does by this means give us property, does also bound that property too. 'God has given us all things richly' (1 Tim. vi. 17), is the voice of reason confirmed by inspiration. But how far has he given it us? To enjoy. As much as any one can make use of to any advantage of life before it spoils, so much he may by his labour fix a property in whatever is beyond this is more than his share, and belongs to others. Nothing was made by God for man to spoil or destroy. And thus considering the plenty of natural provisions there was a long time in the world, and the few spenders, and to how small a part of that provision the industry of one man could extend itself, and engross it to the prejudice of others – especially keeping within the bounds, set by reason, of what might serve for his use – there could be then little room for quarrels or contentions about property so established.

32. But the chief matter of property being now not the fruits of the earth, and the beasts that subsist on it, but the earth itself, as that which takes in and carries with it all the rest, I think it is plain that property in that, too, is acquired as the former. As much land as a man tills, plants, improves, cultivates, and can use the produce of, so much is his property. He by his labour does as it were enclose it from the common ...

33. Nor was this appropriation of any parcel of land, by improving it, any prejudice to any other man, since there was still enough and as good left; and more than the eye unprovided could use. So that in effect there was never the less left for others because of his enclosure for himself. For he that leaves as much as another can make use of, does as good as take nothing at all. Nobody could think himself injured by the drinking of another man, though he took a good draught, who had a whole river of the same water left him to quench his thirst; and the case of land and water, where there is enough of both, is perfectly the same.

34. God gave the world to men in common; but since he gave it them for their benefit, and the greatest conveniences of life they were capable to draw from it, it cannot be supposed he meant it should always remain common and uncultivated. He gave it to the use of the industrious and rational (and labour was to be his title to it), not to the fancy or covetousness of the quarrelsome and contentious. He that had as good left for his improvement as was already taken up, needed not complain, ought not to meddle with what was already improved by another's labour; if he did, it is plain he desired the benefit of another's pains, which he had no right to, and not the ground which God had given him in common with others to labour on, and whereof there was as good left as that already possessed, and more than he knew what to do with, or his industry could reach to …

46   … He that gathered a hundred bushels of acorns or apples had thereby a property in them; they were his goods as soon as gathered. He was only to look that he used them before they spoiled, else he took more than his share, and robbed others; and, indeed, it was a foolish thing, as well as dishonest, to hoard up more than he could make use of. If he gave away part to anybody else, so that it perished not uselessly in his possession, these he also made use of; and if he also bartered away plums that would have rotted in a week, for nuts that would last good for his eating a whole year, he did no injury; he wasted not the common stock, destroyed no part of the portion of goods that belonged to others, so long as nothing perished uselessly in his hands. Again, if he would give his nuts for a piece of metal, pleased with its colour, or exchange his sheep for shells, or wool for a sparkling pebble or a diamond, and keep those by him all his life, he invaded not the right of others; he might heap up as much of these durable things as he pleased, the exceeding of the bounds of his just property not lying in the largeness of his possessions, but the perishing of anything uselessly in it.

47. And thus came in the use of money – some lasting thing that men might keep without spoiling, and that, by mutual consent, men would take in exchange for the truly useful but perishable supports of life.

48. And as different degrees of industry were apt to give men possessions in different proportions, so this invention of money gave them the opportunity to continue and enlarge them …

Document 7.6

Jean-Jacques Rousseau on the Origins of Property

For Rousseau (1712–78) the right to property derives from the natural right which everyone has to provide for their own survival. When land came to be divided up, this principle found common expression in 'the right of first occupant'. The institution of civil society changed the individual acts of occupation into valid rights – one of the benefits of civil association is that it transforms possession into property. The following extract is taken from The Social Contract (1762).

Each member of the community gives himself to it, as of the moment when it is formed, just as he is – himself and all his resources, among which are the goods he possesses.

This does not mean that when he thus gives himself his possessions change hands and thus change character, or that they are transformed into property of the sovereign. On the contrary: Since the city's might is incomparably greater than that of the individual, public possession is likewise stronger and more irrevocable, in actual fact, than a possession as such – though not necessarily, at least in the eyes of outsiders more legitimate, for the following reason: The state, over against its members, controls all the latter's goods under the terms of the social contract, which serves as the basis of all rights within it. But it controls them over against other powers only by virtue of the right of the first occupant, which is conveyed to it by the individuals concerned.

The right of the first occupier, though less fictitious than the right of the strongest, becomes a genuine right only where the right of property has been established. Each man has from nature, to be sure, a right to everything he needs. The positive act that makes a man the owner of such and such property has, however, the effect of excluding him from all other property. Once his property claim has been made effective, that is to say, he must confine himself to the property in question, and he accordingly retains no right to that which is held in common. That is why the right of the first occupier, though so very flimsy in the state of nature, is venerable in the eyes of everyone in civil society: Respecting it is a matter not so much of respecting what belongs to someone else as of respecting what does not belong to oneself.

Speaking in general terms, the following conditions must be fulfilled in order to make good the right of the first occupier to a given parcel of land: First, the land in question must not yet be inhabited by anybody. Secondly, one must occupy only that amount that one needs for one's subsistence. Thirdly, one must take possession of that amount not by going through some idle ritual, but by working and cultivating it – this being the only evidence of ownership that, in the absence of positive title, ought to be respected by others.

When we base the right of the first occupier on need and labor are we not, in point of fact, pushing it as far as it can go? Are we – in other words – entitled to regard this right as unlimited? In order for a man to put himself forward, once and for all, as the owner of a parcel of common land, shall he have merely to set foot on it? If a man is mighty enough to put other men off that piece of land for a single moment – shall this suffice to deprive those others, for aye and ever, of the right to come back to it? Where the result is to deprive the rest of mankind of the living-space and sustenance nature gives to all men in common, how can a man or a people – without committing a punishable act of encroachment – take possession of, and so place beyond the reach of others, a vast territory? When Nunez Balboa stood on the shore and took possession, in the name of the Castillian crown, of the entire Southern Sea, along with the whole of South America, did that indeed suffice not only to dispossess every last one of South America's inhabitants, but also to keep out every last one of the world's princes? If so, the ritual was gone through a mite too often, inasmuch as His Catholic Majesty had only to sit in his cabinet and take possession of the entire universe at a single blow – the sole catch being that he would subsequently have had to carve back out of his empire whatever other princes had already owned.

How the holdings of individuals, physically contiguous and pooled by contract, become the territory of the body politic, is clear enough. How the power of the sovereign spreads from the subjects to the land they occupy, and thus comes to be power over property as well as over persons, is clear enough also. This places the possessors in a position of greater dependency, and makes their very resources serve as guarantees of their fidelity.

The advantage this confers was apparently not fully understood by the monarchs of ancient times: By styling themselves merely king of the Persians, king of the Scythians, king of the Macedonians, etc., they showed themselves to be, in their own eyes, rulers over certain men rather than rulers over certain territories. The kings of our day, who know their trade better than their predecessors, call themselves king of France, king of Spain, king of England, etc. With so firm a hold on the land, they are quite sure of keeping a firm grip on its inhabitants.

The strange thing about this act of alienation is that the community, when it receives the goods of the individuals who make it up, does not divest them of those goods. Far from it: It simply guarantees for them the lawful ownership thereof, transforming mere possession into genuine right, and occupancy into property. The possessors are, for that reason, thenceforth regarded as depositaries of common wealth, so that their rights are not only respected by all the members of the state but also protected against outsiders with all the state's might. And, that being the case, the said possessors have, as a result of a surrender that is advantageous to the body politic but still more advantageous to them, so to speak acquired all that they have given up – a paradox which, as we shall see below, is easy to explain in the light of the distinction between the sovereign's and the owner's rights with respect to a given parcel of land.

I have assumed, up to this point, a community formed by men who already possess goods.

Another possibility is that of a number of men who begin to unite in a body politic before they possess anything at all, subsequently take possession of a piece of land large enough for them all, and either use it in common or divide it up among themselves – perhaps in equal parts, perhaps in unequal ones, with the shares being fixed by the sovereign. On either showing, each individual's right over his own holding is always subservient to the community's right over all the holdings – failing which the social bond would lack permanence, and the exercise of sovereignty would lack genuine power.

I shall close the present chapter, and the present book as well, with an observation that should serve as the basis of the entire social system: the basic pact, instead of merely destroying the equality of the state of nature, does the opposite of that. It substitutes a moral and legitimate equality for such physical inequality as nature has been able to produce among men – so that, while possibly unequal in strength or wit they all become equal as a matter of contract and of right. (Under bad governments this equality is merely ostensible, i.e., an illusion: it serves only to perpetuate the poor man's poverty and the rich man's possession). Laws, in actual practice, are invariably useful to those who possess and damaging to those who do not – from which it follows that the social condition is a benefit to man only when all own something and none owns the least bit too much.

Document 7.7

Edmund Burke on Inheritance and Property

The following observations were made by Edmund Burke (see also document 1.9) (1729–97) in his celebrated attack on the French Revolution, *Reflections on the Revolution in France* (1790). In his view, interference with the ownership of private property threatened the stability of society.

The characteristic essence of property, formed out of the combined principles of its acquisition and conservation, is to be unequal. The great masses, therefore, which excite envy, and tempt rapacity, must be put out of the possibility of danger. Then they form a natural rampart about the lesser properties in all their gradations. The same quantity of property which is by the natural course of things divided among many has not the same operation. Its defensive power is weakened as it is diffused. In this diffusion each man's portion is less than what, in the eagerness of his desires, he may flatter himself to obtain by dissipating the accumulations of others. The plunder of the few would, indeed, give but a share inconceivably small in the distribution to the many. But the many are not capable of making this calculation; and those who lead them to rapine never intend this distribution.

The power of perpetuating our property in our families is one of the most valuable and interesting circumstances belonging to it, and that which tends to the most to the perpetuation of society itself. It makes our weakness subservient to our virtue; it grafts benevolence even upon avarice. The possessors of family wealth, and of the distinction which attends hereditary possession (as most concerned in it), are the natural securities for this transmission. With us the House of Peers is formed upon this principle. It is wholly composed of hereditary property and hereditary distinction, and made, therefore, the third of the legislature, and, in the last event, the sole judge of all property in all its subdivisions. The House of Commons, too, though not necessarily, yet in fact, is always so composed, in the far greater part. Let those large proprietors be what they will (and they have their chance of being amongst the best), they are, at the very worst, the ballast in the vessel of the commonwealth. For though hereditary wealth, and the rank which goes with it, are too much idolized by creeping sycophants, and the blind, abject admirers of power, they are too rashly slighted in shallow speculations of the petulant, assuming, short-sighted coxcombs of philosophy. Some decent, regulated preeminence, some preference (not exclusive appropriation) given to birth, is neither unnatural nor unjust, nor impolitic.

Document 7.8

Sir Walter Scott in Defence of A Propertied Franchise

Sir Walter Scott (1771–1832) is primarily known as a historical novelist. The following extract is from *The Visionary* (1819), a tract in defence of the existing social and political order.

Capital is the superfluity of the wealthy, but it is the very sustenance of the poor, who live by the various modes in which it is employed; nor can the selfishness of the capitalist devise any mode of disposing it, by which, in his own despite, (were he wicked enough to nourish a hatred against the human race,) the poor would not be fed, clothed and supported out of his fortune. Let any man sit down and devise an expenditure of capital in such a manner as that, ultimately, it shall not be distributed among the body of the community, and he will find he has undertaken a task almost impossible. The most useless, perhaps would be that of hoarding large quantities of what are called precious metals; yet even the existence of these, though unproductive in themselves, would increase the credit of the state and the hoards of the miser would augment the general wealth of the country. The plan of those short-sighted and suspicious individuals who would annihilate commerce, learning and all its professions, together with the various modes of acquiring wealth, which have so much increased the population and comports of the country, in order to destroy every means of support, saving that which can be afforded by a barren and ill-cultivated soil, must commence with dispeopling the land of three-fifths of its inhabitants, and end by starving the greater part of those who might remain.

The subject of Radical Reform and Universal Suffrage, is only worthy of being treated … with scorn and derision. The general principle of the British Constitution devolves the choice of the members of the legislature on men of a certain property. The reason is, that the bulk and the mass of the population are rendered incapable of the due exercise of an elective franchise, by their want of education and violence of passion, as well as by their dependent situation, which must place their votes at the command of those who pay them daily wages to pay daily bread. The free nations of antiquity, to whose practice we are so fond of appealing, had a short cut for this; nine-tenths of their population were slaves, and as such, considered not merely as without franchise, but as the goods and chattels of their masters. With more justice, and more humanity, the law of Britain limits the elective franchise to those possessed of certain property, which is ascertained by various arbitrary rules, as the election is more or less popular, while the Constitution extends to all the subjects alike the benefits and protection of equal law.

Property is chosen as the basis of the elective franchise, because it is the most tangible mark of the capacity necessary to exercise it, as well as the most certain sign of the independence of situation, from which, if possible, it should never be divided. The person of property, if it is inherited, must probably have received education, or, if it is acquired by his own industry, he must probably possess talent of some sort or other. In either event, he cannot plead dependence as an excuse for degrading himself by corruption … An enlargement of the elective privilege, which should bring the fickle, unthinking and brutal mob into the field, would be a measure which must speedily terminate in military despotism, to which men have fled, in all ages and countries, as an evil whose terrors were incalculably less than those of a factious and furious democracy.

Document 7.9

Daniel Webster on Government and Property

Daniel Webster (1782–1852), US constitutional lawyer, Senator, Secretary of State between 1841 and 1843 and one of the most famous orators in American history, made the speech from which this extract is taken in the Massachusetts Convention in 1820. He believed that extension of the suffrage would enable the enfranchised masses to invade the rights of private property.

The true principle of a free and popular government would seem to be so to construct it as to give to all, or at least to a very great majority, an interest in its preservation. To found it, as other things are founded, on men's interest. The stability of government requires that those who desire its continuance should be more powerful than those who desire its dissolution. This power, of course, is not always to be measured by mere numbers. Education, wealth, talents, are all parts and elements of the general aggregate of power; but numbers, nevertheless, constitute ordinarily the most important consideration, unless indeed there be a military force in the hands of the few, by which they can control the many. In this country we have actual existing systems of government, in the protection of which it would seem a great majority, both in numbers and in other means of power and influence, must see their interest. But this state of things is not brought about merely by written political constitutions, or the mere manner of organizing the government; but also by the laws which regulate the descent and transmission of property. The freest government, if it could exist, would not be long acceptable, if the tendency of the laws were to create a rapid accumulation of property in few hands, and to render the great mass of the population dependent and penniless. In such a case the popular power must break in upon the rights of property, or else the influence of property must limit and control the exercise of popular power. Universal suffrage, for example, could not long exist in a community, where there was great inequality of property. The holders of estates would be obliged in such case, either, in some way, to restrain the right of suffrage; or else such right of suffrage would, ere long divide the property. In the nature of things, those who have not property, and see their neighbours possess much more than they think them to need, cannot be favorable to laws made for the protection of property. When this class becomes numerous, it grows clamorous. It looks on property as its prey and plunder, and is naturally ready, at all times, for violence and revolution.

It would seem, then, to be the part of political wisdom to found government on property; and to establish such distribution of property, by the laws which regulate its transmission and alienation, as to interest the great majority of society in the protection of the government. This is, I imagine, the true theory and the actual practice of our republican institutions. With property divided, as we have it, no other government than that of a republic could be maintained, even were we foolish enough to desire it. There is reason, therefore, to expect a long continuance of our systems. Party and passion, doubtless, may prevail at times, and much temporary mischief be done. Even modes and forms may be changed, and perhaps for the worse. But a great revolution, in regard to property, must take place, before our governments can be moved from their republican basis, unless they be violently struck off by military power. The people possess the property, more emphatically than it could ever be said of the people of any other country, and they can have no interest to overturn a government which protects that property by equal laws.

If the nature of our institutions be to found government on property, and that it should look to those who hold property for its protection, it is entirely just that property should have its due weight and consideration, in political arrangements. Life, and personal liberty, are, no doubt, to be protected by law; but property is also to be protected by law, and is the fund out of which the means for protecting life and liberty are usually furnished. We have no experience that teaches us, that any other rights are safe, where property is not safe. Confusion and plunder are generally in revolutionary commotions not far before banishment, imprisonment and death. It would be monstrous to give even the name of government, to any association, in which the rights of property should not be competently secured. The disastrous revolutions which the world has witnessed, those political thunderstorms, and earthquakes which have overthrown the pillars of society from their very deepest foundations, have been revolutions against property …

Document 7.10

Karl Marx and Friedrich Engels on the Abolition of Private Property

The following extract is taken from the *Communist Manifesto* which was first published in February 1848 (a year which saw revolutions across a large part of

Europe) and predicted the emancipation of the working-class from class domination. The analysis of property was essential to the authors' argument. They put forward the view that the changes in forms of property were the main characteristic of the evolution of different socio-economic formations in history and rejected the assumption that the nineteenth-century 'bourgeois' forms were the norm.

All property relations in the past have continually been subject to historical change consequent upon the change in historical conditions.

The French Revolution, for example, abolished feudal property in favour of bourgeois property.

The distinguishing feature of Communism is not the abolition of property generally, but the abolition of bourgeois property. But modern bourgeois private property is the final and most complete expression of the system of producing and appropriating products that is based on class antagonisms, on the exploitation of the many by the few.

In this sense, the theory of the Communists may be summed up in the single sentence: Abolition of private property.

We Communists have been reproached with the desire of abolishing the right of personally acquiring property as the fruit of a man's own labour, which property is alleged to be the groundwork of all personal freedom, activity and independence.

Hard-won, self-acquired, self-earned property! Do you mean the property of the petty artisan and of the small peasant, a form of property that preceded the bourgeois form? There is no need to abolish that; the development of industry has to a great extent already destroyed it, and is still destroying it daily.

Or do you mean modern bourgeois private property?

But does wage-labour create any property for the labourer?

Not a bit. It creates capital, i.e. that kind of property which exploits wage-labour, and which cannot increase except upon condition of begetting a new supply of wage-labour for fresh exploitation. Property, in its present form, is based on the antagonism of capital and wage-labour. Let us examine both sides of this antagonism.

To be a capitalist, is to have not only a purely personal, but a social, status in production. Capital is a collective product, and only by the united action of many members, nay, in the last resort, only by the united action of all members of society, can it be set in motion.

Capital is therefore not a personal, it is a social power.

When, therefore, capital is converted into common property, into the property of all members of society, personal property is not thereby transformed into social property. It is only the social character of the property that is changed. It loses its class character.

Let us now take wage-labour.

The average price of wage-labour is the minimum wage, i.e. that quantum of the means of subsistence which is absolutely requisite to keep the labourer in bare existence as a labourer. What, therefore, the wage-labourer appropriates by means of his labour, merely suffices to prolong and reproduce a bare existence. We by no means intend to abolish this personal appropriation of the products of labour, an appropriation that is made for the maintenance and reproduction of human life, and that leaves no surplus with which to command the labour of others. All that we want to do away with is the miserable character of this appropriation under which the labourer lives merely to increase capital, and is allowed to live only in so far as the interest of the ruling class requires it.

In bourgeois society, living labour is but a means to increase accumulated labour. In communist society, accumulated labour is but a means to widen, to enrich, to promote the existence of the labourer.

In bourgeois society, therefore, the past dominates the present; in Communist society, the present dominates the past. In bourgeois society capital is independent and has individuality, while the living person is dependent and has no individuality.

And the abolition of this state of things is called by the bourgeois, abolition of individuality and freedom! And rightly so. The abolition of bourgeois individuality, bourgeois independence, and bourgeois freedom is undoubtedly aimed at.

By freedom is meant, under the present bourgeois conditions of production, free trade, free selling and buying.

But if selling and buying disappears, free selling and buying disappears also. This talk about free selling and buying, and all the other 'brave words' of our bourgeoisie about freedom in general have a meaning, if any, only in contrast with restricted selling and buying, with the fettered traders of the Middle Ages, but have no meaning when opposed to the Communist abolition of buying and selling, of the bourgeois conditions of production, and of the bourgeoisie itself.

You are horrified at our intending to do away with private property. But in your existing society, private property is already done away with for nine-tenths of the population; its existence for the few is solely due to its non-existence in the hands of those nine-tenths. You reproach us, therefore, with intending to do away with a form of property, the necessary condition for whose existence is the non-existence of any property for the immense majority of society.

Document 7.11

Henry George on the Injustice of Private Property in Land

Henry George (1839–97) was born in Philadelphia, subsequently migrating to California where he became a journalist. His major work, *Progress and Poverty*, (1879), argued that the root of America's economic problem, increasing want in the face of increasing wealth, lay in the monopoly of land. Rent deprived labour and capital of a fair return. His solution was not confiscation of property, but of rent through taxation. He instituted the Single Tax Movement and also called for municipal ownership of public utilities.

When it is proposed to abolish private property in land the first question that will arise is that of justice. Though often warped by habit, superstition, and selfishness into the most distorted forms, the sentiment of justice is yet fundamental to the human mind, and whatever dispute arouses the passions of men, the conflict is sure to rage, not so much as to the question 'Is it wise?' as to the question 'Is it right?' …

What constitutes the rightful basis of property? What is it that enables a man to justly say of a thing, 'It is mine!' From what springs the sentiment which acknowledges his exclusive right as against all the world? Is it not, primarily, the right of a man to himself, to the use of his own powers, to the enjoyment of the fruits of his own exertions? Is it not this individual right which springs from and is testified to by the natural facts of individual organization – the fact that each particular pair of hands obey a particular brain and are related to a particular stomach; the fact that each man is a definite, coherent, independent whole – which alone justifies individual ownership? As a man belongs to himself, so his labor when put in concrete form belongs to him.

And for this reason, that which a man makes or produces is his own, as against all the world – to enjoy or to destroy, to use, to exchange, or to give. No one else can rightfully claim it, and his exclusive right to it involves no wrong to any one else. Thus there is to everything produced by human exertion a clear and indisputable title to exclusive possession and enjoyment, which is perfectly consistent with justice, as it descends from the original producer, in whom it is vested by natural law. The pen with which I am writing is justly mine. No other human being can rightfully lay claim to it, for in me is the title of the producers who made it. It has become mine, because transferred to me by the stationer, to whom it was transferred by the importer, who obtained the exclusive right to it by transfer from the manufacturer, in whom, by the same process of purchase, vested the rights of those who dug the material from the ground and shaped it into a pen. Thus, my exclusive right of ownership in the pen springs from the natural right of the individual to the use of his own faculties …

This right of ownership that springs from labor excludes the possibility of any other right of ownership. If a man be rightfully entitled to the produce of his labor, then no one can be rightfully entitled to the ownership of anything which is not the produce of his labor, or the labor of some one else from whom the right has passed to him. If production give to the producer the right to the exclusive possession and enjoyment, there can rightfully be no exclusive possession and enjoyment of anything not the production of labor, and the recognition of private property in land is a wrong. For the right to the produce of labor cannot be enjoyed without the right to the free use of the opportunities offered by nature, and to admit the right of property in these is to deny the right of property in the produce of labor. When non-producers can claim as rent a portion of the wealth created by producers, the right of the producers to the fruits of their labor is to that extent denied …

The moment this distinction is realized, that moment is it seen that the sanction which natural justice gives to one species of property is denied to the other; that the rightfulness which attaches to individual property in the produce of labor implies the wrongfulness of individual property in land; that, whereas the recognition of the one places all men upon equal terms, securing to each the due reward of his labor, the recognition of the other is the denial of the equal rights of men, permitting those who do not labor to take the natural reward of those who do.

Whatever may be said for the institution of private property in land, it is therefore plain that it cannot be defended on the score of justice. The equal right of all men to the use of land is as clear as their equal right to breathe the air – it is a right proclaimed by the fact of their existence. For we cannot suppose that some men have a right to be in this world and others no right …

Document 7.12

Ramsay MacDonald on Communal Property

James Ramsay MacDonald (1866–1937) was leader of the Labour Party and first British Labour Prime Minister. The following extract is taken from *Socialism: Critical and Constructive* (1921).

The personal enjoyment of property possible to the mass of the people is from collective and not from individual ownership. The significance of this is seen if one considers, say, public parks. Within the administrative county of London there are 4100 acres devoted to parks. These are laid out in woods, arbours, gardens, recreation grounds, walks and so on, and this use is only possible by the massing together of what, on a division into private property, would be millions of mud puddles not big enough to swing a cat by the tail without trespassing. Divided into the number of people who as Londoners really own them, the park area of London only gives a little over four square yards to each. The same is true of museums, picture galleries and such things, where the value of the possessions divided into private property would not, on distribution, allow a new German oleograph to be added to the horrors of our kitchen walls. A very little per head, massed together for common use, puts the discriminating user in a superior position to that of the millionaire. Communal property, however, whilst enlivening the communal interests of the individual and enabling him to understand what community means and how its well-being is his own well-being, is not by itself a sufficient motive for industry. It belongs to a better class of motive than the purely personal one, and we may hope that in time that class will be predominant, but that is not yet.

Document 7.13

Morris Cohen on Property as Power

Morris Cohen (1880–1947) was a leading US jurist and philosophy professor. The points below were originally made in a lecture to the Cornell Law School in 1927. His view that property amounts to a right to impose one's will over others led him on to argue that the state should set limits to it in the interests of society at large.

Any one who frees himself from the crudest materialism readily recognizes that as a legal term 'property' denotes not material things but certain rights.

In the world of nature apart from more or less organized society, there are things but clearly no property rights.

Further reflection shows that a property right is not to be identified with the fact of physical possession. Whatever technical definition of property we may prefer, we must recognize that a property right is a relation not between an owner and a thing, but between the owner and other individuals in reference to things. A right is always against one or more individuals. This becomes unmistakably clear if we take specifically modern forms of property such as franchises, patents, goodwill, etc., which constitute such a large part of the capitalized assets of our industrial and commercial enterprises.

The classical view of property as a right over things resolves it into component rights such as the *jus utendi, jus disponendi*, etc. But the essence of private property is always the right to exclude others. The law does not guarantee me the physical or social ability of actually using what it calls mine. By public regulations it may indirectly aid me by removing certain general hindrances to the enjoyment of property. But the law of property helps me directly only to exclude others from using the things that it assigns to me. If, then, somebody else wants to use the food, the house, the land, or the plough that the law calls mine, he has to get my consent. To the extent that these things are necessary to the life of my neighbour, the law thus confers on me a power, limited but real, to make him do what I want. If Laban has the sole disposal of his daughters and his cattle, Jacob must serve him if he desires to possess them. In a regime where land is the principal source of obtaining a livelihood, he who has the legal right over the land receives homage and service from those who wish to live on it.

The character of property as sovereign power compelling service and obedience may be obscured for us in a commercial economy by the fiction of the so-called labour contract as a free bargain and by the frequency with which service is rendered indirectly through a money payment. But not only is there actually little freedom to bargain on the part of the steel-worker or miner who needs a job, but in some cases the medieval subject had as much power to bargain when he accepted the sovereignty of his lord. Today I do not directly serve my landlord if I wish to live in the city with a roof over my head, but I must work for others to pay him rent with which he obtains the personal services of others. The money needed for purchasing things must for the vast majority be acquired by hard labour and disagreeable service to those to whom the law has accorded dominion over the things necessary for subsistence.

To a philosopher this is of course not at all an argument against private property. It may well be that compulsion in the economic as well as the political realm is necessary for civilized life. But we must not overlook the actual fact that dominion over things is also imperium over our fellow human beings.

The extent of the power over the life of others which the legal order confers on those called owners is not fully appreciated by those who think of the law as merely protecting men in their possession. Property law does more. It determines what men shall acquire. Thus, protecting the property rights of a landlord means giving him the right to collect rent, protecting the property of a railroad or a public-service corporation means giving it the right to make certain charges.

Document 7.14

Charles Lindblom on Private Property and Authority

Charles Edward Lindblom (born 1917), author, among other works, of *The Intelligence of Democracy* and *Politics and Markets*, has shown special interest in the relationship between market power and political power and privilege.

What are the specific conditions we seek to impose in order to constrain and direct rulers in suitable ways? The list is familiar and understandable.

1. That when authority is granted it be accompanied by responsibility of that authority to act. No power without responsibility.

2. That authority be granted to a role player not a named person. Thus we confer authority on a prime minister; the authority is granted to whoever qualifies for that role.

3. That one who holds authority use it for assigned public purposes but not for his private purposes.

4. That the holder of authority cannot transfer it to another, although he can delegate some of it to subordinates under his supervision. And it does not pass to his inheritors, as traditional royal power passes to offspring.

5. That the holder of the authority use it only for limited prescribed purposes.

6. That the exercise of authority be subject to a large body of procedural rules that assure 'due process'.

These six conditions specify the elementary or fundamental requirements of acceptable rulers or acceptable acts of rule over us. Let us look at the list again to see what unacceptable practices we have ruled out. Here I will, point by point, rewrite the list to specify not what is required but what we intend to prohibit.

1. A grant of authority that imposes no responsibility to act.

2. Authority that is granted to named persons rather than role players.

3. Authority that is used for private purposes.

4. Holders of authority who are free to transfer it to other persons as they wish by giving it away, selling it or passing it to offspring.

5. Authority that is broadly granted so that it can be used to pursue a wide variety of purposes. Thus authority that can be used to gain authority, including authority to create a machine.

6. Authority that is subject to relatively few procedural rules. The many restrictions of 'due process' do not apply to it.

I believe that most of us would say that such a list as this one describes a thoroughly unacceptable set of rules for persons in authority. The list seems to characterize an earlier set of preconstitutional rules no longer considered acceptable in constitutional or democratic systems. It seems to describe irresponsible power.

But consider. What is the contemporary significance of this second list? Where have we seen it? Is there something familiar about it, aside from its characterization of times past? Take note that each rule in the second list specifies a right – for example, a right to use authority for private purpose.

The second list is a set of rules or rights known as the law of private property. Private property in the means of production is a set of rules that confers authority over the society's resources. The rules impose no responsibility to act or to employ the resources in any public interest. Authority is granted to named persons, may be used for private purposes, can be given away, sold, bequeathed. And its exercise is subject to few procedural rules, unlike the due process rules that constrain governmental authorities.

Document 7.15

C.B. Macpherson on Common Property, Private Property, State Property

Crawford Brough Macpherson (1911–87) was a Canadian democratic theorist. He was particularly interested in the political questions associated with property and the way in which the development of political theory in the seventeenth and eighteenth centuries reflected the growth of a capitalist market society. He also related his historical perceptions of 'possessive individualism' to contemporary political issues.

The definition of property as an enforceable claim of a person to some use or benefit of something is often taken to rule out the idea of common property. But a little analysis will show that it does not.

Society or the state may declare that some things – for example, common lands, public parks, city streets, highways – are for common use. The right to use them is then a property of individuals, in that each member of the society has an enforceable claim to use them. It need not be an unlimited claim. The state may, for instance, have to ration the use of public lands, or it may limit the kinds of uses anyone may make of the streets or of common waters (just as it now limits the use anyone may make of his private property), but the right to use the common things, however limited, is a right of individuals.

This point needs some emphasis, for it can easily be lost sight of. The fact that we need some such term as 'common property,' to distinguish such rights from the exclusive individual rights which are private property, may easily lead to our thinking that such common rights are not individual rights. But they are. They are the property of individuals, not of the state. The state indeed creates and enforces the right which each individual has in the things the state declares to be for common use. But so does the state create and enforce the exclusive rights which are private property. In neither case does the fact that the state creates the right make the right the property of the state. In both cases what is created is a right of individuals. The state creates the rights, the individuals have the rights. Common property is created by the guarantee to each individual that he will not be excluded from the use or benefit of something; private property is created by the guarantee that an individual can exclude others from the use or benefit of something. Both kinds of property, being guarantees to individual persons, are individual rights.

In the case of private property the right may, of course, be held by an artificial person, that is, by a corporation or an unincorporated grouping created or recognized by the state as having the same (or similar) property rights as a natural individual. The property which such a group has is the right to the use and benefit, and the right to exclude non-members from the use and benefit, of the things to which the group has a legal title. Corporate property is thus an extension of individual private property.

Both the kinds of property we have noticed so far are thus, directly or by extension, individual rights. Both are rights of distinct natural or artificial persons. We have now to notice that there is another kind of property which appears not to be an individual right at all. This may be called 'state property': it consists of rights which the state has not only created but has kept for itself or has taken over from private individuals or corporations. The right to use the airwaves for radio and television communication, for instance, may be retained wholly or partially by the state, as it is in countries with publicly owned and operated broadcasting systems. Again, various enterprises, e.g. railways and airlines, are in many countries owned by the state. The rights which the state holds and exercises in respect of these things, the rights which comprise the state's property in these things, are akin to private property rights, for they consist of the right to the use and benefit, and the right to exclude others from the use and benefit, of something. In effect, the state itself is taking and exercising the powers of a corporation: it is acting as an artificial person.

Now state property, as just described, does not give the individual citizen a direct right to use, nor a right not to be excluded from, the assets held by the state acting as a corporation. Air France and British Railways are not freely available to all the citizens of those countries; a state-owned railway is apt to be as jealous of its property as is a privately owned one. State property, then, is not common property as we have defined it: state property is not an individual right not to be excluded. It is a corporate right to exclude. As a corporate right to exclude others it fits the definition of (corporate) private property.

It may seem paradoxical to call it a kind of private property, for by definition it is the property of the whole state. The paradox disappears when we notice that the state, in any modern society, is not the whole body of citizens but a smaller body of persons who have been authorized (whether by the whole body of citizens or not) to command the citizens. Although Idealist philosophers, in order to emphasize their belief that every state ought to be (or that the good or true state is) a community of all the citizens, may define the state as a community of all, political realists have always seen that the state is in fact the persons who are acknowledged by the citizens to have the right to command them. This was more obviously true of the state before the rise of democracy – Louis XIV could say, not unrealistically, 'L'état, c'est moi' – but it is just as true of democratic states: the body of persons that is authorized by the citizens in a democracy is not the whole body of citizens. It acts in their name, but it is not they. And it is the body that holds the rights called state property. When the state is seen in this way it becomes perfectly intelligible that the state can have a corporate right to exclude others, including citizens, from the use or benefit of something, in just the same way as it permits a private owner to do.

State property, then, is to be classed as corporate property, which is exclusive property, and not as common property, which is non-exclusive property. State property is an exclusive right of an artificial person.

Two points emerge from this analysis of the three kinds of property. One is that all three kinds – common, private, and state property – are rights of persons, either natural individuals or artificial persons. The other is that common property, rather than being ruled out by the very concept of property as rights (enforceable claims) of persons, turns out to be the most unadulterated kind of property. For common property is always a right of the natural individual person, whereas the other two kinds of property are not always so: private property may be a right of either a natural or an artificial person, and state property is always a right of an artificial person.

In the light of this analysis it is apparent that the concept of property as enforceable claims of persons to some use or benefit of something cannot logically be confined to exclusive private property.

QUESTIONS FOR DISCUSSION

1. Can the propertyless be full and responsible citizens?
2. To what extent should individual property rights limit the powers of government?
3. Is there any basis for property rights other than convention and custom?
4. Is private property irresponsible authority?
5. 'The slogan that property is a human right can be employed only disingenuously to legitimize the massive inequality that we find in modern capitalist countries'. Do you agree?

NOTES

1 For these limits see C. Donahue, 'The Future of the Concept of Property Predicted from its Past', in J.R. Pennock and J.W. Chapman (eds), *Nomos XXII. Property* (New York, New York University Press, 1980), pp. 35–6.
2 A. Ryan, *The Political Theory of Property* (Oxford, Blackwell, 1984), p. 11.
3. R. Schlatter, Private Property (London, George Allen & Unwin, 1951), p.273

FURTHER READING

R. Schlatter, *Private Property – the History of an Idea* (London, Allen and Unwin, 1951) is a useful survey. On changing attitudes to the claims of the poor see I. Hont and M. Ignatieff, 'Need and Justice in the Wealth of Nations', in *Wealth and Virtue* (Cambridge, Cambridge University Press, 1983). T. Horne, *Property Rights and Poverty: Political Arguments in Britain 1605–1834*, (Chapel Hill NC, University of North Carolina Press, 1990) argues for the persistence of the claims of the poor. Of particular interest on seventeenth-century England there are C.B. Macpherson's *The Political Theory of Possessive Individualism* (Oxford, Clarendon Press, 1962) and J. Tully's *A Discourse on Property: John Locke and his Adversaries*, (Cambridge, Cambridge University Press, 1980). A. Ryan, *The Political Theory of Property* (Oxford, Blackwell, 1984) distinguishes between instrumentalist and self-development approaches. On the philosophical premises see: L.C. Becker, *Property Rights: Philosophic Foundations* (London, Routledge & Kegan Paul, 1977) and A. Carter, *The Philosophical Foundations of Property Rights* (Hemel Hempstead, Harvester Wheatsheaf, 1989). On the theory of property see A. Reeve, *Property* (Basingstoke, Macmillan, 1986), J. Waldron, *The Right to Private Property* (Oxford, Oxford University Press, 1988), A. Ryan, *Property* (Milton Keynes, Open University Press, 1987).

8

THE STATE AND SOVEREIGNTY

INTRODUCTION

The concepts of state and sovereignty were formulated to answer old questions about who has the right and power to command?, over whom is that command exercised?, and what is the extent of the right and power to command? Yet the concepts are comparatively novel, dating from the sixteenth century. According to this modern conception, the sovereign state is the supreme power, subject to the rule neither of some external power nor of a rival power within its own territorial boundaries. It is part of the novelty of these concepts that they were linked together. Sovereignty was defined as an essential attribute of statehood.

Sovereignty was also construed as an essentially legislative power. Although all political forms have recognized the act of legislation as a vital part of the political process, rulers and ruling bodies had typically been assigned both legislative and judicial power. Kings were supreme magistrates and parliaments were as much, if not more, courts of law as legislative bodies. The transition from a mixed judicial-legislative power to a stricter emphasis upon legislation was vital to the modern concept of sovereignty and the sovereign state. To construe the supreme political authority as a judicial one left open the possibility that the law stood above the sovereign. That had indeed been the predominant assumption. The law, not the sovereign, was truly supreme. By defining sovereignty as essentially legislative, the new doctrine sought to exclude this possibility. The sovereign as the fount of law was above the law. Being able to change the law at will, the sovereign could not in any meaningful sense be said to be bound by the law.

These two key characteristics of the modern conception were first laid down unequivocally by the sixteenth-century Frenchman Jean Bodin.[1] Although the Roman Empire had seen the formulation of most of the elements of the concept of sovereignty, these formulations were submerged by the complex diffusion of power throughout the Middle Ages. It was only with the centralization of power at the beginning of the modern era that the conditions occurred for a revival and refinement of these conceptions. During the medieval period power was limited by the overarching authority of Christianity, by the division of power between church and temporal ruler and by the existence of corporate privileges and rights. The inhabitants of medieval states faced their rulers not as an undifferentiated mass of subjects, but as bearers of rights which they enjoyed by virtue of their status as members of religious and secular bodies.

The emergence of the modern conceptions of state and sovereignty was bound up with the growth of state power which gradually suppressed these local and corporate autonomies or confined them to limits defined by the central power. The Italian, Niccolò Machiavelli, stands out as an advocate of this pursuit of power. For Machiavelli, the task was to cheat the onset of political decay which threatened all states for as long as possible. In this the Prince was absolved of respect for normal morality. Yet Machiavelli did not normally use the term state in its modern sense. Following customary usage he referred to the state or condition of a city or Prince. In a similar way modern American Presidents deliver addresses on the 'state of the nation'.

The triumph of the term 'state' was a slow one. Even Bodin wrote of *la république* more than of *l'état*. The term sovereignty, although long established to identify the ruler, also struggled to gain acceptance as indicating an abstract and absolute power. It did not gain acceptance in Germany until the early nineteenth century. But a German ruler did provide one of the most succinct expressions of a key characteristic of the modern state: its abstract character. Recognition of this enabled Frederick the Great to describe himself as 'the first servant of the state'. The identification of ruler and state had given way to an abstract concept apparently independent of the individuals and institutions through which alone state power can be exercised. It is, of course, this abstraction from the actual men and levers of power which makes it so difficult to agree upon a definition of the state.

While Bodin can be ascribed authorship of the modern conception, he was not entirely consistent, retaining, for example, the old conception that sovereigns were bound by the laws of nature and God. The sixteenth-century English political theorist, Thomas Hobbes, was more consistent and more radical. Hobbes sought to strip away the last vestiges of restraint. He argued that men would agree to abandon a state of nature by a covenant appointing a sovereign. That agreement, however, was made between the future subjects of the sovereign. There was no contract whatsoever between subject and sovereign'. The point of this insistence was to rule out any recourse to older contractarian arguments. If it was admitted that a contract existed between subject and sovereign there was the possibility of the subject renouncing allegiance on the grounds the sovereign had violated the contract.

For all their insistence upon the indivisibility of sovereignty and their denial of the traditional restraint upon the exercise of power, neither Bodin or Hobbes was an advocate of tyranny. Both wrote against the background of civil war. Both were desperately seeking to persuade their contemporaries that the sovereign state was the only guarantee of security. Only by elevating a sovereign above themselves could men be preserved from the ravages of civil war.

Hobbes and Bodin were concerned to cut off the intellectual justification for rebellion. But the doctrine of sovereignty, which they did so much to develop, was also deployed to justify rebellion. Using essentially the same characteristics of sovereignty, an indivisible essential attribute of the state entailing unrestricted legislative competence, others bestowed this power upon the people themselves. Governments might exercise power in trust but they could not appropriate that power. This strategy was employed by John Locke to set limits to the authority of parliament as well as the executive. In accordance with the new doctrine, he insisted 'there can be but *one Supream Power*, which is *the Legislative* ... yet the Legislative being only a Fiduciary Power to act for certain ends, there remains still *in the People a Supream Power* to remove or *alter the Legislative*'.[2]

The assertion of the sovereignty of the people was to be taken one stage further by the French philosopher Jean-Jacques Rousseau. For Rousseau there could be no question of delegating legislative power. The people were sovereign and hence must exercise that sovereign power and legislate for themselves. Sovereign and subject were one and the same. Or, to use Rousseau's terms, the body politic was Sovereign in its active capacity as legislator and was the State in its passive capacity. The individuals making up the body politic were citizens when they legislated and subjects in that they were subject to the laws thus made.

There were, then, two uses of the concept of sovereignty. One set the sovereign over the people, the other located sovereignty in the people. These two diverse applications of the concept of sovereignty clashed at the time of the American War of Independence. Dr Johnson set out from the principle that there 'must in every society be some power or other from which there is no appeal' (see document 8.4). Whether or not British policy in the American colonies was right was, he implied, irrelevant. To resist was to dispute where sovereignty lay and hence to undermine the foundations of society. Johnson had set out from the need for a sovereign power and assumed that sovereignty lay with the Crown. In defence of the colonists, Richard Price argued that sovereignty must lie with the people or community, and argued that there was no way in which this sovereignty could be alienated. Both men had proceeded logically, each extrapolating from different traditions of the idea of sovereignty. For Johnson what mattered was that the sovereign existed and must not be challenged. For Price what mattered, to adopt Rousseau's terminology, was that citizens and subjects must be one and the same.

In his argument Price noted that tyranny was bad enough when practised within a state, it was bound to be worse when exercised by one community over another. He might have added that it would be worse still when these two communities did not share the same political concepts, including concepts of state and sovereignty. This complication was one which many western European states were inevitably confronted with by virtue of their acquisition of colonies including cultures distinct from their own. It was this discrepancy which Edmund Burke seized upon with great rhetorical skill and not a little equivocation. In his indictment of Warren Hastings he managed to accuse Hastings of both usurping the sovereignty of parliament and of laying claim a kind of sovereignty not recognized by the peoples over whom he ruled.

Even within single political communities the concepts of state and sovereignty were to be pushed to the point where they revoked the peace and security its sixteenth- and seventeenth-century advocates had sought. The fascist state radicalized the centralization of power to the point where it could not only brook no rival, but to the point where it could respect no limit. The claim to be exempt from any limitation had been inherent in the claims made for the modern state from the start. It would, however, be mistaken to extrapolate from those early assertions to the deification of the state by Italian fascists. The heart of the modern doctrine of state and sovereignty lay in the assertion that the sovereign state recognizes no superior. The heart of the doctrine of the fascist state lay in the assertion that 'It wants to remake, not the forms of human life, but its content, man, character, faith'. The ambition of the fascists was so extensive that their vision could only be realized by reversing many of the achievements of the modern state. In place of the separation of ruler and office the fascists elevated the leader, the Duce or Führer, to a position where the state was nothing more than an emanation of the leader's will. In the place of peace and security they instituted a permanent pursuit of internal and external enemies.

The underlying purpose of the concept of sovereignty was similarly inverted by the authoritarian German political theorist, Carl Schmitt. Schmitt took up an undeniable problem with the concept of sovereignty. The difficulty, as the difference between Johnson and Price in the eighteenth century shows, is that it can only command allegiance if there is no dispute about where sovereignty is located. Johnson's response to this dilemma amounted to claiming that merely to raise this question was to dispute the existence of sovereignty. In a sense he was right. Where there is fundamental disagreement as to where sovereignty lies there will, in effect, be at least two possible locations and two potential sovereigns. Schmitt, however, defined sovereignty as the power to decide when this critical situation had arisen. The sovereign, according to this account, is whoever can set aside all law and constitution and declare a state of emergency, and define who counts as friend and who as foe. In other words, sovereignty is effectively redefined as the right to declare a reversion to the state of nature.

The modern twin concepts of state and sovereignty were formulated primarily from an approach to political life which focuses upon considerations of security.

Alternative approaches, concerned, for example, with the just distribution of goods, are based upon a radically different conception of the political condition. For the latter, the political condition of man is governed by a shortage of goods. Principles and procedures must, therefore, be established for the allocation of goods. For the authors of the modern conceptions of state and sovereignty the basic political condition was insecurity. Danger not desire, fear of violence not of hunger were the dominant themes.

DOCUMENTS

Document 8.1

Niccolò Machiavelli on the Means by which Rulers can Increase their States' Power

Machiavelli (1496–1527) had been secretary of the magistracy in the Florentine Republic and ambassador during a period in which the Florentines were trying to safeguard their domains and recover Pisa. *The Prince* (1513) and *The Discourses on the First Ten Books of Titus Livy* (1513–17), his best-known political works, were written after his loss of office and combined his awareness of contemporary Italian politics with Renaissance Humanist fascination with classical antiquity. *The Prince* is particularly concerned with the role of force and the means by which rulers can maintain and increase their territories and power in difficult times. The following extract is taken from *The Prince*.

A prince should therefore have no other aim or thought, nor take up any other thing for his study, but war and its organisation and discipline, for that is the only art that is necessary to one who commands, and it is of such virtue that it not only maintains those who are born princes, but often enables men of private fortune to attain to that rank. And one sees, on the other hand, that when princes think more of luxury than of arms, they lose their state. The chief cause of the loss of states, is the contempt of this art, and the way to acquire them is to be well versed in the same.

Francesco Sforza, through being well armed, became, from private status, Duke of Milan; his sons, through wishing to avoid the fatigue and hardship of war, from dukes became private persons. For among other evils caused by being disarmed, it renders you contemptible; which is one of those disgraceful things which a prince must guard against, as will be explained later. Because there is no comparison whatever between an armed and a disarmed man; it is not reasonable to suppose that one who is armed will obey willingly one who is unarmed; or that any unarmed man will remain safe among armed servants. For one being disdainful and the other suspicious, it is not possible for them to act well together. And therefore a prince who is ignorant of military matters, besides the other misfortunes already mentioned, cannot be esteemed by his soldiers, nor have confidence in them.

He ought, therefore, never to let his thoughts stray from the exercise of war; and in peace he ought to practise it more than in war, which he can do in two ways: by action and by study. As to action, he must, besides keeping his men well disciplined and exercised, engage continually in hunting, and thus accustom his body to hardships; and meanwhile learn the nature of the land, how steep the mountains are, how the valleys debouch, where the plains lie, and understand the nature of rivers and swamps. To all this he should devote great attention. This knowledge is useful in two ways. In the first place, one learns to know one's country, and can the better see how to defend it. Then by means of the knowledge and experience gained in one locality, one can easily understand any other that it may be necessary to observe; for the hills and valleys, plains and rivers of Tuscany, for instance, have a certain resemblance to those of other provinces, so that from a knowledge of the country in one province one can easily arrive at a knowledge of others. And that prince who is lacking in this skill is wanting in the first essentials of a leader; for it is this which teaches how to find the enemy, take up quarters, lead armies, plan battles and lay siege to towns with advantage.

Philopeomen, prince of the Achaei, among other praises bestowed on him by writers, is lauded because in times of peace he thought of nothing but the methods of warfare, and when he was in the country with his friends, he often stopped and asked them: if the enemy were on that hill and we found ourselves here with our army, which of us would have the advantage? How could we safely approach him maintaining our order? If we wished to retire, what ought we to do? If they retired, how should we follow them? And he put before them as they went along all the contingencies that might happen to an army, heard their opinion, gave his own, fortifying it by argument; so that thanks to these constant reflections there could never happen any incident when actually leading his armies for which he was not prepared.

But as to exercise for the mind, the prince ought to read history and study the actions of eminent men, see how they acted in warfare, examine the causes of their victories and defeats in order to imitate the former and avoid the latter, and above all, do as some men have done in the past, who have imitated some one, who has been much praised and glorified, and have always kept his deeds and actions before them, as they say Alexander the Great imitated Achilles, Caesar Alexander, and Scipio Cyrus. And whoever reads the life of Cyrus written by Xenophon, will perceive in the life of Scipio how gloriously he imitated the former, and how, in chastity, affability, humanity, and liberality Scipio conformed to those qualities of Cyrus as described by Xenophon.

A wise prince should follow similar methods and never remain idle in peaceful times, but industriously make good use of them, so that when fortune changes she may find him prepared to resist her blows, and to prevail in adversity …

Document 8.2

Jean Bodin on Sovereignty

Bodin (1529/30–96), French jurist and political thinker, developed his definition of sovereignty as the undivided power to make general laws against the background of the French Wars of Religion, during which a strong Protestant Huguenot minority advanced the legitimacy of resistance to the Catholic monarchy. Without such a legal power a state could not be held properly to exist.

Sovereignty is that absolute and perpetual power vested in a commonwealth which in Latin is termed *majestas* … The term needs careful definition, because although it is the distinguishing mark of a commonwealth, and an understanding of its nature is fundamental to any treatment of politics, no jurist or political philosopher has in fact attempted to define it …

I have described it as perpetual because one can give absolute power to a person or group of persons for a period of time, but that time expired they become subjects once more. Therefore even while they enjoy power, they cannot properly be regarded as sovereign rulers, but only as the lieutenants and agents of the sovereign ruler, till the moment comes when it pleases the prince or the people to revoke the gift. The true sovereign remains always seized of his power. Just as a feudal lord who grants lands to another retains his eminent domain over them, so the ruler who delegates authority to judge and command, whether it be for a short period, or during pleasure, remains seized of those rights of jurisdiction actually exercised by another in the form of a revocable grant, or precarious tenancy. For this reason the law requires the governor of a province, or the prince's lieutenant, to make a formal surrender of the authority committed to him, at the expiration of his term of office. In this respect there is no difference between the highest officer of state and his humblest subordinate. If it were otherwise, and the absolute authority delegated by the prince to a lieutenant was regarded as itself sovereign power, the latter could use it against his prince who would thereby forfeit his eminence, and the subject could command his lord, the servant his master. This is a manifest absurdity, considering that the sovereign is always excepted personally, as a matter of right, in all delegations of authority, however extensive. However much he gives there always remains a reserve of right in his own person, whereby he may command or intervene by way of prevention, confirmation, evocation, or any other way he thinks fit, in all matters delegated to a subject, whether in virtue of an office or a commission. Any authority exercised in virtue of an office or a commission can be revoked, or made tenable for as long or short a period as the sovereign wills …

A perpetual authority therefore must be understood to mean one that lasts for the lifetime of him who exercises it. If a sovereign magistrate is given office for one year, or for any other predetermined period, and continues to exercise the authority bestowed on him after the conclusion of his term, he does so either by consent or by force and violence. If he does so by force, it is manifest tyranny. The tyrant is a true sovereign for all that. The robber's possession by violence is true and natural possession although contrary to the law, for those who were formerly in possession have been disseized. But if the magistrate continues in office by consent, he is not a sovereign prince, seeing that he only exercises power on sufferance. Still less is he a sovereign if the term of his office is not fixed, for in that case he has no more than a precarious commission …

What bearing have these considerations on the case of the man to whom the people has given absolute power for the term of his natural life? One must distinguish. If such absolute power is given him simply and unconditionally, and not in virtue of some office or commission, nor in the form of a revocable grant, the recipient certainly is, and should be acknowledged to be, a sovereign. The people has renounced and alienated its sovereign power in order to invest him with it and put him in possession, and it thereby transfers to him all its powers, authority, and sovereign rights, just as does the man who gives to another possessory and proprietary rights over what he formerly owned …

Let us now turn to the other term of our definition and consider the force of the word absolute. The people or the magnates of a commonwealth can bestow simply and unconditionally upon someone of their choice a sovereign and perpetual power to dispose of their property and persons, to govern the state as he thinks fit, and to order the succession, in the same way that any proprietor, out of his liberality, can freely and unconditionally make a gift of his property to another. Such a form of gift, not being qualified in any way, is the only true gift, being at once unconditional and irrevocable. Gifts burdened with obligations and hedged with conditions are not true gifts. Similarly, sovereign power given to a prince charged with conditions is neither properly sovereign, nor absolute, unless the conditions of appointment are only such as are inherent in the laws of God and of nature …

If we insist however that absolute power means exemption from all law whatsoever, there is no prince in the world who can be regarded as sovereign, since all the princes of the earth are subject to the laws of God and of nature, and even to certain human laws common to all nations …

On the other hand, it is the distinguishing mark of the sovereign that he cannot in any way be subject to the commands of another, for it is he who makes law for the subject, abrogates law already made, and amends obsolete law …

For all laws, ordinances, letters patent, privileges, and grants whatsoever issued by the prince, have force only during his own lifetime, and must be expressly, or at least tacitly confirmed by the reigning prince who has cognizance of them … In proof of which, it is the custom of this realm for all corporations and corporate bodies to ask for the confirmation of their privileges, rights, and jurisdictions, on the accession of a new king. Even Parliaments and high courts do this, as well as individual officers of the crown.

If the prince is not bound by the laws of his predecessors, still less can he be bound by his own laws. One may be subject to laws made by another, but it is impossible to bind oneself in any matter which is the subject of one's own free exercise of will. As the law says, 'there can be no obligation in any matter which proceeds from the free will of the undertaker'. It follows of necessity that the king cannot be subject to his own laws. Just as, according to the canonists, the Pope can never tie his own hands, so the sovereign prince cannot bind himself, even if he wishes. For this reason edicts and ordinances conclude with the formula 'for such is our good pleasure', thus intimating that the laws of a sovereign prince, even when founded on truth and right reason, proceed simply from his own free will.

It is far otherwise with divine and natural laws. All the princes of the earth are subject to them, and cannot contravene them without treason and rebellion against God. His yoke is upon them, and they must bow their heads in fear and reverence before His divine majesty. The absolute power of princes and sovereign lords does not extend to the laws of God and of nature. He who best understood the meaning of absolute power, and made kings and emperors submit to his will, defined his sovereignty as a power to override positive law; he did not claim power to set aside divine and natural law.

But supposing the prince should swear to keep the laws and customs of his country, is he not bound by that oath? One must distinguish. If a prince promises in his own heart to obey his own laws, he is nevertheless not bound to do so, any more than anyone is bound by an oath taken to himself. Even private citizens are not bound by private oaths to keep agreements. The law permits them to cancel them, even if the agreements are in themselves reasonable and good. But if one sovereign prince promises another sovereign prince to keep the agreements entered into by his predecessors, he is bound to do so even if not under oath, if that other prince's interests are involved. If they are not, he is not bound either by a promise, or even by an oath.

The same holds good of promises made by the sovereign to the subject, even if the promises were made prior to his election (for this does not make the difference that many suppose). It is not that the prince is bound either by his own laws or those of his predecessors. But he is bound by the just covenants and promises he has made, whether under oath to do so or not, to exactly the same extent that a private individual is bound in like case.

Document 8.3

Thomas Hobbes, *Leviathan*

Thomas Hobbes (1588–1679) published *Leviathan* in 1651 during the Commonwealth. The following extracts deal with the issue which is central to his theory. In every political order, he argued, there must be a sovereign power to enforce the covenant to peace that men have made to ensure their self-preservation, which is so threatened in the state of nature. 'Covenants without the sword', he said, 'are but words and of no strength to secure a man at all'. His conception was novel in that it allowed no legal limitation on the sovereign power, which was indivisible. At the same time man's right to self-preservation remained and this considerably qualified the absolutist tenor of his thought.

OF THE CAUSES, GENERATION, AND DEFINITION OF A COMMONWEALTH

a) The final cause, end, or design of men, who naturally love liberty, and dominion over others, in the introduction of that restraint upon themselves, in which we see them live in commonwealths, is the foresight of their own preservation, and of a more contented life thereby; that is to say, of getting themselves out from that miserable condition of war, which is necessarily consequent, as hath been shown (Part I, chapter 13), to the natural passions of men, when there is no visible power to keep them in awe, and tie them by fear of punishment to the performance of their convenants, and observation of laws of nature.

For the laws of nature, as justice, equity, modesty, mercy, and, in sum, doing to others, as we would be done to, of themselves, without the terror of some power to cause them to be observed, are contrary to our natural passions, that carry us to partiality, pride, revenge, and the like. And covenants, without the sword, are but words, and of no strength to secure a man at all. Therefore notwithstanding the laws of nature (which every one hath then kept, when he has the will to keep them, when he can do it safely) if there be no power erected, or not great enough for our security; every man will, and may lawfully rely on his own strength and art, for caution against all other men ...

Nor is it the joining together of a small number of men, that gives them this security; because in small numbers, small additions on the one side or the other, make the advantage of strength so great, as is sufficient to carry the victory; and therefore gives encouragement to an invasion. The multitude sufficient to confide in for our security, is not determined by any certain number, but by comparison with the enemy we fear; and is then sufficient, when the odds of the enemy is not of so visible and conspicuous moment, to determine the event of war, as to move him to attempt.

And be there never so great a multitude; yet if their actions be directed according to their particular judgements, and particular appetites, they can expect thereby no defence, nor protection, neither against a common enemy, nor against the injuries of one another. For being distracted in opinions concerning the best use and application of their strength, they do not help but hinder one another; and reduce their strength by mutual opposition to nothing: whereby they are easily, not only subdued by a very few that agree together; but also when there is no common enemy, they make war upon each other, for their particular interests ...

It is true, that certain living creatures, as bees, and ants, live sociably one with another, which are therefore by Aristotle numbered amongst political creatures; and yet have no other direction, than their particular judgments and appetites; nor speech, whereby one of them can signify to another, what he thinks expedient for the common benefit: and therefore some man may perhaps desire to know, why mankind cannot do the same. To which I answer, First, that men are continually in competition for honour and dignity, which these creatures are not; and consequently amongst men there ariseth on that ground, envy and hatred, and finally war; but amongst these not so.

Secondly, that amongst these creatures, the common good differeth not from the private; and being by nature inclined to their private, they procure thereby the common benefit. But man, whose joy consisteth in comparing himself with other men, can relish nothing but what is eminent.

Thirdly, that these creatures, having not, as man, the use of reason, do not see, nor think they see any fault, in the administration of their common business; whereas amongst men, there are very many, that think themselves wiser, and abler to govern the public, better than the rest; and these strive to reform and innovate, one this way another that way; and thereby bring it into distraction and civil war ...

Lastly, the agreement of these creatures is natural; that of men, is by covenant only, which is artificial: and therefore it is no wonder if there be somewhat else required, besides covenant, to make their agreement constant and lasting; which is a common power, to keep them in awe, and to direct their actions to the common benefit.

The only way to erect such a common power, as may be able to defend them from the invasion of foreigners, and the injuries of one another, and thereby to secure them in such sort, as that by their own industry, and by the fruits of the earth, they may nourish themselves and live contentedly; is, to confer all their power and strength upon one man, or upon one assembly of men, that may reduce all their wills, by plurality of voices, unto one will: which is as much as to say, to appoint one man, or assembly of men, to bear their person; and every one to own, and acknowledge himself to be author of whatsoever he that so beareth their person, shall act, or cause to be acted, in those things which concern the common peace and safety; and therein to submit their wills, every one to his will, and their judgement. This is more than consent, or concord; it is a real unity of them all, in one and the same person, made by covenant of every man with every man, in such manner, as if every man should say to every man, 'I authorize and give up my right of governing myself, to this man, or to this assembly of men, on this condition, that thou give up thy right to him, and authorize all his actions in like manner.' This done, the multitude so united in one person, is called a COMMONWEALTH, in Latin *CIVITAS*. This is the generation of that great LEVIATHAN, or rather, to speak more reverently, of that immortal God, to which we owe under the immortal god, our peace and defence. For by this authority, given him by every particular man in the commonwealth, he hath the use of so much power and strength conferred on him, that by terror thereof, he is enabled to form the wills of them all, to peace at home, and mutual aid against their enemies abroad. And in him consisteth the essence of the commonwealth; which, to define it, is one person, of whose acts a great multitude, by mutual covenants one with another, have made themselves every one the author, to the end he may use the strength and means of them all, as he shall think expedient, for their peace and common defence.

And he that carrieth this person, is called SOVEREIGN, and said to have sovereign power; and every one besides, his SUBJECT.

The attaining to this sovereign power, is by two ways. One, by natural force; as when a man maketh his children, to submit themselves, and their children to his government, as being able to destroy them if they refuse; or by war subdueth his enemies to his will, giving them their lives on that condition. The other, is when men agree amongst themselves, to submit to some man, or assembly of men, voluntarily, on confidence to be protected by him against all others. This latter, may be called a political commonwealth, or commonwealth by institution; and the former, a commonwealth by acquisition. And first, I shall speak of a commonwealth by institution.

b) *OF THE RIGHTS OF SOVEREIGNS BY INSTITUTION*

From [the] institution of a commonwealth are derived all the rights, and faculties of him, or them, on whom the sovereign power is conferred by the consent of the people assembled ...

[Thus] because the right of bearing the person of them all, is given to him they make sovereign, by covenant only of one to another, and not of him to any of them; there can happen no breach of covenant on the part of the sovereign; and consequently none of his subjects, by any pretence of forfeiture, can be freed from his subjection ... The opinion that any monarch receiveth his power by covenant, that is to say, on condition, proceedeth from want of understanding this easy truth, that covenants being but words and breath, have no force to oblige, contain, constrain, or protect any man, but what it has from the public sword ...

[Further], because every subject is by this institution author of all the actions, and judgements of the sovereign instituted; it follows, that whatsoever he doth, it can be no injury to any of his subjects; nor ought he to be by any of them accused of injustice. For he that doth anything by authority from another, doth therein no injury to him by whose authority he acteth: but by this institution of a commonwealth, every particular man is author of all the sovereign doth: and consequently he that complaineth of injury from his sovereign, complaineth of what whereof he himself is author ...

Consequently to that which was said last, no man that hath sovereign power can justly be put to death, or otherwise in any manner by his subjects punished ...

And because the end of this institution, is the peace and defence of them all; and whosoever has right to the end, has right to the means; it belongeth of right, to whatsoever man, or assembly that hath the sovereignty, to be judge both of the means of peace and defence, and also of the hindrances, and disturbances of the same; and to do whatsoever he shall think necessary to be done, both beforehand, for the preserving of peace and security, by prevention of discord at home, and hostility from abroad; and, when peace and security are lost, for the recovery of the same.

And therefore ... it is annexed to the sovereignty, to be judge of what opinions and doctrines are averse, and what conducing to peace; and consequently, on what occasions, how far, and what men are to be trusted withal, in speaking to multitudes of people; and who shall examine the doctrines of all books before they be published. For the actions of men proceed from their opinions; and in the well-governing of opinions, consisteth the well-governing of men's actions, in order to their peace, and concord. And though in matter of doctrine, nothing ought to be regarded but the truth; yet this is not repugnant to regulating the same by peace. For doctrine repugnant to peace, can no more be true, than peace and concord can be against the law of nature ...

[Also] is annexed to the sovereignty, the whole power of prescribing the rules, whereby every man may know, what goods, and how great forces are to be assembled, armed, and paid for that end; and to levy money upon the subjects, to defray the expenses thereof. For the power by which the people are to be defended, consisteth in their armies; and the strength of an army, in the union of their strength under one command; which command the sovereign instituted, therefore hath …

c) OF DOMINION PATERNAL AND DESPOTICAL

A commonwealth by acquisition, is that, where the sovereign power is acquired by force; and it is acquired by force, when men simply, or many together by plurality of voices, for fear of death, or bonds, do authorise all the actions of that man, or assembly, that hath their lives and liberty in his power.

And this kind of dominion, or sovereignty, differeth from sovereignty by institution, only in this, that men who choose their sovereign, do it for fear of one another, and not of him whom they institute: but in this case, they subject themselves, to him they are afraid of. In both cases they do it for fear …

But the rights and consequences of sovereignty, are the same in both … [The sovereign] cannot be accused by any of his subjects, of injury; he cannot be punished by them; he is judge of what is necessary for peace; and judge of doctrines; he is sole legislator; and supreme judge of controversies; and of the times, and occasions of war, and peace; to him it belongeth to choose magistrates, counsellors, commanders, and all other officers, and ministers; and to determine of rewards, and punishment, honour and order. The reasons whereof, are the same which are alleged in the precedent chapter, for the same rights, and consequences of sovereignty by institution …

So that it appeareth plainly, to my understanding, … that the sovereign power, whether placed in one man, as in monarch, or in one assembly of men, as in popular and aristocratical commonwealths, is as great, as possibly men can be imagined to make it. And though of so unlimited a power, men may fancy many evil consequences, yet the consequences of the want of it, which is perpetual war of every man against his neighbour, are much worse.

The condition of man in this life shall never be without inconvenience; but there happeneth in no commonwealth any great inconvenience, but what proceeds from the subjects' disobedience, and breach of those covenants, from which the commonwealth hath its being …

Document 8.4

Dr Samuel Johnson, Taxation no Tyranny

Dr Johnson (1709–84), English literary critic, lexicographer and journalist, also showed a close interest in contemporary politics. The following is an extract from a pamphlet, published in 1775, justifying King George III's coercion of the American colonists. In his view the American principle of no taxation without representation was fallacious. Millions of British people were taxed yearly without representation. The significance of this passage is its assertion of the legal omnicompetence of Parliament, a principle which he grasped in advance of most of his contemporaries.

The colonies of England differ no otherwise from those of other nations, than as the English constitution differs from theirs. All government is ultimately and essentially absolute, but subordinate societies may have more immunities, or individuals greater liberty, as the operations of government are differently conducted. An Englishman in the common course of life and action feels no restraint. An English colony has very liberal powers of regulating its own manners and adjusting its own affairs. But an English individual may by the supreme authority be deprived of liberty, and a colony divested of its powers, for reasons of which that authority is the only judge.

In sovereignty there are no gradations. There may be limited royalty, there may be limited consulship; but there can be no limited government. There must in every society be some power or other from which there is no appeal, which admits no restrictions, which pervades the whole mass of the community, regulates and adjusts all subordination, enacts laws or repeals them, erects or annuls judicatures, extends or contracts privileges, exempts itself from question or control, and bounded only by physical necessity.

By this power, wherever it subsists, all legislation and jurisdiction is animated and maintained. From this all legal rights are emanations, which, whether equitably or not, may be legally recalled. It is not infallible, for it may do wrong; but it is irresistible, for it can be resisted only by rebellion, by an act which makes it questionable what shall be thenceforward the supreme power.

An English colony is a number of persons, to whom the King grants a charter permitting them to settle in some distant country, and enabling them to constitute a corporation, enjoying such powers as the charter grants, to be administered in such forms as the charter prescribes. As a corporation they make laws for themselves, but as a corporation subsisting by a grant from higher authority, to the control of that authority they continue subject.

As men are placed at a greater distance from the Supreme Council of the kingdom, they must be entrusted with ampler liberty of regulating their conduct by their own wisdom. As they are more secluded from easy recourse to national judicature, they must be more extensively commissioned to pass judgment on each other.

For this reason our more important and opulent colonies see the appearance and feel the effect of a regular legislature, which in some places has acted so long with unquestioned authority, that it has been forgotten whence that authority was originally derived.

To their charters the colonies owe, like other corporations, their political existence. The solemnities of legislation, the administration of justice, the security of property, are all bestowed upon them by the royal grant. Without their charter there would be no power among them, by which any law could be made, or duties enjoined, any debt recovered, or criminal punished.

A charter is a grant of certain powers or privileges given to a part of the community for the advantage of the whole, and is therefore liable by its nature to change or to revocation. Every act of government aims at publick good. A charter, which experience has shewn to be detrimental to the nation, is to be repealed; because general prosperity must always be preferred to particular interest. If a charter be used to evil purposes, it is forfeited, as the weapon is taken away which is injuriously employed.

The charter therefore by which provincial governments are constituted, may be always legally, and where it is either inconvenient in its nature, or misapplied in its use, may be equitably repealed; by such repeal the whole fabrick of subordination is immediately destroyed, and the constitution sunk at once into a chaos: the society is dissolved into a tumult of individuals, without authority to command, or obligation to obey; without any punishment of wrongs but by personal resentment, or any protection of right but by the hand of the possessor.

Document 8.5

Richard Price on the Authority of one Country Over Another

Richard Price (1723–91), a Welsh dissenting clergyman, was one of the most cogent writers in defence of the American and French Revolutions. An imperial relationship, he argued, was only justifiable as long as those living under such rule countenanced it. He was a fearless spokesman for inalienable human rights based on justice, and his writings illustrate emergent democratic thought. His sermon-pamphlet, *Discourse on the Love of our Country*, prompted Edmund Burke to write his *Reflections on the Revolution in France* (1790).

From the nature and principles of civil liberty, as they have been now explained, it is an immediate and necessary inference that no one community can have any power over the property or legislation of another community which is not incorporated with it by a just and adequate representation. Then only, it has been shewn, is a state free when it is governed by its own will. But a country that is subject to the legislature of another country in which it has no voice, and over which it has no control, cannot be said to be governed by its own will. Such a country, therefore, is in a state of slavery. And it deserves to be particularly considered that such a slavery is worse, on several accounts, than any slavery of private men to one another, or of kingdoms to despots within themselves. Between one state and another there is none of that fellow-feeling that takes place between persons in private life. Being detached bodies that never see one another, and residing perhaps in different quarters of the globe, the state that governs cannot be a witness to the sufferings occasioned by its oppressions; or a competent judge of the circumstances and abilities of the people who are governed. They must also have in a great degree separate interests; and the more the one is loaded the more the other may be eased. The infamy likewise of oppression, being in such circumstances shared among a multitude, is not likely to be much felt or regarded. On all these accounts there is, in the case of one country subjugated to another, little or nothing to check rapacity; and the most flagrant injustice and cruelty may be practised without remorse or pity. I will add that it is particularly difficult to shake off a tyranny of this kind. A single despot, if a people are unanimous and resolute, may be soon subdued. But a despotic state is not easily subdued, and a people subject to it cannot emancipate themselves without entering into a dreadful and, perhaps, very unequal contest.

I cannot help observing farther, that the slavery of a people to internal despots may be qualified and limited; but I don't see what can limit the authority of one state over another. The exercise of power in this case can have no other measure than discretion, and, therefore, must be indefinite and absolute.

Once more, it should be considered that the government of one country by another can only be opposed by a military force, and, without such a support must be destitute of all weight and efficiency.

This will be best explained by putting the following case. There is, let us suppose, in a province subject to the sovereignty of a distant state, a subordinate legislature consisting of an assembly chosen by the people; a council chosen by that assembly; and a governor appointed by the sovereign state, and paid by the province. There are, likewise, judges and other officers, appointed and paid in the same manner, for administering justice agreeably to the laws by the verdicts of juries fairly chosen.

This forms a constitution seemingly free, by giving the people a share in their own government and some check on their rulers. But, while there is a higher legislative power to the control of which such a constitution is subject, it does not itself possess liberty, and therefore cannot be of any use as a security to liberty; nor is it possible that it should be of long duration. Laws offensive to the province will be enacted by the sovereign state. The legislature of the province will remonstrate against them. The magistrates will not execute them. Juries will not convict upon them, and, consequently, like the Pope's Bulls which once governed Europe, they will become nothing but forms and empty sounds to which no regard will be shewn. In order to remedy this evil and to give efficiency to its government, the supreme state will naturally be led to withdraw the governor, the council, and the judges from the control of the province by making them entirely dependent on itself for their pay and continuance in office, as well as for their appointment. It will also alter the mode of chusing juries on purpose to bring them more under its influence. And in some cases, under the pretence of the impossibility of gaining an impartial trial where government is resisted, it will perhaps ordain that offenders shall be removed from the province to be tried within its own territories. And it may even go so far in this kind of policy as to endeavour to prevent the effects of discontents by forbidding all meetings and associations of the people except at such times, and for such particular purposes, as shall be permitted them.

Thus will such a province be exactly in the same state that Britain would be in were our first executive magistrate, our House of Lords, and our judges, nothing but the instruments of a sovereign democratical power; were our juries nominated by that power; or were we liable to be transported to a distant country to be tried for offences committed here; and restrained from calling any meetings, consulting about any grievances, or associating for any purposes, except when leave should be given us by a Lord Lieutenant or Viceroy.

It is certain that this is a state of oppression which no country could endure, and to which it would be vain to expect, that any people should submit an hour without an armed force to compel them.

The late transactions in Massachusett's Bay are a perfect exemplification of what I have now said. The government of Great Britain in that province has gone on exactly in the train I have described; till at last it became necessary to station troops there not amenable to the civil power; and all terminated in a government by the sword. And such, if a people are not sunk below the character of men, will be the issue of all government in similar circumstances.

It may be asked, 'Are there not causes by which one state may acquire a rightful authority over another, though not consolidated by an adequate representation?' I answer that there are no such causes. All the causes to which such an effect can be ascribed are conquest, compact, or obligations conferred.

Much has been said of the right of conquest; and history contains little more than accounts of kingdoms reduced by it under the dominion of other kingdoms, and of the havock it has made among mankind. But the authority derived from hence, being founded on violence, is never rightful. The Roman Republic was nothing but a faction against the general liberties of the world; and had no more right to give law to the provinces subject to it than thieves have to the property they seize, or to the houses into which they break. Even in the case of a just war undertaken by one people to defend itself against the oppressions of another people, conquest gives only a right to an indemnification for the injury which occasioned the war and a reasonable security against future injury.

Neither can any state acquire such an authority over other states in virtue of any compacts of cessions. This is a case in which compacts are not binding. Civil liberty is, in this respect, on the same footing with religious liberty. As no people can lawfully surrender their religious liberty by giving up their right of judging for themselves in religion, or by allowing any human beings to prescribe to them what faith they shall embrace, or what mode of worship they shall practise, so neither can any civil societies lawfully surrender their civil liberty by giving up to any extraneous jurisdiction their power of legislating for themselves and disposing their property. Such a cession, being inconsistent with the unalienable rights of human nature, would either not bind at all, or bind only the individuals who made it. This is a blessing which no one generation of men can give up for another, and which, when lost, a people have always a right to resume.

Had our ancestors in this country been so mad as to have subjected themselves to any foreign community, we could not have been under any obligation to continue in such a state. And all the nations now in the world who, in consequence of the tameness and folly of their predecessors, are subject to arbitrary power have a right to emancipate themselves as soon as they can.

If neither conquest nor compact can give such an authority, much less can any favours received or any services performed by one state for another. Let the favour received be what it will, liberty is too dear a price for it. A state that has been obliged is not, therefore, bound to be enslaved. It ought, if possible, to make an adequate return for the services done to it, but to suppose that it ought to give up the power of governing itself and the disposal of its property, would be to suppose, that, in order to show its gratitude, it ought to part with the power of ever afterwards exercising gratitude. How much has been done by this kingdom for Hanover?

But no one will say that on this account we have a right to make the laws of Hanover; or even to draw a single penny from it without its own consent.

After what has been said, it will, I am afraid, be trifling to apply the preceding arguments to the case of different communities which are considered as different parts of the same empire. But there are reasons which render it necessary for me to be explicit in making the application.

What I mean here is just to point out the difference of situation between communities forming an empire; and particular bodies of classes of men forming different parts of a kingdom. Different communities forming an empire have no connexions which produce a necessary reciprocation of interests between them. They inhabit different districts and are governed by different legislatures. On the contrary, the different classes of men within a kingdom are all placed on the same ground. Their concerns and interests are the same, and what is done to one part must affect all. These are situations totally different and a constitution of government that may be consistent with liberty in one of them may be entirely inconsistent with it in the other. It is, however, certain that, even in the last of these situations, no one part ought to govern the rest. In order to a fair and equal government, there ought to be a fair and equal representation of all that are governed; and as far as this is wanting in any government, it deviates from the principles of liberty, and becomes unjust and oppressive. But in the circumstances of different communities, all this holds with unspeakably more force. The government of a part in this case becomes complete tyranny, and subjection to it becomes complete slavery.

Document 8.6

Edmund Burke at the Trial of Warren Hastings

Edmund Burke (1729–97) instigated the impeachment of Warren Hastings for corruption and abuse of power. Governor-General of Bengal between 1772 and

1785, in 1787 Hastings argued that it was inappropriate to apply Western standards of legality and authority to government in India. He was subsequently acquitted, after a seven-year trial before the House of Lords.

... I will first beg your lordships to take notice of the utter contempt with which he treats all our Acts of Parliament. Speaking of the absolute sovereignty which he would have you believe is exercised by the princes of India, he says, 'The sovereignty which they assumed, it fell to my lot very unexpectedly to exert, and whether or not such power or powers of that nature were delegated to me by any Act of Parliament, I confess myself too little of a lawyer to pronounce', and so on. This is the manner in which he treats an act of parliament! In the place of Acts of Parliament he substitutes his own arbitrary will. This he contends is the sole law of the country he governed, as laid down in what he calls the arbitrary institutes of Ghinges Khan and Tamerlane. This arbitrary will he claims, to the exclusion of the Gentoo law, the Mahomedan law, and the law of his own country ...

On the one side, your lordships have the prisoner declaring that the people have no laws, no rights, no usages, no distinctions of rank, no sense of honour, no property; in short, that they are nothing but a herd of slaves to be governed by the arbitrary will of a master. On the other side, we assert that the direct contrary is true. And to prove our assertion we have referred you to the Institutes of Ghinges Khan and of Tamerlane: we have referred you to the Mahomedan law, which is binding upon all, from the crowned head to the meanest subject; a law interwoven with a system of the wisest, the most learned, and most enlightened jurisprudence that perhaps ever existed in the world. We have shown you, that it is not the rights of the people which are nothing, but rather the rights of the sovereign which are so. The rights of the people are everything, as they ought to be in the true and natural order of things. God forbid that these maxims should trench upon sovereignty, and its true, just, and lawful prerogative; on the contrary, they ought to support and establish them. The sovereign's rights are undoubtedly sacred rights, and ought to be so held in every country in the world; because exercised for the benefit of the people and in subordination to that great end for which alone God has vested power in any man or any set of men ...

He next alleges with reference to one particular case, that he received this sovereignty from the Vizier Sujah Dowlah, who, he pretends, was sovereign, with an unlimited power over the life, goods, and property of Cheit Sing. This we positively deny. Whatever power the supreme sovereign of the empire had, we deny that it was delegated to Sujah Dowlah. He never was in possession of it. He was a vizier of the empire; he had a grant of certain lands for the support of that dignity, and we refer you to the institutes of Timour, to the institutes of Akbar, to the institutes of Mahomedan law, for the powers of delegated governors and viceroys. You will find that there is not a trace of sovereignty in them; but that they are, to all intents and purposes, mere subjects; and consequently, as Sujah Dowlah had not these powers, he could not transfer them to the India Company.

His master, the Mogul emperor, had them not. I defy any man to show an instance of that emperor's claiming any such thing as arbitrary power; much less can it be claimed by a rebellious viceroy who had broken loose from his sovereign's authority, just as this man broke loose from the authority of Parliament. The one had not a right to give, nor the other to receive, such powers; but whatever rights were vested in the Mogul, they cannot belong either to Sujah Dowlah, to Mr. Hastings, or to the Company. These latter are expressly bound by their compact to take care of the subjects of the empire, and to govern them according to law, reason, and equity; and when they do otherwise, they are guilty of tyranny, of a violation of the rights of the people, and of rebellion against their sovereign.

Document 8.7

G.W.F. Hegel on Sovereignty

Georg Wilhelm Friedrich Hegel (1770–1831), an influential philosopher and political theorist, drew a clear distinction between the state and civil society. The state was not merely an instrumental, but an ethical entity and an end in itself. These considerations led him to reject the radical idea of the sovereignty of the people. The extract is from his *Philosophy of Right*.

The usual sense, however, in which men have recently begun to speak of the 'sovereignty of the people's' is that it is something opposed to the sovereignty existent in the monarch. So opposed to the sovereignty of the monarch, the sovereignty of the people is one of the confused notions based on the wild idea of the 'people'. Taken without its monarch and the articulation of the whole which is the indispensable and direct concomitant of the monarchy, the people is a formless mass and no longer a state. It lacks every one of those determinate characteristics – sovereignty, government, judges, magistrates, class-divisions, etc. – which are to be found only in a whole which is inwardly organized. By the very emergence into a people's life of moments of this kind which have a bearing on an organization, on political life, a people ceases to be that indeterminate abstraction which, when represented in a quite general way, is called the 'people'.

Document 8.8

A.V. Dicey on the Sovereignty of Parliament

Albert Venn Dicey (1835–1922), British jurist, is best known for his classic treatise on constitutional law, *Introduction to the Study of the Law of the Constitution*. This book dealt with what he described as the guiding principles which pervaded the modern Constitution of England, the Sovereignty of Parliament, the Rule of Law and the coexistence of law with constitutional convention. There has been considerable discussion over the application of his analysis in changed circumstances. A particular point of controversy has concerned the question whether a sovereign legislature, as described by Dicey in Britain, is capable of protecting its own legislation from repeal by enacting a special manner and form for legislation of special importance.

The sovereignty of Parliament is (from a legal point of view) the dominant characteristic of our political institutions ... Parliament means, in the mouth of a lawyer ... the Queen, the House of Lords, and the House of Commons; these three bodies acting together may be aptly described as the 'Queen in Parliament', and constitute Parliament. The principle of Parliamentary sovereignty means neither more nor less than this, namely, that Parliament thus defined has, under the English constitution, the right to make or unmake any law whatever; and, further, that no person or body is recognised by the law of England as having a right to override or set aside the legislation of Parliament.

A law, may, for our present purpose, be defined as 'any rule which will be enforced by the courts.' The principle then of Parliamentary sovereignty may, looked at from its positive side, be thus described: Any Act of Parliament, or any part of an Act of Parliament, which makes a new law, or repeals or modifies an existing law, will be obeyed by the courts. The same principle, looked at from its negative side, may be thus stated: There is no person or body of persons who can, under the English constitution, make rules which override or derogate from an Act of Parliament, or which (to express the same thing in other words) will be enforced by the courts in contravention of an Act of Parliament. Some apparent exceptions to this rule no doubt suggest themselves. But these apparent exceptions ... are resolvable into cases in which Parliament either directly or indirectly sanctions subordinate legislation ...

A large proportion of English law is in reality made by the judges ... This judicial legislation might appear, at first sight, inconsistent with the supremacy of Parliament. But this is not so. English judges do not claim or exercise any power to repeal a Statute, whilst Acts of Parliament may override and constantly do override the law of the judges. Judicial legislation is, in short, subordinate legislation, carried on with the assent and subject to the supervision of Parliament ...

The actual exercise of authority by ... Parliament is bounded or controlled by two limitations. Of these the one is an external, the other is an internal limitation ... The combined influence both of the external and of the internal limitation on legislative sovereignty is admirably stated in Leslie Stephen's *Science of Ethics*, whose chapter on 'Law and Custom' contains one of the best statements to be met with of the limits placed by the nature of things on the theoretical omnipotence of sovereign legislatures.

'Lawyers are apt to speak as though the legislature were omnipotent, as they do not require to go beyond its decisions. It is, of course, omnipotent in the sense that it can make whatever laws it pleases, inasmuch as a law means any rule which has been made by the legislature. But from the scientific point of view, the power of the legislature is of course strictly limited. It is limited, so to speak, both from within and from without; from within, because the legislature is the product of a certain social condition, and determined by whatever determines the society; and from without, because the power of imposing laws is dependent upon the instinct of subordination, which is itself limited. If a legislature decided that all blue-eyed babies should be murdered, the preservation of blue-eyed babies would be illegal; but legislators must go mad before they could pass such a law, and subjects be idiotic before they could submit to it'.

Document 8.9

Benito Mussolini on the Fascist State

Benito Mussolini (1883–1945), the Italian Facist leader co-authored with Giovanni Gentile a major article on Fascism in the *Enciclopedia Italiana* in 1932. The following is an extract. Fascism was characterized by exaltation of the totalitarian state, nationalism, hostility to democracy and liberalism, the cult of leader and glorification of struggle and war.

7. Against individualism, the Fascist conception is for the State; and it is for the individual in so far as he coincides with the State, which is the conscience and universal will of man in his historical existence. It is opposed to classical Liberalism, which arose from the necessity of reacting against absolutism, and which brought its historical purpose to an end when the State was transformed into the conscience and will of the people. Liberalism denied the State in the interests of the particular individual; Fascism reaffirms the State as the true reality of the individual. And if liberty is to be the attribute of the real man, and not of that abstract puppet envisaged by individualistic Liberalism, Fascism is for liberty. And for the only liberty which can be a real thing, the liberty of the State and of the individual within the State. Therefore, for the Fascist, everything is in the State, and nothing human or spiritual exists, much less has value, outside the State. In this sense Fascism is totalitarian, and the Fascist State, the synthesis and unity of all values, interprets, develops and gives strength to the whole life of the people.

8. Outside the State there can be neither individuals nor groups (political parties, associations, syndicates, classes). Therefore Fascism is opposed to Socialism, which confines the movement of history with and ignores the unity of classes established in one economic and moral reality in the State; and analogously it is opposed to class syndicalism. Fascism recognizes the real exigencies for which the socialist and syndicalist movement arose, but while recognizing them wishes to bring them under the control of the State and give them a purpose within the corporative system of interests reconciled within the unity of the State.

Individuals form classes according to the similarity of their interests, they form syndicates according to differentiated economic activities within these interests; but they form first, and above all, the State, which is not to be thought of numerically as the sum-total of individuals forming the majority of a nation. And consequently Fascism is opposed to Democracy, which equates the nation to the majority, lowering it to the level of that majority; nevertheless it is the purest form of democracy if the nation is conceived, as it should be, qualitatively and not quantitatively, as the most powerful idea (most powerful because most moral, most coherent, most true) which acts within the nation as the conscience and the will of a few, even of One, which ideal tends to become active within the conscience and the will of all – that is to say, of all those who rightly constitute a nation by reason of nature, history or race, and have development and spiritual formation as one conscience and one sole will. Not a race, nor a geographically determined region, but as a community historically perpetuating itself, a multitude unified by a single idea, which is the will to existence and to power: consciousness of itself, personality.

10. This higher personality is truly the nation in so far as it is the State. It is not the nation that generates the State, as according to the old naturalistic concept which served as the basis of the political theories of the national States of the nineteenth century. Rather the nation is created by the State, which gives to the people, conscious of its own moral unity, a will and therefore an effective existence. The right of a nation to independence derives not from a literary and ideal consciousness of its own being, still less from a more or less unconscious and inert acceptance of a de facto situation, but from an active consciousness, from a political will in action and ready to demonstrate its own rights: that is to say, form a state already coming into being. The State, in fact, as the universal ethical will, is the creator of right.

11. The nation as the State is an ethical reality which exists and lives in so far as it develops. To arrest its development is to kill it. Therefore the State is not only the authority which governs and gives the form of laws and the value of spiritual life to the individuals, but it is also a power that makes its will felt abroad, making it known and respected, in other words, demonstrating the fact of its universality in all the necessary directions of its development. It is consequently organization and expansion, at least virtually. Thus it can be likened to the human will which knows no limits to its development and realizes itself in testing its own limitlessness.

12. The Fascist State, the highest and most powerful form of personality, is a force, but a spiritual force, which takes over all the forms of the moral and intellectual life of man. It cannot therefore confine itself simply to the functions of order and supervision as Liberalism desired. It is not simply a mechanism which limits the sphere of the supposed liberties of the individual. It is the form, the inner standard and the discipline of the whole person; it saturates the will as well as the intelligence. Its principle, the central inspiration of the human personality living in the civil community, pierces into the depths and makes its home in the heart of the man of action as well as of the thinker, of the artist as well as of the scientist: it is the soul of the soul.

13. Fascism, in short, is not only the giver of laws and the founder of institutions, but the educator and promoter of spiritual life. It wants to remake, not the forms of human

life, but its content, man, character, faith. And to this end it requires discipline and the authority that can enter into the spirits of men and there govern unopposed. Its sign, therefore, is the Lictors' rods, the symbol of unity, of strength and justice.

Document 8.10

Carl Schmitt on the Definition of Sovereignty

Carl Schmitt (1888–1985) was a German political and legal theorist. His theory of 'Decisionism' emphasized the sovereign state, the power of the executive and the need, in particular, for executive action in exceptional circumstances. He was a constitutional adviser to the German Government in the last years of the Weimar Republic (1930–33). He designated the President as the 'defender of the Constitution' and supported government through emergency decree under Article 48 of the Weimar Constitution. He subsequently became a controversial figure because of his support for the Third Reich. His ideas have recently attracted renewed interest.

Sovereign is he who decides on the exception.

Only this definition can do justice to a borderline concept. Contrary to the imprecise terminology that is found in popular literature, a borderline concept is not a vague concept, but one pertaining to the outermost sphere. This definition of sovereignty must therefore be associated with a borderline case and not with routine. It will soon become clear that the exception is to be understood to refer to a general concept in the theory of the state, and not merely to a construct applied to any emergency decree or state of siege.

The assertion that the exception is truly appropriate for the juristic definition of sovereignty has a systematic, legal-logical foundation. The decision on the exception is a decision in the true sense of the word. Because a general norm, as represented by an ordinary legal prescription, can never encompass a total exception, the decision that a real exception exists cannot therefore be entirely derived from this norm.

From a practical or a theoretical perspective, it really does not matter whether an abstract scheme advanced to define sovereignty (namely, that sovereignty is the highest power, not a derived power) is acceptable. About an abstract concept there will in general be no argument, least of all in the history of sovereignty. What is argued about is the concrete application, and that means who decides in a situation of conflict what constitutes the public interest or interest of the state, public safety and order, *le salut public*, and so on. The exception, which is not codified in the existing legal order, can at best be characterized as a case of extreme peril, a danger to the existence of the state, or the like. But it cannot be circumscribed factually and made to conform to a preformed law.

It is precisely the exception that makes relevant the subject of sovereignty, that is, the whole question of sovereignty. The precise details of an emergency cannot be anticipated, nor can one spell out what may take place in such a case, especially when it is truly a matter of an extreme emergency and of how it is to be eliminated. The precondition as well as the content of jurisdictional competence in such a case must necessarily be unlimited. From the liberal constitutional point of view, there would be no jurisdictional competence at all. The most guidance the constitution can provide is to indicate who can act in such a case. If such action is not subject to controls, if it is not hampered in some way by checks and balances, as is the case in a liberal constitution, then it is clear who the sovereign is. He decides whether there is an extreme emergency as well as what must be done to eliminate it. Although he stands outside the normally valid legal system, he nevertheless belongs to it, for it is he who must decide whether the constitution needs to be suspended in its entirety. All tendencies of modern constitutional development point toward eliminating the sovereign in this sense.

There exist a number of historical presentations that deal with the development of the concept of sovereignty, but they are like textbook compilations of abstract formulas from which definitions of sovereignty can be extracted. Nobody seems to have taken the trouble to scrutinize the often-repeated but completely empty phraseology used to denote the highest power by the famous authors of the concept of sovereignty. That this concept relates to the critical case, the exception, was long ago recognized by Jean Bodin. He stands at the beginning of the modern theory of the state because of his work 'Of the True Marks of Sovereignty' (chapter 10 of the first book of the *Republic*) rather than because of his often-cited definition ('sovereignty is the absolute and perpetual power of a republic'). He discussed his concept in the context of many practical examples, and he always returned to the question: To what extent is the sovereign bound to laws, and to what extent is he responsible to the estates? To this last, all-important question he replied that commitments are binding because they rest on natural law; but in emergencies the tie to general natural principles ceases. In general, according to him, the prince is duty bound toward the estates or the people only to the extent of fulfilling his promise in the interest of the people; he is not so bound under conditions of urgent necessity. These are by no means new theses. The decisive point about Bodin's concept is that by referring to the emergency, he reduced his analysis of the relationships between prince and estates to a simple either/or.

This is what is truly impressive in his definition of sovereignty; by considering sovereignty to be indivisible, he finally settled the question of power in the state. His scholarly accomplishment and the basis for his success thus reside in his having incorporated the decision into the concept of sovereignty. Today there is hardly any mention of the concept of sovereignty that does not contain the usual quotation from Bodin. But nowhere does one find cited the core quote from that chapter of the Republic. Bodin asked if the commitments of the prince to the estates or the people dissolve his sovereignty. He answered by referring to the case in which it becomes necessary to violate such commitments, to change laws or to suspend them entirely according to the requirements of a situation, a time, and a people. If in such cases the prince had to consult a senate or the people before he could act he would have to be prepared to let his subjects dispense with him. Bodin considered this an absurdity because, according to him, the estates were not masters over the laws; they in turn would have to permit their prince to dispense with them. Sovereignty would thus become a play between two parties: sometimes the people and sometimes the prince would rule, and that would be contrary to all reason and all law. Because the authority to suspend valid law – be it general or in a specific case – is so much the actual mark of sovereignty, Bodin wanted to derive from this authority all other characteristics (declaring war and making peace, appointing civil servants, right of pardon, final appeal, and so on).

Document 8.11

F.H. Hinsley, *Sovereignty*

Sir Francis Harry Hinsley (born 1918), past Professor of the History of International Relations at Cambridge University brings the eye of a historian specializing in international relations to this concept. The following extract is taken from *Sovereignty*, 2nd edition (1986).

The concept of sovereignty originated in the closer association of the developing state and the developing community which became inevitable when it was discovered that power had to be shared between them. The function of the concept was to provide the only formula which could ensure the effective exercise of power once the division of power or collaboration of forces had become inescapable. It was on this account that, to begin with, it placed the sovereignty in the rulership. As the community became still more complex the thesis of the sovereignty of the ruler was challenged by the thesis of the sovereignty of the people and even by the thesis that the state and notion of sovereignty were dispensable; but these arguments could not meet the primary need to ensure the effective exercise of power, the more so as the growing complexity of the community was serving to emphasize the importance of the state. If this need was to be met, the only remaining recourse was to locate sovereignty in the body politic which the community and the state together composed, the community being regarded as wholly or partly the source of sovereignty and the state as the sole instrument which exercised it. Greater complexity in the forms, the procedures and the concept of the state facilitated the adoption of this solution, or at any rate followed from it, as did a further tightening of the association between the state and the community. But it is safe to say that far from destroying the dichotomy between the community and the state or eliminating confrontation between them, the central developments in these developments in modern times – the rise of legislatures, the introduction of representation, the extension of suffrages and the insertion of constitutional features into the basis, the composition and the procedures of government – necessitated the notion that sovereignty resided in the body-politic as a means of preserving the precondition of effective action in and for the community, the sovereignty of the state.

Document 8.12

Robert Nozick on the Minimal State

Robert Nozick (born 1938) is an American libertarian theorist who has argued for a strictly minimal state role, arguing, among other things, that principles of state redistribution of private property means the violation of fundamental rights.

Our main conclusions about the state are that a minimal state, limited to the narrow functions of protection against force, theft, fraud, enforcement of contracts, and so on, is justified; that any more extensive state will violate persons' rights not to be forced to do certain things, and is unjustified ... Two noteworthy implications are that the state may not use its coercive apparatus for the purpose of getting some citizens to aid others, or in order to prohibit activities to people for their own good or protection.

A protective agency dominant in a territory does satisfy the two crucial necessary conditions for being a state. It is the only generally effective enforcer of a prohibition on others' using unreliable enforcement procedures (calling them as it sees them), and it oversees these procedures. And the agency protects those non clients in its territory whom it prohibits from using self-help enforcement procedures on its clients, in their dealings with its clients, even if such protection must be financed (in apparent redistributive fashion) by its clients. It is morally required to do this by the principle of compensation, which requires those who act in self-protection in order to increase their own security to compensate those they prohibit from doing risky acts which might actually have turned out to be harmless for the disadvantages imposed upon them. We noted ... that whether the provision of protective services for some by others was 'redistributive' would depend on the reasons for it. We now see such provision need not be redistributive since it can be justified on other than redistributive grounds, namely, those provided for in the principle of compensation.

QUESTIONS FOR DISCUSSION

1. To what extent is the idea of the sovereignty of the state applicable today, where crucial decisions may be taken by supranational organizations and some multi-nationals dispose of more wealth than small states?
2. Who had the better argument: Richard Price or Samuel Johnson?
3. Do you agree with Bodin's definition of sovereignty?
4. Are the sovereignty of the state and the freedom of its citizens compatible?
5. What is the difference between a sovereign state and a protection racket?

NOTES

1 See Quentin Skinner, *The Foundations of Modern Political Thought* (Cambridge, Cambridge University Press, 1978), Vol. 2.
2 Quoted by Julian H. Franklin, *John Locke and the Theory of Sovereignty* (Cambridge,Cambridge University Press, 1978), p. 94.

FURTHER READING

A good historical survey of the concept of sovereignty is provided in F.H. Hinsley, *Sovereignty* (Cambridge, Cambridge University Press, 1986). Older general accounts still worth reading include B. de Jouvenal, *Sovereignty* (Cambridge, Cambridge University Press, 1957). The origins of the modern state are traced in J. Shennan, *The Origins of the Modern European State 1450–1725* (London, Hutchinson, 1974) and the same author's *Liberty and Order in Early Modern Europe: The Subject and the State 1650–1800* (London, Longman, 1986). Q. Skinner, *The Foundations of Modern Political Thought* (Cambridge, Cambridge University Press, 1978) is an influential account. See also Skinner's contribution to Terence Ball, James Farr and Russell L. Hanson (eds), *Political Innovation and Conceptual Change* (Cambridge, Cambridge University Press, 1989). For a recent survey of these issues see A. Harding, 'The Origins of the Concept of the State', *History of Political Thought*, Vol. 15 (1994). On the use of sovereignty to justify resistance see Julian H. Franklin, *John Locke and the Theory of Sovereignty* (Cambridge, Cambridge University Press, 1978). For a defence of Hobbes see George Shelton, *Morality and Sovereignty in the Philosophy of Hobbes* (New York, St. Martin's Press, 1992). There are a large number of general accounts and surveys of the state. Among older works see R.M. McIver, *The Modern State* (Oxford, Clarendon Press, 1967) and A.P. D'Entreves, *The Notion of the State* (Oxford, Clarendon Press, 1964). For more recent surveys see A. Vincent, *Theories of the State* (Oxford, Blackwell, 1987), D. Held, *Political Theory and the Modern State* (Oxford, Polity, 1990) and M. Carnoy, *State and Political*

Theory (Princeton, Princeton University Press, 1984). K. Dyson, *The State Tradition in Western Europe* (Oxford, Oxford University Press, 1980) is very detailed and should be consulted after reading some of the general accounts. There is a growing literature on the controversial figure of Carl Schmitt. Richard Wolin, 'Carl Schmitt. The Conservative Revolutionary. Habitus and the Aesthetics of Horror', *Political Theory*, Vol. 20 (1992) is an excellent assessment.

9

THE IDEA OF REVOLUTION

INTRODUCTION

The term revolution is now used so extensively that it is in danger of being devalued. alongside the great political revolutions in France and Russia, and the Industrial Revolution, we readily refer to scientific revolutions, artistic revolutions and even revolutions in dress and music. Yet the word also retains an emotive power, especially when individuals are identified as 'revolutionaries'. The word revolution, according to one commentator, is 'used either as a bogy or a banality, depending on whether it is seen as a sinister plot or reduced to a mere synonym for change'.[1]

The word itself did not originally have any political implications at all. In the late medieval period it was used predominantly to refer to the movement of heavenly bodies. Only gradually did it acquire a broader meaning of change and then a specifically political significance. Traces of the use of the word in a political sense can be found as far back as the fourteenth century. However, it was not until the late seventeenth century that contemporaries widely agreed on describing political events as revolutions. Even then the term signified a restoration of a previous regime as much as anything else. Thus contemporaries described the restoration of the monarchy in England in 1660 as a revolution.

The comparative novelty of the word does not necessarily mean that earlier periods were unfamiliar with the experience. Two aspects which we would readily recognize as at least typically associated with revolution were evident in discussion of the right of resistance: an overt challenge to existing authority and the use of violence in that challenge. The key issues were: when was resistance justified and who was entitled to decide that it was justified? The answers were not easy. Too tight a restriction would condemn the subjects of government to perpetual subjection. Too permissive an answer would incite arbitrary revolt. In Christian Europe there was one obvious criterion which could justify revolt. Princes supposedly derived their authority from God and were, by the same token, themselves subject to God. Divine commandment rather than human law was ultimately supreme. The prince who undermined religion could therefore be resisted. Indeed the twelfth-century philosopher, John of Salisbury, went further. To kill a tyrant was, he wrote, a 'glorious act'.

The justification of rebellion in defence of one's religion was to take on a new dimension as the unity of medieval Christendom was fragmented by the Reformation. With the emergence of the Protestant creeds the possibility arose that the prince and his subjects might be of different religions. Protestant subjects consequently rebelled against Catholic princes, as for example Protestant Netherlanders rebelled against the Catholic monarch, Philip II of Spain. Catholic subjects also rebelled against Protestant princes. A second argument was that rebellion was justified when the prince broke his oath to the people. The two justifications were often entwined since political authority was so enmeshed in a religious hierarchy which culminated in God. The author of the famous tract *Vindicae contra tyrannos* (1579), however, clearly distinguished between two oaths: one binding God, the king and the people; the other being between the king and the people alone.

The second question, who was to decide when rebellion was justified?, was equally problematic. Defenders of the right of resistance had to guard against the charge that they were inciting revolt. Moreover, as Aquinas pointed out, premature rebellion might mean not only the death of the rebels but also worsen the lot of the subjects of a now vengeful prince. The most prevalent answer was to restrict the decision to the 'inferior magistrates', that is to an élite of public officials. The fear was, in part, that if the decision was left to private individuals, it would be taken for arbitrary reasons. It would, in Edward Sexby's words, 'subvert all government'. In part, the fear was that the discontented lower ranks of society might make too ready a use of the right of resistance.

These restraints have not been recognized by all. As the individual came to be seen as the locus and recipient or holder of rights and as individual conscience displaced communal custom, individual judgement was thrust to the fore, but usually with a significant change in the meaning of resistance. The nineteenth-century American, Henry Thoreau, for instance, had no doubt that individual conscience must prevail. The fact that a majority of his fellow citizens might disagree with the course of action dictated by his conscience made no difference. But Thoreau advocated resistance in the form of civil disobedience. He did not advocate violence.

Civil disobedience has become the most prominent form of resistance in modern democracies. All forms of civil disobedience abjure violence but within this common assumption it can take distinct forms. Civil disobedience can take the form advocated by Thoreau. Although peaceful, he explicitly repudiated governmental authority. A different, more moderate form does not challenge the government *per se* but refuses to abide by a particular law, as for example Americans refused to acknowledge the call to fight in Vietnam or as people in the United Kingdom refused to pay the Poll Tax. In both cases the majority of dissenters repudiated the policy but not the legitimacy of the government.

While we can see one trend in which the right of resistance has become more moderate, we can see another trend, culminating in our modern sense of revolution, in which it has become more extensive. Even prior to the adoption of the term revolution the actions and ambitions of rebels could be very extensive. The Anabaptists in Münster prohibited the use of money and instituted polygamy in their brief rule in 1534–35. Their revolt, which resembled much later revolutions in some respects, was marked by a radical millenarianism which also surfaced in the Peasant War in Germany of 1525 and the English Civil War. Although the term revolution was being widely used in the eighteenth century, usually in the plural to refer to a series of political disorders, it was the French Revolution which was to fuse together several themes into the idea of *the* Revolution. The Revolution entailed violent political disorder, belief in significant political and cultural progress, the idea of revolution as a deliberate political act, the supposition that the revolution was of universal significance and the idea that the revolution had been an inevitable consequence of the misery of the people.[2] From then on it was difficult to use the term revolution without conjuring up the images and events of the French Revolution.

The French Revolution provided a kind of model for revolution. The novelty of the French experience forcibly impressed itself upon contemporaries. The nineteenth-century historian, Alexis de Tocqueville, was born too late to witness the Revolution but he was clearly impressed by the momentous character of the French Revolution, although he also shrewdly pointed to its links with the earlier religious movements. The French Revolution impressed contemporaries not only because of the extent of the political disorder, but also because it succeeded, for a while at least, in establishing a new regime committed to the cause of the Revolution. It was, in this sense, more successful than any other revolution until the Russian and Chinese revolutions of the twentieth century. As nineteenth- and twentieth-century political theorists reflected upon the frequent failure of revolutions, the obstacle to revolution and indeed the limits of the French Revolution, their conception of what a revolution, a true break with the past, would have to involve became more and more extensive. Indicative of this are the works of disparate figures like Karl Marx, his bitter opponent the anarchist Michael Bakunin and the twentieth-century philosopher, Herbert Marcuse.

Marx and other socialists insisted that the merely political French Revolution had not gone far enough. The problem lay with the economic structure of society. That too would have to be transformed. Anarchists like Bakunin went even further, challenging the need for the idea of authority at all. In the twentieth century the failure of revolution in industrialized Western Europe at the end of the First World War and then the moderation of socialist parties and the decline of radical opposition to the existing social order in the West, pushed advocates of revolution to even more radical, and often desperate, conceptions.

Among the innovations of the French Revolution was the figure of the revolutionary, the man whose profession was revolution. The idea that revolutions needed leaders was in itself not new. The Englishman Francis Bacon had warned governments to ensure 'that there be no likely or fit head whereunto discontented persons may resort, and under whom they may join ...' (see document 9.4). But the figure of the revolutionary was more than just a likely leader. He was committed to the revolution as his own cause. The difficulty was that these would-be leaders found that the people were more hesitant. Faced with this dilemma, the professional revolutionaries could turn to study the underlying causes of revolution, although they usually turned out to be poor predictors of revolution. Alternatively, they could seek to carry through the revolution with a small band of followers, a strategy associated with the name of the Frenchman Auguste Blanqui. But this reduced the prospects of success and was difficult to reconcile with the extent of their aims.

The more the revolution was seen as involving a transformation not just of the political structure but of the economy and society, the more necessary widespread participation in the revolution was seen to be. The professional revolutionary was obliged therefore, like Lenin, to seek to inculcate the idea of revolution before the event. Radical action required that men be made into revolutionaries first. Not all revolutionaries were happy with this position. Too great an emphasis upon the guiding role of the revolutionary leaders risked, among other things, turning the revolutionary into a manipulator rather than a liberator of men. The revolution was, after all, supposed to be a qualitative leap in human and social progress, not merely to replace one set of rulers by another.

The lot of the revolutionary was indeed fraught with risks. Revolutions, successful or unsuccessful, have never developed according to the initial expectations of their would-be leaders. Several of the latter have usually fallen victim not just to defenders of the old order but to more radical, or more moderate, co-revolutionaries. Consequently, those who survived the revolutionary process, like Leon Trotsky, have been left charging that the revolution was betrayed by their former colleagues.

If the course of the revolution was difficult to predict, so too was its occurrence in the first place. Attempts to explain revolutions long predate the association of the term with political disorder and the transformation of regimes. Two early and diverse approaches can be found in the work of Machiavelli and Francis Bacon. Machiavelli looked for a pattern of events and found it in a cyclical movement through a limited number of forms of government. In distinction to more modern explanations, there is, despite the emphasis upon change, little sense of historical progress in Machiavelli's scheme. That would have to wait until the eighteenth century. Only as observers began to see history as being a unified and progressive chronological development could revolutions be located within this overarching framework. But there is at least one modern element in Machiavelli's account. There is a strong element of necessity in his scheme, not because forms of government are crushed beneath the wheels of history, but because they decay.

Bacon took a more pragmatic approach, focusing, as Machiavelli did elsewhere, upon the diversity of factors which could induce 'seditions and troubles' – like Machiavelli he did not use the term revolution in its modern sense. It is clear that there was much that he thought governments could do to avert revolution. It is equally clear that he thought bad policy could provoke revolt where there had been none. An innovative policy could be as dangerous as a conservative one.

When the Frenchman Proudhon considered ways in which governments might avert revolution, the change in underlying assumptions was substantial. Bacon had picked out many factors with which we are now familiar – political oppression, economic inequality, overpopulation, unpopular innovations to name a few – but revolution was something to be avoided. For Proudhon, revolution was a fact of life. The only choice was whether to manage it, to have a controlled and peaceful revolution, or to resist it and provoke violent conflict.

Karl Marx, more than any other, developed the idea of the historical inevitability of revolution, although his extensive writings on the subject reflect the complexity and indeterminacy of the revolutionary process. Marx was sure at least that the existing capitalist system would collapse. In more optimistic moments he asserted that the proletarian revolution would promptly triumph. But on other occasions Marx was keenly aware that there was a gap between the collapse of the old order and the triumph of a new order. In the two key revolutions of the twentieth century the gap between the collapse of the old order and the emergence of the new regime proved to be quite different, only eight months in Russia but some forty years in the case of China.[3]

For followers of Marx this problem was compounded by their assumption that there was a set pattern of social development, that feudal and agrarian societies would first undergo a revolution by which the bourgeoisie would attain power, and would undergo a process of capitalist industrialization before the desired proletarian revolution came on to the agenda. As Lenin found in 1917 this schedule did not seem to fit the reality of developments in Russia.

Since the French Revolution the idea of revolution has been predominantly associated with what we would label as the left wing. Revolution has been seen as the cause of the oppressed and the poor, or the cause of those who claimed to speak and act on behalf of the oppressed and the poor. Revolution has meant an attack upon privilege and tradition in the name of progress, equality and liberty. Before the adoption of the term revolution, and indeed before the political use of the words left and right emerged, it had been clear that revolution could be associated with the defence of traditions, especially religious traditions, and that revolution could be a restoration.

In the twentieth century, however, a new phenomenon arose which had little connection with these earlier understandings of revolution but was implacably opposed to the tradition inaugurated by the French Revolution. Twentieth-century fascists have provided commentators on the idea of revolution with a substantial problem. They proclaimed they were revolutionaries but despised the revolutionary tradition; they alternately espoused the violent overthrow of the existing political system and shunned a direct clash with the state and triumphed, where they did, only with the collusion of conservative élites; they proclaimed that they would create a new 'fascist' man but looked back to the past, to some primeval state of racial purity in the case of Adolf Hitler, or to the glories of imperial Rome in the case of Benito Mussolini. The contradictions and systematic ambiguities bemused the fascists themselves – as the comments of the one-time National Socialist Hermann Rauschning indicate (see document 9.17).

The idea of revolution is an emotive and problematic one for several reasons. Primary among these is the connection of revolution with political violence. The association is strong enough for one of the leaders of the opposition to the Communist regime in Poland to reject the common label of East European Revolutions for the events of 1989 precisely on the grounds that they were largely non-violent. Yet the threat, and usually the reality, of violence, are difficult to avoid. Whether men spoke of revolution and had in mind a replay of the French Revolution, or spoke of resistance against tyrants, they were, to varying degrees, challenging the idea of political order. Or rather they were opposing one political order in the name of another. The vacuum between the two is the space in which political violence can take place.

The fault, if fault it is, does not necessarily lie solely with the revolutionaries. Bacon had warned that failure to 'give moderate liberty for griefs and discontentments to evaporate' was to invite sedition. Alexander Hamilton argued that the Americans had exhausted all other alternatives: they had no choice but slavery or resort to arms. Proudhon warned against blind resistance to 'gradual revolution' which would only issue in violent conflict. The modern world is in some respects more averse to political violence – despite the unprecedented loss of life in this century. We are now more likely to call for an international tribunal to sit in judgement upon murderous dictators than to join with John of Salisbury in proclaiming 'it is a lawful and glorious act to slay public tyrants'. But then John of Salisbury was concerned with the abuse of authority. The injustice which justified resistance lay in the conduct of the ruler. In modern revolutions the injustice is more likely to seem to be located in the political, social and economic system.

DOCUMENTS

Document 9.1

John of Salisbury on Tyrannicide

John of Salisbury (*c*. 1115/20–80) was Bishop of Chartres from 1176. Earlier he had written *Policraticus* (1159) from which the extract is taken. He sent the book to Thomas Becket in Toulouse. Becket was murdered in Canterbury Cathedral in 1170 at the instigation of the king. *Policraticus* dealt primarily with men's behaviour rather than with the institutions of government and was intended as a guide for princes and courtiers.

> OF THE COHESION AND MUTUAL DEPENDENCE OF THE HEAD AND MEMBERS OF THE COMMONWEALTH; AND THAT THE PRINCE IS AS IT WERE THE LIKENESS OF DEITY; AND OF THE CRIME OF LÈSE MAJESTÉ, AND OF THE OBLIGATIONS OF FEALTY.

For myself, I am satisfied and persuaded that loyal shoulders should uphold the power of the ruler; and not only do I submit to his power patiently, but with pleasure, so long as it is exercised in subjection to God and follows His ordinances. But on the other·hand if it resists and opposes the divine commandments, and wishes to make me share in its war against God; then with unrestrained voice I answer back that God must be preferred before any man on earth. Therefore inferiors should cleave and cohere to their superiors, and all the limbs should be in subjection to the head; but always and only on condition that religion is kept inviolate …

> That by the authority of the divine page it is a lawful and glorious act to slay public tyrants, provided that the slayer is not bound by fealty to the tyrant, or does not for some other reason sacrifice justice and honour thereby.

The well-known narrative of the Books of Kings and Chronicles shows, according to the authority of Jerome, that Israel was oppressed by tyrants from the beginning and that Juda had none but wicked kings save only David, Josiah and Ezechiah. Yet I can easily believe that Solomon and perhaps some of the others in Juda recovered when God recalled them to the true way. And I will be readily persuaded that tryants instead of legitimate princes were rightly deserved by a stiff-necked and stubborn people who always resisted the Holy Spirit, and by their gentile abominations provoked to wrath not Moyses only, the servant of the law, but God Himself, the Lord of the law. For tyrants are demanded, introduced, and raised to power by sin, and are excluded, blotted out, and destroyed by repentance. And even before the time of their kings, as the Book of Judges relates, the children of Israel were time without number in bondage to tyrants, being visited with affliction on many different occasions in accordance with the dispensation of God, and then often, when they cried aloud to the Lord, they were delivered. And when the allotted time of their punishment was fulfilled, they were allowed to cast off the yoke from their necks by the slaughter of their tyrants; nor is blame attached to any of those by whose valour a penitent and humbled people was thus set free, but their memory is preserved in affection by posterity as servants of the Lord ...

The histories teach, however, that none should undertake the death of a tyrant who is bound to him by an oath or by the obligation of fealty. For we read the Sedechias, because he disregarded the sacred obligation of fealty, was led into captivity; and that in the case of another of the kings of Juda whose name escapes my memory, his eyes were plucked out because, falling into faithlessness, he did not keep before his sight God, to whom the oath is taken; since sureties for good behaviour are justly given even to a tyrant.

But as for the use of poison, although I see it sometimes wrongfully adopted by infidels, I do not read that it is ever permitted by any law. Not that I do not believe that tyrants ought to be removed from our midst, but it should be done without loss of religion and honour.

Document 9.2

St Thomas Aquinas on Tyranny

Thomas Aquinas (1225–74) played a major part in the revival of Aristotelian thought. Part of that revival involved an emphasis upon the concept of the citizen rather than the subject. This, in turn, facilitated the idea of popular government and resistance, although justifications of resistance were still heavily constrained. The extract is taken from *On Princely Government*, a text unfinished at Aquinas's death.

Since government by one person, being the best, is to be preferred; and since, as we have shown, there is always a danger that it will develop into tyranny, which is the worst government, every precaution must be taken to provide the community with a ruler who will not become a tyrant. In the first place it is necessary that whoever of the possible candidates is proclaimed king shall be of such character that it is unlikely that he will become a tyrant ... Next, a monarch should be so constituted that there is no opportunity for the king, once he is reigning, to become a tyrant. And, at the same time the kingly power should be so restricted that he could not easily turn to tyranny. The steps to be taken to this end will be considered later. Finally, we must consider the action to be taken should a king become tyrannical.

If the tyranny be not excessive it is certainly wiser to tolerate it in limited measure, at least for a time, rather than to run the risk of even greater perils by opposing it. For those who take action against a tyrant may fail in their object, and only succeed in rousing the tyrant to greater savagery. Even when action against a tyrant meets with success, this very fact breeds strife and grave discord among the populace, either in the moment of rebellion or after his overthrow when opinion in the community is factiously divided as to the new form of government ...

It seems then, that the remedy against the evils of tyranny lies rather in the hands of public authority than in the private judgement of individuals. In particular, where a community has the right to elect a ruler for itself, it would not be contrary to justice for the community to depose the king whom it has elected, nor to curb his power should he abuse it to play the tyrant. Nor should the community be accused of disloyalty for thus deposing a tyrant, even after a previous promise of constant fealty; for the tyrant lays himself open to such treatment by his failure to discharge the duties of his office as governor of the community, and in consequence his subjects are no longer bound by their oath to him ...

If on the other hand the right to appoint a king over a certain community belongs to some superior, then the remedy against tyrannical excess must be sought from him. Thus the Jews made complaint to Caesar Augustus against Archelaus, when the latter began to rule in the place of his father, Herod, in Judea and had begun to imitate his father's evil ways ...

Finally, when there is no hope of human aid against tyranny, recourse must be made to God the King of all, and the helper of all who call upon Him in the time of tribulation.

Document 9.3

Niccolò Machiavelli on the Causes of Revolt

Machiavelli's (see introduction to document 5.1) *Discourses* were inspired by Livy's history of Rome. In them he argued for the revival of the values of republican Rome. He broke off writing the *Discourses* to write *The Prince*, returning to them in 1515. They were first published in 1531 after Machiavelli's death. The extract reflects the prevalent cyclical view of political change.

Others – and with better judgement many think – say that there are six types of government, of which three are very bad, and three are good in themselves but easily become corrupt, so that they too must be classed as pernicious. Those that are good are the three above mentioned. Those that are bad are the other three, which depend on them, and each of them is so like the one associated with it that it easily passes from one form to the other. For *Principality* easily becomes *Tyranny*. From *Aristocracy* the transition to *Oligarchy* is an easy one. *Democracy* is without difficulty converted into *Anarchy*. So that if anyone who is organizing a commonwealth sets up one of the three first forms of government, he sets up what will last but for a while; since there are no means whereby to prevent it passing into its contrary, on account of the likeness which in such a case virtue has to vice.

These variations of government among men are due to chance. For in the beginning of the world, when its inhabitants were few, they lived for a time scattered like the beasts. Then, with the multiplication of their offspring, they drew together and, in order the better to be able to defend themselves, began to look about for a man stronger and more courageous than the rest, made him their head, and obeyed him.

It was thus that men learned how to distinguish what is honest and good from what is pernicious and wicked, for the sight of someone injuring his benefactor evoked in them hatred and sympathy and they blamed the ungrateful and respected those who showed gratitude, well aware that the same injuries might have been done to themselves. Hence to prevent evil of this kind they took to making laws and to assigning punishments to those who contravened them. The notion of justice thus came into being.

In this way it came about that, when later on they had to choose a prince, they did not have recourse to the boldest as formerly, but to one who excelled in prudence and justice.

But when at a yet later stage they began to make the prince hereditary instead of electing him, his heirs soon began to degenerate as compared with their ancestors, and forsaking virtuous deeds, considered that princes have nought else to do but to surpass other men in extravagance, lasciviousness, and every other form of licentiousness. With the result that the prince came to be hated, and, since he was hated, came to be afraid, and from fear soon passed to offensive action, which quickly brought about a tyranny.

From which, before long, was begotten the source of their downfall; for tyranny gave rise to conspiracies and plots against princes, organized not by timid and weak men, but by men conspicuous for their liberality, magnanimity, wealth and ability, for such men could not stand the dishonourable life the prince was leading. The masses, therefore, at the instigation of these powerful leaders, took up arms against the prince, and, when he had been liquidated, submitted to the authority of those whom they looked upon as their liberators. Hence the latter, to whom the very term 'sole head' had become odious, formed themselves into a government. Moreover, in the beginning, mindful of what they had suffered under a tyranny, they ruled in accordance with the laws which they had made, subordinated their own convenience to the common advantage, and, both in private matters and public affairs, governed and preserved order with the utmost diligence.

But when the administration passed to their descendants who had no experience of the changeability of fortune, had not been through bad times, and instead of remaining content with the civic equality then prevailing, reverted to avarice, ambition and to seizing other men's womenfolk, they caused government by an aristocracy to become government by an oligarchy in which civic rights were entirely disregarded; so that in a short time there came to pass in their case the same thing as happened to the tyrant, for the masses, sick of their government, were ready to help anyone who had any sort of plan for attacking their rulers; and so there soon arose someone who with the aid of the masses liquidated them.

Then, since the memory of the prince and of the injuries inflicted by him was still fresh, and since, having got rid of government by the few, they had no desire to return to that of a prince, they turned to a democratic form of government, which they organized in such a way that no sort of authority was vested either in a few powerful men or in a prince.

And, since all forms of government are to some extent respected at the outset, this democratic form of government maintained itself for a while but not for long, especially when the generation that had organized it had passed away. For anarchy quickly supervened, in which no respect was shown either for the individual or for the official, and which was such that, as everyone did what he liked, all sorts of outrages were constantly committed. The outcome was inevitable. Either at the suggestion of some good man or because this anarchy had to be got rid of somehow, principality was once again restored. And from this there was, stage by stage, a return to anarchy, by way of the transitions and for the reasons assigned.

This, then, is the cycle through which all commonwealths pass, whether they govern themselves or are governed. But rarely do they return to the same form of government, for there can scarce be a state of such vitality that it can undergo often such changes and yet remain in being. What usually happens is that, while in a state of commotion in which it lacks both counsel and strength, a state becomes subject to a neighbouring and better organized state. Were it not so, a commonwealth might go on for ever passing through these governmental transitions.

Document 9.4

Francis Bacon on the Causes of Sedition

Francis Bacon (1561–1626) was the son of Nicholas Bacon, Lord Chancellor and nephew of Lord Burghley. He did not, however, attain high office himself until the reign of James I, under whom he became Attorney General (1612 and 1617) and Lord Chancellor (1617). He was impeached in 1621 and stripped of his offices. Bacon was an advocate of a scientific approach to politics but the *Essays* reflect a more pragmatic awareness of the contingencies of politics. The *Essays* were first published in 1598 but subsequently enlarged and revised. The final, third edition appeared in 1625.

The causes and motives of seditions are, innovation in religion, taxes, alteration of laws and customs, breaking of privileges, general oppression, advancement of unworthy persons, strangers, dearths, disbanded soldiers, factions grown desperate; and whatsoever in offending people joineth and knitteth them in a common cause.

For the remedies, there may be some general preservatives, whereof we will speak: as for the just cure, it must answer to the particular disease; and so be left to counsel rather than rule.

The first remedy, or prevention, is to remove, by all means possible, that material cause of sedition whereof we spake, which is, want and poverty in the estate: to which purpose serveth the opening and well-balancing of trade; the cherishing of manufactures; the banishing of idleness; the repressing of waste and excess, by sumptuary laws; the improvement and husbanding of the soil; the regulating of prices of things vendible; the moderating of taxes and tributes, and the like. Generally, it is to be foreseen that the population of a kingdom (especially if it be not mown down by wars) do not exceed the stock of the kingdom which should maintain them: neither is the population to be reckoned only by number; for a smaller number, that spend more and earn less, do wear out an estate sooner than a greater number that live lower and gather more: therefore the multiplying of nobility, and other degrees of quality, in an over proportion to the common people, doth speedily bring a state to necessity; and so doth likewise an overgrown clergy, for they bring nothing to the stock; and, in like manner, when more are bred scholars than preferments can take off ...

Above all things, good policy is to be used, that the treasure and moneys in a state be not gathered into few hands; for, otherwise, a state may have a great stock, and yet starve: and money is like muck, not good except it be spread. This is done chiefly by suppressing, or, at least, keeping a strait hand upon the devouring trades of usury, engrossing great pasturages, and the like ...

To give moderate liberty for griefs and discontentments to evaporate (so it be without too great insolency or bravery), is a safe way: for he that turneth the humours back, and maketh the wound bleed inwards, endangereth malign ulcers and pernicious imposthumations ...

Certainly, the politic and artificial nourishing and entertaining of hopes, and carrying men from hopes to hopes, is one of the best antidotes against the poison of discontentments: and it is a certain sign of a wise government and proceeding, when it can hold men's hearts by hopes, when it cannot by satisfaction; and when it can handle things in such manner as no evil shall appear so peremptory but that it hath some outlet of hope; which is the less hard to do, because both particular persons and factions are apt enough to flatter themselves, or at least to brave that which they believe not.

Also the foresight and prevention, that there be no likely or fit head whereunto discontented persons may resort, and under whom they may join, is a known, but an excellent point of caution. I understand a fit head to be one that hath greatness and reputation, that hath confidence with the discontented party, and upon whom they turn their eyes, and that is thought discontented in his own particular: which kind of persons are either to be won and reconciled to the state, and that in a fast and true manner; or to be fronted with some other of the same party that may oppose them, and so divide the reputation. Generally, the dividing and breaking of all factions and combinations that are adverse to the state, and setting them at distance, or, at least, distrust amongst themselves, is not one of the worst remedies; for it is a desperate case, if those that hold with the proceeding of the state be full of discord and faction, and those that are against it be entire and united. Surely princes had need in tender matters and ticklish times to beware what they say, especially in these short speeches, which fly abroad like darts, and are thought to be shot out of their secret intentions; for as for large discourses, they are flat things, and not so much noted.

Lastly, let princes, against all events, not be without some great person, one or rather more, of military valour, near unto them, for the repressing of seditions in their beginnings; for without that, there useth to be more trepidation in court upon the first breaking out of troubles than were fit; and the state runneth the danger of that which Tacitus saith: *Atque is habitus animorum fuit, ut pessimum facinus auderent pauci, plures vellent, omnes paterentur* [And such was the state of feeling, that a few dared to perpetrate the worst of crimes; more wished to do so, – all submitted to it]: but let such military persons be assured, and well reputed of, rather than factious and popular; holding also good correspondence with the other great men in the state, or else the remedy is worse than the disease.

Document 9.5

Edward Sexby, *Killing No Murder. Whether it be Lawful to Kill a Tyrant*

Edward Sexby (1616–58) was a Leveller. He served in Cromwell's armies and spoke for the radicals at the Putney Debates with the army commanders. He later conspired against Oliver Cromwell who is the target of *Killing No Murder. Whether it be Lawful to Kill a Tyrant* (1657). Sexby died in prison.

In deciding this Question Authors very much differ as far as it concerns supreme Magistrates, who degenerate into Tyrants. Some think they are to be borne with as bad Parents; and place them in the Number of those Mischiefs that have no other Cure but our Patience. Others think they may be questioned by that Supreme Law of the People's Safety; and that they are answerable to the People's Representatives for the Breach of their Trust. But none, of sober Sense makes private Persons Judges of their Actions: which were, indeed, to subvert all Government. But, on the other side, I find none, that have not been frighted or corrupted out of their reason, that have been so great Enemies to common Justice and the Liberty of Mankind as to give any Kind of Indemnity to a Usurper who can pretend no Title, but that of being stronger, nor challenge the People's Obedience upon any other Obligation but that of their Necessity and Fear. Such a Person, as one out of all bounds of human protection, all men make the Ishmael, against whom is every Man's Hand, as his is against every Man. To him they give no more Security than Cain, his Fellow Murderer and Oppressor, promised to himself, to be destroyed by him that found him first.

The Reason why a Tyrant's Case is particular, and why, in that, every Man hath that vengeance given him, which in other Cases, is reserved to GOD and the Magistrate, cannot be obscure, if we rightly consider what a Tyrant is, what his Crimes are, and in what State he stands with the Commonwealth, and with every Member of it. And certainly, if we find him an Enemy to all human Society, and a Subverter of all Laws, and one that by the Greatness of his Villainies secures himself against all ordinary Course of Justice, we shall not at all think it strange, if then he have no Benefit from human Society, no Protection from the Law, and if, in his Case, Justice dispenses with her forms ...

In the next Place, let it be considered, that a Tyrant, making himself above all Law, and defending his Injustice by a Strength which no Power of Magistrates is able to oppose, he becomes above all Punishment, above all other Justice than that he receives from the Stroke of some generous Hand. And, certainly, the Safety of Mankind were but ill provided for, if there were no Kind of Justice to reach great Villainies, but Tyrants should be immanitate scelerum tuti, secured by the Greatness of their Crimes. Our laws would be then but Cobwebs indeed, made only to catch Flies, but not to hold Wasps or Hornets; And it might be then said of all Commonwealths, what was said of Athens, that there only small Thieves were hanged, but the great Ones were free, and condemned the rest. But he that will secure himself of all Hands must know he secures himself from none. He that flies Justice in the Court must expect to find it in the Street: And he that goes against every Man arms every Man against himself.

Document 9.6

John Locke on the Dissolution of Government

John Locke (see introduction to document 1.5) began the *Two Treatises of Government* at the time of the Exclusion Crisis 1679–81) when a Parliamentary attempt to exclude James, the Catholic son of Charles II, from the throne failed and Charles dissolved Parliament. Locke went into exile in 1683 and only returned when James II was deposed in favour of William and Mary (1688)

He that will with any clearness speak of the dissolution of government ought, in the first place, to distinguish between the dissolution of the society and the dissolution of the government. That which makes the community, and brings men out of the loose state of nature into one politic society, is the agreement which every one has with the rest to incorporate and act as one body, and so be one distinct commonwealth. The usual and almost only way whereby this union is dissolved, is the inroad of foreign force making a conquest upon them. For in that case (not being able to maintain and support themselves as one entire and independent body) the union belonging to that body which consisted therein must necessarily cease, and so every one return to the state he was in before, with a liberty to shift for himself and provide for his own safety as he thinks fit in some other society. Whenever the society is dissolved, it is certain the government of that society cannot remain. Thus conquerors' swords often cut up governments by the roots, and mangle societies to pieces, separating the subdued or scattered multitude from the protection of and dependence on that society which ought to have preserved them from violence ...

Besides this overturning from without, governments are dissolved from within.

First, when the legislative is altered.

When any one or more shall take upon them to make laws, whom the people have not appointed so to do, they make laws without authority, which the people are not therefore bound to obey; by which means they come again to be out of subjection, and may constitute to themselves a new legislative, as they think best, being in full liberty to resist the force of those who without authority would impose anything upon them. Every one is at the disposure of his own will when those, who had by the delegation of the society the declaring of the public will, are excluded from it, and others usurp the place who have no such authority or delegation ...

In these and the like cases, when the government is dissolved, the people are at liberty to provide for themselves by erecting a new legislative, differing from the other, by the change of persons, or form, or both, as they shall find it most for their safety and good. For the society can never, by the fault of another, lose the native and original right it has to preserve itself, which can only be done by a settled legislative, and a fair and impartial execution of the laws made by it. But the state of mankind is not so miserable that they are not capable of using this remedy, till it be too late to look for any. To tell people they may provide for themselves by erecting a new legislative, when by oppression, artifice, or being delivered over to a foreign power, their old one is gone, is only to tell them they may expect relief when it is too late, and the evil is past cure. This is in effect no more than to bid them first be slaves, and then to take care of their liberty; and when their chains are on tell them they may act like free men. This, if barely so, is rather mockery than relief; and men can never be secure from tyranny if there be no means to escape it till they are perfectly under it. And therefore it is that they have not only a right to get out of it, but to prevent it ...

There is therefore, secondly, another way whereby governments are dissolved, and that is when the legislative or the prince, either of them, act contrary to their trust.

First, The legislative acts against the trust reposed in them when they endeavour to invade the property of the subject, and to make themselves or any part of the community masters or arbitrary disposers of the lives, liberties, or fortunes of the people.

The reason why men enter into society is the preservation of their property; and the end why they choose and authorise a legislative is that there may be laws made, and rules set, as guards and fences to the properties of all the members of the society, to limit the power and moderate the dominion of every part and member of the society. For since it can never be supposed to be the will of the society that the legislative should have a power to destroy that which every one designed secure by entering into society, and for which the people submitted themselves to legislators of their own making, whenever the legislators endeavour to take away and destroy the property of the people, or to reduce them to slavery under arbitrary power, they put themselves into a state of war with the people, who are thereupon absolved from any further obedience, and are left to the common refuge which God hath provided for all men against force and violence.

Document 9.7

Alexander Hamilton, *A Full Vindication*

Alexander Hamilton (1755–1804) was a military leader in the American War of Independence after which he became a lawyer. He was the author, along with James Madison and John Jay of the *Federalist Papers* (1787–88) and later served as Secretary to the Treasury (1789–95). He died after a duel with a political opponent. *A Full Vindication* (1744) was written, when Hamilton was only nineteen, before the outbreak of war, in reply to 'Free Thoughts ... by a Farmer'. The 'Farmer' was in fact Samuel Seabury (1729–86), a loyalist cleric.

What, then, is the subject of our controversy with the mother country? It is this: Whether we shall preserve that security to our lives and properties, which the law of nature, the genius of the British constitution, and our charters, afford us; or whether we shall resign them into the hands of the British House of Commons, which is no more privileged to dispose of them than the Great Mogul? ... The Parliament claims a right to tax us in all cases whatsoever: its late acts are in virtue of that claim ...

The design of electing members to represent us in general Congress, was, that the wisdom of America might be collected in devising the most proper and expedient means to repel this atrocious invasion of our rights. It has been accordingly done. Their decrees are binding upon all, and demand a religious observance ...

If it should be objected, that they have not answered the end of their election, but have fallen upon an improper and ruinous mode of proceeding, I reply by asking, Who shall be the judge? Shall any individual oppose his private sentiment to the united counsels of men, in whom America has reposed so high a confidence? The attempt must argue no small degree of arrogance and self-sufficiency ...

The only scheme of opposition, suggested by those who have been and are averse from a non-importation and non-exportation agreement, is, by REMONSTRANCE and PETITION. The authors and abettors of this scheme have never been able to invent a single argument to prove the likelihood of its succeeding. On the other hand, there are many standing facts and valid considerations against it.

In the infancy of the present dispute, we had recourse to this method only. We addressed the throne in the most loyal and respectful manner, in a legislative capacity; but what was the consequence? Our address was treated with contempt and neglect …

There is less reason now than ever to expect deliverance, in this way, from the hand of oppression …

What can we represent which has not already been represented? What petitions can we offer, that have not already been offered? The rights of America, and the injustice of parliamentary pretensions, have been clearly and repeatedly stated, both in and out of parliament. No new arguments can be framed to operate in our favour … Upon the whole, it is morally certain, this mode of opposition would be fruitless and defective …

This being the case, we can have no recourse but in a restriction of our trade, or in a resistance *vi et armis*. It is impossible to conceive any other alternative. Our Congress, therefore, have imposed what restraint they thought necessary. Those who condemn or clamour against it, do nothing more, nor less, than advise us to be slaves …

Document 9.8

Condorcet, 'On the Meaning of the Term "Revolutionary"'

The Marquis de Condorcet (1743–94) was a French aristocrat who supported the Revolution. He was a mathematician and educational reformer. His most famous work is his *Esquisse d'un tableau historique du progrès de l'esprit humain*, written at the height of the terror, in which he prophesied indefinite progress and enlightenment. There is a certain irony in his justification of ruthlessness in 'On the Meaning of the Term "Revolutionary"' (1793), for Condorcet was soon to fall victim to the Revolution.

From revolution we have derived revolutionary, and the general meaning of this word expresses everything which appertains to a revolution.

But we have made it our own, in that one of the states, which was oppressed for a long time by despotism, has made in a few years, the only republic where liberty has been based entirely on equal rights. Thus the word revolutionary can only be applied to revolutions which have liberty as their object.

We say a man is revolutionary when he is bound to the principles of revolution, when he acts for it and is prepared to sacrifice himself to maintain it.

A revolutionary spirit is one which is fit to produce and to direct a revolution made in the interests of liberty.

A revolutionary law is one whose object is to maintain this revolution and to accelerate or to regulate its progress.

A revolutionary measure is one which can ensure the success of the revolution.

We understand therefore that these laws and measures are not of the kind which are suitable for a peaceful society; they are characteristically appropriate only to a revolutionary period, however useless or unjust in another ...

When a country recovers its liberty, when this revolution is a fact, but is not yet completed, there naturally exist a large number of men who wish to produce a revolution in reverse – *a counter-revolution*, and who, merged with the mass of citizens, could become dangerous if they were allowed to act together, and to gather to them all those who share their ideas but are restrained by fear or idleness. Here, therefore, is a danger against which one is justified in defending oneself; thus, all actions, however insignificant, which increase this danger, may become subject to a repressive law, and all actions which forestall them, can legitimately be required of the citizens.

The social pact has for its object the equal and total enjoyment of human rights. It is founded on the mutual guarantee of these rights. But this guarantee ceases with respect to those who wish to dissolve it. Consequently, when it is established that such people exist in a society, one has the right to find means to discover them, and when they are discovered, one need only be restrained by the limits of the natural right of defence. The same applies if a more precious right is threatened; if, in order to preserve it, one has to sacrifice the exercise of a less important right. For such a right ceases to exist, because it would be nothing more, to him who claimed it, than the freedom to violate in others a more precious right.

In the fire of London, in 1666, the fire was not cut off, because the law forbade the demolition of houses. Furniture and goods belonging to absentees were allowed to burn, because it was forbidden to break in doors. Let us not imitate this example ...

Let us not imagine that we can justify all excesses by 'necessity, the excuse of tyrants'. But let us also beware of slandering the friends of liberty by judging the laws they have adopted, and the measures that they propose, merely by rules which are true, ultimately, only for peaceful times.

If zeal, even for the most just of causes, sometimes becomes culpable, let us remember that moderation is not always wisdom.

Let us make revolutionary laws, but to accelerate the time when we would have no more need of them. Let us adopt revolutionary measures, not to prolong or make bloody the revolution, but to complete it and to hasten its end.

Alteration in the meaning of words indicates an alteration in the things themselves.

Aristocracy signifies government by wise men. Old men governed by their authority and experience, poor and small tribes. A small number of rich men governed with arrogance these tribes transformed into opulent and populous towns. From that time aristocracy became the exact synonym for tyranny.

Document 9.9

Henry David Thoreau, 'Resistance to Civil Government'

Henry David Thoreau (1817–62) was born in Concord, Massachusetts. His hostility to the state was induced by his hatred of slavery and his opposition to the war between the United States of America and Mexico (1846–48). The extract is from his 'Resistance to Civil Government' (1849). Thoreau was imprisoned overnight for refusing to pay his taxes in protest against the Mexican war.

I do not hesitate to say, that those who call themselves Abolitionists should at once effectually withdraw their support, both in person and property, from the government of Massachusetts, and not wait till they constitute a majority of one, before they suffer the right to prevail through them. I think that it is enough if they have God on their side, without waiting for that other one. Moreover, any man more right than his neighbors constitutes a majority of one already.

    … I know this well, that if one thousand, if one hundred, if ten men whom I could name, – if ten *honest* men only, – ay, if one HONEST man, in this State of Massachusetts, *ceasing to hold slaves*, were actually to withdraw from this co-partnership, and be locked up in the county jail therefore, it would be the abolition of slavery in America. For it matters not how small the beginning may seem to be …

    Under a government which imprisons any unjustly, the true place for a just man is also a prison. The proper place to-day, the only place which Massachusetts has provided for her freer and less desponding spirits, is in her prisons, to be put out and locked out of the State by her own act, as they have already put themselves out by their principles. It is there that the fugitive slave, and the Mexican prisoner on parole, and the Indian come to plead the wrongs of his race should find them; on that separate, but more free and honorable ground, where the State places those who are not *with* her, but *against* her, – the only house in a slave State in which a free man can abide with honor. If any think that their influence would be lost there, and their voices no longer afflict the ear of the State, that they would not be as an enemy within its walls, they do not know how by how much truth is stronger than error, nor how much more eloquently and effectively he can combat injustice who has experienced a little in his own person. Cast your whole vote, not a strip of paper merely, but your whole influence. A minority is powerless while it conforms to the majority; it is not even a minority then; but it is irresistable when it clogs by its whole weight. If the alternative is to keep all just men in prison, or give up war and slavery, the State will not hesitate which to choose. If a thousand men were not to pay their tax-bills this year, that would not be a violent and bloody measure, as it would be to pay them, and enable the State to commit violence and shed innocent blood. This is, in fact, the definition of a peaceable revolution, if any such is possible … But even suppose blood should flow. Is there not a sort of blood shed when the conscience is wounded?

... I have never declined paying the highway tax, because I am as desirous of being a good neighbor as I am of being a bad subject; and as for supporting schools, I am doing my part to educate my fellow-countrymen now. It is for no particular item in the tax-bill that I refuse to pay it. I simply wish to refuse allegiance to the State, to withdraw and stand aloof from it effectually. I do not care to trace the course of my dollar, if I could, till it buys a man or a musket to shoot one with, – the dollar is innocent, – but I am concerned to trace the effects of my allegiance. In fact, I quietly declare war with the State, after my fashion, though I will still make what use and get what advantage of her I can, as is usual in such cases.

Document 9.10

Alexis de Tocqueville, *The Ancien Régime and the French Revolution*

Alexis de Tocqueville (1805–59) (see document 3.13) published *The Ancien Régime and the French Revolution* in 1856. He acknowledges the novelty of the Revolution but then goes on to point to its precedents.

All mere civil and political revolutions have had some country for their birthplace, and have remained circumscribed within its limits. The French Revolution, however, had no territorial boundary – far from it; one of its effects has been to efface as it were all ancient frontiers from the map of Europe. It united or it divided mankind in spite of laws, traditions, characters, and languages, turning fellow-countrymen into enemies, and foreigners into brothers; or rather, it formed an intellectual country common to men of every nation, but independent of all separate nationalities.

We should search all the annals of history in vain for a political revolution of the same character; that character is only to be found in certain religious revolutions. And accordingly it is to them that the French Revolution must be compared, if any light is to be thrown upon it by analogy.

Schiller remarks, with truth, in his 'History of the Thirty Years' War', that the great Reformation of the sixteenth century had the effect of bringing together nations which scarcely knew each other, and of closely uniting them by new sympathies. Thus it was that Frenchmen warred against Frenchmen, while Englishmen came to their assistance; men born on the most distant shores of the Baltic penetrated into the very heart of Germany in order to defend Germans of whose existence they had never heard until then. International wars assumed something of the character of civil wars, whilst in every civil war foreigners were engaged. The former interests of every nation were forgotten in behalf of new interests: territorial questions were succeeded by questions of principle. The rules of diplomacy, were involved in inextricable confusion, greatly to the horror and amazement of the politicians of the time. The very same thing happened in Europe after 1789.

The French Revolution was then a political revolution, which in its operation and its aspect resembled a religious one. It had every peculiar and characteristic feature of a religious movement; it not only spread to foreign countries, but it was carried thither by preaching and by propaganda. It is impossible to conceive a stranger spectacle than that of a political revolution which inspires proselytism, which its adherents preach to foreigners with as much ardour and passion as they have shown in enacting it at home. Of all the new and strange things displayed to the world by the French Revolution, this assuredly is the newest. On penetrating deeper into this matter, we shall most likely discover that this similarity of effects must be produced by a latent similarity of causes.

The general character of most religions is, that they deal with man by himself, without taking into consideration whatever the laws, the traditions, and the customs of each country may have added to his original nature. Their principal aim is to regulate the relations of man towards God, and the rights and duties of men towards each other, independently of the various forms of society. The rules of conduct which they inculcate apply less to the man of any particular country or period than to man as a son, a father, a servant, a master or a neighbour. Being thus based on human nature itself, they are applicable to all men, and at all times, and in all places. It is owing to this cause that religious revolutions have so often spread over such vast spheres of action, and have seldom been confined, like political revolutions, to the territory of a single nation, or even of a single race. If we investigate this subject still more closely, we shall find that the more any religion has possessed the abstract and general character to which I refer, the wider has it spread, in spite of all differences of laws, of climate, and of races ...

The French Revolution proceeded, as far as this world is concerned, in precisely the same manner that religious revolutions proceed with regard to the next; it looked upon the citizen in the abstract, irrespective of any particular society, just as most religions looked upon man in general independently of time or country. It did not endeavour merely to define what were the especial rights of a French citizen, but what were the universal duties and rights of all men in political matters.

It was by thus recurring to that which was least peculiar and, we might almost say, most natural in the principles of society and of government that the French Revolution was rendered intelligible to all men, and could be imitated in a hundred different places.

Document 9.11

Proudhon, *General Idea of Revolution in the Nineteenth Century*

Pierre-Joseph Proudhon (1809–65) has been claimed by both anarchists and socialists. After a childhood marked by poverty he became an apprentice compositor in his home town of Besançon. He gained notoriety with *What is Property?* (1840) which opened with the assertion that property is theft. His ideas were invoked by many French socialists in the second half of the nineteenth century, often in opposition to Marxist socialism. The extract is from *General Idea of Revolution in the Nineteenth Century* (1851).

A revolution is a force against which no other force, be it human or divine, can prevail. By its nature it gains strength and grows through the very opposition it encounters. A revolution may be directed, restrained or retarded … The wisest course in politics is to give way to it inch by inch so that instead of proceeding by leaps and bounds, humanity's eternal evolution may proceed imperceptibly and without causing an upheaval. One cannot stem the tide of revolution, deceive it, distort it, and still less can one defeat it. The more you repress it, the more you are tightening its spring, and the more irresistible you are making its action; so much so that for an idea to be successful it is quite immaterial whether it be persecuted, harassed or suppressed when it first appears, or whether it develops and spreads without hindrance.

In the first instance revolutions claim to be voicing the people's grievances, and indicting a corrupt state of affairs in which the poor are always the first to suffer. It is not in the nature of the masses to revolt, except against what harms them physically or morally. Are these grounds for repression, vengeance or persecution? What folly! Any government whose policy is to evade the aspirations of the masses and reject their grievances condemns itself out of its own mouth. It is like the evil-doer who tries to overcome his remorse by committing further crimes. At each outrage the pangs of conscience become more terrible until finally the criminal's reason gives way and delivers him up to the executioner.

There is, as I have said, only one way of averting the dangers of revolution. It is by making revolution legitimate. The people suffer and are discontented with their lot. They are like men groaning in sickness, or children crying in their cradles. Anticipate their wants, listen to their grievances, discover the causes, the consequences, and exaggerate these if need be. Then set about healing the patient immediately and constantly. In these conditions revolution will take place without causing disruption, as part of the natural and proper development of the old order. Nobody will notice it or suspect that it is taking place. The grateful people will look upon you as their benefactor, their representative, their leader. This was how, in 1789, Louis XVI was greeted by the National Assembly and the people as the Restorer of Public Liberty. At his hour of glory Louis XVI, who was more powerful than his forebear Louis XIV, could have secured his house for centuries. He could have used the Revolution as a means of government, but the fool saw it only as an infringement of his rights. He carried this inconceivable blindness with him to the scaffold.

Alas, it seems that peaceful revolution is too ideal a thing for man, with his bellicose nature, to accept. Events seldom follow the most natural and least destructive course, although there is ample opportunity for them to do so. Just as the origins of revolution lie in the urgency of people's needs, so those of the forces of reaction are to be found in the authority of custom. The status quo always wants to prescribe against poverty, and this is why reaction initially gains the ascendancy that the revolution comes to enjoy in the end. As a result of this advance in opposite directions, in which one man's gain invariably means another man's loss, a violent struggle is much to be feared.

Two things militate against gradual revolution: vested interests and the pride of the government.

Document 9.12

Michael Bakunin on Anarchism

Michael Alexandrovich Bakunin (1814–76) was a leader of a revolt in Dresden in 1849 after which he was imprisoned in Saxony, Austria and Russia. Exiled to Siberia in 1857 he escaped in 1861. He participated in several revolutionary risings and conspiracies in Italy and France. The extract is from the *National Catechism*, one of three documents setting out the programme of the International Revolutionary Association (International Brotherhood). These documents also set out Bakunin's anarchism. Bakunin and his followers were opponents of the Marxists (see document 2.10).

The spread and depth of this revolution will more or less differ in each country, according to the political and social situation and the level of revolutionary development. Nevertheless, there are CERTAIN PRINCIPLES which can today attract and inspire the masses to action, regardless of their nationality or the condition of their civilization. These principles are:

1. The land is the common property of society. But its fruits and use shall be open only to those who cultivate it by their labour; accordingly, ground rents must be abolished.

2. Since all social wealth is produced by labour, he who consumes without working, if able to work, is a thief.

3. Only honest people should be entitled to political rights. Such rights shall belong only to the workers ...

4. Today no revolution can succeed in any country if it is not at the same time both a political and a social revolution. Every exclusively political revolution – be it in defence of national independence or for internal change, or even for the establishment of a republic – that does not aim at the immediate and real political and economic emancipation of people will be a false revolution. Its objectives will be unattainable and its consequences reactionary.

5. The Revolution must be made not *for* but *by* the people and can never succeed if it does not enthusiastically involve all the masses of the people, that is, in the rural countryside as well as in the cities.

6. Organized by the idea and the identity of a common programme for all countries; coordinated by a secret organization which will rally not a few, but all, countries into a single plan of action; unified, furthermore, by simultaneous revolutionary uprisings in most of the rural areas and in the cities, the Revolution will from the beginning assume and retain a LOCAL character. And this in the sense that it will not originate with a preponderance of the revolutionary forces of a country spreading out, or focused from, a single point or centre, or ever take on the character of a bourgeois quasi-revolutionary expedition in Roman imperial style (i.e. sending dictatorial commissars to impose the 'party line'). On the contrary, the Revolution will burst out from all parts of a country. It will thus be a true people's revolution involving everybody – men, women, and children – and it is this that will make the Revolution invincible.

7. At the outset (when the people, for just reasons, spontaneously turn against their tormentors) the Revolution will very likely be bloody and vindictive. But this phase will not last long and will never (degenerate into) cold, systematic terrorism … It will be a war, not against particular men, but primarily against the antisocial institutions upon which their power and privileges depend.

8. The Revolution will therefore begin by destroying, above all, all the institutions and all the organizations, churches, parliaments, tribunals, administration, banks, universities, etc., which constitute the lifeblood of the State. The State must be entirely demolished and declared bankrupt, not only financially, but even more politically, bureaucratically, militarily (including its police force). At the same time, the people in the rural communes as well as in the cities will confiscate for the benefit of the Revolution all state property. They will also confiscate all property belonging to the reactionaries and will burn all deeds of property and debts, declaring null and void every civil, criminal, judicial, and official document and record, leaving each in the status quo possession (of property). This is the manner in which the Social Revolution will be made, and once the enemies of the Revolution are deprived of all their resources it will no longer be necessary to invoke bloody measures against them. Further, the unnecessary employment of such unfortunate measures must inevitably lead to the most horrible and formidable reaction.

9. The Revolution being localized, it will necessarily assume a FEDERALIST CHARACTER. Thus, upon overthrowing the established government, the communes must reorganize themselves in a revolutionary manner, electing the administrators and revolutionary tribunals on the basis of universal suffrage and on the principle that all officials must be made directly and effectively responsible to the people.

10. In order to prepare for this revolution it will be necessary to conspire and to organize a strong secret association coordinated by an international nucleus.

Document 9.13

Karl Marx on the Inevitability of Revolution

The extract is from *Capital* Volume 1 (1867), the only part of *Capital* to be published in Marx's lifetime. Marx (see document 4.10) describes how the triumph of capitalism leads to its own overthrow. The implication that capitalism had to triumph before the proletarian revolution came on to the agenda created problems for later socialists (see document 9.16).

... the transformation of the individualized and scattered means of production into socially concentrated means of production, the transformation, therefore, of the dwarf-like property of the many into the giant property of the few, and the expropriation of the great mass of the people from the soil, from the means of subsistence and from the instruments of labour, this terrible and arduously accomplished expropriation of the mass of the people forms the pre-history of capital ...

As soon as this metamorphosis has sufficiently decomposed the old society throughout its depth and breadth, as soon as the workers have been turned into proletarians, and their means of labour into capital, as soon as the capitalist mode of production stands on its own feet, the further socialization of labour and the further transformation of the soil and other means of production into socially exploited and therefore communal means of production takes on a new form. What is now to be expropriated is not the self-employed worker, but the capitalist who exploits a large number of workers.

This expropriation is accomplished through the action of the immanent laws of capitalist production itself, through the centralization of capitals. One capitalist always strikes down many others. Hand in hand with this centralization, or this expropriation of many capitalists by a few, other developments take place on an ever-increasing scale, such as the growth of the cooperative form of the labour process, the conscious technical application of science, the planned exploitation of the soil, the transformation of the means of labour into forms in which they can only be used in common, the economizing of all means of production by their use as the means of production of combined, socialized labour, the entanglement of all peoples in the net of the world market, and, with this, the growth of the international character of the capitalist regime. Along with the constant decrease in the number of capitalist magnates, who usurp and monopolize all the advantages of this process of transformation, the mass of misery, oppression, slavery, degradation and exploitation grows; but with this there also grows the revolt of the working class, a class constantly increasing in numbers, and trained, united and organized by the very mechanism of the capitalist process of production. The monopoly of capital becomes a fetter upon the mode of production which has flourished alongside and under it. The centralization of the means of production and the socialization of labour reach a point at which they become incompatible with their capitalist integument. This integument is burst asunder. The knell of capitalist private property sounds. The expropriators are expropriated.

Document 9.14

Karl Marx on the Forms of Class Conflict

The extract is from one of Marx's letters to Friedrich Bolte (23 November 1871), a leader of working class groups in America. In it Marx (see document 4.10) comments on the political aspect of revolution (cf. document 9.12).

The ultimate object of the political movement of the working class is, of course, the conquest of political power for this class, and this naturally requires that the organisation of the working class, an organisation which arises from its economic struggles, should obviously reach a certain level of development.

On the other hand, however, every movement in which the working class as a *class* confronts the ruling classes and tries to constrain them by pressure from without is a political movement. For instance, the attempt by strikes, etc., in a particular factory or even in a particular trade to compel individual capitalists to reduce the working day, is a purely economic movement. On the other hand, the movement to force through an eight-hour, etc. *law* is a *political* movement. And in this way, out of the separate economic movements of the workers there grows up everywhere a *political* movement, that is to say, a *class* movement, with the object of enforcing its interests in a general form, in a form possessing general, socially coercive force. While these movements presuppose a certain degree of previous organisation, they are in turn equally a means of developing this organisation.

Where the working class is not yet far enough advanced in its organisation to undertake a decisive campaign against the collective power, i.e., the political power, of the ruling classes, it must at any rate be trained for this by continual agitation against this power and by a hostile attitude toward the policies of the ruling classes. Otherwise it remains a plaything in their hands, as the September revolution in France showed, and as is also proved to a certain extent by the game that Mr. Gladstone & Co. have been able to play in England up to the present time.

Document 9.15

V.I. Lenin on the Working Class

Vladimir Ilyich Ulyanov (1870–1924) took the name of Lenin as a code name. His brother had been executed for conspiracy to assassinate the Tsar. Lenin became a Marxist and leader of a faction of the Russian Social Democrats who claimed the title Bolshevik (majority). He returned to Russia from exile in April 1917 and became head of government after the Bolsheviks seized power in November. Within a few years, however, Lenin suffered a series of heart attacks, dying in 1924. The extract is from *What is to be Done?* (1902). The book was a critique of 'economism' which Lenin defined as a pragmatic adaption of revolutionary aims to the immediate concerns and grievances of the working class.

We have said that *there could not yet be* Social-Democratic consciousness among the workers. It could only be brought to them from without. The history of all countries shows that the working class, exclusively by its own effort, is able to develop only trade union consciousness, i.e., the conviction that it is necessary to combine in unions, fight the employers and strive to compel the government to pass necessary labour legislation, etc. The theory of Socialism, however, grew out of the philosophic, historical and economic theories that were elaborated by the educated representatives of the propertied classes, the intellectuals. According to their social status, the founders of modern scientific Socialism, Marx and Engels, themselves belonged to the bourgeois intelligentsia. In the very same way, in Russia, the theoretical doctrine of Social-Democracy arose quite independently of the spontaneous growth of the working-class movement, it arose as a natural and inevitable outcome of the development of ideas among the revolutionary socialist intelligentsia …

Since there can be no talk of an independent ideology being developed by the masses of the workers themselves in the process of their movement the *only* choice is: either the bourgeois or the socialist ideology. There is no middle course (for humanity has not created a 'third' ideology, and, moreover, in a society torn by class antagonisms there can never be a non-class or above-class ideology). Hence, to belittle the socialist ideology *in any way*, to *turn away from it in the slightest degree* means to strengthen bourgeois ideology. There is a lot of talk about spontaneity, but the *spontaneous* development of the working-class movement leads to its becoming subordinated to the bourgeois ideology …

But why, the reader will ask, does the spontaneous movement, the movement along the line of the least resistance, lead to the domination of the bourgeois ideology? For the simple reason that the bourgeois ideology is far older in origin than the socialist ideology; because it is more fully developed and because it possesses *immeasurably* more opportunities for being spread. And the younger the socialist movement is in any given country, the more vigorously must it fight against all attempts to entrench non-socialist ideology, and the more strongly must the workers be warned against those bad counsellors who shout against 'overrating the conscious element,' etc.

Document 9.16

V.I. Lenin on Revolutionary Tactics

Lenin (see introduction to document 9.15) arrived in Petrograd on 3 April 1917, after the collapse of the old regime. His assessment of the situation caused consternation among fellow Bolsheviks. Lenin published the *Letters on Tactics*, from which the extract is taken, in preparation for the All-Russian Party Conference of 20 April which only partly endorsed Lenin's stance.

'Our theory is not a dogma, but a guide to action', Marx and Engels always said, rightly ridiculing the mere memorising and repetition of 'formulas', that at best are capable only of marking out *general* tasks, which are necessarily modifiable by the *concrete* economic and political conditions of each particular *period* of the historical process ...

I define the 'special feature of the present situation in Russia' as a period of *transition* from the first stage of the revolution to the second ...

What, then, is the first stage?

It is the passing of state power to the bourgeoisie.

Before the February–March revolution of 1917, state power in Russia was in the hands of one old class, namely, the feudal landed nobility, headed by Nicholas Romanov.

After the revolution, the power is in the hands of *different* class, a new class, namely, the *bourgeoisie*.

The passing of state power from one *class* to another is the first, the principal, the basic sign of a *revolution*, both in the strictly scientific and in the practical political meaning of that term.

To this extent, the bourgeois, or the bourgeois-democratic, revolution in Russia is *completed*.

But at this point we hear a clamour of protest from people who readily call themselves 'old Bolsheviks'. Didn't we always maintain, they say, that the bourgeois-democratic revolution is completed only by the 'revolutionary-democratic dictatorship of the proletariat and the peasantry'? Is the agrarian revolution, which is also a bourgeois-democratic revolution, completed? Is it not a fact, on the contrary, that it has *not even* started? ...

According to the old way of thinking, the rule of the bourgeoisie could and should be *followed* by the rule of the proletariat and the peasantry, by their dictatorship.

In real life, however, things have *already* turned out differently; there has been an extremely original, novel and unprecedented *interlacing of the one with the other*. We have side by side, existing together, simultaneously, *both* the rule of the bourgeoisie (the government of Lvov and Guchkov) and a revolutionary-democratic dictatorship of the proletariat and the peasantry, which is *voluntarily* ceding power to the bourgeoisie, voluntarily making itself an appendage of the bourgeoisie.

Document 9.17

Hermann Rauschning, *Revolution of Nihilism*

Hermann Rauschning (1887–1982) joined the Nazi Party in Danzig – then a free state – in 1932. He soon gained Hitler's confidence and after the Nazi electoral success in the 28 May Danzig parliamentary election was appointed President of the Danzig Senate. He later fell out of favour and fled to Switzerland. *Revolution of Nihilism* was one of a series of books by Rauschning which emphasized the ruthless character of the Nazis.

What, then, are the aims of National Socialism which are being achieved one after another? Certainly not the various points of its programme; even if some of these are carried out, this is not the thing that matters. The aim of National Socialism is the complete revolutionizing of the technique of government, and complete dominance over the country by the leaders of the movement. The two things are inseparably connected: the revolution cannot be carried out without an élite ruling with absolute power, and this élite can maintain itself in power only through a process of continual intensification of the process of revolutionary disintegration. National Socialism is an unquestionably genuine revolutionary movement in the sense of a final achievement on a vaster scale of the 'mass rising' dreamed of by Anarchists and Communists. But modern revolutions do not take place through fighting across improvised barricades, but in disciplined acts of destruction. They follow irrational impulses, but they remain under rational guidance and command. Their perilousness lies in their ordered destructiveness – it is a misuse on a vast scale of the human desire for order – and in the irrationality and incalculability of their pressure for the 'victory of the revolutionary new order.' This pressure is completely uncalculated, unconsidered, the pressure of men with no programme but action, instinctive in the case of the best troops of the movement; but the part played in it by its controlling élite is most carefully and coolly considered down to the smallest detail. There was and is no aim that National Socialism has not been ready for the sake of the movement to abandon or to proclaim at any time.

The National Socialist revolution, at the outset a nationalist seizure of power, is viewed much too much in the light of historic precedents. There are no criteria and no precedents for the new revolutions of the twentieth century. The revolutionary dictatorship is a new type, in its cynical, unprincipled policy of violence. The outsider overlooks above all the essential distinction between the mass and the élite in the new revolutions. This distinction is vital in every field. That which is intended for the mass is not applicable to the élite. Programme and official philosophy, allegiance and faith, are for the mass. Nothing commits the élite – no philosophy, no ethical standard. It has but one obligation, that of absolute loyalty to comrades, to fellow-members of the initiated élite. This fundamental distinction between élite and mass does not seem to have been sufficiently clearly realized, but it is just this that explains many inconsistencies, many things done, that leave the outsider dumbfounded.

Document 9.18

Herbert Marcuse, 'Re-examination of the Concept of Revolution'

Herbert Marcuse (1898–1979) was born in Berlin. He joined the radical Institute for Social Research in 1933. He went into exile, settling in America where he worked for the Institute, then for the US Government before holding several academic posts. In the late 1960s he enjoyed considerable popularity among radical students. The extract is taken from his 'Re-examination of the Concept of Revolution' (1969).

Opposition in the Metropoles

The character of the opposition in the centre of corporate capitalism is concentrated in the two opposite poles of the society: in the ghetto population (itself not homogeneous), and in the middle-class intelligentsia, especially among the students.

Common to these different and even conflicting groups is the total character of the refusal and rebellion:

1. Insistence on a break with the continuity of domination and exploitation – no matter in what name; insistence not only on new institutions, but on self-determination;

2. Distrust of all ideologies, including socialism made into an ideology;

3. Rejection of the pseudo-democratic process sustaining the dominion of corporate capitalism.

This 'unorthodox' character of the opposition is itself expressive of the structure of corporate capitalism (the 'integration' of the majority of the underlying population). Neither of the two oppositional groups constitutes the 'human basis' of the social process of production – for Marx a decisive condition for the historical agent of the revolution.

They do not make up the majority of the population.

They are faced with hostility (and resentment) among organized labour (still the human basis of capitalist production and the source of surplus value, and therefore still the potential agent of a possible revolution) and they are not effectively organized, neither on the national nor on the international level …

Working Class and Revolution

By itself, this opposition cannot be regarded as agent of radical change; it can become such an agent only if it is sustained by a working class which is no longer the prisoner of its own integration and of a bureaucratic trade-union and party apparatus supporting this integration. If this alliance between the new opposition and the working classes does not materialize, the latter may well become, in part at least, the mass basis of a neo-fascist regime.

Conclusion: the *Marxian concept of a revolution* carried by the majority of the exploited masses, culminating in the 'seizure of power' and in the setting up of a proletarian dictatorship which initiates socialization, *is 'overtaken' by the historical development*: it pertains to a stage of capitalist productivity and organization which has been overtaken; it does not project the higher stage of capitalist productivity, including the productivity of destruction, and the terrifying concentration of the instruments of annihilation and of indoctrination in the hands of the powers that be.

However, this 'invalidation' of the Marxian concept is an authentic and accurate *Aufhebung*; the truth of the concept is preserved and reaffirmed on the level actually attained by the historical development. The revolutionary proletariat becomes an agent of change where it still is the human basis of the social process of production, namely, in the predominantly agrarian areas of the Third World, where it provides the popular support for the national liberation fronts.

And these areas, and these forces are not external to the capitalist system. They are an essential part of its global space of exploitation, they are areas and forces which this system cannot allow to go and shift into that other orbit (of socialism or communism), because it can survive only if its expansion is not blocked by any superior power. The National Liberation movements are expressive of the *internal contradictions* of the global capitalist system ...

The ever more blatant contradiction between the vast social wealth and its wasteful and destructive use, between the potential of freedom and the actuality of repression, between the possible abolition of alienated labour and the capitalist need to sustain it, may well lead to a gradual dysfunction of the society, a decline of the morale which normally assures the day-to-day performance and the compliance with the required pattern of behaviour, at work and at leisure. This may awaken the consciousness of the use of technical progress as instrument of domination.

The events of May and June in France have shown to what extent these tensions in the established society can loosen the grip of capitalist and trade union integration, and promote the alliance between working class groups and the militant intelligentsia.

The concept of revolution must take into account this eventuality of the diffuse, apparently 'spontaneous', disintegration of the system, the general loosening of its cohesion – an expression of the objective obsolescence of alienated labour, of the pressure for the liberation of man from his function as agent (and servant) of the process of production: the revolution may be seen as a crisis of the system in 'affluence' and superfluity.

The Agents of Change

In such a crisis, the historical agents of change would emerge – and they would not be identical with any of the traditional classes. But the 'qualification' of these agents can be gauged if we recall the perhaps most decisive element in the Marxian concept, namely, that the historical subject of revolution must be the 'definite negation' also in the sense that this subject is a social class free from, that is, not contaminated by the exploitative needs and interests of man under capitalism, that it is the subject of essentially different, 'humanistic' needs and values.

   This is the notion of the rupture with the continuum of domination, the qualitative difference of socialism as a new form and way of life, not only rational development of the productive forces, but also the redirection of progress toward the ending of the competitive struggle for existence, not only abolition of poverty and toil, but also reconstruction of the social and natural environment as a peaceful, beautiful universe: *total transvaluation of values, transformation of needs and goals.* This implies *still another change in the concept of revolution*, a break with the continuity of the technical apparatus of productivity which, for Marx, would extend (freed from capitalist abuse) to the socialist society. Such *'technological' continuity* would *constitute a fateful link between capitalism and socialism*, because this technical apparatus has, in its very structure and scope, become an apparatus of control and domination. *Cutting this link* would mean, not to regress in the technical progress, but to reconstruct the technical apparatus in accordance with the needs of free men, guided by their own consciousness and sensibility, by their autonomy. This autonomy would call for a decentralized apparatus of rational control on a reduced basis – reduced because no longer inflated by the requirements of exploitation, aggressive expansion, and competition, held together by solidarity in co-operation.

QUESTIONS FOR DISCUSSION

1. Do you agree that 'it is a lawful and glorious act to slay public tyrants'
2. Do revolutions break out because governments fail to adapt to change or because they try to implement change too rapidly?
3. How would you recognize a revolution?
4. When is revolution justified?
5. How far should a minority go in resisting what it believes are unjust governments?

NOTES

1 Hal Draper, *Karl Marx's Theory of Revolution. Volume II The Politics of Social Classes* (New York, Monthly Review Press, 1978), p. 17
2 These characteristics are taken from Keith Michael Baker, *Inventing the French Revolution* (Cambridge, Cambridge University Press, 1990)
3 On the importance of this see John Dunn, 'Revolution', in Terence Ball, James Farr and Russell L. Hanson (eds), *Political Innovation and Conceptual Change* (Cambridge, Cambridge University Press, 1986), pp. 346–9.

FURTHER READING

Most general surveys of revolution concentrate on modern, usually nineteenth- and twentieth-century ideas. A brief account stretching from ancient Egypt onwards is, however, provided by Peter Calvert, *Revolution* (London, Pall Mall, 1970). Relevant collections of documents include Krishan Kumar (ed.), *Revolution. The Theory and Practice of a European Idea* (London, Weidenfeld and Nicolson, 1971). Helpful accounts of the origins and development of the term can be found in Arthur Hatto, '"Revolution": An Enquiry into the Usefulness of an Historical Term', *Mind*, Vol. 58 (1949), pp. 495–517 and Vernon F. Snow, 'The Concept of Revolution in Seventeenth-Century England', *The Historical Journal*, Vol. 5 (1962), pp. 167–90. There is considerable dispute about which events qualify as 'revolutions' and especially about whether modern, post-1789, revolutions differ radically from previous occurrences. For some contrasting views see the incisive contribution by John Dunn, 'Revolution', in Terence Ball, James Farr and Russell L. Hanson (eds), *Political Innovation and Conceptual Change* (Cambridge, Cambridge University Press, 1989), pp. 333–56, Perez Zagorin, *Rebels and Rulers*, 2 Vols (Cambridge, Cambridge University Press, 1982) and Charles Tilly, *European Revolutions 1492–1992* (Oxford, Blackwell, 1993). On the use of the term before and during the French Revolution see Keith Michael Baker, *Inventing the French Revolution*

(Cambridge, Cambridge University Press, 1990). For an interesting attempt to distinguish the *coup d'état* from a revolution see David C. Rapaport, 'Coup d'état: The View of the Men Firing Pistols', in Carl J. Friedrich (ed.), *Revolution* (New York, Atherton Press, 1966), pp. 53–74. Carl Cohen, *Civil Disobedience. Conscience, Tactics and the Law* (New York, Columbia University Press, 1971) distinguishes between its subject and revolution. On Marx see Hal Draper, *Karl Marx's Theory of Revolution*, especially Volume II, *The Politics of Social Classes* (New York, Monthly Review Press, 1978), although readers unfamiliar with Marx's work might start with the comments in a general account such as Michael Evans, *Karl Marx* (London, Allen and Unwin, 1975). On the problematic case of fascism see Jeremy Noakes, 'Nazism and Revolution', in Noel O'Sullivan (ed.), *Revolutionary Theory and Political Reality* (Brighton, Wheatsheaf, 1983), pp. 73–100.

10

DEMOCRACY AND POPULAR REPRESENTATION

INTRODUCTION

Although the meaning of democracy, 'rule by the people' from the ancient Greek 'demokratia' coined in the fifth century BC, appears simple, it has proved a much disputed term, both as an ideal and in its procedural implications. The complex arrangements of Greek democracy began to emerge in 508/7 BC with the reforms of the Athenian aristocrat, Kleisthenes. In its fully developed form, Athenian democracy was a system of citizen self-rule in a society in which the great majority of the population were not citizens. Each citizen was equally entitled to attend, vote and speak at gatherings of the assembly, which decided all the major issues in the city-state or *polis* by simple majority vote. Every Athenian citizen who had reached the age of 30 was eligible and expected to staff one of the multitude of official positions and to sit and deliberate in the courts which both decided disputes and confirmed or overruled novel items of legislation passed by the assembly. Many citizens would find themselves, sooner or later, acting for a day as head of the Athenian council, the official executive body, although they might only occupy it for a day in their life. On the face of it, this system seemed contrived to minimize the abuse of political power.

This participatory democracy was very different from the representative democracy of the nineteenth and twentieth centuries. It was poorly regarded by the aristocratic philosophers and historians of ancient Greece notably, by Plato and Aristotle. Aristotle, for instance advocated a government mixing monarchical, aristocratic and democratic elements (see documents 3.1, 3.2 and 10.1) They depicted democracy as rule by the poor and ignorant, leading to anarchy and then, by consequence, to tyranny. Aristotle regarded it as a source of political instability, with polarization of the rich and poor. The argument advanced in favour of this democracy was that it made freedom possible. Its critics claimed that it was intrinsically corrupting and that this freedom was destructive even to its supposed beneficiaries.

This negative assessment of democracy was still the predominant view in the eighteenth century and was shared by the creators of the American Constitution.

In *The Federalist,* James Madison, assuming that democracy involved direct rule by citizens, wrote that 'democracies have ever been found incompatible with personal security, or the rights of property; and have in general been as short in their lives as they have been violent in their deaths'.[1] The emphasis, to begin with, in America was not on democracy but on representative institutions. In Britain, people described their system as one of representative and responsible government.

The term democracy, used in a positive sense, was only beginning to enter regular political discourse at the end of the eighteenth century. The only constitution openly to proclaim itself democratic was that of the Helvetic Republic of 1798. One of the major obstacles which the term and the idea faced was the problem of size. The original models of democratic government in ancient Greece had been the city-states and the consensus was that democracy was possible only in such relatively small political communities. It was not an option for the modern European states. The prospects of democracy were rescued by something which had not formed part of the democratic tradition: the concept of representation. Not long after the turn of the century, the Frenchman, Destutt de Tracy, claimed that 'Representative democracy ... is democracy rendered practicable for a long time and over a great extent of territory'. He added that it was a 'new invention'.

Thus, the term 'democracy' in its modern sense came into use in the course of the nineteenth century to describe a system of representative government in which the representatives are chosen by free competitive elections and most male citizens are entitled to vote. This state of affairs was reached in the United States of America during the 1830s and 1840s. In Britain the franchise was successively broadened in 1832, 1867 and 1884. Women in Britain only received the vote after the First World War and in France in 1946. The last two centuries have seen both the spread of the ideal of democracy and changes, such as the growth of public education, which have made informed popular participation in the political process increasingly viable, at least in the form of participation in elections.

The slow progress made by the extension of the franchise indicates the reservations which were held about the idea of universal suffrage. One such reservation predated the modern idea of democracy and found unusually clear expression in the Putney Debates during the English Civil War. Here, the Levellers advanced the proposition that the franchise should be considered a natural right. Their opponents insisted with equal vigour that it should be restricted to those who had a stake in the country (see document 10.2 and compare with the nineteenth-century statements, documents 10.5 to 10.8).

This reservation was still very much alive in the nineteenth century, although additional arguments for extending the franchise had entered the field. In the views of James Stuart Mill and Jeremy Bentham in nineteenth-century England, the key to good government could be found in two propositions. First, there was the principle of 'self-preference' by which it was affirmed that everyone will know what will promote their own happiness; and, secondly that of 'utility' by which it was claimed that the right and proper end of government is to promote 'the greatest happiness of the greatest number' of citizens. These propositions established a case for parliamentary reform independent of such ideas as natural rights. John Stuart Mill recommended the extension of the vote to working-class citizens provided they paid taxes and could pass a literacy test, but argued that this should be accompanied by the granting of multiple votes to citizens who had a higher education or were in skilled and professional occupations. (For the views of a prominent Victorian critic of democracy see 10.9 in which the author, Sir James FitzJames Stephen, denies that democracy will lead to equality.)

Lurking behind many nineteenth-century attempts to restrict democracy was the fear that it would amount to the tyranny of the majority (see document 10.4). This fear had waned by the end of the century, although it has never entirely disappeared. The twentieth century saw the breakthrough of radical extensions of the franchise and, at first, the apparent triumphal march of democracy. It should not be forgotten though that the second quarter of the century saw a violent reaction against democracy. It was, to use the title of a book by Harold Laski, a time of 'democracy in crisis' (see document 10.12).

In contemporary analyses of democracy there are basically two alternative approaches. On the one hand, we can start with the observation of usage and political practice (the empirical approach) which leads to definition in terms of institutions and processes. On the other hand, we can spell out our democratic ideals (the idealist approach) and consider what the practical implications of these may be. The idealist approach was questioned by Joseph Schumpeter, who argued that a democratic system is best identified in institutional and procedural terms.

Schumpeter's main target was the Rousseauian tradition and the idea of the general will. The general will was supposed to identify and affirm the common good of society, although Rousseau himself thought that this was possible only in small communities. For Schumpeter this idea of a common good was a dangerous illusion (see his analysis of the classical doctrine of democracy in document 10.10). At the end of the day Schumpeter claimed that the only viable form of democracy consisted of the periodic selection, by means of elections, between competing élites. It was the victorious élite which would rule, not the citizens.

Schumpeter's account has acquired considerable influence because it consciously emphasized the gap between the elected and the electors, the representatives and the represented. With the increasing role of disciplined parties and the power of executives over legislatures it was suggested by Lord Hailsham that, in the United Kingdom, an 'elected dictatorship' had emerged (see document 10.14).

The relationship between representative and electors has been disputed since at least the eighteenth century. On the one hand, it has been argued that representatives should be delegates acting according to a mandate. The power of the rhetoric of the mandate is reflected now when party leaders proclaim that they have a mandate from the people. This idea has some plausibility in the context of a parliamentary system dominated by disciplined parties. It runs contrary, though, to the accepted constitutional doctrine that the government of the country has a responsibility to protect and advance the interests of the whole nation, not just to look after the interests of its own political supporters. This is particularly so since a victorious party rarely gets the support of an overall majority of electors, even where they have been elected by a minority of the electors.

Other trends have also caused concern. There have always been worries in representative democracies about the apportioning of electoral districts, the type of electoral system used, e.g., proportional representation, and the rules governing the conduct of elections. These have been compounded in recent years by concern about low levels of voter turnout, deficient official accountability and lack of basic information about the political system held by voters. These trends have brought forth calls for reform, including the wider use of referenda. The advocacy of referenda 'in turn' is often part of a broader call for a return to the older idea of direct participation. Democracy has been used not only to describe a system of government, but also to describe other social relationships. For instance, in the American sense a democratic society is one without hereditary class or caste distinctions in which there should be something approaching equality of opportunity for all citizens. The principles of the protection of minority rights and civil liberties and the rule of law (see document 1.12) are also generally associated with democracy, although, logically, they are not an essential part of the concept.

Discussion of democracy has also been complicated by the fact that the term has also been appropriated by governments and states which are anything but democratic in the pluralist sense – for instance the Soviet Constitution of 1936. Some institutions were established which took the outward form of democracies although these were impotent in the face of the official monopoly of power by the Communist Party. The weakness of the democratic credentials of the Soviet Union may seem evident, but the position is not always so clear. When a UNESCO conference on democracy met in 1950 more than fifty nations, completely diverse in their political systems, insisted that they (and sometimes only they) were democracies. Democracy, like the concept of justice, is claimed by all, although its universal appeal is of a much more recent date. The consequence is that the term must be defined more specifically if it is to have any substantive meaning.

DOCUMENTS

Document 10.1

Aristotle on Democracy

For Aristotle (384–321 BC) (see document 1.1), the dominant principle in democracy is freedom. It is the majority of the freeborn who rule in a democracy and the majority are usually to be identified with the poor who rule in their own interest. Aristotle believed that the political conflicts of his day were principally due to a clash between two economic groups, the rich and the poor, who supported two different types of constitution (oligarchy and democracy) animated by different political principles (wealth and freedom).

The basis of a democratic state is liberty; which, according to the common opinion of men, can only be enjoyed in such a state; – this they affirm to be the great end of every democracy. One principle of liberty is for all to rule and be ruled in turn, and indeed democratic justice is the application of numerical not proportionate equality; whence it follows that the majority must be supreme, and that whatever the majority approve must be the end and the just. Every citizen, it is said, must have equality, and therefore in a democracy the poor have more power than the rich, because there are more of them, and the will of the majority is supreme. This, then, is one note of liberty which all democrats affirm to be the principle of their state. Another is that a man should live as he likes. This, they say, is the privilege of a freeman, since, on the other hand, not to live as a man likes is the mark of a slave. This is the second characteristic of democracy, whence has arisen the claim of men to be ruled by none, if possible, or, if this is impossible, to rule and be ruled in turns; and so it contributes to the freedom based upon equality.

Such being our foundation and such the principle from which we start, the characteristics of democracy are as follows: the election of officers by all out of all; and that all should rule over each, and each in his turn over all; that the appointment to all offices, or to all but those which require experience and skill, should be made by lot; that no property qualification should be required for offices, or only a very low one; that a man should not hold the same office twice, or not often, or in the case of few except military offices; that the tenure of all offices, or of as many as possible, should be brief; that all men should sit in judgement, or that judges selected out of all should judge, in all matters, or in most and in the greatest and most important – such as the scrutiny of accounts, the constitution, and private contracts; that the assembly should be supreme over all causes, or at any rate over the most important, and the magistrates over none or only over a very few. Of all magistracies, a council is the most democratic when there is not the means of paying all the citizens, but when they are paid even this is robbed of its power; for the people then draw all cases to themselves, as I said in the previous discussion. The next characteristic of democracy is payment for services; assembly, law–courts, magistrates, everybody receives pay, when it is to be had; or when it is not to be had for all, then it is given to the law- courts and to the state assemblies, to the council and to the magistrates, or at least to any of them who are compelled to have their meals together. And whereas oligarchy is characterized by, birth, wealth, and education, the notes of democracy appear to be the opposite of these – low birth, poverty, mean employment. Another note is that no magistracy is perpetual, but if any such have survived some ancient change in the constitution it should be stripped of its power, and the holders should be elected by lot and no longer by vote. These are the points common to all democracies; but democracy and democracies in their truest form are based upon the recognized principle of democratic justice, that all should count equally; for equality implies that the poor should have no more share in the government than the rich, and should not be the only rulers, but that all should rule equally according to their numbers. And in this way men think that they will secure equality and freedom in their state …

Document 10.2

The Levellers: The Putney Debates

The Putney Debates (October–November 1647), from which the following extract is taken, are an early example of the discussion as to whom should be entrusted with the vote. The Leveller movement campaigned, among other things, for a major extension of the franchise (how much they wanted it widened has been the subject of a lively historical controversy). Lieutenant-General Ireton, Oliver Cromwell's son-in-law was speaking in the General Council of the Army at Putney on behalf of established society and property and against the enfranchisement of the unpropertied. Rainsborough and Wildman, leading Levellers, advanced the idea of paramount natural rights. The issue was fundamental: were political rights and institutions shaped by constitutional compacts and historic entitlements, or were political rights based on natural law?

(From the second day's debate in the General Council of the Army, Putney Church, 29 October 1647)

The Paper called the Agreement read. Afterwards the first Article read by itself.

Commissary (General) Ireton: The exception that lies in it is this: it is said, they are to be distributed according to the number of the inhabitants, 'The people of England', etc. And this does make me think, that the meaning is that every man that is an inhabitant is to be equally considered, and to have an equal voice in the election of those representers, the persons that are for the general representative, and if that be the meaning then I have something to say against it, but if it be only that those people that by the civil constitution of this kingdom, which is original and fundamental, and beyond which I am sure no memory of record does go.

Mr Pettus (Maximilian Petty): We judge that all inhabitants that have not lost their birthright should have an equal voice in elections.

Rainsborough: I desired that those that had engaged in it, for really I think that the poorest he that is in England has a life to live as the greatest he; and therefore truly, sir, I think it's clear, that every man that is to live under a government ought first by his own consent to put himself under that government; and I do think that the poorest man in England is not at all bound in a strict sense to that government that he has not had a voice to put himself under; and I am confident that, when I have heard the reasons against it, that something will be said to answer those reasons, insomuch that I should doubt whether I was an Englishman or no, that should doubt of these things.

Ireton: That's this:

Give me leave to tell you, that if you make this the rule, I think you must fly for refuge to an absolute natural right, and you must deny all civil right; and I am sure it will come to that in the consequence. This, I perceive, is pressed as that which is so essential and due, the right of the people of this kingdom, and as they are the people of this kingdom, distinct and divided from other people, as that we must for this right lay aside all other considerations. This is so just; this is so due; this is so right to them; and those that they must thus choose, and that those that they do thus choose, must have such a power of binding all, and loosing all, according to those limitations. This is pressed as so due, and so just, as is argued that it is an engagement paramount all others, you must break it; so look upon these as thus held out to us; so it was held out by the gentlemen that brought it yesterday.

For my part, I think it is no right at all. I think that no person has a right to an interest or share in the disposing of the affairs of the kingdom, and in determining or choosing those that shall determine what laws we shall be ruled by here, no person has a right to this that has not a permanent fixed interest in this kingdom, and those persons together are properly the represented of this kingdom who, taken together, and consequently are to make up the representers of this kingdom; are the representers who, taken together, do comprehend whatsoever is of real of permament interest in the kingdom, and I am sure there is otherwise (I cannot tell what), otherwise any man can say why a foreigner coming in amongst us, or as many as will coming in amongst us, or by force or otherwise settling themselves here, or at least by our permission having a being here, why they should not as well lay claim to it as any other.

We talk of birthright. Truly, birthright there is thus much claim: men may justly have by birthright, by their very being born in England, that we should not seclude them out of England. That we should not refuse to give them air and place and ground, and the freedom of the highways and other things, to live amongst us, not any man that is born here, though he in birth or by his birth there come nothing at all that is part of the permanent interest of this kingdom to him. That I think is due to a man by birth. But that by a man's being born here he shall have a share in that power that shall dispose of the lands here, and of all things here, I do not think it a sufficient ground.

But I am sure if we look upon that which is the utmost, within man's view, of what was originally the constitution of this kingdom, upon that which is most radical and fundamental, and which if you take away, there is no man has any land, any goods, you take away any civil interest, and that is this: that those that choose the representers for the making of laws by which this state kingdom are to be governed are the persons who, taken together, do comprehend the local interest of this kingdom; that is, the persons in whom all land lies, and those in corporations in whom all trading lies. This is the most fundamental constitution of this kingdom, and which if you do not allow, you allow none at all. This constitution has limited and determined it, that only those shall have voices in elections.

It is true, as was said by a gentleman near me. 'The meanest man in England ought to have.' I say this: that those that have the meanest local interest, that man that has but forty shillings a year, he has as great (a) voice in the election of a knight for the shire as he that has ten thousand a year or more, if he had never so much, and therefore there is that regard had to it. But this still the constitution of this government has had an eye to, and what other government has not an eye to the foundation of the power that's given to the representers in those who have a permanent and a local interest in the kingdom, and who, taken altogether, do comprehend the whole, and if we shall go to take away this,we shall plainly go to take away all property and interest that any man has, either in land by inheritance, or in estate by possession, or anything else, if you take away this fundamental part of the civil constitution ...

Document 10.3

Noah Webster to Joseph Priestley, A Representative Republic

Noah Webster (1758–1843), American lexicographer and author, among other works, of the *American Dictionary of the English Language*. His political writings included *Ten Letters to Dr .Joseph Priestley* (1800) and the following extract is taken from the third letter. Priestley (1733–1804), an English scientist, educationalist and dissenting minister, had emigrated to Pennsylvania in 1794 after his house and laboratory had been destroyed by a mob hostile to sympathizers with the French Revolution.

By democracy is intended a government where the legislative powers are exercised directly by all the citizens, as formerly in Athens and Rome. In our country this power is not in the hands of the people but of their representatives. The powers of the people are principally restricted to the direct exercise of the rights of suffrage. Our form of government has acquired the appelation of a Republic, by way of distinction, or rather of a representative Republic.

Hence the word Democrat has been used as synonymous with the word Jacobin in France; and by an additional idea, which arose from the attempt to control our government by private popular associations, the word has come to signify a person who attempts an undue opposition to, or influence over, government by means of private clubs, secret intrigues, or by public popular meetings which are extraneous to the constitution. By Republicans we understand the friends of our Representative Governments, who believe that no influence whatever should be exercised in a state which is not directly authorized by the Constitution and laws.

Document 10.4

Benjamin Constant, *Principles of Politics*

Benjamin Constant (Henri Benjamin Constant de Rebecque) (1767–1830) was a Swiss-born French Liberal who was exiled for most of Napoleon I's rule. His social and political thought was in many respects a sustained commentary on Rousseau's ideas. He criticized the latter for sacrificing the rights of the individual to the omnipotence of the state, and argued for a representative system (his preference was for a parliamentary monarchy) as the surest means of safeguarding individual independence. The following extract is taken from *Principles of Politics* (1815).

The error of those who, sincere in their love of freedom, have attributed unlimited power to the sovereign people, comes of the manner in which their ideas about politics have been formed. They have seen in history a few men, or even one man alone, possessed of immense and very harmful power; and their anger has turned against the possessors of power and not against power itself. Instead of destroying it, they dreamt only of displacing it. It was a scourge, but they looked upon it as something to be conquered. They endowed society as a whole with it. And it passed perforce from the whole to the majority, and from the majority into the hands of a few men, and often of one man alone; and it has done as much harm as before. Manifold examples, objections, arguments and facts have been used to condemn all political institutions. Certainly, in a society where the people's sovereignty is accepted as a basic principle, no man and no class may subject the others to his or their particular will; but it is not true that society as a whole possesses over its members an unlimited sovereignty.

The generality of citizens constitute the sovereign in the sense that no individual, no fraction, no partial association can assume the sovereignty unless it has been delegated to him or them. But it does not follow that the citizens generally, or those in whom they have vested the sovereignty, may dispose absolutely of the lives of individuals. On the contrary, there is a part of life which necessarily remains personal and independent, which of right is beyond the competence of society. Sovereignty can be only limited and relative. At the point where personal independence and life begin, the jurisdiction of the sovereign ceases. If society goes beyond this point, it is as guilty as the despot whose only title is the sword of the destroyer; society cannot pass beyond the sphere of its competence without usurpation, nor the majority without factiousness. The assent of the majority is not always enough to make its acts legitimate: there are some which nothing can justify. When authority commits such actions, it matters little from what source the authority is alleged to come, or whether it belongs to an individual or a nation; even when it is exercised by the whole nation, except for the citizen oppressed, it is not the more legitimate for that. Rousseau failed to recognize this truth, and his error has made of his Social Contract, so often invoked in favour of liberty, the most terrible support of all kinds of despotism. He defines the contract made by society with its members as the complete and unreserved alienation of each individual with all his rights to the community. To reassure us about the consequences of so absolute a surrender of all aspects of our life to an abstract being, he tells us that the sovereign, that is to say the social body, cannot injure either its members in general or any one of them in particular; that, since each gives himself entire, the condition is the same for all, and none has an interest in making it burdensome to others; that each in giving himself to all gives himself to nobody, that each acquires over all his associates the rights which he grants to them, and gains the equivalent of all that he loses together with greater power to preserve what he has. But he forgets that all these preservative attributes which he confers on the abstract being he calls the sovereign derive from its including within it all individuals without exception. But, as soon as the sovereign has to make use of the power belonging to him – that is to say, as soon as authority has to be organized for practical purposes – the sovereign, since he cannot himself exercise it, must delegate it; and all these attributes disappear. Since the action taken in the name of all is willy nilly done by one person or by a few, it is not true that in giving oneself to all one gives oneself to no one; on the contrary one gives oneself to those who act in the name of all. Whence it follows that, in giving oneself entire, one does not enter a condition which is equal for all, because there are some who alone benefit from the sacrifice of others. It is not true that no one has an interest in making the condition a burden to others, since there are associates to whom the condition does not apply. It is not true that all the associates acquire over others the rights which they grant to them over themselves; they do not all gain the equivalent of what they lose, and what results from their sacrifice is, or may be, the establishment of a power which takes from them what they have. Rousseau himself took fright at these consequences. Appalled by the immensity of the social power he had created, he did not know in what hands to place that monstrous power, and could find as a safeguard against the danger inseparable from sovereignty thus conceived only an expedient which made its exercise impossible.

He declared that sovereignty could not be alienated or delegated or represented; which amounted to saying that it could not be exercised. This was to annihilate the principle he had just proclaimed.

But see how much more frank the partisans of despotism are when they start from this principle which supports and favours them. Hobbes, the ablest man who ever reduced despotism to a system, was zealous to admit that sovereignty is unlimited in order to conclude therefrom that the absolute rule of one man is legitimate. Sovereignty, he says, is absolute; this truth has always been recognized, even by the promoters of sedition or civil war: their intention was not to destroy sovereignty but to transfer it. Democracy is an absolute sovereignty in the hands of all; aristocracy an absolute sovereignty in the hands of a few; monarchy an absolute sovereignty in the hands of only one person. The people could divest themselves of this absolute sovereignty in favour of a monarch, who thus became its legitimate possessor …

Where sovereignty is unlimited, there is no way of protecting the individual against the government. It is in vain that you claim to subject governments to the general will. It is they who give utterance to that will, and all precautions become illusory. The people, says Rousseau, are sovereign in one respect, and subjects in another; but in practice these two respects merge into one another. Authority can easily oppress the people taken as subjects in order to compel them in their sovereign capacity to express a will prescribed to them by authority.

No political organization can remove this danger. It is in vain that you separate the powers: if the sum total of power is unlimited, the separate powers have only to make an alliance, and there is despotism without a remedy. What matters is not that our rights should be inviolable by one power without the approval of another, but that the violation be forbidden to all the powers. It is not enough that executive agents should have to invoke a grant of authority by the legislator; the legislator must be able to grant them authority to act only within a legitimate sphere. It is of little moment that the executive power should not have the right to act without the backing of the law, if limits are not set to that backing; if it is not laid down that there are matters about which the lawmaker may not make law – or, in other words, that sovereignty is limited, and there are decisions which neither the people nor their delegates have the right to make.

It is this that must be proclaimed; this, the important truth, the essential principle, to be established.

No authority on earth is unlimited; whether it resides in the people, or in the men who claim to be their representatives, or in kings, whatever their title to rule, or in the law, which, being only the expression of the people's or the prince's will (depending on the form of government), must be confirmed within the same limits as that will.

Citizens possess rights independently of all social or political authority, and every authority which violates these rights becomes illegitimate. These rights are freedom of person, of religious worship, and of opinion (including its publication), the enjoyment of property, and security, against arbitrary power. No one in authority can infringe these rights without destroying his own title to authority …

We owe to public tranquillity many sacrifices; and we should be morally to blame if, by holding inflexibly to our rights, we resisted all laws which appeared to us to impair them; but no duty binds us to those pretended laws whose corrupting influence threatens the noblest aspects of life, to the laws which not only restrict our legitimate rights but require of us actions contrary to the eternal principles of justice and compassion which man cannot cease to observe without degrading and belying his nature.

So long as a law, though a bad one, does not tend to deprave us, so long as the encroachments of authority require only sacrifices which do not make us vile or cruel, we can submit. We then make compromises which affect only ourselves. But if the law should require us to tread underfoot our affections or our duties; if, on the pretext of an extraordinary and factitious sacrifice, in favour either of the monarchy or the republic (as the case may be), it should forbid loyalty to friends in misfortune; if it should require us to betray our allies, or even to persecute vanquished enemies, anathema upon the promotion of injustices and crimes thus covered with the name of law!

Whenever a law appears unjust, it is a positive, general, unrestricted duty not to become an executor of it. This force of inertia entails neither upheavals, nor revolutions, nor disorders.

Nothing justifies the man who gives his support to a law which he believes is iniquitous.

Document 10.5

The Chartist *Northern Star*

The People's Charter of 1838 had comprised six points: manhood suffrage, annual parliaments, equal electoral districts, vote by ballot, payment of members and abolition of members' property qualification. The following extract is an editorial from the Chartist leader, Feargus O'Connor's *Northern Star*, published on 2 January 1841. It expressed a basic tenet of nineteenth-century radicalism, that political authority was delegated upwards from the people, something popularized earlier by Tom Paine in *The Rights of Man* (1791).

… We would regard the subject in a more general and useful form, by the light of reason and experience, hanging our faith on the individual opinion of neither this person nor that. From one principle alone, we feel convinced, may be deduced every rational and true proposition relating to a democratic government – and that principle is:

'The people are the source of all power'.

Is this assertion well founded? Let us try it by the common, yet excellent, hypothesis of a transition from a state of nature to a state of society. Men first unite together for protection and mutual advantage; they feel the necessity of having some head, or leader, to control the vicious and reward the meritorious; they, therefore, by the general voice, and for the general good, invest one or more of their fellow-beings with superior authority; these persons, thus privileged, may admit others to their councils, and to a share in their power; but yet this alters not the source of that power; it must, if traced up, be found to spring originally from the people, the public, the nation at large.

From the establishment of the above truth flow many valuable maxims. First. All who are affected by this power are entitled to a voice in its creation. This assertion, so strongly supported by reason and common sense, receives additional strength from the supposition, on which we are proceeding; for, how can we conceive a body of men, just associated from a state of wild nature, all equal, all free, delegating a power to one individual above the rest, for the government of all, without at the same time believing that he was nominated and elected by all? To aver the contrary would be absurd and contradictory to that self-interest which reigns so powerfully in the human mind. Secondly. Power springing from the people must be responsible to the people. In other words, the channels must be referrable to their source. We cannot fancy that any men would be such fools, and so blind to their own advantage, as to delegate unlimited and irresponsible authority to any individual as to say, 'Cut off our heads, spoil our property, ruin the country; we give all into your hands; we throw ourselves upon your generous mercy; we reserve no license of revocation to ourselves'.

The Crown, the Ministers, and the Parliament, are all trustees for the nation; they have peculiar privileges delegated for the sake of the prosperity of the country, not for their own sakes.

Thirdly. Any power exerted to the disadvantage and detriment of the country at large is illegal, and without any authority. The people do not confer strength for their own injury, but for their own good; they do not furnish weapons for their own destruction, but implements for their preservation; they limit the power of their rulers to the wants of the ruled; they bestow it for the general prosperity, and, therefore, there is no power delegated for injury and injustice. Many more important corollaries might be deduced, but these are sufficient for our present subject. Well, then, what government approaches most nearly to these necessary qualities of a free constitution? Under the now existing forms we have no hesitation in giving the palm to a republic; but if our constitution, in its mixed monarchical form, were to be rendered sufficiently democratic; if every member of the State had a voice in its public affairs; if Universal Suffrage prevailed, and the whole people were, in truth, recognised as the legitimate source of all power, then we believe the requisite advantages would follow, that their delegates would be responsible to the nation at large, and exert their powers, thus bestowed, for the good of the whole community.

Let the whole country; let every class then be assured of this, that in the present age and the present character and opinion of the nation, the only means of avoiding a republic is by infusing the true spirit of rational democracy into our constitution, and giving to every Briton his rights as a human being, and his privileges as a freeman.

Document 10. 6

John Stuart Mill, *Considerations on Representative Government*

John Stuart Mill (1806–73) (see document 5.7) published his *Considerations on Representative Government* in 1861. It was in many respects the keystone of his career as a political theorist. It set the parameters for the discussion of the prospects and perils of democracy for another twenty years. To prevent the majority swamping the minority, he offered a system of proportional representation, and of plural voting which entitled the educated to additional votes. He tried to balance two things – widespread participation and progressive government on the one hand, and the influence of the intellectual and moral élite on the other. The following extract is taken from Chapter VII – 'Of True and False Democracy, Representation of All and Representation of the Majority Only'.

There is no difficulty in showing that the ideally best form of government is that in which the sovereignty, or supreme controlling power in the last resort, is vested in the entire aggregate of the community; every citizen not only having a voice in the exercise of that ultimate sovereignty, but being, at least occasionally, called on to take an actual part in the government, by the personal discharge of some public function, local or general [...].

The ideally best form of government, it is scarcely necessary to say, does not mean one which is practicable or eligible in all states of civilization, but the one which, in the circumstances in which it is practicable and eligible, is attended with the greatest amount of beneficial consequences, immediate and prospective. A completely popular government is the only polity which can make out any claim to this character. It is pre-eminent in both the departments between which the excellence of a political constitution is divided. It is both more favourable to present good government, and promotes a better and higher form of national character, than any other polity whatsoever.

Its superiority in reference to present well-being rests upon two principles, of as universal truth and applicability as any general propositions which can be laid down respecting human affairs. The first is, that the rights and interests of every or any person are only secure from being disregarded, when the person interested is himself able, and habitually disposed, to stand up for them. The second is, that the general prosperity attains a greater height, and is more widely diffused, in proportion to the amount and variety of the personal energies enlisted in promoting it.

Putting these two propositions into a shape more special to their present application; human beings are only secure from evil at the hands of others, in proportion as they have the power of being; and are, self-protecting; and they only achieve a high degree of success in their struggle with Nature, in proportion as they are self-dependent, relying on what they themselves can do, either separately or in concert, rather than on what others do for them.

The former proposition - that each is the only safe guardian of his own rights and interests – is one of those elementary maxims of prudence, which every person, capable of conducting his own affairs, implicitly acts upon, wherever he himself is interested. Many, indeed, have a great dislike to it as a political doctrine, and are fond of holding it up to obloquy, as a doctrine of universal selfishness. To which we may answer, that whenever it ceases to be true that mankind, as a rule, prefer themselves to others, and those nearest to them to those more remote, from that moment Communism is not only practicable, but the only defensible form of society; and will, when that time arrives, be assuredly carried into effect. For my own part, not believing in universal selfishness, I have no difficulty in admitting that Communism would even now be practicable among the élite of mankind, and may become so among the rest. But as this opinion is anything but popular with those defenders of existing institutions who find fault with the doctrine of the general predominance of self-interest, I am inclined to think they do in reality believe, that most men consider themselves before other people. It is not, however, necessary to affirm even thus much, in order to support the claim of all to participate in the sovereign power. We need not suppose that when power resides in an exclusive class, that class will knowingly and deliberately sacrifice the other classes to themselves; it suffices that, in the absence of its natural defenders, the interest of the excluded is always in danger of being overlooked; and, when looked at, is seen with very different eyes from those of the persons whom it directly concerns. In this country, for example, what are called the working classes may be considered as excluded from all direct participation in the government. I do not believe that the classes who do participate in it, have in general any intention of sacrificing the working classes, and err rather by too lavish and indiscriminating beneficence; nor do I believe that any rulers in history have been actuated by a more sincere desire to do their duty towards the poorer portion of the countrymen. Yet does Parliament, or almost any of the members composing it, ever for an instant look at any question with the eyes of a working man? When a subject arises in which the labourers as such have an interest, is it regarded from any point of view but that of the employers of labour? I do not say that the working men's view of these questions is in general nearer to the truth than the other; but it is sometimes quite as near; and in any case it ought to be respectfully listened to, instead of being, as it is, not merely turned away from, but ignored. On the question of strikes, for instance, it is doubtful if there is so much as one among the leading members of either House, who is not firmly convinced that the reason of the matter is unqualifiedly on the side of the masters, and that the men's view of it is simply absurd. Those who have studied the question, know well how far this is from being the case; and in how different, and how infinitely less superficial a manner the point would have to be argued, if the classes who strike were able to make themselves heard in Parliament.

It is an inherent condition of human affairs, that no intention, however sincere, of protecting the interests of others, can make it safe or salutary to tie up their own hands. Still more obviously true is it, that by their own hands only can any positive and durable improvement of their circumstances in life be worked out. Throughout the joint influence of these two principles, all free communities have both been more exempt from social injustice and crime, and have attained more brilliant prosperity, than any others, or than they themselves after they lost their freedom.

Document 10.7

Mrs Hugo Read, *A Plea for Women*

The following extract is taken from a pamphlet published in 1843 in Edinburgh. *A Plea for Women* was subtitled a *Vindication of the Importance and the Extent of her natural Sphere of Action.*

The ground on which equality is claimed for all men is of equal force for all women … It is the possession of the noble faculties of reason and conscience which elevates man above the brutes, and invests him with this right of exercising supreme authority over himself … He feels that he has a right to have all those duties exercised by others towards him, which his conscience tells him he ought to exercise towards others; hence the natural and equal rights of men … without distinction of sex …

The exercise of those rights would be useful in two ways: it would tend to enable and elevate the mind; and it would secure the temporal interest of those who exercise it. No doubt can be entertained of the debasing nature of slavery … Likewise, it is found that when one class legislates for any other class, it attends first to the bearing of that legislation on its own class interests … The many laws which have been obliged to be passed to protect women from their nearest male relatives are a sufficient answer [to the claim that women are virtually represented in Parliament] … Those laws, then, are in themselves a convincing proof, first, that woman requires representation, and second, that she is not represented …

We do not mean to assert that man and woman are strictly the same in their nature, or the character of their minds; but simply, that in the grand characteristics of their nature they are the same, and that where they differ, it is in the minor features; that they resemble far more than they differ from each other … And by equality, we mean equal civil and legal rights; such an equality as will prevent the rich or wise man from having more power over his fellow-creatures than his riches and wisdom naturally gives him. And from this rule we can see no reason whatever for excluding the female half of the race. The weaker they are, the greater is their need of equal rights, that they may not fall under the tyranny of the stronger portion of their race.

Document 10.8

Barbara Bodichon on the Benefit from the Vote

Barbara Bodichon (1827–91) was a strong Victorian campaigner for women's rights, including enfranchisement. She was one of the founders of the Women's Suffrage Committee of 1866. The following extract is taken from *Reasons for and Against the Enfranchisement of Women*, published in the same year.

THE VOTE FOR WOMEN: A Natural Right

Among all the reasons for giving women votes, the one which appears to me the strongest, is that of the influence it might be expected to have in increasing public spirit … And I know no better means, at this present time, of counteracting the tendency to prefer narrow private ends to the public good, than this of giving to all women, duly qualified, a direct and conscious participation in political affairs. Give some women votes, and it will tend to make all women think seriously of the concerns of the nation at large, and their interest having once been fairly roused, they will take pains, by reading and by consultation with persons better informed than themselves, to form sound opinions. As it is, women of the middle class occupy themselves but little with anything beyond their own family circle. They do not consider it any concern of theirs, if poor men and women are ill-nursed in workhouse infirmaries, and poor children ill-taught in work house schools. If the roads are bad, the drains neglected, the water poisoned, they think it is all very wrong, but it does not occur to them that it is their duty to get it put right, they think it is men's business, not theirs, to look after such things. It is this belief – so narrowing and deadening in its influence – that the exercise of the franchise would tend to dissipate. The mere fact of being called upon to enforce an opinion by a vote, would have an immediate effect in awakening a healthy sense of responsibility. There is no reason why these women should not take an active interest in all the social questions – education, public health, prison discipline, the poor laws, and the rest – which occupy Parliament, and by bringing women into hearty co-operation with men, we gain the benefit not only of their work, but of their intelligent sympathy. Public spirit is like fire: a feeble spark of it may be fanned into a flame, or it may very easily be put out. And the result of teaching women that they have nothing to do with politics, is that their influence goes towards extinguishing the unselfish interest – never too strong – which men are disposed to take in public affairs.

Document 10.9

Sir James Fitzjames Stephen, *Liberty, Equality, Fraternity*

The following extract is taken from *Liberty, Equality, Fraternity*, published in 1873. Stephen (1829–94) was also one of the leading Conservative thinkers of

the Victorian period. He denounced democracy as a 'substitute religion'; and here
questions the argument that universal suffrage will lead to equality.

I now proceed to the most important of the remaining senses of the word 'equality' —
the equal distribution of political power. This is perhaps the most definite sense which can
be attached to the vague general word 'equality'. It is undoubtedly true that for several
generations a process has been going on all over our own part of the world which may
be described, not inaccurately, as the subdivision of political power. The accepted theory
of government appears to be that everybody should have a vote, that the Legislature
should be elected by these votes, and that it should conduct all the public business of the
country through a committee which succeeds for the time in obtaining its confidence.
This theory, beyond all question, has gone forth, and is going forth conquering and to
conquer. The fact of its triumph is as clear as the sun at noonday, and the probability that
its triumphs will continue for a longer time than we need care to think about it as strong
as any such probability can well be. The question is, what will a reasonable man think of
it? I think he will criticize it like any other existing fact, and with as little partiality on either
side as possible; but I am altogether at a loss to understand how it can rouse enthusiastic
admiration in any one whatever. It certainly has done so for some reason or other. Nearly
every newspaper, and a very large proportion of modern books of political speculation,
regard the progress of democracy, the approaching advent of universal suffrage, with
something approaching to religious enthusiasm. To this I for one object.

In the first place, it will be well to point out a distinction which, though perfectly clear
and of the utmost importance, is continually overlooked. Legislate how you will, establish
universal suffrage, if you think proper, as a law which can never be broken. You are still as
far as ever from equality. Political power has changed its shape but not its nature. The
result of cutting it up into little bits is simply that the man who can sweep the greatest
number of them into one heap will govern the rest. The strongest man in some form or
other will always rule. If the government is a military one, the qualities which make a man
a great soldier will make him a ruler. If the government is a monarchy, the qualities which
kings value in counsellors, in generals, in administrators, will give power. In a pure
democracy the ruling men will be the wirepullers and their friends; but they will no more
be on an equality with the voters than soldiers or Ministers of State are on an equality
with the subjects of a monarchy. Changes in the form of a government alter the
conditions of superiority much more than its nature. In some ages a powerful character,
in others cunning, in others powers of despatching business, in others eloquence, in
others a good hold upon current commonplaces and facility in applying them to practical
purposes will enable a man to climb on to his neighbours' shoulders and direct them this
way or that; but in all ages and under all circumstances the rank and file are directed by
leaders of one kind or another who get the command of their collective force. The
leading men in a trade union are as much the superiors and rulers of the members of
the body at large, and the general body of the members are as much the superiors and

rulers of each individual member, as the master of a family or the head of a factory is the ruler and superior of his servants or work-people.

Document 10.10

Joseph Schumpeter on the Classical Doctrine of Democracy

Joseph Schumpeter (1883–1950) was an Austrian economist and social scientist who subsequently became Professor of Economics at Harvard. The following extract is from *Capitalism, Socialism and Democracy* (1942). He distinguished the 'classical doctrine' described below, in which democracy is viewed as dependent upon a shared notion of the common good, from a revised theory in which the competition for votes is analogous to the interest-based competition of economic markets.

The Common Good and the Will of the People

The eighteenth-century philosophy of democracy may be couched in the following definition: the democratic method is that institutional arrangement for arriving at political decisions which realizes the common good by making the people itself decide issues through the election of individuals who are to assemble in order to carry out its will. Let us develop the implications of this.

It is held, then, that there exists a Common Good, the obvious beacon light of policy, which is always simple to define and which every normal person can be made to see by means of rational argument. There is hence no excuse for not seeing it and in fact no explanation for the presence of people who do not see it except ignorance – which can be removed – stupidity and anti-social interest. Moreover, this common good implies definite answers to all questions so that every social fact and every measure taken or to be taken can unequivocally be classed as 'good' or 'bad'. All people having therefore to agree, in principle at least, there is also a Common Will of the people (will of all reasonable individuals) that is exactly coterminous with the common good or interest or welfare or happiness. The only thing, barring stupidity and sinister interests, that can possibly bring in disagreement and account for the presence of an opposition is a difference of opinion as to the speed with which the goal, itself common to nearly all, is to be approached. Thus every member of the community, conscious of that goal, knowing his or her mind, discerning what is good and what is bad, takes part, actively and responsibly, in furthering the former and fighting the latter and all the members taken together control their public affairs.

It is true that the management of some of these affairs requires special aptitudes and techniques and will therefore have to be entrusted to specialists who have them. This does not affect the principle, however, because these specialists simply act in order to carry out the will of the people exactly as a doctor acts in order to carry out the will of the patient to get well. It is also true that in a community of any size, especially if it displays the phenomenon of division of labor, it would be highly inconvenient for every individual citizen to have to get into contact with all the other citizens on every issue in order to do his part in ruling or governing. It will be more convenient to reserve only the most important decisions for the individual citizens to pronounce upon – say by referendum – and to deal with the rest through a committee appointed by them – an assembly or parliament whose members will be elected by popular vote. This committee or body of delegates, as we have seen, will not represent the people in a legal sense but it will do so in a less technical one – it will voice, reflect or represent the will of the electorate. Again as a matter of convenience, this committee being large, may resolve itself into smaller ones for the various departments of public affairs. Finally, among these smaller committees there will be a general-purpose committee, mainly for dealing with current administration, called cabinet or government, possibly with a general secretary or scapegoat at its head, a so-called prime minister.

As soon as we accept all the assumptions that are being made by this theory of the polity – or implied by it – democracy indeed acquires a perfectly unambiguous meaning and there is no problem in connection with it except how to bring it about. Moreover we need only forget a few logical qualms in order to be able to add that in this case the democratic arrangement would not only be the best of all conceivable ones, but that few people would care to consider any other. It is no less obvious however that these assumptions are so many statements of fact every one of which would have to be proved if we are to arrive at that conclusion. And it is much easier to disprove them.

There is, first, no such thing as a uniquely determined common good that all people could agree on or be made to agree on by the force of rational argument. This is due not primarily to the fact that some people may want things other than the common good but to the much more fundamental fact that to different individuals and groups the common good is bound to mean different things. This fact, hidden from the utilitarian by the narrowness of his outlook on the world of human valuations, will introduce rifts on questions of principle which cannot be reconciled by rational argument because ultimate values – our conceptions of what life and what society should be – are beyond the range of mere logic. They may be bridged by compromise in some cases but not in others. Americans who say, 'We want this country to arm to its teeth and then to fight for what we conceive to be right all over the globe' and Americans who say, 'We want this country to work out its own problems which is the only way it can serve humanity' are facing irreducible differences of ultimate values which compromise could only maim and degrade.

Secondly, even if a sufficiently definite common good – such as for instance the utilitarian's maximum of economic satisfaction – proved acceptable to all, this would not imply equally definite answers to individual issues. Opinions on these might differ to an extent important enough to produce most of the effects of 'fundamental' dissension about ends themselves. The problems centering in the evaluation of present versus future satisfactions, even the case of socialism versus capitalism, would be left still open, for instance, after the conversion of every individual citizen to utilitarianism. 'Health' might be desired by all, yet people would still disagree on vaccination and vasectomy. And so on.

The utilitarian fathers of democratic doctrine failed to see the full importance of this simply because none of them seriously considered any substantial change in the economic framework and the habits of bourgeois society. They saw little beyond the world of an eighteenth-century ironmonger. But, third, as a consequence of both preceding propositions, the particular concept of the will of the people or the 'volonté generale' that the utilitarians made their own vanishes into thin air. For that concept presupposes the existence of a uniquely determined common good discernible to all. Unlike the romanticists the utilitarians had no notion of that semi-mystic entity endowed with a will of its own – that 'soul of the people' which the historical school of jurisprudence made so much of. They frankly derived their will of the people from the wills of individuals. And unless there is a center, the common good, toward which, in the long run at least, all individual wills gravitate, we shall not get that particular type of 'natural' 'volonté generale'. The utilitarian center of gravity, on the one hand, unifies individual wills, tends to weld them by means of rational discussion into the will of the people and, on the other hand, confers upon the latter the exclusive ethical dignity claimed by the classic democratic creed. This creed does not consist simply in worshiping the will of the people as such but rests on certain assumptions about the 'natural' object of that will which object is sanctioned by utilitarian reason. Both the existence and the dignity of this kind of 'volonté generale' are gone as soon as the idea of the common good fails us. And both the pillars of the classical doctrine inevitably crumble into dust.

Document 10.11

G.D.H. Cole on Democracy and Representation

G.D.H. Cole (1889–1959), a Guild Socialist and leading Left-wing intellectual advocated a doctrine of industrial and Socialist self-government as an alternative to Capitalism on the one hand and State Socialism on the other. He was Reader in Economics at Oxford and later Professor of Social and Political Theory. His persistent advocacy of a decentralized, pluralist Socialism seemed eccentric in his own lifetime, but his ideas have subsequently aroused renewed interest. The following is taken from the *Social Theory* (1920).

There is in our own day an almost general prejudice in favour of democracy. Almost everybody is a 'democrat', and the name of democracy is invoked in support of the most diverse social systems and theories. This general acceptance of the name of democracy, even by persons who are obviously not in any real sense 'democrats', is perhaps largely to be explained by the fact that the idea of democracy has become almost inextricably tangled up with the idea of representative government, or rather with a particular theory of representative government based on a totally false theory of representation.

This false theory is that one man can 'represent' another or a number of others, and that his will can be treated as the democratic expression of their wills. Stated in this form, the theory admits of only one answer. No man can represent another man, and no man's will can be treated as a substitute for, or representative of, the wills of others.

This may look, at first sight, like a complete denial of every form of representative government, and an affirmation of the futility of all elections. It is, however, nothing of the sort; it is not an attack upon, or an attempt to destroy the theoretic basis of, representative government, but an attempt to restate the theory of representation in a truer form. In order that it may be fully understood, we must bring it into relation to the doctrine of function. We have seen that, just as every action of an individual aims at some specific object, so men form and enter associations in pursuit of specific objects which can be best pursued in common by or through an organized group. Every association, then, has a specific object or objects, and it is in pursuit of some or all of these objects that men consent to be members of the association.

Every association which sets before itself any object that is of more than the most rudimentary simplicity finds itself compelled to assign tasks and duties, and with these powers and a share of authority, to some of its members in order that the common object may be effectively pursued. It elects, perhaps, a secretary, a president, a treasurer, and an executive committee, and empowers these persons to act on behalf of the association in certain definite ways and within certain limits. In the smaller and more localized associations, much of the control of the proceedings of the association may remain in the hands of the general body of the members; but as soon as it becomes too large or too dispersed for a general meeting to transact business, or if the members are too preoccupied with other affairs to make it their constant concern, the detailed regulation of its proceedings passes largely into the hands of a comparatively small number of its members, officers, committee men, delegates, or representatives. In the largest and most complex form of association, such as the state, the ordinary member is reduced to a mere voter, and all the direction of actual affairs is done by representatives – or misrepresentatives.

At the best, representative government gives rise to many inconveniences, to what Walt Whitman described as 'the neverending audacity of elected persons', and Rousseau as 'the tendency of all government to deteriorate'. With these inconveniences we shall have to deal at a later stage; but here we are concerned only to make clear the nature of the representative relation as it exists in such associations as we have spoken of.

In the majority of associations, the nature of the relation is clear enough. The elected person – official, committee man, or delegate – makes no pretension of substituting his personality for those of his constituents, or of representing them except in relation to a quite narrow and clearly defined purpose or group of purposes which the association exists to fulfil. There is, then, in these cases, no question of one man taking the place of many; for what the representative professes to represent is not the whole will and personalities of his constituents, but merely so much of them as they have put into the association, and as is concerned with the purposes which the association exists to fulfil.

This is the character of all true representation. It is impossible to represent human beings as selves or centres of consciousness; it is quite possible to represent, though with an inevitable element of distortion which must always be recognized, so much of human beings as they themselves put into associated effort for a specific purpose.

True representation, therefore, like true association, is always specific and functional, and never general and inclusive. What is represented is never man, the individual, but always certain purposes common to groups of individuals. That theory of representative government which is based upon the idea that individuals can be represented as wholes is a false theory, and destructive of personal rights and social well-being.

The fact that a man cannot be represented as a man seems so obvious that it is difficult to understand how many theories of government and democracy have come to be built upon the idea that he can. Each man is a centre of consciousness and reason, a will possessed of the power of self-determination, an ultimate reality. How can one such will be made to stand in place of many? How can one man, being himself, be at the same time a number of other people? It would be a miracle if he could; but it is a risky experiment to base our social system upon a hypothetical miracle.

Document 10.12

Harold Laski, *Democracy in Crisis*

The following extract from *Democracy in Crisis* (1933) reflects the mood of political and economic anxiety which accompanied the slump and the rise of Fascism in Europe. Harold Laski (1893–1950), who abandoned Liberal collectivism for neo-Marxism, was Professor of Political Science at the London School of Economics and subsequently Chairman of the Labour Party.

Political democracy developed in response to the demand for the abrogation of privilege. In modern European history its cause was the liberation of a commercial middle class from domination by a landholding aristocracy. To free itself, that middle class formulated a body of liberal generalisations which culminated in the widespread grant of universal suffrage. Their underlying philosophy was the well-known Benthamite argument, that since each man in a political democracy was to count for one, and not more than one, and since each was, on the whole, the best judge of his own interest, universal suffrage would permit the translation of the majority will into the substance of legislation. Sinister interest, it was urged, belonged only to a few; privilege could not resist the onset of numbers. Representative democracy, on the basis of equal and universal suffrage, would mean the creation of a society in which the equal interest of men in the results of the social process would be swiftly recognised. The rule of democracy was to be the rule of reason. The party which best grasped the purpose of the electorate would win a majority in the legislature, and it would use the normal, constitutional forms to give effect to that purpose.

The flaw in the argument was an obvious one. It assumed the absolute validity of the form of the political state regardless of the economic character of the society it was supposed to represent. It did not see that each economic regime gives birth to a political order which represents the interests of those who dominate the regime, who possess in it the essential instruments of economic power. In a feudal society, broadly speaking, sovereignty belonged to the owners of land; custom was registered, legislation was made, in their interest. In a capitalist society, quite similarly, sovereignty belonged to the owners of capital; and custom was registered, legislation made, in their interest also. The simplest test of this truth in any society is the analysis of the working of the Courts. And if their decisions be scrutinised, it will always be found that, in the last analysis, they are inexplicable except upon the basis of their effort to defend the sovereignty of the owners of economic power. The framework of a legal system is always geared to that end. Liberty means liberty within the law, and the purpose of the law is the protection of some given status quo. Its substance is always the result of a struggle to widen an existing basis of privilege. Those who share in this may on occasion be tempted to the surrender of an occasional outwork; they have always defended to the last the possession of the inner citadel.

It is in the perspective of these general truths that the history of parliamentary democracy must be set. It has been successful in the difficult task of enabling the outworks of the capitalist system to be surrendered to its opponents; it has at no point solved the central problem of the inner citadel's surrender. It has discovered ways and means of graceful compromise, wherever compromise has been possible; it has not proved that it forms the natural road to a new equilibrium when the differences between men are ultimate. For we have to acknowledge the grim fact that, at the parting of the ways, men in the possession of actual sovereignty choose to fight rather than to abdicate. In Great Britain, no doubt, the genius for compromise has been peculiarly outstanding, though that is most largely due to the fact that the ultimate issues have never been raised. In other European countries this has not been the case, and a break with the old legal order has invariably become imperative in order to find the necessary conditions of a new equilibrium. The power to compromise while compromise is still possible is perhaps the rarest quality in history.

And if the character of the struggle involved in the historic process be analysed, its root will be found always to lie in the unending problem of equality. Those who are denied access to privilege seek to destroy privilege. It may present itself under the most various forms – religious, social, economic, political. It may be accepted for a period as part of an order of nature; the abolition of the prerogatives of the House of Lords was hardly thinkable to the eighteenth century. But, sooner or later, those excluded from privilege resent their exclusion, and it is then only a matter of time before they attack it. And unless they can be convinced that the maintenance of the privilege is directly associated with their own good, the choice offered to the society is always one between concession and violence.

Document 10.13

Friedrich von Hayek on the Justification of Democracy

Friedrich August von Hayek (1899–1992), previously to leaving Austria in 1930, was Director of the Austrian Institute for Economic Research. In *The Constitution of Liberty* (1960), from which the extract below is taken, he reformulated the traditional conception of economic liberalism to exclude various measures of state intervention. He argued that over the long run such interventions were incompatible with the rule of law.

If democracy is a means rather than an end, its limits must be determined in the light of the purpose we want it to serve. There are three chief arguments by which democracy can be justified, each of which may be regarded as conclusive. The first is that, whenever it is necessary that one of several conflicting opinions should prevail and when one would have to be made to prevail by force if need be, it is less wasteful to determine which has the stronger support by counting numbers than by fighting. Democracy is the only method of peaceful change that man has yet discovered.

The second argument, which historically has been the most important and which is still very important, though we can no longer be sure that it is always valid, is that democracy is an important safeguard of individual liberty. It was once said by a seventeenth-century writer that 'the good of democracy is liberty, and the courage and industry which liberty begets'. This view recognizes, of course, that democracy is not yet liberty; it contends only that it is more likely than other forms of government to produce liberty. This view may be well founded so far as the prevention of coercion of individuals by other individuals is concerned: it can scarcely be to the advantage of a majority that some individuals should have the power arbitrarily to coerce others. But the protection of the individual against the collective action of the majority itself is another matter. Even here it can be argued that, since coercive power must in fact always be exercised by a few, it is less likely to be abused if the power entrusted to the few can always be revoked by those who have to submit to it. But if the prospects of individual liberty are better in a democracy than under other forms of government, this does not mean that they are certain. The prospects of liberty depend on whether or not the majority makes it its deliberate object. It would have little chance of surviving if we relied on the mere existence of democracy to preserve it.

The third argument rests on the effect which the existence of democratic institutions will have on the general level of understanding of public affairs. This seems to me the most powerful. It may well be true, as has been often maintained, that, in any given state of affairs, government by some educated élite would be a more efficient and perhaps even a more just government than one chosen by majority vote. The crucial point, however, is that, in comparing the democratic form of government with others, we cannot take the understanding of the issues by the people at any time as a datum. It is the burden of the argument of Tocqueville's great work, 'Democracy in America', that democracy is the only effective method of educating the majority. This is as true today as it was in his time. Democracy is, above all, a process of forming opinion. Its chief advantage lies not in its method of selecting those who govern but in the fact that, because a great part of the population takes an active part in the formation of opinion, a correspondingly wide range of persons is available from which to select. We may admit that democracy does not put power in the hands of the wisest and best informed and that at any given moment the decision of a government by an élite might be more beneficial to the whole; but this need not prevent us from still giving democracy the preference. It is in its dynamic, rather than in its static, aspects that the value of democracy proves itself. As is true of liberty, the benefits of democracy will show themselves only in the long run, while its more immediate achievements may well be inferior to those of other forms of government.

Document 10.14

Lord Hailsham on Elective Dictatorship

Lord Hailsham (Quintin Hogg) (born 1907), Conservative MP and Lord Chancellor, is one of the most persuasive Conservative polemicists of the post-Second World War period. His publications include *The Left was Never Right* (1945) and *The Case for Conservatism* (1947). More recently, his constitutional thought has attracted notice for his support for a new Bill of Rights. The following extract is taken from his Dimbleby Lecture of 1976.

We are sometimes unaware that our constitution is unique. There is nothing quite like it, even among nations to whom we have given independence ... The point is not that all other nations have what is called, in a literal sense, a 'written constitution'. After all, much of our own constitution is in writing, and much more could be reduced to writing if we wanted, without making any appreciable change. No, the point is that the powers of our own Parliament are absolute and unlimited. And in this, we are almost alone. All other free nations impose limitations on their representative assemblies. We impose none on ours. Parliament can take away a man's liberty or his wife without a trial ... It can prolong its own life, and in our own time, has done so twice, quite properly, during two world wars.

No doubt, in recent times, Parliament has not abused these particular powers. Nonetheless, the point I am making is that, as a result of the changes in its operation and structure, the absence of any legal limitation on the powers of Parliament has become quite unacceptable. And the questions which I desire to leave for your consideration are, first, whether the time has not come to end or modify this legal theory, and, secondly, whether and how it is possible to do so.

Of course, this doctrine of absolute sovereignty of Parliament has been fully recognised for very many years, judges may pass judgment on the acts of ministers ... To this extent, the rule of law applies and prevails here as in other free countries. But once the courts are confronted with an Act of Parliament, all they can do is to ascertain its meaning, if they can, and then apply it as justly and mercifully as the language of the law permits. So, of the two pillars of our constitution, the rule of law and the sovereignty of Parliament, it is the sovereignty of Parliament which is paramount in every case.

The limitations on it are only political and moral. They are found in the consciences of members, in the necessity for periodical elections, and in the so-called checks and balances inherent in the composition, structure and practice of Parliament itself.

Only a revolution, bloody or peacefully contrived, can put an end to the situation which I have just described. We live under an elective dictatorship, absolute in theory, if Hitherto thought tolerable in practice. How far it is still tolerable is the question I want to raise for discussion ...

To begin with, there has been a continuous enlargement of the scale and range of government itself. Then there has been a change in the relative influence of the different elements in government, so as to place all the effective powers in the hands of one of them; in other words, the checks and balances, which in practice used to prevent abuse, have now disappeared. So both sets of changes have operated in the same direction – to increase the extent to which elective dictatorship is a fact, and not just a lawyer's theory.

Until comparatively recently, Parliament consisted of two effective chambers. Now, for most practical purposes, it consists of one. Until recently, the powers of government within Parliament were largely controlled either by the opposition or by its own back-benchers. It is now largely in the hands of the government machine, so that the government controls Parliament, and not Parliament the government. Until recently, debate and argument dominated the parliamentary scene. Now, it is the whips and the party caucus.

Let me develop one or two of these points. [First] the scale and range of modern government ... Consider two simple tests: the mass of annual legislation, and the size of the annual Budget. Before the First World War, the then Liberal government was content to pass a single slim volume of legislation in a year ... In 1911, there were not more than about 450 pages, and that was a heavy year. For 1975 ... there were over 13,000 pages of legislation ...

It must be remembered, moreover, that these changes are cumulative. Even allowing for repeals and amendments, those 13,000 pages of 1975 represent a huge addition to the corpus of British law, and that had already reached an all-time high by 1974. So, year by year, there are substantially more, and more complicated, laws to obey.

Another example. When Gladstone was Prime Minister, he was able to spend about five months of the year at his country home in North Wales ... Today, if a prime minister takes time off to spend a weekend on the water on his yacht, there is an immediate outcry that he is only working part-time, as if the quality of his statesmanship were a direct result of the quantity of his output ...

Then look at the Budget. I suppose that, at the turn of the century, it could be expected never to exceed £100 million in any one year. By the end of the Second World War, we were already spending 25 times as much as before the First. But now, we are spending something like £50,000 millions in the annual Budget every year, and, of course, one in every four is borrowed and not being paid back. With local government expenditure, two-thirds of our annual income is spent by public authority ...

Changes on this scale, even taking full account of the fall in the value of money, really represent alterations in the character of our institutions, and not simply differences of degree. At the same time, the checks and balances have largely disappeared. Power has centralised itself more and more in the Commons, more and more on the government side of the House, more and more on the front benches, while the time allotted for debate of individual measures has become progressively less and less. As between the two Houses, the Commons, for many years, have been quite properly the dominant partner. They are elected; so they are entitled to control the finance and give the political colour to the government of the day. But the process has now developed to the point at which the sovereignty of Parliament has virtually become the sovereignty of the House of Commons.

I am not, of course, in the least suggesting that the House of Lords is useless, or that its influence in modifying the details of legislation is without value, or that the effect of its debates in moulding opinion is negligible. But I do say that it is not an effective balancing factor, and cannot, in practice, control the advancing powers of the executive. Its influence on government is far weaker than that of the senates in other countries, like America ...

But how far are the Commons really masters in their own House? Not so long ago, influence was fairly evenly balanced between government and opposition, and between front and back benches. Today, the centre of gravity has moved decisively towards the government side of the House, and on that side, to the members of the government itself. The opposition is gradually being reduced to impotence, and the government majority, where power resides, is itself becoming a tool in the hands of the cabinet. Back-benchers, where they show promise, are soon absorbed into the administration, and so lose their powers of independent action ... In present conditions, the whole absolute powers of Parliament, except in a few matters, like divorce or abortion, are wielded by the cabinet alone, and sometimes by a relatively small group within the cabinet.

To begin with, the actual members of the government, with their parliamentary private secretaries, are one of the largest and most disciplined single groups in the House. They number, I suppose, not much short of 130, out of the 300-odd members of the government party, and not one, so long as he retains his position, can exercise an independent judgment.

But far more important than numbers is the disproportionate influence of ministers in debate, as a result of their possession of the civil service brief. The increasing complexity of public affairs makes meticulous research and specialisation almost indispensable for speaking in Parliament. The decreasing leisure and increasing economic pressures upon private members, few of whom live upon their parliamentary salaries, make it more and more difficult to bring a minister to book. Even when he is wrong, he can usually make it look sufficiently as if he were right to get his own supporters into the lobby when the bell rings ...

So the sovereignty of Parliament has increasingly become, in practice, the sovereignty of the Commons and the sovereignty of the Commons has increasingly become the sovereignty of the government, which, in addition to its influence in Parliament, controls the party whips, the party machine, and the civil service. This means that what has always been an elective dictatorship in theory, but one in which the component parts operated, in practice, to control one another, has become a machine in which one of those parts has come to exercise a predominant influence over the rest.

QUESTIONS FOR DISCUSSION

1. Can one say that a political system is partially democratic if the right to participate is confined to one section of the population?
2. Do you agree that only a small minority of individuals can be 'rulers' in modern highly populated countries?
3. Should liberty or democracy be given precedence where they clash?
4. Has the idea of representation really solved the problem of size for democracies?
5. Do you agree with Schumpeter's account of democracy?

NOTES

1 Alexander Hamilton, James Madison, John Jay, *The Federalist Papers* (New York, Mentor, 1961), p. 81.
2 Robert A. Dahl, *Democracy and its Critics* (New Haven, Yale University Press, 1989),p. 29.

FURTHER READING

For a very informative series of chapters on the history of democracy see J. Dunn (ed.), *Democracy: The Unfinished Journey 503 BC – 1993 AD* (Oxford, Oxford University Press, 1992). For a broader overview of the history of democracy see R. Dahl, *Democracy and its Critics*, (New Haven, Yale University Press, 1989). For examples of early positive uses of the terms democracy and democrat see Chapter 1 of R.R. Palmer, *The Age of Democratic Revolution. The Challenge* (Princeton NJ, Princeton University Press, 1959). J.L. Talmon, *The Origins of Totalitarian Democracy* (London, Secker and Warburg, 1955) is a criticism of the collectivist impulse in democratic thought. For nineteenth-century views see Jon Roper, *Democracy and Its Critics. Anglo-American Democratic Thought in the Nineteenth Century* (London, Unwin Hyman, 1989). An excellent survey of the difficulties of democracy in the twentieth century is provided by K.D. Bracher, *The Age of Ideologies* (London, Methuen, 1985). An influential reformulation of the concept of democracy is provided by Joseph A. Schumpeter, *Capitalism, Socialism and Democracy* (London, Allen & Unwin, 1943). There is a large number of useful general accounts and assessments: see Anthony H. Birch, *The Concepts and Theories of Modern Democracy* (London, Routledge. 1993); A. Arblaster, *Democracy*, (Milton Keynes, Open University Press, 1982), D. Held, *Models of Democracy* (Oxford, Polity, 1987); J. Lively, *Democracy and Illusion* (London, Longman, 1973); C.B. Macpherson, *Democratic Theory*, (Oxford, Oxford University Press 1973); G. Sartori, *The Theory of Democracy Revisited*,

(Chatham NJ, Chatham House, 1987). For a useful attempt to classify theories of democracy see C.B. Macpherson, *The Life and Times of Liberal Democracy* (Oxford, Oxford University Press, 1977). On the procedural implications of democracy see in particular V. Bogdanor and D. Butler, *Democracy and Elections: Electoral Systems and their Consequences* (Cambridge, Cambridge University Press, 1983) and M. Harrop and W. Miller, *Elections and Voters: A Comparative Introduction* (Basingstoke, Macmillan, 1987). A brief but helpful approach to assessing the democratic credentials of the United Kingdom is provided by D. Beetham, *The Democratic Audit of the United Kingdom* (London, The Charter 88 Trust, 1993).

11

THE STATE AND THE ECONOMY

INTRODUCTION

The close connection between the political and the economic is evident to us today in several ways. First, it is clear that the prospects of democratically elected governments are determined in large part by the development of the economy under their stewardship. Indeed, even undemocratic regimes, as the recent events in the former Soviet Union and Eastern Europe show, can be undermined by inadequate economic progress. Secondly, the relationship between the state and the economy is itself highly contentious. Both high levels of state intervention and low levels of state intervention have been blamed for economic failure, or, alternatively, been ascribed the credit for economic success. Furthermore, all of the ideas presented earlier, ideas of authority, rights, liberty, justice, and so on, have been applied to describe the relationship between state and economy or to suggest how the relationship ought to be modified. To that extent, the economic is inescapably political.

Yet there is also a tension between the political and the economic. It was apparent in the Greek contrast between the household – the word economic is derived from the Greek *oikonomos*, manager of a household – and the city-state. But our understanding of the distinction between economic and political arose more recently, with the rapid expansion of international trade from the sixteenth century onwards and attempts to understand this process in terms of the new scientific methods.[1] Observers were beginning to see economic processes, the exchange of goods, the movement of capital, the rise and fall of prices, as being ruled by laws similar to those which governed the world of nature. Many were also impressed by the growing wealth of their societies and were advocating limits to the extent of government intervention in the economy in order to ensure increased prosperity. The founder of modern political economy, Adam Smith, reflected this trend when he wrote that, 'The causes of this improvement, in the productive powers of labour, and the order, according to which its produce is naturally distributed among the different ranks and conditions of men in the society, make the subject of the First Book of this Inquiry,[2] Although Smith was a sharp critic of some of the deficiencies of this 'natural' distribution, and even more so of the motives of the 'mercantile classes', the main message of his Inquiry, *The Wealth of Nations*, was that governments ought to interfere as little as possible. In broader terms, Smith was expressing a view of the state and the economy as two separate realms.[3] The separation, according to Karl Marx, had a profound effect on both. Indeed, he insisted that the character of the modern state was defined precisely by this separation from the economic, by the contrast between the public (the political) and the private (the economic). It is this basic contrast which lies behind subsequent disputes about the relationship between state and economy. The contrast is reflected in the modern disciplines of economics and politics, in the predilection of the former to begin with the concept of exchange and of the latter to begin with power or authority. Whether with Marx the separation of state and economy is seen as ultimately misguided and pernicious in its effects, or with Smith as the only sure road to prosperity, it forms the starting point of debate up to the present day.

One problem, which had been the focus of debate long before Smith, is that the ability of the state to perform its other functions, especially that of defending itself against other states, is dependent upon the performance of its economy. The relevance of the economy to the military capacity of the state has increased (see Chapter 12). Alongside its impact upon the population of the state and the physical health of the citizens, the level of industrialization and degree of self-sufficiency all play a role in the influence of the economy upon military capacity. The influence, it has been argued, is not one way. The state, including the military capacity of the state, has played a significant role in economic development. The nineteenth-century German political economist, Friedrich List was one of a number of advocates of state intervention. Although he accepted the desirability of free trade, in the long run he argued that, faced with more advanced competitors, a state should protect its infant industries until they were well-enough developed to be able to withstand the challenge of international competition.

It is an argument which has been repeated with great frequency, especially by the underdeveloped states of the Third World. In putting forward his defence of the legitimate role of the state, List also attacked the basic focus of the new economics, that is, market exchange. It distracted attention, he claimed, from the contribution made by the political and judicial system, the educational and cultural establishment to the well-being of the nation and hence to the strength of the state.

The threat of other states, to either the economic development of one's own state or its capacity to defend itself, is only one source of pressure for intervention. During the nineteenth century opinion became increasingly concerned about the fate of those who did not share in the rising prosperity of the nation. The ill, the unemployed, those too poor to afford adequate housing or education needed the intervention of the state. So too did the nation as a whole if railways, canals, roads, postal systems, telegraph systems and so on, were to be provided. Although the development of the modern welfare state would have to wait until after the Second World War, the arguments for and against it had been raised long before. Despite, by modern contemporary standards, the paucity of provision in the nineteenth century, critics of intervention were already sounding the alarm. The fears they voiced have been re-expressed with little change in recent years.

According to the critics of intervention, the state and its agents wrongly presume to know what individuals need better than those individuals themselves. Secondly, when the state intervenes it often takes upon itself the role of entrepreneur, but the state, it is argued, is a bad businessman. Thirdly, it is claimed that some problems cannot be remedied at all by state intervention or that in attempting to solve one problem the state only creates another. A fourth fear is of the growth of bureaucracy associated with the growth of intervention. Bureaucrats are said to have a vested interest in the expansion of the state and pose a threat to the liberty of citizens. The concern of the critics with liberty typically takes on a broader form. The threat is supposed to come not only from the power of a potentially oppressive bureaucracy. Bureaucracy and regulation also undermine the virtues of self-reliance and initiative which are fostered by free exchange on the market. More forthright critics, like the nineteenth-century liberal, Herbert Spencer, added that the successful deserved to prosper; the unsuccessful deserved to go under. That, he said, was progress. The final defence against the encroachment of the state involves recourse to rights. If we have a right to something, is the state any more entitled to take it away from us for the benefit of someone else than a common thief is entitled to take it from us?

The critics notwithstanding, from the late nineteenth century onwards the state did increasingly intervene in all industrialized societies. The extent of intervention, the method of intervention and the perceived legitimacy of intervention varied from nation to nation. Broadly speaking, intervention was more likely to be seen as legitimate in countries with a strong sense of the state as an organized public power and where a high value was placed upon the state's responsibility for ensuring social solidarity or consensus. States, primarily the Anglo-Saxon states of Britain and the United States of America, with comparatively weak senses of the state and greater suspicion of government, found it correspondingly more difficult to accept the legitimacy of intervention.[4]

Despite these differences, the increase of intervention in the interests of national welfare continued and began to affect concepts of the state. In Germany this led to a revival of the idea of the *Sozialstaat*, in France it led to Leon Duguit's idea of a 'service' state. In both cases the concept is justified not just by the existence of needs, by the relief of suffering, but by the desire to maintain social solidarity or consensus. In advocating the idea of service as definitive of the functions and character of the state Duguit was purposefully challenging the definition of the state in terms of sovereignty. Not the sovereign command but organization should and, he believed, would define the state. In England the socialist, G. D. H. Cole (see also document 10.11), was also led to question the traditional concept of the state, although he was more ready to recognize the persistence of a conflict of interests and the need to maintain the traditional institutions and ideas of statehood alongside the democratically organized power of the producers. He argued, that is, for a division of power between the state and trade unions, each with redefined powers. Both Duguit and Cole were seeking to close the gap between the political and economic, albeit in different ways.

The strength, that is military strength, of the state, economic development, the existence of poverty and deprivation, and social consensus have all been invoked to question, in varying degrees, the separation of state and economy. In all of these cases the basic arguments for and against were formulated before the First World War. The most radical challenge to the separation of state and economy had, however, not been the subject of much discussion. Although Marxists had long inscribed the planned economy upon their banner they had given little detailed thought to what would happen to the economy on the 'day after the revolution'. In fact the debate on a planned economy was to be initiated by senior officials in the wartime German government. The German government, like the governments of its opponents in the First World War, had been forced to regulate the economy to an unprecedented extent, in the interest of prosecuting the war. Drawing on this experience, these German officials formulated a concept of a *Planwirtschaft* for the postwar period. But this was to be a capitalist planned economy. As the victorious Marxists in the new Soviet Union made clear, a Communist planned economy would have to involve more than just the organization of production. Capitalists too could, hypothetically, suppress competition and organize production. The Communist planned economy would also have to end the exploitation of one class by another.

The Soviet Union naturally formed a prime point of reference in much of the debate about planned economies, their relative efficiency or inefficiency, the extent of inequality and the impact upon political and civil liberty. But this has not been the sole point of reference. While the Marxists had substituted planning for the market in the interests of social justice, others sought to introduce planning as an antidote to market failure, in the interests of preserving the market and its associated benefits. The interwar period was rich in such schemes but the one which was to gain intellectual ascendency, if only after the Second World War, was put forward by the British economist, John Maynard Keynes. For both

Keynes and William Beveridge, who was the main intellectual force behind the postwar British welfare state, the task was both to justify intervention and to set limits to it. For Keynes and Beveridge the target was the scourge of unemployment. For much of the postwar period the Keynesian compromise of limited planning prevailed, even in countries with historic antipathies to intervention like the United States of America. But not all accepted that the compromise was possible. Planning, insisted Friedrich von Hayek, cannot be had piecemeal, at least not without destroying the benefits of competition. Hayek's views have experienced a revival as, over the last two decades, the Keynesian consensus has fragmented. Moreover, the Soviet model of a planned economy has now been discredited. The question, which Hayek answered in the negative, remains: is it possible, or desirable, to find a middle way between competition and central direction?

One of Hayek's objections to the search for a middle way was that it would facilitate industrial monopolies. The suspicion that industrialists would, given the chance, undermine competition and put their own interests before the interest of the nation is an old and persistent fear. None other than Adam Smith warned that any suggestion made by the 'mercantile classes',

> ought always to be listened to with great precaution, and ought never to be adopted till after having been long and carefully examined, not only with the most scrupulous, but with the most suspicious attention. It comes from an order of men, whose interest is never exactly the same with that of the public, who have generally an interest to deceive and even oppress the public, and who accordingly have, upon many occasions, both deceived and oppressed it.[5]

Claims that the 'mercantile classes' or industrialists have divergent interests from the public and have the power to impose their own interests have come from the most varied sources. Here, the German Chancellor and aristocratic landowner, Bismarck, could join the impoverished farmers of the American mid-west, whose Populist Party manifesto of 1892 called for public ownership of the railways (see documents 11.4 and 11.6). Suspicion of the selfish interests of industrialists and financiers has tended to focus more strongly upon particular groups: railway companies in the nineteenth century and oil companies in the twentieth have been particular targets. Banks are a perennial object of suspicion. Alongside accusations that they abuse their market power, colluding in cartels or trusts to avoid competition and impose excessive prices, are charges of insufficient patriotism in wartime or a too ready willingness to supply potential enemies with war material in peacetime. More directly related to the general question of the relation between state and economy is the suspicion that industrialists, often operating through pressure groups, exercise undue influence over governments. A different criticism concerns the structural position which businesses occupy in predominantly capitalist societies. According to the contemporary American political economist, Charles E. Lindblom, business interests do not need to conspire to enjoy governmental favour. Their authority over economic resources suffices to ensure that governments will typically give them preference.

The separation of state and economy, of state authority and the authority derived from private property is a facet of most industrialized societies. Yet the precise delimitation between the two has been a constant source of dispute. Both advocates of the separation and critics as well, as those who have sought a middle way, have constantly had to argue for their preferred option.

DOCUMENTS

Document 11.1

Adam Smith, *The Wealth of Nations*

Adam Smith (1723–90) taught at Edinburgh before becoming Professor of Logic (1751) and then Professor of Moral Philosophy (1752) at Glasgow, where he published *The Theory of Moral Sentiment* (1759). He published *The Wealth of Nations* (1766) on returning from a tour of France as tutor to the Duke of Buccleuch. In 1777 he was appointed Commissioner of Customs in Edinburgh. Smith's *Wealth of Nations* was a contribution to a fierce debate over the consequences of the burgeoning commercial society. It also came to be regarded as the foundation of modern economics.

Great nations are never impoverished by private, though they sometimes are by public prodigality and misconduct. The whole, or almost the whole public revenue, is in most countries employed in maintaining unproductive hands. Such are the people who compose a numerous and splendid court, a great ecclesiastical establishment, great fleets and armies, who in time of peace produce nothing, and in times of war acquire nothing which can compensate the expense of maintaining them, even while the war lasts. Such people, as they themselves produce nothing, are all maintained by the produce of other men's labour ... Those unproductive hands, who should be maintained by a part only of the spare revenue of the people, may consume so great a share of their whole revenue, and thereby oblige so great a number to encroach upon their capitals, upon the funds destined for the maintenance of productive labour, that all the frugality and good conduct of individuals may not be able to compensate the waste and degradation of produce occasioned by this violent and forced encroachment.

This frugality and good conduct, however, is upon most occasions, it appears from experience, sufficient to compensate, not only the private prodigality and misconduct of individuals, but the public extravagance of government. The uniform, constant, and uninterrupted effort of every man to better his condition, the principle from which public and national, as well as private opulence is originally derived, is frequently powerful enough to maintain the natural progress of things towards improvement, in spite both of the extravagance of government and of the greatest errors of administration. Like the unknown principle of animal life, it frequently restores health and vigour to the constitution, in spite, not only of the disease, but of the absurd prescriptions of the doctor.

Karl Marx on the Separation of State and Economy

The extract is from 'Critical Notes on the Article "The King of Prussia and Social Reform. By a Prussian"' (1844) by Karl Marx (see introduction to document 4.10) The self-styled 'Prussian' was Arnold Ruge. In his 'Critical Notes' Marx attacked prevailing assumptions about the separation of the state and the economy.

From a *political* point of view the *state* and the *organization of society* are not *two* different things. The state is the organization of society. In so far as the state acknowledges the existence of *social* grievances it locates their origins either in the *laws of nature* over which no human agency has control, or in *private life*, which is independent of the state, or else in *malfunctions of the administration* which is dependent on it. Thus England finds poverty to be based on the *law of nature* according to which the population must always outgrow the available means of subsistence. From another point of view it explains *pauperism* as the consequence of the *bad will of the poor*, just as the King of Prussia explains it in terms of the *unchristian feelings of the rich* and the Convention explains it in terms of the *counter-revolutionary and suspect attitudes* of the *proprietors*. Hence England punishes the poor, the King of Prussia exhorts the rich and the Convention beheads the proprietors.

Lastly, *all* states seek the cause in *fortuitous* or *intentional defects in the administration* and hence the cure is sought in administrative measures. Why? Because the *administration* is the *organizing* agency of the state.

The contradiction between the vocation and the good intentions of the administration on the one hand and the means and powers at its disposal on the other cannot be eliminated by the state, except by abolishing itself; for the state is based on this contradiction. It is based on the contradiction between *public* and *private life*, between *universal* and *particular* interests. For this reason, the state must confine itself to *formal*, *negative* activities, since the scope of its own power comes to an end at the very point where civil life and work begin. Indeed, when we consider the consequences arising from the social nature of civil life, of private property, of trade, of industry, of the mutual plundering that goes on between the various groups in civil life, it becomes clear that the *law of nature* governing the administration is *impotence*. For the fragmentation, the depravity and the *slavery of civil society* is the natural foundation of the *modern* state, just as the civil society of slavery was the natural foundation of the state in *antiquity*. The existence of the state is inseparable from the existence of slavery. The state and slavery in antiquity – frank and open *classical* antitheses – were not more closely *welded* together than the modern state and the cut-throat world of modern business – sanctimonious *Christian* antitheses. If the modern state desired to abolish the *impotence* of its administration it would have to abolish contemporary *private life*. And to abolish private life it would have to abolish itself, since it exists *only* as the antithesis of private life. However, no *living* person believes the defects of his existence to be based on the *principle*, the essential nature of his own life; they must instead be grounded in circumstances *outside* his own life. *Suicide* is contrary to nature. Hence the state cannot believe in the *intrinsic* impotence of its administration, i.e. of itself. It can *only* perceive formal, contingent defects in it and try to remedy them. If these modifications are inadequate, well, that just shows that social ills are natural imperfections, independent of man, they are a *law of God*, or else, the will of private individuals is too degenerate to meet the good intentions of the administration halfway. And how perverse private individuals are! They grumble about the government when it places limits on freedom and yet demand that the government should prevent the inevitable consequences of that freedom!

The more powerful a state and hence the *more political* a nation, the less inclined it is to explain the *general* principle governing *social* ills and to seek out their causes by looking at the *principle of the state*, i.e. at the *actual organization of society* of which the state is the active, self-conscious and official expression. *Political* understanding is just *political* understanding because its thought does not transcend the limits of politics. The sharper and livelier it is, the more incapable is it of comprehending social problems. The *classical* period of political understanding is the *French Revolution*. Far from identifying the principle of the state as the source of social ills, the heroes of the French Revolution held social ills to be the source of political problems. Thus Robespierre regarded great wealth and great poverty as an obstacle to *pure democracy*. He therefore wished to establish a universal system of *Spartan* frugality. The principle of politics is the will. The more one-sided, i.e. the more perfect, *political* understanding is, the more completely it puts its faith in the *omnipotence* of the will; the blinder it is towards the *natural* and spiritual *limitations* of the will, the more incapable it becomes of discovering the real source of the evils of society. No further arguments are needed to prove that when the 'Prussian' claims that 'the political understanding' is destined 'to uncover the roots of social want in Germany' he is indulging in vain illusions.

Document 11.3

Friedrich List on Classical Political Economy

Friedrich List (1789–1846) was a German economist and advocate of the *Zollverein* (customs union) between the states of Germany. List put forward an influential defence of economic protectionism – although he saw this as a purely temporary measure – in his *National System of Political Economy* (1846). In the extract he also calls into question the basic assumptions of classical political economy, as formulated by Adam Smith and David Ricardo (1772–1823). John Ramsay McCulloch (1789–1864) was a popularizer of Ricardo's views. Jean-Baptiste Say (1767–1832) was a French economist.

The popular school of economists would have us believe that politics and political power cannot be taken into consideration in political economy. So far as it makes only values and exchange the subjects of its investigations, this may be correct; we can define the ideas of value and capital, profit, wages, and rent; we can resolve them into their elements, and speculate on what may influence their rising or falling etc without thereby taking into account the political circumstances of the nation. Clearly, however, these matters appertain as much to private economy as to the economy of whole nations. We have merely to consider the history of Venice, of the Hanseatic League, of Portugal, Holland, and England, in order to perceive what reciprocal influence material wealth and political power exercise on each other ...

We now see into what extraordinary mistakes and contradictions the popular school has fallen in making material wealth or value of exchange the sole object of its investigations, and by regarding mere bodily labour as the sole productive power.

The man who breeds pigs is, according to this school, a productive member of the community, but he who educates men is a mere non-productive. The maker of bagpipes or jews-harps for sale is a productive, while the great composers and virtuosos are non-productive simply because that which they play cannot be brought into the market. The physician who saves the lives of his patients does not belong to the productive class, but on the contrary the chemist's boy does so, although the values of exchange (viz. the pills) which he produces may exist only for a few minutes before they pass into a valueless condition. A Newton, a Watt, or a Kepler is not so productive as a donkey, a horse, or a draught-ox (a class of labourers who have been recently introduced by McCulloch into the series of the productive members of human society) ...

The errors and contradictions of the prevailing school to which we have drawn attention, can be easily corrected from the standpoint of *the theory of the productive powers*. Certainly those who fatten pigs or prepare pills are productive, but the instructors of youths and of adults, virtuosos, musicians, physicians, judges, and administrators, are productive in a much higher degree. The former *produce values of exchange*, and the latter *productive powers*, some by enabling the future generation to become producers, others by furthering the morality and religious character of the present generation, a third by ennobling and raising the powers of the human mind, a fourth by preserving the productive powers of his patients, a fifth by rendering human rights and justice secure, a sixth by constituting and protecting public security, a seventh by his art and by the enjoyment which it occasions fitting men the better to produce values of exchange. In the doctrine of mere values, these *producers of the productive powers* can of course only be taken into consideration so far as their services are rewarded by values of exchange; and this manner of regarding their services may in some instances have its practical use, as e.g. in the doctrine of public taxes, inasmuch as these have to be satisfied by values of exchange. But whenever our consideration is given to the nation (as a whole and in its international relations) it is utterly insufficient, and leads to a series of narrow-minded and false views.

The prosperity of a nation is not, as Say believes, greater in the proportion in which it has amassed more wealth (i.e. values of exchange), but in the proportion in which it has more *developed its powers of production*. Although laws and public institutions do not produce immediate values, they nevertheless produce productive powers, and Say is mistaken if he maintains that nations have been enabled to become wealthy under all forms of government, and that by means of laws no wealth can be created. The foreign trade of a nation must not be estimated in the way in which individual merchants judge it, solely and only according to the theory of values (i.e. by regarding merely the gain at any particular moment of some material advantage); the nation is bound to keep steadily in view all these conditions on which its present and future existence, prosperity, and power depend.

The nation must sacrifice and give up a measure of material property in order to gain culture, skill, and powers of united production; it must sacrifice some present advantages in order to insure to itself future ones. If, therefore, a manufacturing power developed in all its branches forms a fundamental condition of all higher advances in civilisation, material prosperity, and political power in every nation (a fact which, we think, we have proved from history); if it be true (as we believe we can prove) that in the present conditions of the world a new unprotected manufacturing power cannot possibly be raised up under free competition with a power which has long since grown in strength and is protected on its own territory; how can anyone possibly undertake to prove by arguments only based on the mere theory of values, that a nation ought to buy its goods like individual merchants, at places where they are to be had the cheapest – that we act foolishly if we manufacture anything at all which can be got cheaper from abroad – that we ought to place the industry of the nation at the mercy of the self-interest of individuals – that protective duties constitute monopolies, which are granted to the individual home manufacturers at the expense of the nation? It is true that protective duties at first increase the price of manufactured goods; but it is just as true, and moreover acknowledged by the prevailing economical school, that in the course of time, by the nation being enabled to build up a completely developed manufacturing power of its own, those goods are produced more cheaply at home than the price at which they can be imported from foreign parts. If, therefore, a sacrifice of *value* is caused by protective duties, it is made good by the gain of a *power of production*, which not only secures to the nation an infinitely greater amount of material goods, but also industrial independence in case of war. Through industrial independence and the internal prosperity derived from it the nation obtains the means for successfully carrying on foreign trade and for extending its mercantile marine; it increases its civilisation, perfects its institutions internally, and strengthens its external power. A nation capable of developing a manufacturing power, if it makes use of the system of protection, thus acts quite in the same spirit as that landed proprietor did who by the sacrifice of some material wealth allowed some of his children to learn a productive trade.

Otto von Bismarck on the Role of the State

Otto von Bismarck (1815–98) was a Junker (Prussian landowner) and diplomat before becoming Chief Minister of Prussia in 1862. Under his guidance, most of the German states were united in 1871 and he became Chancellor of the new Empire. The Germanic states were noted for their willingness to intervene in the economy in the interest of the national economy. The extract is from a letter of 7 February 1879 to the *Bundesrat* (upper chamber).

The regulation of freights on railways, which are public roads, is of far-reaching importance for the economic interests of the nation, and nobody must be damaged or be artificially limited in their use. The Government will no longer be able to abstain from promoting the public interest by creating those conditions which are necessary for the requirements of our national industries. The railways are public roads for traffic turned into a monopoly by the State, but they can be used by only one corporation. By granting to these corporations certain privileges, such as that of expropriation, i.e. powers of compulsory purchase, of police powers and of raising capital by public subscription, the State has ceded to the railways part of its power. This part of its power was ceded to the railways not in the interest of the proprietors of the railways, but in that of the general public; therefore it follows that the management of a railway cannot be left entirely to the discretion of the railway companies themselves. Their management must be regulated in accordance with the requirement of the public welfare and general traffic ...

Therefore it follows that railway charges must not be fixed solely in order to obtain the largest possible profit. The State must not only consider the interest of the shareholders in determining railway freights, but it has also to see that the well-being of the population as a whole is fostered and promoted, and that thus the vitality of the nation will be strengthened.

At any rate it damages the interest of the community if a railway company takes no notice of these larger considerations. Hence the arguments which can be raised against the system of private railways as such are strengthened ... Railways must not be allowed, by arbitrarily fixed tariffs, to develop industries in certain parts and to obstruct or destroy other industries in other parts of the country. Even the most far-seeing railway directors ... cannot realize the consequences which a policy of discriminating tariffs may have later on, although such a policy may prove beneficial in the immediate future ... and several railway boards have already begun to understand that it is not their vocation to act the part of Providence, to alter the natural conditions of demand and supply, and to dominate trade and industry, but that it is their duty to serve them ...

In railway matters changes are taking place of historical necessity which have already been observed in the general development of nations. New economic factors have arisen, and have grown up without State interference, but soon the interest in these institutions has become so great and so general that their further direction can no longer safely be left to the egotism and arbitrariness of irresponsible individuals, but must be brought into harmony with the general interest of the country.

Document 11.5

Herbert Spencer, *The Man versus the State*

Herbert Spencer (1820–1903) began his career as a railway engineer and subsequently became a columnist for *The Economist*. After 1853 he lived from his writing and several legacies. Spencer was a life-long opponent of state intervention. In his later years he was also influenced by Social Darwinism. The extract is taken from his *The Man versus the State* (1884).

The blank form of an inquiry daily made is – 'We have already done this; why should we not do that?' And the regard for precedent suggested by it, is ever pushing on regulative legislation. Having had brought within their sphere of operation more and more numerous businesses, the Acts restricting hours of employment and dictating the treatment of workers are now to be made applicable to shops. From inspecting lodging-house to limit the numbers of occupants and enforce sanitary conditions, we have passed to inspecting all houses below a certain rent in which there are members of more than one family, and are now passing to a kindred inspection of all small houses ...

And then, avowedly proceeding on the precedents furnished by the church, the school, and the reading-room, all publicly provided, it is contended that 'pleasure, in the sense it is now generally admitted, needs legislating for and organizing at least as much as work'.

Not precedent only prompts this spread, but also the necessity which arises for supplementing ineffective measures, and for dealing with the artificial evils continually caused. Failure does not destroy faith in the agencies employed, but merely suggests more stringent use of such agencies or wider ramifications of them. Laws to check intemperance, beginning in early times and coming down to our own times, not having done what was expected, there come demands for more thorough-going laws, locally preventing the sale altogether; and here, as in America, these will doubtless be followed by demands that prevention shall be made universal. All the many appliances for 'stamping out' epidemic diseases not having succeeded in preventing outbreaks of smallpox, fevers, and the life, a further remedy is applied for in the shape of police-power to search houses for diseased persons, and authority for medical officers to examine any one they think fit, to see whether he or she is suffering from an infectious or contagious malady. Habits of improvidence having for generations been cultivated by the Poor-Law, and the improvident enabled to multiply, the evils produced by compulsory charity are now proposed to be met by compulsory insurance.

The extension of this policy, causing extension of corresponding ideas, fosters everywhere the tacit assumption that Government should step in whenever anything is not going right. 'Surely you would not have this misery continue!' exclaims some one, if you hint a demurer to much that is now being said and done. Observe what is implied by this exclamation. It takes for granted, first, that all suffering ought to be prevented, which is not true: much of the suffering is curative, and prevention of it is prevention of a remedy. In the second place, it takes for granted that every evil can be removed: the truth being that, with the existing defects of human nature, many evils can only be thrust out of one place or form into another place or form – often being increased by the change. The exclamation also implies the unhesitating belief, here especially concerning us, that evils of all kinds should be dealt with by the State. There does not occur the inquiry whether there are at work other agencies capable of dealing with evils, and whether the evils in question may not be among those which are best dealt with by these other agencies. And obviously, the more numerous governmental interventions become, the more confirmed does this habit of thought grow, and the more loud and perpetual the demands for intervention.

Every extension of the regulative policy involves an addition to the regulative agents – a further growth of officialism and an increasing power of the organization formed of officials ...

A comparatively small body of officials, coherent, having common interests, and acting under central authority, has an immense advantage over an incoherent public which has no settled policy, and can be brought to act unitedly only under strong provocation. Hence an organization of officials, once passing a certain stage of growth, becomes less and less resistible; as we see in the bureaucracies of the Continent.

Not only does the power of resistance of the regulated part decrease in a geometrical ratio as the regulating part increases, but the private interests of many in the regulated part itself, make the change of ratio still more rapid. In every circle conversations show that now, when the passing of competitive examinations renders them eligible for the public service, youths are being educated in such ways that they may pass them and get employment under Government. One consequence is that men who might otherwise reprobate further growth of officialism, are led to look on it with tolerance, if not favourably, as offering possible careers for those dependent on them and those related to them. Any one who remembers the numbers of upper-class and middle-class families anxious to place their children, will see that no small encouragement to the spread of legislative control is now coming from those who, but for the personal interests thus arising, would be hostile to it ...

The foregoing discussions have, I think, shown that the dictates of utility, and, consequently, the proper actions of governments, are not to be settled by inspection of facts on the surface, and acceptance of their *prima facie* meanings; but are to be settled by reference to, and deductions from, fundamental facts. The fundamental facts to which all rational judgments of utility must go back, are the facts that life consists in, and is maintained by, certain activities; and that among men in a society, these activities, necessarily becoming mutually limited, are to be carried on by each within the limits thence arising, and not carried on beyond those limits: the maintenance of the limits becoming, by consequence, the function of the agency which regulates society. If each, having freedom to use his powers up to the bounds fixed by the like freedom of others, obtains from his fellow-men as much for his services as they find them worth in comparison with the services of others — if contracts uniformly fulfilled bring to each the share thus determined, and he is left secure in person and possessions to satisfy his wants with the proceeds; then there is maintained the vital principle alike of individual life and of social life. Further, there is maintained the vital principle of social progress; inasmuch as, under such conditions, the individuals of most worth will prosper and multiply more than those of less worth. So that utility, not as empirically estimated but as rationally determined, enjoins this maintenance of individual rights; and, by implication, negatives any course which traverses them.

Here, then, we reach the ultimate interdict against meddling legislation. Reduced to its lowest terms, every proposal to interfere with citizens' activities further than by enforcing their mutual limitations, is a proposal to improve life by breaking through the fundamental conditions to life. When some are prevented from buying beer that others may be prevented from getting drunk, those who make the law assume that more good than evil will result from interference with the normal relation between conduct and consequences, alike in the few ill-regulated and the many well-regulated. A government which takes fractions of the incomes of multitudinous people, for the purpose of sending to the colonies some who have not prospered here, or for building better industrial dwellings, or for making public libraries and public museums, etc., takes for granted that, not only proximately but ultimately, increased general happiness will result from transgressing the essential requirement to general happiness — the requirement that each shall enjoy all those means to happiness which his actions, carried on without aggression, have brought him. In other cases we do not thus let the immediate blind us to the remote. When asserting the sacredness of property against private transgressors, we do not ask whether the benefit to a hungry man who takes bread from a baker's shop, is or is not greater than the injury inflicted on the baker: we consider, not the special effects, but the general effects which arise if property is insecure. But when the State exacts further amounts from citizens, or further restrains their liberties, we consider only the direct and proximate effects, and ignore the indirect and distant effects. We do not see that by accumulated small infractions of them, the vital conditions of life, individual and social, come to be so imperfectly fulfilled that the life decays.

The Populist Manifesto and the Expansion of the Role of Government

American populism was rural in origin, although it also appealed to some industrial workers. From a background of Farmers' Alliances formed in the 1880s, People's Parties emerged in the early 1890s. A successful electoral campaign in Kansas in 1890 marked the upswing of the populist movement. The extract is from the Omaha Platform of the 1892 party convention. The People's Party went into decline in the second half of the 1890s. The radicalism of the populists caused some alarm at the time.

The conditions which surround us best justify our co-operation; we meet in the midst of a nation brought to the verge of moral, political, and material ruin. Corruption dominates the ballot-box, the Legislatures, the Congress, and touches even the ermine of the bench. The people are demoralized; most of the States have been compelled to isolate the voters at the polling places to prevent universal intimidation and bribery. The newspapers are largely subsidized or muzzled, public opinion silenced, business prostrated, homes covered with mortgages, labour impoverished, and the land concentrating in the hands of capitalists. The urban workmen are denied the right to organize for self-protection, imported pauperized labour beats down their wages, a hireling standing army, unrecognized by our laws, is established to shoot them down, and they are rapidly degenerating into European conditions. The fruits of the toil of millions are boldly stolen to build up colossal fortunes for a few, unprecedented in the history of mankind; and the possessors of these, in turn, despise the Republic and endanger liberty. From the same prolific womb of governmental injustice we breed the two great classes – tramps and millionaires ...

We believe that the power of government – in other words, of the people – should be expanded (as in the case of the postal service) as rapidly and as far as the good sense of an intelligent people and the teachings of experience shall justify, to the end that oppression, injustice, and poverty shall eventually cease in the land ...

We declare, therefore –

First – That the union of the labour forces of the United States this day consummated shall be permanent and perpetual; may its spirit enter into all hearts for the salvation of the Republic and the uplifting of mankind.

Second – Wealth belongs to him who creates it, and every dollar taken from industry without an equivalent is robbery. 'If any will not work, neither shall he eat.' The interests of rural and civil labour are the same; their enemies are identical.

Third – We believe that the time has come when the railroad corporations will either own the people or the people must own the railroads; and should the government enter upon the work of owning and managing all railroads, we should favour an amendment to the constitution by which all persons engaged in the government service shall be placed under a civil-service regulation of the most rigid character, so as to prevent the increase of the power of the national administration by the use of such additional government employees.

FINANCE – We demand a national currency, safe, sound, and flexible issued by the general government only, a full legal tender for all debts, public and private, and that without the use of banking corporations; a just, equitable, and efficient means of distribution direct to the people, at a tax not to exceed 2 per cent. per annum. to be provided as set forth in the sub-treasury plan of the Farmers' Alliance, or a better system; also by payments in discharge of its obligations for public improvements.

Document 11.7

Leon Duguit on the Service State

Leon Duguit (1859–1928) was a French jurist whose ideas were influential in the interwar years, especially among socialist public servants. His *Law in the Modern State* (1911) defined the state in terms of its social and economic functions rather than in terms of the concept of sovereignty.

Public services are those activities that the government is bound to perform. What are the nature and extent of these functions? To this question, as I pointed out in 1911, no general answer is possible. 'The content of public services is always varying and in a state of flux. It is even difficult to define the general direction of such change. All that can be said is that with the development of civilisation the number of activities related to public need grows and as a consequence the number of public services grows also. That is logical enough. Indeed, civilisation itself is simply the growth of all kinds of needs that can be satisfied in the least time. As a consequence, governmental intervention becomes normally more frequent with the growth of civilisation simply because government alone can make civilisation a thing of meaning.'

I have observed above that the government must at every time perform three functions: (1) National defence; (2) the maintenance of internal security and order, and (3) justice. Today these services are not enough. There are indeed some economists of the study antiquated enough to say that the state has no other function than defence, police and justice, and that all other activities must be left to individual arrangement which usually assures a satisfaction of all social needs. For such theories the facts are too strong; the modern attitude refuses to accept them. It has other demands, as, for example, a demand that the state no longer regard education as a private affair and, in the material field, that the state organise the work of charity.

The profound economic and industrial change that has taken place over the world has created new governmental obligations. The clear interdependence of peoples, the solidarity of economic interests, growing commercial relations, the circulation on all hands of intellectual ideas and scientific discoveries, impose on the state the duty of organizing such public services as will permanently assure international communication. So in the modern state the postal and telegraph system has become a public service of primary importance. That service, indeed, brings out clearly the legal nature of the obligation internally and internationally, that is imposed upon the modern state. It shows the solidarity of the rights and obligations by which nations are linked together.

Within each state, an economic transformation has occurred which may be briefly characterised by saying that in almost every field of activity a national economy has replaced a domestic economy. As a result, men of the same social group are made more dependent upon one another even for their daily and elementary needs. For these purposes the family group is hardly sufficient. Its external relations have become essential and the activity of those relations is too vital to admit of interruption. It has become the business of government to ensure their permanence.

Examples could be given to repletion. The time has passed when each man was his own public carrier. Today to whatever social class he belongs he looks for transportation, whether of himself or of his possessions, to groups charged with this service. Both our habits and our economic needs cannot suffer even the shortest suspension; and this makes plain every day the greater necessity of organizing transportation into a public service. In the great towns we need tramways and a public motor service; throughout the country we need railway service. Transportation, like the post office, tends to become international in character. Not only public lighting but also private have been similarly transformed. The peasant in the Hinterland of Auvergne and Brittany is no longer content with the little oil or wax candle by which his parents' home was lighted. The time is not far distant when every house will demand electric light. So soon as this becomes a primary need it will create a new subject of public service ...

We need not insist on these economic considerations. What they show in brief is how law evolves under the empire above all of economic needs. I have shown how the theory of sovereignty suffered eclipse immediately it was understood that the duty of the state was something more than defence and internal tranquillity. It is today clear that the policy of the state must be determined by its total environment. A public service, then, may be defined as follows: Any activity that has to be governmentally regulated and controlled because it is indispensable to the realisation and development of social solidarity is a public service so long as it is of such a nature that it cannot be assured save by governmental intervention.

Were there need of a formal criterion by which such service as needs to be publicly organized could be determined, I should suggest that it is to be found in the social disorder that results in the suspension even for a short time of that service. In October, 1910, for example, the French railway strike, partial and short-lived though it was, showed clearly that railroad transport has every element of a public service. Similarly, the

English miners' strike of 1912, by the disaster that it might well have entailed, showed that the time is coming when the coal miners must be organised as a public service, and when Mr. Asquith persuaded parliament to impose upon the coal owners the duty of establishing a minimum wage he took the first step towards their transformation into a public service.

Document 11.8

G.D.H. Cole on Guild Socialism

George Douglas Howard Cole (1889–1959) (see document 10.11) was a major influence on the ideas of Guild Socialism which flourished between 1917 and the early 1920s. In the extract from his *Self-Government in Industry* (1917) Cole sought to define Guild Socialism.

I do not deny, as indeed, no one can deny if he desires to call himself either National Guildsman or Guild Socialist, that industry is not everything, and that industrial democracy cannot be truly national unless it is responsible in some sense to the community as a whole. What I do most emphatically deny is that this ultimate court of appeal is the State, in any sense in which the term is ordinarily understood. Of course, if by 'State' is meant merely any ultimate body, there is no more to be said: in this sense everyone who is not an Anarchist is an advocate of State Sovereignty. But if the sovereignty of the State means the sovereignty of Parliament with its subordinate local bodies, then I maintain that it is utterly inconsistent with the principle on which Guild Socialism rests.

Parliament, Municipal and County Councils, School Boards, Boards of Guardians and the like, in fact, the whole complex machine which we call the State, are territorial associations, elected on a territorial basis by all the persons recognised as citizens who live within a definite locality. One and all, they are based upon the fact of living together, even if some relics of a different system survive, or if the territorial basis has become purely nominal, as in the House of Lords.

The bond between persons who live together is, in its material aspect, the fact that they are users or consumers in common of commodities and services. Parks, roads, houses, water and many other 'public utilities' are consumed in common by all the dwellers within such and such an area. The sovereignty of the territorial association therefore means the sovereignty of the consumer – a fact which is continually recognised and acclaimed by Collectivists.

The Guild idea, as applied to industry, is in essence a denial of the industrial sovereignty of the organised consumers, that is, of territorial associations. It repudiates the industrial sovereignty of Parliament. But this does not mean either that it rejects the idea of communal sovereignty, or that it finds its sovereign within the Guilds themselves.

Anarchism set out to destroy State Sovereignty without replacing it: Syndicalism denied the sovereignty of the State only to enthrone the General Confederation of Labour in its stead. Guild Socialists, recognising that a purely industrial sovereign is no advance on a purely political sovereign, must create a political theory to fit the Guild idea.

Collectivism, we have seen, is the practical equivalent of State Sovereignty. It is not generally realised how completely Syndicalism is an inversion of Collectivism. The one asserts the absolute sovereignty of the consumers, of the territorial association: the other the sovereignty, no less absolute, of the producers, of the professional associations. Criticised for leaving out the producers, Collectivists will ask what it matters, since producers and consumers are, or would be in a Socialist Society, the same people; criticised for neglecting the consumers, Syndicalists make precisely the same reply …

A stable community, recognising the rights and personality of all sections of consumers and producers alike, can only be secured if both the State and the Trade Unions take on new functions, and are invested with control in their respective spheres. Collectivism which is not supplemented by strong Trade Unions will be merely State bureaucracy on a colossal scale; Trade Unions not confronted by a strong and democratised State might well be no less tyrannous than a supreme State unchecked by any complementary association.

The proper sphere of the industrial organisation is the control of production and of the producers' side of exchange: its function is industrial in the widest sense, and includes such matters as directly concern the producer as a producer – in his work, the most important and serviceable part of his daily life. It has no claim to decide 'political' questions: for its right rests upon the fact that it stands for the producer, and that the producers ought to exercise direct control over production.

The proper sphere of the State in relation to industry is the expression of those common needs and desires which belong to men as consumers or users of the products of industry. It has no claim to decide producers' questions or to exercise direct control over production; for its right rests upon the fact that it stands for the consumers, and that the consumers ought to control the division of the national product, or the division of income in the community …

The Guild must preserve the right and the economic resource to withdraw its labour; the State must rely, to check unjust demands, on its equal voice in the decision of points of difference, and on the organised opinion of the community as a whole. As a last resort the preservation of equality between the two types of organisation involves the possibility of a deadlock; but it is almost impossible to imagine such a deadlock arising in an equalitarian Society.

Document 11.9

N.I. Bukharin and E.A. Preobrazhensky, *ABC of Communism*

Nikolai Ivanovich Bukharin (1888–1938) joined the Russian Social Democratic Party in 1906. A leading party member and economist he was driven from high office by Stalin in 1929 and was killed after a show trial in 1938. Evgenii Alekseevich Preobrazhensky (1886–1937) joined the party in 1903 but never gained the prominence of Bukharin. Generally regarded as a member of the left-wing opposition to Stalin, he was arrested in the mid-1930s. Their *ABC of Communism* was written as a commentary on the new 1919 programme of the Russian Communist Party. For ten years it was widely distributed as an authoritative guide to the Communist Party programme.

Let us examine this society more closely.

The basis of communist society must be the social ownership of the means of production and exchange. Machinery, locomotives, steamships, factory buildings, warehouses, grain elevators, mines, telegraphs and telephones, the land, sheep, horses, and cattle, must all be at the disposal of society. All these means of production must be under the control of society as a whole, and not as at present under the control of individual capitalists or capitalist combines. What do we mean by 'society as a whole'? We mean that ownership and control is not the privilege of a class but of all the persons who make up society. In these circumstances society will be transformed into a huge working organization for cooperative production. There will then be neither disintegration of production nor anarchy of production. In such a social order, production will be organized. No longer will one enterprise compete with another; the factories, workshops, mines, and other productive institutions will all be subdivisions, as it were, of one vast people's workshop, which will embrace the entire national economy of production. It is obvious that so comprehensive an organization presupposes a general plan of production. If all the factories and workshops together with the whole of agricultural production are combined to form an immense cooperative enterprise, it is obvious that everything must be precisely calculated. We must know in advance how much labour to assign to the various branches of industry; what products are required and how much of each it is necessary to produce; how and where machines must be provided. These and similar details must be thought out beforehand, with approximate accuracy at least; and the work must be guided in conformity with our calculations. This is how the organization of communist production will be effected. Without a general plan, without a general directive system, and without careful calculation and book-keeping, there can be no organization. But in the communist social order, there is such a plan.

Mere organization does not, however, suffice. The essence of the matter lies in this, that the organization shall be a cooperative organization of *all* the members of society. The communist system, in addition to affecting organization, is further distinguished by the fact that *it puts an end to exploitation*, that *it abolishes the division of society into classes*. We might conceive the organization of production as being effected in the following manner: a small group of capitalists, a capitalist combine, controls everything; production has been organized, so that capitalist no longer competes with capitalist; conjointly they extract surplus value from the workers, who have been practically reduced to slavery.

Here we have organization, but we also have the exploitation of one class by another. Here there is a joint ownership of the means of production, but it is joint ownership by one class, an exploiting class. This is something very different from communism, although it is characterized by the organization of production. Such an organization of society would have removed only one of the fundamental contradictions, the anarchy of production. But it would have strengthened the other fundamental contradiction of capitalism, the division of society into two warring halves; the class war would be intensified. Such a society would be organized along one line only; on another line, that of class structure, it would still be rent asunder. Communist society does not merely organize production; in addition, it frees people from oppression by others. It is organized throughout.

Document 11.10

Herbert Hoover on the American Economic System

Herbert Hoover (1874-1964) was a mining engineer and successful director of mining companies before entering politics. He was Secretary of Commerce (1921–28) and was nominated Republican candidate for the 1928 Presidential campaign which he won. The extract is from a campaign speech given on 22 October 1928. The speech forms part of the American debate over the meaning of liberalism.

During the war we necessarily turned to the government to solve every difficult economic problem. The government having absorbed every energy of our people for war, there was no other solution. For the preservation of the state the Federal Government became a centralized despotism which undertook unprecedented responsibilities, assumed autocratic powers, and took over the business of citizens. To a large degree we regimented our whole people temporarily into a socialistic state. However justified in time of war if continued in peace-time it would destroy not only our American system but with it our progress and freedom as well.

When the war closed, the most vital of all issues both in our own country and throughout the world was whether governments should continue their wartime ownership and operation of many instrumentalities of production and distribution. We were challenged with a peace-time choice between the American system of rugged individualism and a European philosophy of diametrically opposed doctrines – doctrines of paternalism and State Socialism. The acceptance of these ideas would have meant the destruction of self-government through centralization of government. It would have meant the undermining of the individual initiative and enterprise through which our people have grown to unparalleled greatness.

The Republican Party from the beginning resolutely turned its face away from these ideas and these war practices ... When the Republican Party came into full power it went at once resolutely back to our fundamental conception of the state and the rights and responsibilities of the individual. Thereby it restored confidence and hope in the American people, it freed and stimulated enterprise, it restored the government to its position as an umpire instead of a player in the economic game. For these reasons the American people have gone forward in progress while the rest of the world has halted, and some countries have even gone backwards. If anyone will study the causes of retarded recuperation in Europe, he will find much of it due to stifling of private initiative on one hand, and overloading of the government with business on the other.

There has been revived in this campaign, however, a series of proposals which, if adopted, would be a long step toward the abandonment of our American system and a surrender to the destructive operation of governmental conduct of commercial business. Because the country is faced with difficulty and doubt over certain national problems – that is prohibition, farm relief, and electrical power – our opponents propose that we must thrust government a long way into the business which give rise to these problems. In effect, they abandon the tenets of their own party and turn to state socialism as a solution for the difficulties presented by all three. It is proposed that we shall change from prohibition to the state purchase and sale of liquor. If their agricultural relief program means anything, it means that the government shall directly or indirectly buy and sell and fix prices of agricultural products. And we are to go into the hydro-electric power business. In other words, we are confronted with a huge program of government in business.

There is, therefore, submitted to the American people a question of fundamental principle. That is: shall we depart from the principles of our American political and economic system, upon which we have advanced beyond all the rest of the world, in order to adopt methods based on principles destructive of its very foundations? And I wish to emphasize the seriousness of these proposals. I wish to make my position clear; for this goes to the very roots of American life and progress.

I should like to state to you the effect that this projection of government in business would have upon our system of self-government and our economic system. That effect would reach to the daily life of every man and woman. It would impair the very basis of liberty and freedom not only for those left outside the fold of expanded bureaucracy but for those embraced within it.

Let us first see the effect upon self-government. When the Federal Government undertakes to go into commercial business it must at once set up the organization and administration of that business, and it immediately finds itself in a labyrinth, every alley of which leads to the destruction of self-government.

Commercial business requires a concentration of responsibility. Self-government requires decentralization and many checks and balances to safeguard liberty. Our Government to succeed in business would need to become in effect a despotism. There at once begins the destruction of self-government ...

It is a false liberalism that interprets itself into the government operation of commercial business. Every step of bureaucratizing of the business of our country poisons the very roots of liberalism – that is, political equality, free speech, free assembly, free press, and equality of opportunity. It is the road not to more liberty, but to less liberty. Liberalism should be found not striving to spread bureaucracy but striving to set bounds to it. True liberalism seeks all legitimate freedom first in the confident belief that without such freedom the pursuit of all other blessings and benefits is vain. That belief is the foundation of all American progress, political as well as economic.

Liberalism is a force truly of the spirit, a force proceeding from the deep realization that economic freedom cannot be sacrificed if political freedom is to be preserved. Even if Governmental conduct of business could give us more efficiency instead of less efficiency, the fundamental objection to it would remain unaltered and unabated. It would destroy political equality. It would increase rather than decrease abuse and corruption. It would stifle initiative and invention. It would undermine the development of leadership. It would cramp and cripple the mental and spiritual energies of our people. It would extinguish equality and opportunity. It would dry up the spirit of liberty and progress. For these reasons primarily it must be resisted. For a hundred and fifty years liberalism has found its true spirit in the American system, not in the European systems.

I do not wish to be misunderstood in this statement. I am defining a general policy. It does not mean that our government is to part with one iota of its national resources without complete protection to the public interest. I have already stated that where the government is engaged in public works for purposes of flood control, of navigation, of irrigation, of scientific research or national defense, or in pioneering a new art, it will at times necessarily produce power or commodities as a by-product. But they must be a by-product of the major purpose, not the major purpose itself.

Document 11.11

John Maynard Keynes, *General Theory of Employment, Interest and Money*

John Maynard Keynes (1883–1946) was a civil servant before becoming an academic in 1911. He returned to government service in both World Wars and played a leading role in the negotiations leading to agreement on an International Monetary Fund. Highly critical of orthodox economic policies in the interwar years, he put forward an alternative approach in his *General Theory of Employment, Interest and Money* (1936). His ideas dominated the postwar consensus on economic policy until the 1970s.

In some other respects the foregoing theory is moderately conservative in its implications. For whilst it indicates the vital importance of establishing certain central controls in matters which are now left in the main to individual initiative, there are wide fields of activity which are unaffected. The State will have to exercise a guiding influence on the propensity to consume partly through its scheme of taxation, partly by fixing the rate of interest, and partly, perhaps, in other ways. Furthermore, it seems unlikely that the influence of banking policy on the rate of interest will be sufficient by itself to determine an optimum rate of investment. I conceive, therefore, that a somewhat comprehensive socialisation of investment will prove the only means of securing an approximation to full employment; though this need not exclude all manner of compromises and of devices by which public authority will co-operate with private initiative. But beyond this no obvious case is made out for a system of State Socialism which would embrace most of the economic life of the community. It is not the ownership of the instruments of production which it is important for the State to assume. If the State is able to determine the aggregate amount of resources devoted to augmenting the instruments and the basic rate of reward to those who own them, it will have accomplished all that is necessary. Moreover, the necessary measures of socialisation can be introduced gradually and without a break in the general traditions of society ...

To put the point concretely, I see no reason to suppose that the existing system seriously misemploys the factors of production which are in use. There are, of course, errors of foresight; but these would not be avoided by centralising decisions. When 9,000,000 men are employed out of 10,000,000 willing and able to work, there is no evidence that the labour of these 9,000,000 men is misdirected. The complaint against the present system is not that these 9,000,000 men ought to be employed on different tasks, but that tasks should be available for the remaining 1,000,000 men. It is in determining the volume, not the direction, of actual employment that the existing system has broken down ...

But there will still remain a wide field for the exercise of private initiative and responsibility. Within this field the traditional advantages of individualism will still hold good.

Let us stop for a moment to remind ourselves what these advantages are. They are partly advantages of efficiency – the advantages of decentralisation and of the play of self-interest. The advantage to efficiency of the decentralisation of decisions and of individual responsibility is even greater, perhaps, than the nineteenth century supposed; and the reaction against the appeal to self-interest may have gone too far. But, above all, individualism, if it can be purged of its defects and its abuses, is the best safeguard of personal liberty in the sense that, compared with any other system, it greatly widens the field for the exercise of personal choice. It is also the best safeguard of the variety of life, which emerges precisely from this extended field of personal choice, and the loss of which is the greatest of all the losses of the homogeneous or totalitarian state. For this variety preserves the traditions which embody the most secure and successful choices of former generations; it colours the present with the diversification of its fancy; and, being the handmaid of experiment as well as of tradition and of fancy, it is the most powerful instrument to better the future.

Whilst, therefore, the enlargement of the functions of government, involved in the task of adjusting to one another the propensity to consume and the inducement to invest, would seem to a nineteenth-century publicist or to a contemporary American financier to be a terrific encroachment on individualism, I defend it, on the contrary, both as the only practicable means of avoiding the destruction of existing economic forms in their entirety and as the condition of the successful functioning of individual initiative.

For if effective demand is deficient, not only is the public scandal of wasted resources intolerable, but the individual enterpriser who seeks to bring these resources into action is operating with the odds loaded against him. The game of hazard which he plays is furnished with many zeros, so that the players *as a whole* will lose if they have the energy and hope to deal all the cards.

Document 11.12

William Beveridge on Planning

William Henry Beveridge (1879–1963) was a journalist, civil servant and academic. He was appointed chairman of the Committee on Social and Allied Services in 1941 – largley to remove the fractious Beveridge from a more prominent post. The Committee's Report (1942), soon known as the 'Beveridge Report', formed the basis of the acts establishing the British welfare state. *Full Employment in a Free Society* (1944), from which the extract is taken, was published without government assistance or cooperation. The extract is a contribution to a widespread debate on the nature and extent of planning.

48. In the Report on Social Insurance and Allied Services, I set out a Plan for Social Security. The present Report sets out not a 'Plan' but a 'Policy' for Full Employment. The difference of wording is due, in part, to the different circumstances in which the two Reports have been prepared, one with all the help that His Majesty's Government and all the departments under their control could give me, and the other without that help. With the same help, this second Report could have dealt with many practical details which are now omitted from it.

49. But the difference of wording, between 'Plan' and 'Policy' does not arise simply or mainly from differences in the conditions under which the two Reports were prepared. It reflects also a fundamental difference between the problems to be solved. Social Security today can be made the subject of a definite Plan and of legislation to give effect to that Plan. It lies wholly within the power of each National Government; once a decision has been taken to abolish Want by comprehensive unified social insurance as the principal method, once a few issues of equity between older and newer contributors have been settled, the rest is administrative and actuarial detail: the Plan should be as definite as

possible, so that every citizen, knowing just what he may expect from social insurance, can plan his personal spending and saving to suit his special needs.

50. Prevention of Idleness enforced by mass unemployment is a different task. Detailed legislation is neither needed nor useful. It is a problem of adjusting State action to the free activities of the citizens of that State and to the policies of other States. It involves one large decision of principle – acceptance by the State of a new responsibility to the individual – and the setting up of an agency of the State with powers adequate for the discharge of that responsibility. But the course which that agency should pursue cannot be laid down in advance. As is said in concluding Part IV of this Report, pursuit of full employment is not like the directed flight of an aircraft on a beam; it is a difficult navigation, in which a course must be steered among shifting, unpredictable, and to a large extent, uncontrollable currents and forces. All that can be done is to see that the pilot has the necessary controls, and an instrument board to tell him when and how to use the controls. It is necessary also that the pilot should always have the will to sue the controls by which alone he can reach his destination.

Document 11.13

Friedrich von Hayek, *The Road to Serfdom*

Friedrich August von Hayek (1899–1992) was born in Vienna. He held academic posts in Vienna, London, Chicago, Freiburg and Salzburg. An economist, his first avowedly political book was *The Road to Serfdom* (1944). Its ideas ran counter to the general trend at the time but it now enjoys a considerable reputation on the right. The idea of a Third Way was much discussed in Europe in the 1930s and 1940s.

The successful use of competition as the principle of social organisation precludes certain types of coercive interference with economic life, but it admits of others which sometimes may very considerably assist its work and even requires certain kinds of government action. But there is good reason why the negative requirements, the points where coercion must not be used, have been particularly stressed. It is necessary in the first instance that the parties in the market should be free to sell and buy at any price at which they can find a partner to the transaction, and that anybody should be free to produce, sell, and buy anything that may be produced or sold at all. And it is essential that the entry into the different trades should be open to all on equal terms, and that the law should not tolerate any attempts by individuals or groups to restrict this entry by open or concealed force. Any attempt to control prices or quantities of particular commodities deprives competition of its power of bringing about an effective co-ordination of individual efforts, because price changes then cease to register all the relevant changes in circumstances and no longer provide a reliable guide for the individual's actions …

Yet, though all the changes we are observing tend in the direction of a comprehensive central direction of economic activity, the universal struggle against competition promises to produce in the first instance something in many respects even worse, a state of affairs which can satisfy neither planners nor liberals: a sort of syndicalist or 'corporative' organisation of industry, in which competition is more or less suppressed but planning is left in the hands of the independent monopolies of the separate industries. This is the inevitable first result of a situation in which the people are united in their hostility to competition but agree on little else. By destroying competition in industry after industry, this policy puts the consumer at the mercy of the joint monopolist action of capitalists and workers in the best organised industries. Yet, although this is a state of affairs which in wide fields has already existed for some time, and although much of the muddled (and most of the interested) agitation for planning aims at it, it is not a state which is likely to persist or can be rationally justified. Such independent planning by industrial monopolies would, in fact, produce effects opposite to those at which the argument for planning aims. Once this stage is reached the only alternative to a return to competition is the control of the monopolies by the state, a control which, if it is to be made effective, must become progressively more complete and more detailed ...

If we are nevertheless rapidly moving towards such a state this is largely because most people still believe that it must be possible to find some Middle Way between 'atomistic' competition and central direction. Nothing indeed seems at first more plausible, or is more likely to appeal to reasonable people, than the idea that our goal must be neither the extreme decentralisation of free competition, nor the complete centralisation of a single plan, but some judicious mixture of the two methods. Yet mere common sense proves a treacherous guide in this field. Although competition can bear some admixture of regulation, it cannot be combined with planning to any extent we like without ceasing to operate as an effective guide to production. Nor is 'planning' a medicine which, taken in small doses, can produce the effects for which one might hope from its thoroughgoing application. Both competition and central direction become poor and inefficient tools if they are incomplete; they are alternative principles used to solve the same problem, and a mixture of the two means that neither will really work and that the result will be worse than if either system had been consistently relied upon. Or, to express it differently, planning and competition can be combined only by planning for competition, but not by planning against competition.

Document 11.14

Charles Lindblom on Democracy and Economy

Charles Edward Lindblom (born 1917) has taught at the Universities of Minnesota and Yale. Although Lindblom was originally an economist his work straddles the disciplines of economics and politics. He is Sterling Professor of Economics and Political Science (Emeritus) at Yale. The extract is from 'Democracy and Economy', (1983).

This line of argument can be summarized as follows:

1. In market-oriented systems, there are, as we have already seen, two major groups of organizing and coordinating rulers: those who exercise state authority and those who exercise authority derived from the rules of private property: in short, government officials and business officials. Both are essential to us all.

2. The second group, business officials, cannot be commanded to discharge their essential functions, for they are not assigned responsibility with their authority. (And a general attempt generally to command them would constitute a termination of property rights in the means of production and an abandonment of the market system.)

3. They must be induced, gratified, indulged, or rewarded to give them incentive to perform necessary tasks of social organization or coordination.

4. Sufficient inducement does not arise spontaneously. Historically, and still today in underdeveloped economies, inducements have been provided or strengthened through governmental regulation and supply of credit, appropriate monetary policies; river, railroad, highway and airways development; tax concessions; subsidies; protected markets; development of overseas markets, sometimes through military force; curbing of labour union activity; research and development; occupational training; and the like. Precisely what is needed to stimulate business incentives varies somewhat from decade to decade and from country to country.

5. Weakness of incentives leads to economic stagnation, and specifically to unemployment.

6. Governmental rulers in the democracies are usually fearful of being turned out of office if the economy stagnates and unemployment rises.

7. Hence governments in these systems warp democracy to give high priority to devising such policies as businessmen want. This they are driven to do independently of any electoral pressure from businessmen. Indeed they will often identify needed changes in government policy to stimulate business incentive even before businessmen themselves explicitly ask for them.

8. Businessmen consequently achieve not a complete domination of the state but a degree of control over the state entirely disproportionate to their numbers, hence a degree of control over the state that does not satisfy the requirements of democracy.

QUESTIONS FOR DISCUSSION

1. To what extent can one separate the economy and the state?
2. What are the major criticisms of state intervention in the economy?
3. What does economic planning involve?
4. Is there a 'Middle Way between "atomistic" competition and central direction' of the economy?
5. Is Lindblom right to claim that governments warp democracy to give businessmen the kinds of policies they want?

NOTES

1 See Phyllis Deane, *The State and the Economic System. An Introduction to Political Economy* (Oxford, Oxford University Press, 1989), pp. 3–50
2 Adam Smith, *The Wealth of Nations* (Harmondsworth, 1979), p. 105.
3 This still left a greater need for appropriate institutional backing than many of himodern advocates realize. See N. Rosenberg, 'Some Institutional Aspects of the *Wealth of Nations*', *Journal of Political Economy*, Vol. 68 (1960), pp. 557–70.
4 The contrast is well-illustrated by Douglas E. Ashford: 'When France finally achieved a national social insurance plan in 1945, the *fond de solidarité nationale* remained a charge against all contributors so the state could provide benefits for those without incomes.The principle of self-financing social insurance was never popular in France, while every effort was made to avoid Treasury responsibility in the British 1911 law and the principle of self-financing was maintained as late as the Beveridge national insurance scheme.' *The Emergence of the Welfare State* (Oxford, Basil Blackwell, 1986), p. 103.
5 Smith, *The Wealth of Nations*, p. 359

FURTHER READING

Among recent attempts to deal with the intersection between the political and the economic see James E. Alt and K. Alec Chrystal, *Political Economics* (Brighton, Wheatsheaf, 1983). The work of Charles E. Lindblom marks a major contribution to the debate. See especially *Politics and Markets* (New York, Basic Books, 1977). A good survey of the history of political economy, with a keen grasp of the broader intellectual background, is Phyllis Deane, *The State and the Economic System. An Introduction to Political Economy* (Oxford, Oxford University Press, 1989). Among the histories of economic ideas see Eric Roll, *A History of Economic Thought* (London, Faber and Faber, 1961). G. Poggi, *The Development of the Modern State* (London, Hutchinson, 1978) is a lucid introduction while Kenneth Dyson, *The State Tradition in Western Europe* (Oxford, Martin Robertson, 1978) contains a wealth of information, emphasizing the contrast between societies with a strong and weak sense of the state. The same contrast is evident in Douglas E. Ashford, *The Emergence of the Welfare State* (Oxford, Basil Blackwell, 1986) which concentrates on the British and French cases. See also W.H. Greenleaf, *The British Political Tradition*, Vol. 2 *The Ideological Heritage* (London, Methuen, 1983). The international dimension is surveyed in Evan Luard, *Economic Relationships Among States* (London, Macmillan, 1984). On Adam Smith and the emergence of modern political economy see Istvan Hont and Michael Ignatieff (eds), *Wealth and Virtue. The Shaping of Political Economy in the Scottish Enlightenment* (Cambridge, Cambridge University Press, 1983). The socialist tradition is introduced by Gerd Hardach, Dieter Karras and Ben Fine, *A Short History of Socialist Economic Thought* (London, Edward Arnold, 1978). For the background to American debates see Michael Foley, *American Political Ideas. Traditions and Usage* (Manchester, Manchester University Press, 1991) and for the vagaries of American 'liberalism' see Larry G. Gerber, *The Limits of Liberalism* (New York, New York University Press, 1983). A starting point for the complex debates on planning during the interwar period is provided by Alan Gillie, 'The State, the Market and the Plan', in James Anderson (ed.), *The Rise of the Modern State* (Brighton, Wheatsheaf, 1981), pp. 170–91. Andrew Shonfield, *Modern Capitalism. The Changing Balance of Public and Private Power* (Oxford, Oxford University Press, 1965) remains an indispensable survey covering the European and American experience. This now needs to be supplemented by Scott Lash and John Urry, *The End of Organized Capitalism* (Cambridge, Polity, 1988). On the revolt against Keynsianism see David Green, *The New Right* (Hemel Hempstead, Harvester-Wheatsheaf, 1987).

12

THE INTERNATIONAL ORDER

INTRODUCTION

While political ideas have been formulated, refined and enforced mostly within political communities, interaction between communities has also been a significant factor of political life. This is true today to a greater extent than at any previous period. In seeking to understand and regulate this interaction we employ much the same set of ideas that we employ within political communities: ideas of order, authority, sovereignty, right, justice and so on. Yet, within the modern international order at least, there is a fundamental difference which underlies the development of ideas of international relations. The international order is, at the end of the day, an anarchic one. There is no overarching political authority analogous to that within political communities.

The modern system of states is composed of states each of which claims undisputed authority (internal sovereignty) over its citizens and complete independence from any putative higher authority (external sovereignty). This has suggested to many writers that international political life can best be understood by analogy with the relation between individual men in that hypothetical 'state of nature' which existed prior to the establishment of government. According to this Hobbesian view, states, like individuals within the state of nature, must continually fear for the security of their possessions and their very existence. They must look to their own resources, their own power, for protection. They must act as judges in their own case; for there is no impartial judge to whom they can turn. There is not even, in some versions at least, any law, save that of the stronger, that is the victor, to which states can appeal.

Other commentators draw a different conclusion. They argue that just as men in a 'state of nature' were in fact subject to the constraints of the law of nature, so too are states in their behaviour towards each other. The roots of this view go back at least to the medieval period, before the formation of the modern state system. Even then, when Christendom could claim some overarching authority, violence between political communities called forth attempts to at least restrict the incidence, and intensity, of warfare. Aquinas, amongst others, set down conditions for just wars, seeking to dissuade avaricious and proud rulers from undertaking war without due cause. He did not seek to prohibit war, despite the fact that any violence between Christians was an affront to Christian doctrine.

In seeking to limit the resort to warfare, the just war tradition is confronted not only by the Hobbesian vision where insecurity prompts preparation for war, but is also confronted by a tradition which sets a positive value upon war. According to this interpretation the international realm is an arena in which states or their rulers pursue glory. The positive value set upon reputation rather than mere security is the dominating factor. While earlier it was primarily, but not exclusively, ruling princes who were expected to seek glory on the field of battle, in the later age of nationalism the same ambition was ascribed to nation-states (see documents 12.3 and 12.11).

Within the just war tradition two separate but related issues are at stake. They are identified as *jus ad bellum* and *jus in bello*. The first deals with the right to go to war in the first place. The second deals with the right conduct of warfare. The distinction is important for it opens up the possibility of recognizing wars which have been justly undertaken but in which the conduct of the war is not just. The idea that women, children and prisoners ought not to be slaughtered – if for no other reason than that they are usually judged to be incapable of harming the victorious forces – is an old example of the dictates of *jus in bello*. In the contemporary world of weapons of mass destruction and aerial bombardment the relevance of this restriction is even greater. But so too are the pressures to ignore these restrictions. With the advent of total warfare, in which the entire resources of the nation are committed to the conflict, it has been claimed that the distinction between combatants and innocents is harder and harder to maintain.

The *jus ad bellum* also has its problems. Within the ethical community of Christendom it seemed plausible to presume that it was possible to identify the just and the unjust. But as this ethical community weakened with the divisions of the Reformation, the sixteenth-century lawyer, Alberico Gentili, raised the possibility of both parties entering a war with justice on their side, or, to be more precise, of both parties believing in the justice of their cause and of outsiders lacking the ability to assess the rival claims with any certainty. Referring to Europe's miserable plight, the eighteenth-century philosopher, Rousseau, wrote 'in the absence of any sure clue to guide her, reason is bound, in every case of doubt, to obey the promptings of self-interest – which in itself would make war inevitable, even if all parties desired to be just'.[1]

The idea that raising questions of justice in interstate relations is of little avail has been put forward on several grounds: that it is futile where there is no authority to enforce it; that there is no such thing as an international law at all; or, as with Gentile and Rousseau, that even just states will be drawn into war.

Where justice has seemed to be irrelevant, or at least an uncertain or unreliable guide to conduct, other principles have been invoked.

If justice is ruled out, what should take its place? One answer is the interest of the state or nation. This was the view of the nineteenth-century British politician, Palmerston, although he tacked on considerations of justice for good measure. According to this view, elevated into a universal doctrine by writers of the Realist school who criticized reliance upon international law or morality, all states are potential enemies. Whether they are enemies on any particular occasion depends on whether their interests happen to coincide or conflict with the interests of the state determining its policy. This vision is, once the remnants of the just war tradition are stripped away, one of an amoral and dynamic world. It had been expressed without restraint by Athenian representatives as early as the fifth century BC.

A different response is to look for another way of regulating the conflict of states. If justice will not suffice, either because it is too difficult to determine or because states will subordinate justice to interest, perhaps interest itself can be seen as an amoral regulator. This possibility is taken up in the idea of a balance of power. The idea of the balance of power is far from unequivocal despite the misleading simplicity of the metaphor. Critics were not slow to point out that the idea was used to suggest that where a balance existed states would refrain from aggression. In other words, the balance was supposed to prevent war. But it was also used to suggest that the interests of states would lead them to ally against an increasingly powerful and threatening neighbour and, at some appropriate point, to reduce his power by means of war. Here the instigation of war becomes a central part of maintaining the balance.[2] Whichever of these two, or other, interpretations was taken, the final criterion was the preservation of the system of states. Individual states might disappear, because, according to the version of the balance of power, either the balance temporarily broke down or, by virtue of its very operation, but the system of states in general would be maintained.

During the nineteenth century the central features of this vision, of states, interests, and limited warfare, were being challenged. Up until the nineteenth-century, states had indeed been the primary actors: states not nations, at least not nations in the modern sense of the word. As a sense of national identity grew in importance, the existing arrangement of states was called into question. Critics pointed out that many states were multinational, others were more or less homogenous but did not encompass the entirety of the nation. Furthermore some nations, or putative nations, lacked any state of their own and some of these nations were distributed across several states. For advocates of an international order based upon the coincidence of nations and states, like the Italian nationalist, Mazzini, any other arrangement was a recipe for, and also a justification for, war. Once the desired harmony of nations and states was achieved, peace was supposed to reign. Each nation-state would take its place in the international order and none would encroach upon any other. As recent conflicts demonstrate, this harmony of nation and state is far from achieved: nor is it evident that it is achievable or even desirable.

Quite how nations are defined has remained disputed. The nineteenth-century Frenchman, Renan, although reflecting conceptions of statehood and nationality rooted in the French Revolutionary tradition, was not alone in despairing of finding any sure objective criterion. Nor, as the comments of the British liberal historian, Acton, indicate, have multinational states lacked their defenders (see document 12.10). Even if nationality could be defined and the coincidence of nation and state were held to be desirable, that would still leave the thorny problems of what to do with minorities (see document 4.15) and what to do with those frequent situations where 'nations' are so entwined that no territorial border can readily separate them.

An alternative to looking to nationality and the nation-state as a solution is to look to a refocusing of the idea of interests. Whereas advocates of the balance of power had looked to the interests of states, their critics looked to the interests of peoples. The argument here, as advanced by the nineteenth-century British liberal, Cobden, is that peace and trade between peoples is conducive to mutual economic prosperity and that war was costly, disruptive of trade and hence harmful to the interests of the people. Later supporters of this line claimed that the costs of war were becoming so great that even governments would be unable to escape the logic of the argument. Even where this claim seemed to be refuted – a famous affirmation of it occurred on the eve of the First World War! – the attempt to bind states together by means of their material interests has been a recurrent ambition and one with some evidence of success in recent years.[3]

The limitations of warfare were under increasing strain in the nineteenth century, although few recognized that the future of warfare in twentieth-century Europe was foreshadowed not by the short campaigns of the Austro-Prussian and Franco-Prussian wars of 1866 and 1870, but by the bloody and protracted struggle of the American Civil War. Amidst the carnage of the First World War the old policies of the balance of power and the pursuit of interest were called into question. The Fourteen Points laid down by the American President, Woodrow Wilson, in February 1918, which set out the war aims of the United States of America, were promptly recognized as an attempt to inaugurate a new kind of international order.

Although the Covenant of the League of Nations did not embody all of Wilson's hopes – membership of his own country was vetoed by the United States' Senate – the League did enshrine attitudes which are still part of the contemporary understanding of the international order. The Covenant sought to reassert moral considerations, complete with procedures for adjudication, into the international realm. It sought, by creating an international organization, to provide a form of international authority with some resemblance to domestic political authority.

Ideas of international behaviour were consequently refashioned. Instigating war, for example, was defined as an act of aggression which made states liable to punishment by the collective actions of the members of the League. By providing mechanisms of adjudication and enforcement, the League was seeking to resolve the problem which had dogged the just war tradition. The idea of the League of Nations represents an 'internationalist' approach which stands in direct contrast to the Hobbesian view of the international realm.

The League of Nations was subsequently to be regarded as a deeply flawed organization, a fact which would play an important role in the shaping of the United Nations in the wake of the Second World War. Despite the provisions for enforcement, the League had failed to deal effectively with unequivocal acts of aggression, most notably the Italian Fascist invasion of Abyssinia in 1935. The League and its somewhat better organized successor, raise other questions in addition to that of enforcement. Both organizations can be accused of having misleading names. Neither is composed of nations at all. Both are composed of states. That fact reflects the limits of the achievement of Mazzini's programme. Both organizations, especially the League, called forth criticism which, in some respects, sought to reassert the inescapability of the Hobbesian world of states.

The central issue here is to what extent ideas of right and justice can be applied to the international realm and to what extent states can be expected to adhere to them, if they can be plausibly applied. The issues are thus similar to those already met with in the discussion of rights and justice. Observers who were sceptical of a positive answer, who were soon to label themselves 'Realists', raised several objections to the underlying assumptions of the League and its successor. According to E.H. Carr, the most important assumption was that a harmony of interests could exist among states. In criticizing this assumption, Carr was reiterating the assertion of the balance of power theorists. A second point of criticism was that any particular dispensation in the international order and any particular conception of the requirements of justice would reflect the interests of the predominant power or powers and would be so regarded by those who felt themselves to be disadvantaged by it.

Carr's criticisms were formulated on the eve of the Second World War, with the League of Nations and the Versailles Treaty as the clear embodiments of the supposed standard of justice and Germany as the prime revisionist power. However, his arguments have subsequently been repeated by, for example, Third World states who see themselves as disadvantaged in a political and economic world order designed by, and in the interests of, the industrialized states of the northern hemisphere.

Despite these criticisms, the idea of an international order, like many other concepts, has incorporated more and more aspects of life. In the eighteenth century, Adam Smith could acknowledge that populations far removed from our territories deserved our good wishes but add that since our ability to be of any benefit to them was so small, our obligations were decidedly limited. With improvements in communications, the growth of trade and the sheer resources of some of the world's states, abilities to influence events in even distant parts of the world have increased. So too, as E.F. Penrose (see document 12.15) suspected, has the assumption that states have obligations to other states which go far beyond the requirements to respect each other's integrity and possessions and to keep promises.

DOCUMENTS

Document 12.1

Thucydides, The Pelloponnesian War

Thucydides (*c.*455–400 BC) was an Athenian historian and author of *The Pelloponnesian War*, from which the extract is taken. Melos was caught up in the war between Athens and Sparta. The Melians refused to bow to the Athenian threats but were eventually defeated. The Athenians then killed the men of Melos and sold the women and children into slavery.

Athenians: We on our side will use no fine phrases saying, for example, that we have a right to our empire because we defeated the Persians, or that we have come against you now because of the injuries you have done us – a great mass of words that nobody would believe. And we ask you on your side not to imagine that you will influence us by saying that you, though a colony of Sparta, have not joined Sparta in the war, or that you have never done us any harm. Instead we recommend that you should try to get what it is possible for you to get, taking into consideration what we both really do think; since you know as well as we do that, when these matters are discussed by practical people, the standard of justice depends on the equality of power to compel and that in fact the strong do what they have the power to do and the weak accept what they have to accept …

Melians: So you would not agree to our being neutral, friends instead of enemies, but allies of neither side?

Athenians: No, because it is not so much your hostility that injures us; it is rather the case that, if we were on friendly terms with you, our subjects would regard that as a sign of weakness in us, whereas your hatred is evidence of our power.

Melians: Is that your subjects' idea of fair play – that no distinction should be made between people who are quite unconnected with you and people who are mostly your own colonists or else rebels whom you have conquered?

Athenians: So far as right and wrong are concerned they think that there is no difference between the two, that those who still preserve their independence do so because they are strong, and that if we fail to attack them it is because we are afraid. So that by conquering you we shall increase not only the size but the security of our empire.

Document 12.2

St Thomas Aquinas on the Just War

The extract is from the *Summa Theologica* of Thomas Aquinas (see introduction to documents 1.2 and 7.3).

For a war to be just three conditions are necessary. First, the authority of the ruler within whose competence it lies to declare war. A private individual may not declare war; for he can have recourse to the judgement of a superior to safeguard his rights. Nor has he the right to mobilize the people, which is necessary in war. But since responsibility for public affairs is entrusted to the rulers, it is they who are charged with the defence of the city, realm, or province, subject to them. And just as in punishment of criminals they rightly defend the states against all internal disturbances with the civil arm; as the Apostle says (*Romans*, XIII, 4): 'He beareth not the sword in vain. For he is God's minister: an avenger to execute wrath upon him that doeth evil.' So also they have the duty of defending the state, with the weapons of war, against external enemies. For this reason rulers are told in *Psalm* LXXXI to 'Rescue the poor; and deliver the needy out of the hand of the sinner.' And St. Augustine says in his book, *Contra Faustum* (XXIII, 73): 'The natural order of men, to be peacefully disposed, requires that the power and decision to declare war would lie with the rulers.'

Secondly, there is required a just cause: that is that those who are attacked for some offence merit such treatment. St. Augustine says (Book LXXXIII qu.; *Super Josue*, qu. X): 'Those wars are generally defined as just which avenge some wrong, when a nation or a state is to be punished for having failed to make amends for the wrong done, or to restore what has been taken unjustly.'

Thirdly, there is required a right intention on the part of the belligerents: either of achieving some good object or of avoiding some evil. So St. Augustine says in his book *De Verbis Domini*: 'For the true followers of God even wars are peaceful, not being made for greed or out of cruelty, but from desire of peace, to restrain the evil and assist the good.' So it can happen that even when war is declared by legitimate authority and there is just cause, it is, nevertheless, made unjust through evil intention. St. Augustine says in *Contra Faustum* (LXXIV): 'The desire to hurt, the cruelty of vendetta, the stern and implaccable spirit, arrogance in victory, the thirst for power, and all that is similar, all these are justly condemned in war.'

Document 12.3

Machiavelli on the Pursuit of Glory

The extract is from Machiavelli's *The Prince* (see introduction to document 9.3). Ferdinand of Aragon (1452–1516) conquered the last Moorish kingdom in Spain (Granada) in 1491 and secured control of Naples in 1505. The Moors (Moriscos) expelled in 1502 were those who refused to accept baptism. The final expulsion of the Moors did not take place until 1610. Bernabò Visconti (1354–85) was a Milanese ruler who was eventually killed by his own nephew.

XXI. *How a prince must act to win honour*

Nothing brings a prince more prestige than great campaigns and striking demonstrations of his personal abilities. In our own time we have Ferdinand of Aragon, the present king of Spain. He can be regarded as a new prince, because from being a weak king he has risen to being, for fame and glory, the first king of Christendom. If you study his achievements, you will find that they were all magnificent and some of them unparalleled. At the start of his reign he attacked Granada; and this campaign laid the foundation of his power. First, he embarked on it undistracted, and without fear of interference; he used it to engage the energies of the barons of Castile who, as they were giving their minds to the war, had no mind for causing trouble at home. In this way, without their realizing what was happening, he increased his standing and his control over them. He was able to sustain his armies with money from the Church and the people, and, by means of that long war, to lay a good foundation for his standing army, which has subsequently won him renown. In addition, in order to be able to undertake even greater campaigns, still making use of religion, he turned his hand to a pious work of cruelty when he chased out the Moriscos and rid his kingdom of them: there could not have been a more pitiful or striking enterprise. Under the same cloak of religion he assaulted Africa; he started his campaign in Italy; he has recently attacked France. Thus he has always planned and completed great projects, which have always kept his subjects in a state of suspense and wonder, and intent upon their outcome. And his moves have followed closely upon one another in such a way that he has never allowed time and opportunity in between time for people to plot quietly against them.

It is also very profitable for a prince to give striking demonstrations of his capabilities in regard to government at home, similar to those which are attributed to messer Bernabò of Milan; in the event that someone accomplishes something exceptional, for good or evil, in civil life, he should be rewarded or punished in a way that sets everyone talking. Above all, in all his doing a prince should endeavour to win the reputation of being a great man of outstanding ability.

Document 12.4

Alberico Gentili on the Laws of War

Alberico Gentili (1552–1608) was a Protestant whose family left their native Italy on account of religious persecution. He settled in England and enjoyed the patronage of the Earl of Leicester. He became famous for his argument for ambassadorial immunity when the Spanish Ambassador, Mendoza, was accused of conspiring to overthrow Elizabeth I. The extract is from his *De Jure Belli* (1598).

But may a war be waged with justice on both sides? The learned Piccolomini raises this question somewhere, but does not answer it. Among our jurists Fulgosius maintained the affirmative against the opinion of the others. Alciati has followed Fulgosius in more than one place. I too follow him, but with the proviso that there may be reasonable doubt as to the justice of the cause. This same point has been made by our other jurists and by our theologians, who declare that there is justice on one side in reality, but on the other and on both through justifiable ignorance. Thus, led by the voice of God, the Jews justly made war upon the Canaanites, and the Canaanites also justly resisted the Jews through ignorance of the divine utterance, acting in self-defence. And so Pius the Second wisely replied to the Hungarian envoys, who spoke against the emperor, that he thought that the King of Hungary was not departing from what was honourable; while he knew that the emperor was a lover of justice, however much the two might differ as to sovereignty. For neither of them thought that he had an unjust cause.

It is the nature of wars for both sides to maintain that they are supporting a just cause. In general it may be true in nearly every kind of dispute, that neither of the two disputants is unjust. Aristotle makes an exception only when the inquiry is 'whether the act took place'. And indeed in the case of one's own act our jurists are not in the habit of admitting ignorance as a defence. But they do admit it in the case of another's act, because that happens under different conditions. We are driven to this distinction by the weakness of our human nature, because of which we see everything dimly, and are not cognizant of that purest and truest form of justice, which cannot conceive of both parties to a dispute being in the right. For why, says Maximus of Tyre in this connexion should those whose purposes are just engage in strife with one another? And in fact it is either the unjust who fight with one another or the unjust with the just.

But we for the most part are unacquainted with that truth. Therefore we aim at justice as it appears from man's standpoint. In this way we avoid the objection of Baldus, that when war arises among the contending parties, it is absolutely inevitable that one side or the other is in the wrong. Accordingly we say that if it is evident that one party is contending without any adequate reason, that party is surely practising brigandage and not waging war. All agree on this point, and rightly. And it is quite true that the cause of the party which is in the right receives additional justification from that fact. 'The injustice of an adversary makes war just', writes Augustine, and referring to the Romans he says: 'The injustice of others furnished them with adversaries with whom they could wage just wars.'

But if it is doubtful on which side justice is, and if each side aims at justice, neither can be called unjust. Thus Baldus himself maintains that war between kings is just, whenever the aim on both sides is to retain majesty and justice. Those who contend in the litigation of the Forum justly, that is to say, on a plausible ground, either as defendants or plaintiffs, and lose their case and the verdict, are not judged guilty of injustice. And yet the oath regarding false accusations is taken by both parties. Why should the decision be different in this kind of dispute and in a contest of arms?

Document 12.5

Hugo Grotius on International Law

Huig de Groot (Hugo Grotius) (1583–1645) was already historiographer of Holland by the age of 18. A political protégé of Johan van Oldenbarnevelt (one of the political leaders of the United Provinces) he was tried for treason and imprisoned on Oldenbarenevelt's fall from power and execution in 1619. After a dramatic escape, he was a pensioner of the French court and then, from 1634, Swedish Ambassador to France. Grotius put forward a defence of international law that was not dependent upon theological assumptions. The extract is from his *De Jure belli Ac Pacis Libri Tres* (1625). Aristotle's point about the brigands was that even they had to observe some rule if only with respect to each other.

Many hold, in fact, that the standard of justice which they insist upon in the case of individuals within the state is inapplicable to a nation or the ruler of a nation. The reason for the error lies in this, first of all, that in respect to law they have in view nothing except the advantage which accrues from it, such advantage being apparent in the case of citizens who, taken singly, are powerless to protect themselves. But great states, since they seem to contain in themselves all things required for the adequate protection of life, seem not to have need of that virtue which looks toward the outside, and is called justice.

But ... that law is not founded on expediency alone, there is no state so powerful that it may not some time need the help of others outside itself, either for purposes of trade, or even to ward off the forces of many foreign nations united against it. In consequence we see that even the most powerful peoples and sovereigns seek alliances, which are quite devoid of significance according to the point of view of those who confine law within the boundaries of states. Most true is the saying, that all things are uncertain the moment men depart from law.

If no association of men can be maintained without law, as Aristotle showed in his remarkable illustration drawn from brigands, surely also that association which binds together the human race, or binds many nations together, has need of law; this was perceived by him who said that shameful deeds ought not to be committed even for the sake of one's country.

Document 12.6

Emmerich de Vattel, *Law of Nations*

Emmerich de Vattel (1714–67) was born in Neuchâtel, a Swiss canton then ruled by the King of Prussia. Vattel was a diplomat as well as a philosopher. He became Privy Councillor to Augustus III of Saxony in 1758, the same year in which his

Law of Nations appeared and the third year of the Seven Years War (1756–63) which had begun with the Prussian invasion of Saxony. The plan attributed to Henry IV involved redrawing the map of Europe to create states of roughly equal size and power.

Europe forms a political system in which the Nations inhabiting this part of the world are bound by their relations and various interests into a single body. It is no longer, as in former times, a confused heap of detached parts, each of which had but little concern for the lot of the others, and rarely troubles itself over what did not immediately affect it. The constant attention of sovereigns to all that goes on, the custom of resident ministers, the continual negotiations that take place, make of modern Europe a sort of Republic, whose members – each independent, but all bound together by a common interest – unite for the maintenance of order and the preservation of liberty. This is what has given rise to the well-known principle of the balance of power, by which is meant an arrangement of affairs so that no States shall be in a position to have absolute mastery and dominate over the others.

The surest means of preserving this balance of power would be to bring it about that no State should be much superior to the others, that all the States, or at least the larger part, should be about equal in strength. This idea has been attributed to Henry IV, but it is one that could not be realized without injustice and violence. And moreover, once this equality were established, how could it be regularly maintained by lawful means? Commerce, industry, the military virtues, would soon put an end to it. The right of inheritance, even in favor of women and their descendants, which has been so absurdly established for succession to the throne, but which after all has been established, would overturn your arrangement.

It is simpler, easier, and more just to have recourse to the method just referred to, of forming alliances in order to make a stand against a very powerful sovereign and prevent him from dominating. This is the plan followed by the sovereigns of Europe at the present day. They look upon the two principal powers, who for that very reason are naturally rivals, as destined to act as a mutual check upon each other, and they unite with the weaker of the two, thereby acting as so much weight thrown into the lighter scale in order to make the balance even. The House of Austria has for a long time been the predominant power; now it is the turn of France. England, whose wealth and powerful navy have given her a very great influence, without, however, causing any State to fear for its liberty, since that power appears to be cured of the spirit of conquest – England, I say, has the honor to hold in her hands the political scales. She is careful to maintain them in equilibrium. It is a policy of great wisdom and justice, and one which will be always commendable, so long as she only makes use of alliances, confederations, and other equally lawful means.

Confederations would be a sure means of preserving the balance of power and thus maintaining the liberty of Nations, if all sovereigns were constantly aware of their true interests, and if they regulated their policy according to the welfare of the State. But powerful sovereigns succeed only too often in winning for themselves partisans and allies who are blindly devoted to their designs. Dazzled by the glitter of a present advantage, seduced by their greed, deceived by unfaithful ministers, how many princes become the instruments of a power which will one day swallow up either themselves or their successors. The safest plan, therefore, is either to weaken one who upsets the balance of power, as soon as a favorable opportunity can be found when we can do so with justice … ,or, by the use of all upright means to prevent him from attaining so formidable a degree of power. To this end all Nations should be on their guard above all not to allow him to increase his power by force of arms, and this they are always justified in doing …

Finally, there is no question but that if a formidable prince is clearly entertaining designs of oppression and conquest, if he betrays his plans by preparations or other advances, other Nations have the right to check him; and if the fortune of war be favorable to them, they may profit by the favorable opportunity to weaken and reduce his strength, which upsets the balance of power and constitutes a menace to the common liberty of all.

This right on the part of Nations is still more evident as against a sovereign who is always ready to take to arms without cause and without plausible pretext, and who is thus a constant disturber of the public peace.

This leads us to a special question which is closely connected with the preceding one. When, in the midst of profound peace, a neighbouring sovereign constructs fortresses upon our frontiers, fits out a fleet, increases his troops, assembles a powerful army, fills his magazines, in a word, when he makes preparations for war, are we allowed to attack him in order to ward off the danger with which we believe we are threatened? The answer depends in large part upon the personal character and moral qualities of our neighbor. We must inquire into the reason of his preparations and demand an explanation of them. This is the practice of European Nations; and if there be just cause to suspect his good faith, securities can be demanded from him. A refusal to grant them would be sufficient indication of evil designs and just grounds for preventing them. But if that sovereign has never given evidence of base perfidy, and above all, if we have at the time no quarrel with him, why should we not quietly trust in his word, taking only such precautions as prudence renders indispensable? We should not unwarrantedly presume him capable of covering himself with such infamy by adding the crime of perfidy to that of unjust attack. So long as his good faith is not open to suspicion, we have no right to demand any further security from him.

Still, it is true that if a sovereign continues to keep up a powerful army in time of profound peace, his neighbors can not rest entirely upon his word. Prudence obliges them to be on their guard. Although they may be absolutely certain of his good faith, unforseen difficulties may arise: and shall they leave him the advantage of having in such an event a large and disciplined army, to oppose which they will have nothing but raw recruits? Certainly not, for that would be almost equivalent to putting themselves at his mercy. They are thus forced to imitate him and themselves keep up a large army.

Document 12.7

Richard Cobden on the Balance of Power

Richard Cobden (1804–65) was a supporter of free trade and disarmament and a constant critic of government policy. He was a leader of the Anti-Corn Law League and negotiated the Commercial Treaty with France (1860), reducing tariffs between the two countries. He opposed the Crimean War and refused a post in Palmerston's Cabinet in order to maintain his independence. The extract is from *Russia* (1836) which was published amidst fears of Russian expansion. Friedrich von Gentz (1764–1832) and Henry Brougham (1778–1868) were, along with Vattel, the principal advocates of the balance of power.

The balance of power ... which has served, down to the very year in which we write, and which will, no doubt continue to serve, for years to come, as a pretence for maintaining enormous standing armaments, by land and sea, at a cost of many hundreds of millions of treasure – the balance of power is a chimera! it is not a fallacy, a mistake, an imposture – it is an undescribed, indescribable, incomprehensible nothing; mere words, conveying to the mind not ideas, but sounds like those equally barren syllables which our ancestors put together for the purpose of puzzling themselves about words, in the shape of *Prester John*, of the *philosopher's stone!* We are bound, however, to see what are the best definitions of this theory.

'By this balance', says Vattel, 'is to be understood such a disposition of things as that no one potentate or state shall be able, absolutely, to predominate and prescribe laws to the others.' ...

'What is usually termed a balance of power', says Gentz, 'is that constitution subsisting among neighbouring states, more or less connected with one another, by virtue of which no one among them can injure the independence or essential rights of another without meeting with effectual resistance on some side, and, consequently, exposing itself to danger.'

'The grand and distinguishing feature of the balancing system,' says Brougham, 'is the perpetual attention to foreign affairs which it inculcates; the constant watchfulness over every nation which it prescribes; the subjection in which it places all national passions and antipathies to the fine and delicate view of remote expediency; the unceasing care which it dictates of nations most remotely situated, and apparently unconnected with ourselves; the general union which it has affected of all the European powers, obeying certain laws, and actuated in general by a common principle; in fine, the right of mutual inspection, universally recognised, among civilised states, in the rights of public envoys and residents.'
...

These are the best definitions we have been able to discover of the system denominated the balance of power. In the first place, it must be remarked that, taking any one of these descriptions separately, it is so vague as to impart no knowledge even of the writer's meaning; whilst, if taken together, one contradicts another – Gentz describing it to be 'a constitution subsisting among neighbouring states more or less connected with each other;' whilst Brougham defines it as 'dictating a care of nations most remotely situated and apparently unconnected with ourselves.' Then it would really appear, from the laudatory tone applied to the system by Vattel, who says it is 'such a disposition of things as no one potentate or state *shall be able* absolutely to predominate and prescribe laws to the others;' as well as from the complacent manner in which Brougham states 'the general *union which it has effected* of all the European powers, obeying certain laws, and actuated in general by a common principle' – it would seem, from such assurances as these, that there was no necessity for that 'perpetual attention to foreign affairs,' or that 'constant watchfulness over every nation,' which the latter author tells us, the system 'prescribes and inculcates'. The only one point on which these writers, in common with many other authors and speakers in favour of the balance of power, agree, is in the fundamental delusion that such a system was ever acceded to by the nations of Europe. To judge from the assumption, by Brougham, of a 'general *union* among all the European powers;' from the allusion made by Gentz to that '*constitution* subsisting among neighbouring states;' or from Vattel's reference to 'a *disposition of things*,' etc. – one might be justified in inferring that a kind of federal union had existed for the last century throughout Europe, in which the several kingdoms had found, like the States of America, uninterrupted peace and prosperity …

So far from any such confederation having ever been, by written, verbal, or implied agreement, entered into by the 'European powers, obeying certain laws, and actuated in general by a common principle;' the theory of the balance of power has, we believe, generally been interpreted, by those who, from age to age, have, parrot-like, used the phrase, to be a system invented for the very purpose of supplying the want of such a combination. Regarding it for a moment in this point of view, we should still expect to find that the 'balancing system had, at some period of modern history, been recognised and agreed to by all the Continental states; and that it had created a spirit of mutual concession and guarantee, by which the weaker and more powerful empires were placed upon a footing of equal security, and by which any one potentate or state was absolutely unable to 'predominate over the others.' But, instead, of any such self-denial, we discover that the balance of Europe has merely meant (if it has a meaning) … a desire on the part of the great powers, 'to hold the balance of Europe.' England has, for nearly a century, held the European scales – not with the blindness of the goddess of justice herself, or with a view to the equilibrium of opposite interests, but with a Cyclopean eye to her own aggrandizement. The same lust of conquest has actuated, up to the measure of their abilities, the other great powers …

Upon whatever principle the theory under consideration may have been at first devised … it is certain that it would have been held fatal to the success of the balancing system for any one power, and that one amongst the most civilized, wealthy, and commercial, to have refused to subscribe to its constitution. Yet the United States, (for the number of its inhabitants,) the richest, the most commercial, and, for either attack or defence, the most powerful of modern empires; a country which possesses a wider surface of fertile land than Russia could boast even with the accession of Turkey; and, instead of being imprisoned, like Russia, by the Dardanelles and the Sound, owning five thousand miles of coast, washed by two oceans, and open to the whole world: – *the United States are not parties to the balance of power!* Ignorant as we are of the rule of admission to and exclusion from this balancing system, it would be vain to conjecture why Russia should be entitled, not only to be a member of this union, but to engross its exclusive attention, whilst North America is unknown or not recognised as of any weight in the balance of power. It cannot be, on our part, from closer neighbourhood; for Russia, even at Constantinople, would – commercially and navally speaking – be three times as distant as New York, from Great Britain. Nor on account of the greater amount of the European commerce transacted by Russia. The commerce of the United States with the countries of Europe, is nearly as great in amount as that of the British empire with the Continent ... and three times that of Russia ... It would be difficult to find any other satisfactory answer than that which we are able to give as the reason of this exclusion: *America, with infinite wisdom, refuses to be a party to the 'balance of power.'*

Washington ... seeing the chimerical object for which England, *although an island,* plunged into the contentions of the Continent, with no other result to her suffering people but an enduring and increasing debt – bequeathed, as a legacy to his fellow-citizens, the injunction, that they should never be tempted, by any inducements or provocations, to become parties to the States' system of Europe. And faithfully, zealously, and happily has that testament been obeyed! Down even to our day, the feeling and conviction of the people, and consequently of the Government and the authors of the United States, have constantly increased in favour of a policy from which so much wealth, prosperity, and moral greatness have sprung. America, for fifty years at peace, with the exception of two years of defensive war, is a spectacle of the beneficent effects of that policy which may be comprised in the maxim – As little intercourse as possible betwixt *Governments,* as much connection as possible between the *nations,* of the world.

Document 12.8

Lord Palmerston on the National Interest

Lord Palmerston (1784–1865) was Foreign Secretary (1830–51) and Prime Minister (1855–58 and 1859–65). He held office of one kind or another for a total of 48 years. He made the statement given below in the House of Commons on 1 March 1848. George Canning was Foreign Secretary in 1807–9 and 1822–27.

I hold with respect to alliances, that England is a Power sufficiently strong, sufficiently powerful, to steer her own course, and not to tie herself as an unnecessary appendage to the policy of any other Government. I hold that the real policy of England – apart from questions which involve her own particular interests, political or commercial – is to be the champion of justice and right; pursuing that course with moderation and prudence, not becoming the Quixote of the world, but giving the weight of her moral sanction and support wherever she thinks that justice is, and wherever she thinks that wrong has been done. Firm in pursuing that course, and in pursuing the more limited direction of our own particular interests, my conviction is, that as long as England keeps herself in the right – as long as she wishes to permit no injustice – as long as she labours at legislative interests of her own – and as long as she sympathises with right and justice, she never will find herself altogether alone. She is sure to find some other State, of sufficient power, influence and weight to support and aid her in the course she may think fit to pursue.

Therefore I say that it is a narrow policy to suppose that this country or that is marked out as the eternal ally or the perpetual enemy of England. We have no eternal allies, and we have no perpetual enemies. Our interests are eternal and perpetual, and those interests it is our duty to follow. When we find other countries marching in the same course, and pursuing the same objects as ourselves, we consider them as our friends, and we think for the moment that we are on the most cordial footing; when we find other countries that take a different view, and thwart us in the object we pursue, it is our duty to make allowance for the different manner in which they may follow out the same objects. It is our duty not lightly to engage this country in the frightful responsibilities of war, because from time to time we may find this or that Power disinclined to concur with us in matters where their opinion and ours may fairly differ. That has been, as far as my faculties have allowed me to act upon it, the guiding principle of my conduct. And if I might be allowed to express in one sentence the principle which I think ought to guide an English Minister, I would adopt the expression of Canning, and say that with every British Minister the interests of England ought to be the shibboleth of his policy.

Document 12.9

Giuseppe Mazzini on the Nation State

Giuseppe Mazzini (1805–72) established 'Young Italy' to unite Italy in 1831 but was soon forced into exile and lived mainly in London from 1837. After participating in the 1848–49 revolutions he returned to London. A republican, he regretted the form which Italian Unification took under the House of Savoy. The extract is from his *The Duties of Man* (1858).

... when he [God] gave you a country; when, even as a wise overseer of labour distributes the various branches of employment according to the different capacities of the workmen, he divided Humanity into distinct groups or nuclei upon the face of the earth, thus creating the germ of Nationalities. Evil governments have disfigured the Divine design. Nevertheless you may still trace it, distinctly marked out – at least as far as Europe is concerned – by the course of the great rivers, the direction of the higher mountains, and other geographical conditions. They have disfigured it by their conquests, their greed, and their jealousy even of the righteous power of others; disfigured it so far that, if we except England and France – there is not perhaps a single country whose present boundaries correspond to that Design.

These governments did not, and do not, recognise any country save their own families or dynasty, the egotism of caste. But the Divine design will infallibly be realised. Natural divisions and the spontaneous innate tendencies of the peoples, will take the place of the arbitrary divisions sanctioned by evil governments. The map of Europe will be re-drawn. The countries of the Peoples, defined by the vote of free men, will arise upon the ruins of the countries of kings and privileged castes, and between these countries harmony and fraternity will exist. And the common work of Humanity, of general amelioration, and the gradual discovery and application of its Law of Life, being distributed according to local and general capacities, will be wrought out in peaceful and progressive development and advance.

Then may each one of you, fortified by the power and affection of many millions, all speaking the same language, gifted with the same tendencies, and educated by the same historical tradition, hope even by your own single effort to be able to benefit all Humanity …

In labouring for our own country on the right principle, we labour for Humanity. Our country is the fulcrum of the lever we have to wield for the common good. In abandoning that fulcrum, we run the risk of rendering ourselves useless not only to humanity but to our country itself.

Before men can *associate* with the nations of which humanity is composed, they must have a National existence. There is no true association except among equals. It is only through our country that we can have a recognised *collective* existence.

Document 12.10

Lord Acton in Defence of Multinational States

John Emmerich Edward Dalberg Acton, First Baron Acton (1834-1902) was a Liberal MP and friend of the Liberal leader, Gladstone. He became Professor of History at Cambridge in 1895. 'Nationality' was first published in July 1887. In it Acton cited Mazzini's career as the embodiment of the development of the idea of nationality.

Then began a time when the text simply was, that nations would not be governed by foreigners. Power legitimately obtained, and exercised with moderation, was declared invalid. National rights, like religion, had borne part in the previous combinations, and had been auxiliaries in the struggles for freedom, but now nationality became a paramount claim, which was to assert itself alone, which might put forward as pretexts the rights of rulers, the liberties of the people, the safety of religion, but which, if no such union could be formed, was to prevail at the expense of every other cause for which nations make sacrifices …

It was appealed to in the name of the most contradictory principles of government, and served all parties in succession, because it was one in which all could unite. Beginning by a protest against the dominion of race over race, its mildest and least-developed form, it grew into a condemnation of every State that included different races, and finally became the complete and consistent theory, that the State and the nation must be co-extensive …

In pursuing the outward and visible growth of the national theory we are prepared for an examination of its political character and value. The absolutism which has created it denies equally that absolute right of national unity which is a product of democracy, and that claim of national liberty which belongs to the theory of freedom. These two views of nationality, corresponding to the French and to the English systems, are connected in name only, and are in reality the opposite extremes of political thought. In one case, nationality is founded on the perpetual supremacy of the collective will, of which the unity of the nation is the necessary condition, to which every other influence must defer, and against which no obligation enjoys authority, and all resistance is tyrannical. The nation is here an ideal unit founded on the race, in defiance of the modifying action of external causes, of tradition, and of existing rights. It overrules the rights and wishes of the inhabitants, absorbing their divergent interests in a fictitious unity; sacrifices their several inclinations and duties to the higher claim of nationality, and crushes all natural rights and all established liberties for the purpose of vindicating itself …

Connected with this theory in nothing except in the common enmity of the absolute State, is the theory which represents nationality as an essential, but not a supreme element in determining the forms of the State. It is distinguished from the other, because it tends to diversity and not to uniformity, to harmony and not to unity; because it aims not at an arbitrary change, but at careful respect for the existing conditions of political life, and because it obeys the laws and results of history, not the aspirations of an ideal future. While the theory of unity makes the nation a source of despotism and revolution, the theory of liberty regards it as the bulwark of self-determination, and the foremost limit to the excessive power of the State …

If we take the establishment of liberty for the realisation of moral duties to be the end of civil society, we must conclude that those States are substantially the most perfect which, like the British and Austrian Empires, include various distinct nationalities without oppressing them. Those in which no mixture of races has occurred are imperfect; and those in which its effects have disappeared are decrepit. A State which is incompetent to satisfy different races condemns itself; a State which labours to neutralise, to absorb, or to expel them, destroys its own vitality; a State which does not include them is destitute of the chief basis of self-government. The theory of nationality, therefore, is a retrograde step in history.

Document 12.11

Heinrich von Treitschke on International Law

Heinrich von Treitschke (1834–96) was a German historian and supporter of German unification under Prussian leadership. A National Liberal member of the Reichstag (1871–79), he left the party when Bismarck turned against it. The extract is from his *Politics,* which was first published in 1898, after Treitschke's death. The book was popular among German nationalists.

In order to make no mistake as to the real meaning of international law, we must always remember that it must not run counter to the nature of the State. No State can reasonably be asked to adopt a course which would lead it to destroy itself. Likewise every State in the comity of nations must retain the attributes of sovereignty whose defence is its highest duty even in its international relations. We find the principles of international law most secure in that department of it which does not trench upon questions of sovereignty; that is in the domain of etiquette and of international civil law ...

From this it follows that all the restraints to which States bind themselves by treaty are voluntary, and that all treaties are concluded on the tacit understanding *rebus sic stantibus*. No State ever has, or ever will exist, which is willing to hold to all eternity to the agreements which it signs. No State will ever be in a position to pledge its whole hereafter to a treaty, which cannot fail to be a limitation of its sovereignty; it always intends that the contract shall eventually be annulled, and shall apply only so long as the present circumstances are not wholly altered. This principle is often called inhumane, but its logical conclusion shows it to be the contrary. Only if the State is aware that all its treaties only apply conditionally will it go to work prudently in the making of them. History is not meant to be looked at from the point of view of a judge hearing a civil suit. According to that standard, Prussia, having signed the Treaty of Tilsit, would have been wrong in attacking Napoleon in 1813. But this treaty, like others, had been concluded *rebus sic stantibus*, and, thank God, those *res* had been radically altered some years before. A noble nation was given the chance of shaking off an intolerable yoke, and as soon as a people is aware that their time is come, they have the right to make the attempt.

Politics must never discount the free moral forces in the national life. No State in the world may renounce the 'I' in its sovereignty. If conditions are imposed upon it which impinge upon this, and which it is unable to prevent, then 'the breach is more honoured than the observance.' It is one of the fine things about history that we see nations more easily consoled for their material losses than for injuries to their honour …

When a State recognizes that existing treaties no longer express the actual political conditions, and when it cannot persuade the other Powers to give way by peaceful negotiations, the moment has come when the nations proceed to the ordeal by battle. A State thus situated is conscious when it declares war that it is performing an inevitable duty. The combatant countries are moved by no incentives of personal greed, but they feel that the real position of power is not expressed by existing treaties and that they must be determined afresh by the judgement of the nations, since no peaceful agreement can be reached. The righteousness of war depends simply and solely upon the consciousness of a moral necessity. War is justified because the great national personalities can suffer no compelling force superior to themselves, and because history must always be in constant flux; war therefore must be taken as part of the divinely appointed order …

When a war is actually in progress its guiding political idea is to bring about new conditions of international law which will express the real relative strength of the contending parties and be recognized by both of them. It is, therefore, perfectly equitable to wage war in the most effective manner possible, so that its goal of peace may be reached as quickly as may be. For this reason the blow must be aimed at the enemy's heart, and the use of the most formidable weapons is absolutely justifiable, provided that they do not inflict needless suffering on the wounded. Philanthropists may declaim as much as they like against explosive shells fired into the powder magazines of wooden battle-ships, but still facts remain unchanged. States in conclave have decided what weapons are to be forbidden; the use of explosive bullets for small arms was prohibited at the instance of Russia. It is permissible to take advantage of all the enemy's weak points, and a State may turn treason and mutiny within its enemy's borders to serve its own ends. Nothing but the rapid march of events prevented us in Prussia from making a compact with Hungary in 1866.

It is equally impossible to deny to a belligerent State the right of employing all its troops in the field, whether they be savages or civilized men …

There is one rule of humanity in war which is theoretically of universal application, although it is only practically recognized in land campaigns; namely, that it is States who are fighting, and not their individual citizens. Certain definite signs there must be, therefore, to distinguish those persons who are entitled to fight by authority of the State, and who are to be treated as soldiers. It is an ugly gap in international law that no universal agreement has as yet been reached on this point, although it is the foundation of humanity in war.

Document 12.12

The Covenant of the League of Nations

The Covenant of the League of Nations was incorporated into the peace treaties at the end of the First World War. A major instigator of the Covenant was the American President, Woodrow Wilson. The US Senate, however, refused to ratify the Versailles Treaty and America never joined the League. Although not without some achievements, the League's reputation was undermined by its failure to respond firmly to Italian aggression against Abyssinia in 1935–36.

Article 10

The members of the League undertake to respect and preserve as against external aggression the territorial integrity and existing political independence of all Members of the League. In case of any such aggression or in case of any threat or danger of such aggression the Council shall advise upon the means by which this obligation shall be fulfilled.

Article 12

1. The Members of the League agree that, if there should arise between them any dispute likely to lead to a rupture, they will submit the matter either to arbitration or judicial settlement or to inquiry by the Council …

Article 13

4. …The Members of the League agree that they will carry out in full good faith any award or decision that may be rendered, and that they will not resort to war against a Member of the League which complies therewith …

Article 15

1. If there should arise between members of the League any dispute likely to lead to a rupture, which is not submitted to arbitration or judicial settlement in accordance with Article 13, the Members of the League agree that they will submit the matter to the Council …

Article 16

1. Should any Member of the League resort to war in disregard of its covenants under Articles 12, 13 or 15, it shall *ipso facto* be deemed to have committed an act of war against all other Members of the League, which hereby undertake immediately to subject it to the severance of all trade or financial relations, the prohibition of all intercourse between their nationals and the nationals of the covenant-breaking State, and the prevention of all financial, commercial or personal intercourse between the nationals of the covenant-breaking State and the nationals of any other State, whether a Member of the League or not.

Document 12.13

Alfred Zimmern, *The League of Nations and the Rule of Law*

Sir Alfred Zimmern (1879–1957) was an academic, initially specializing in ancient history. He worked in the Foreign Office in the First World War and later became the first Professor of International Relations at Aberystwyth University. The extract is from his *The League of Nations and the Rule of Law* (1936).

It has been unfortunate for the understanding of the nature and purpose of the Geneva experiment that its English title should have conveyed a false impression. For 'the League of Nations' is a misnomer – a fact which has given rise to much confusion of thought in the English-speaking world. Neither the word 'League' nor the word 'Nations' is accurate. The term 'League', with its philanthropic and humanitarian associations, suggests common action by a band of crusaders and enthusiasts *against* some other party or group or cause. It implies a certain *exclusiveness*, derived from a common attachment to certain particular principles or doctrines. But the essential underlying idea of the League of Nations is its *inclusiveness*. It is a new method or model for *all* states and its membership is intended to be universal. It is framed to be an all-embracing association. This is much more clearly expressed in the French term 'Society' (*Société des Nations*). Much misunderstanding as to aims and methods would have been prevented if this discrepancy between the English and French titles had been avoided. As it is, the English-speaking world must accustom itself to thinking of the League as being no less, and no more, than an all-inclusive association.

This leads us on to the second part of the title. *of* what is this association composed? What are its constituent units? Both texts give the same answer – *Nations*. Both are mistaken. They both misrepresent the membership of the League. Here again is a fruitful cause of confusion.

The term 'nation' opens out a large theme for discussion into which this is not the place to enter. But one thing is quite certain. The members of the League are not nations but states. Membership of the League has nothing to do with nationality or nationhood. It is concerned simply and solely with statehood – that is to say with *political* status. This will be clear at a glance to anyone who consults the list of the actual members of the League. He will find there 'the United Kingdom' and 'the United Socialist Soviet Republics', which are certainly neither of them nations: and he will look in vain for other names, such as 'Scotland' and 'Wales', which should certainly find a place in any true 'association of nations'.

How was it that this strange mistake came to be made? It was not pure oversight. At one of the early sittings of the committee which drafted the Covenant the Brazilian delegate, with characteristic acumen, pointed out that international law knew nothing of nations but only of states. But his protest went unregarded, the general view being that 'nothing was to be gained by modifying wording consecrated by general usage in both languages'. In other words, the majority of the members of the committee were under the sway of a particular political theory, according to which every 'nation' had a *right* to political independence, and they embodied this theory in the superscripture of the Covenant.

The theory in question is neither ancient nor universally accepted. It originated in Western Continental Europe during the latter part of the eighteenth century, its vogue being due to the particular conditions in that area. It is, of course, a revolutionary theory: that is to say, to put it into practice, to make the political organisation of the world conform to it, would involve an upheaval of the existing political arrangements over a large part of the world. Since the committee was drawing up a plan providing for better means of cooperation between existing states, it was not at all within its province to concern itself with the problem of political organisation in general, with such questions as whether Great Britain should, or should not, be broken up into three national units or the Arab peoples, for instance, united into one. But through inertia, or the reluctance of 'practical' men to face an issue of far-reaching principle, the drafters of the Covenant let slip a rare opportunity for clearing out of the way a difficulty of long standing. Thus they carried forward into the post-war world one of the principle causes of confusion and conflict in the interstate politics of nineteenth-century Europe.

However this may be, the League of Nations was never intended to be, nor is it, a revolutionary organisation. On the contrary, it accepts the world of states as it finds it and merely seeks to provide a more satisfactory means for carrying on some of the business which these states transact between one another. It is not even revolutionary in the more limited sense of revolutionising the methods for carrying on interstate business. It does not supersede the older methods. It merely supplements them. The old methods still go on, and were intended by the framers of the Covenant to go on, side by side with the new.

Document 12.14

E.H. Carr on Realism

Edward Hallet-Carr (1892–1982) spent fifteen years in the Foreign Office before becoming Professor of International Politics at Aberystwyth University. He was Assistant Editor of *The Times* (1941–46) and later returned to academic life. The extract is taken from his *The Twenty Years' Crisis 1919–1939* (1939).

The concept of internationalism is a special form of doctrine of the harmony of interests. It yields to the same analysis; and there are the same difficulties about regarding it as an absolute standard independent of the interests and policies of those who promulgate it ...

Just as pleas for 'national solidarity' in domestic politics always come from a dominant group which can use this solidarity to strengthen its own control over the nation as a whole, so pleas for international solidarity and world union come from those dominant nations which may hope to exercise control over a unified world. Countries which are struggling to force their way into the dominant group naturally tend to invoke nationalism against the internationalism of the controlling Powers. In the sixteenth century, England opposed her nascent nationalism to the internationalism of the Papacy and the Empire. Since the beginning of the nineteenth century, Germany has opposed her nascent nationalism to the internationalism first of France, then of Great Britain. This circumstance has made her impervious to those universalist and humanitarian doctrines which were popular in eighteenth-century France and nineteenth-century Britain; and her hostility to internationalism has been further aggravated since 1919, when Great Britain and France endeavoured to create a new 'international order' as a bulwark of their own predominance ... Nevertheless, there is little doubt that Germany, if she became supreme in Europe, would adopt international slogans and establish some kind of international organisation to bolster her power ...

The exposure of the real basis of the professedly abstract principles commonly invoked in international politics is the most damning and most convincing part of the realist indictment of utopianism. The nature of the charge is frequently misunderstood by those who seek to refute it. The charge is not that human beings fail to live up to their principles ... What matters is that these supposedly absolute and universal principles were not principles at all, but the unconscious reflexions of national policy based on a particular interpretation of national interest at a particular time. There is a sense in which peace and co-operation between nations or classes or individuals is a common and universal end irrespective of conflicting interests and politics. There is a sense in which a common interest exists in the maintenance of order, whether it be international order or 'law and order' within the nation. But as soon as the attempt is made to apply these supposedly abstract principles to a concrete political situation, they are revealed as the transparent disguises of selfish vested interests. The bankruptcy of utopianism resides not in any failure to live up to its principles, but in the exposure of its inability to provide any absolute and disinterested standard for the conduct of international affairs.

Document 12.15

E.F. Penrose on International Obligation

E.F. Penrose (1895–1984) was an economist who worked at the Food Research Centre, Stanford University and the International Labour Organization before becoming Special Assistant to the American Ambassador in London (1941–44). The extract is from his *Economic Planning for Peace* (1953). In it he records arguments voiced at the Hot Springs Conference on food distribution in 1943. This was the first formal exercise in planning for the postwar period carried out by the United Nations (i.e., the Allies).

The second question was one of the most difficult of all questions at the conference but though it was not a matter of immediate importance, to some of us it seemed important that it should at least be squarely faced. It was the international counterpart of the national problem of unequal distribution of food within countries. The conference, notably impressed by the example of Great Britain, enthusiastically upheld the principle that governments should be responsible for improving the diets of the people wherever inadequacies are found ... But if this was to be the attitude toward inequality of income and inequality of food consumption *within* a country what was to be said about the same inequalities when they were found on a great scale between nations! In the one case there were differences among the average conditions of different groups within the same nations: in the other there were differences among the average conditions of different national groups in 'one world'. If we agree that the first should be grappled with how long can we ignore the second? If the conscience of the national community is now roused over the consequences of great inequalities among its members, how long can the conscience of the international community remain unaffected by the immense inequalities among the nations?

It was not indeed the mere existence of inequality that aroused uneasiness so much as the combination of inequality with an absolute deficiency of ordinary necessities at the lower end of the scale ...

But the question what should be done about these conditions was not as readily answered in the international as in the domestic sphere. This was not surprising: the inherent difficulties in the first are much greater than those in the second and – almost equally important – few people had yet felt a strong urge to overcome them. The question raised in ancient times, 'Am I my brother's keeper?' was slowly coming to be answered in the affirmative in the twentieth century within some national communities, but few were yet ready to accept, even in principle, the same obligations toward their fellow men – near or far – who acknowledged and lived under other sovereign jurisdictions.

Document 12.16

Hedley Bull, *The Anarchical Society*

Hedley Bull (1932–85) held academic posts in London and Canberra before becoming Professor of International Relations at Oxford University. The extract is taken from his major work, *The Anarchical Society. A Study of Order in World Politics* (1977).

The starting point of international relations is the existence of *states*, or independent political communities, each of which possesses a government and asserts sovereignty in relation to a particular portion of the earth's surface and a particular segment of the human population. On the one hand, states assert, in relation to this territory and population, what may be called internal sovereignty, which means supremacy over all other authorities within that territory and population. On the other hand, they assert what may be called external sovereignty, by which is meant not supremacy but independence of outside authorities ...

The independent political communities that are states in this sense include city-states, such as those of ancient Greece or renaissance Italy, as well as modern nation-states ... They include multinational states, such as the European empires of the nineteenth century, as well as states of a single nationality. They include states whose territory is scattered in parts, such as the oceanic imperial states of Western Europe, as well as states whose territory is a single geographical entity.

There are, however, a great variety of independent political communities that have existed in history and yet are not states in this sense ... The kingdoms and principalities of Western Christendom in the Middle Ages were not states: they did not possess internal sovereignty because they were not supreme over authorities within their territory and population; and at the same time they did not possess external sovereignty since they were not independent of the Pope or, in some cases, the Holy Roman Emperor ...

A *system of states* (or international system) is formed when two or more states have sufficient contact between them, and have sufficient impact on one another's decisions, to cause them to behave – at least in some measure – as parts of a whole ...

A *society of states* (or international society) exists when a group of states, conscious of certain common interests and common values, form a society in the sense that they conceive themselves to be bound by a common set of rules in their relations with one another, and share in the working of common institutions ... By international order is meant a pattern or disposition of international activity that sustains those goals of the society of states that are elementary, primary or universal. What goals, then, are these?

First, there is the goal of preservation of the system and society of states itself. Whatever the divisions among them, modern states have been united in the belief that they are the principal actors in world politics and the chief bearers of rights and duties within it ...

Second, there is the goal of maintaining the independence or external sovereignty of individual states ...

International society has in fact treated the independence of particular states as a goal that is subordinate to the preservation of the society of states itself ...

Third, there is the goal of peace. By this is meant ... the maintenance of peace in the sense of the absence of war among member states of international society as the normal condition of their relationship, to be breached only in special circumstances and according to principles that are generally accepted ...

Fourth, it should be noted that among the elementary or primary goals of the society of states are those which, at the beginning of this chapter, were said to be the common goals of all social life: the limitation of violence resulting in death or bodily harm, the keeping of promises and the stabilisation of possessions by rules of property.

QUESTIONS FOR DISCUSSION

1. Can one still justify war?
2. What is meant by the balance of power?
3. Does the idea of justice have any place in the international realm?
4. 'Only states have a place in the international order. Nations do not, and shouldnot, have a place.' Do you agree?
5. What is the Realist approach to international relations?

NOTES

1 Quoted by Waltz, *Man, the State and War* (New York, Columbia University Press, 1954), pp. 183-4.
2 M. Wright, *Power Politics* (Harmondsworth, Penguin, 1979).
3 Norman Angell argued for the futility of military power in his *The Great Illusion* (1910). See the extract in Evan Luard (ed.), *Basic Texts in International Relations* (London, Macmillan, 1992) pp. 264-7.

FURTHER READING

M.G. Forsyth, H.M.A. Keens-Soper and P. Savigear (eds), *The Theory of International Relations* (London, Allen and Unwin, 1970) includes more extensive extracts from, among others Gentili, Grotius, Vattel and Cobden. Evan Luard (ed.), *Basic Texts in International Relations* (London, Macmillan, 1992) includes short extracts from a very wide range of sources. On the just war theory Michael Walzer, *Just and Unjust Wars. A Moral Argument with Historical Illustrations* (Harmondsworth, Penguin, 1980) remains the most accessible account. The classic statements of Realism are E.H. Carr, *The Twenty Years Crisis*, (London, Macmillan, 1939), and Hans Morgenthau, *Politics Among Nations* (New York, Knopf, 1948), which is more systematic but also more dogmatic. The underlying assumptions about human nature and the international system are discussed in K. Walz, *Man, the State and War* (New York, Columbia University Press, 1954). M. Wright, *Power Politics* (Harmondsworth, Penguin, 1979) is rich in historical illustration. Hedley Bull, *The Anarchical Society,* accepts the Hobbesian starting point but draws different conclusions. More sympathetic to the internationalist approach, although far from uncritical, are F.H. Hinsley, *Power and the Pursuit of Peace* (Cambridge, Cambridge University Press, 1967) and Inis L. Claude, *Swords into Plowshares* (New York, Random House, 1971: 4th edition). There are numerous surveys of the idea of nationalism. Amongst these E.J. Hobsbawm's *Nations and Nationalism since 1870* (Cambridge, Cambridge University Press, 1991) stands out as a brilliant synthesis of the latest research. A survey of the economic dimension of the international order can be found in Evan Luard, *Economic Relationships Among States* (London, Macmillan, 1984).

INDEX